It invites us to believe that God is listening.

The Plain Dealer

The book's strength lies in its balance, with Yancey holding equally important ideals in a beautiful tension: action and meditation, doubt and certainty, and the unchanging God with the God who appears so moved by people's petitions in the Bible that he changes his mind.

Publishers Weekly, starred review

If you feel that there are people who really "get it" about prayer—and then there's *you*, you'll find much here to pique your interest, jump-start your thinking, and impel you to pray.

Discipleship Journal

Yancey works toward a vision of prayer as a kind of "awkward rehearsal" and, ultimately, toward the kind of conversation humankind had with God at the beginning of creation. Highly recommended.

Library Journal

It would be hard to find a better person to guide you through the topic of prayer than Philip Yancey.

Sojourners

It is the rare book about prayer that, rather than inadvertently distracting me from the pursuit of a praying life, actually prompts me to pray.

Books & Culture

Philip Yancey is that rare example of a self-proclaimed recovering fundamentalist who is actually a spiritually healthy human being.

Dallas Morning News

Yancey writes more as a journalist, with a sharp eye for detail and an investigative unwillingness to force conclusions.... One of the chief benefits of Yancey's work is that he'll go where the evidence leads.

Christianity Today

Yancey has now written a winsome and searchingly honest book about prayer.

Kirkus Reviews

Resources by Philip Yancey

The Jesus I Never Knew

What's So Amazing About Grace?

The Bible Jesus Read

Reaching for the Invisible God

Where Is God When It Hurts?

Disappointment with God

The Student Bible, General Edition (with Tim Stafford)

Meet the Bible (with Brenda Quinn)

Church: Why Bother?

Finding God in Unexpected Places

I Was Just Wondering

Soul Survivor

Rumors of Another World

Prayer

A Skeptic's Guide to Faith

Grace Notes

Books by Philip Yancey and Dr. Paul Brand

Fearfully and Wonderfully Made

In His Image

The Gift of Pain

In the Likeness of God

PHILIP YANCEY

PRAYER

DOES IT MAKE ANY DIFFERENCE?

ZONDERVAN®

ZONDERVAN.com/
AUTHORTRACKER
follow your favorite authors

ZONDERVAN

Prayer: Does It Make Any Difference?
Copyright © 2006 by Philip D. Yancey

This title is also available as a Zondervan ebook.
Visit www.zondervan.com/ebooks.

This title is also available in a Zondervan audio edition.
Visit www.zondervan.fm.

Requests for information should be addressed to:
Zondervan, *Grand Rapids, Michigan 49530*

This edition: ISBN 978-0-310-32888-9 (softcover)

Library of Congress Cataloging-in-Publication Data

Yancey, Philip.
    Prayer : does it make any difference? / Philip Yancey.
      p. cm.
    ISBN 978-0-310-27105-5 (alk. paper)
    1. Prayer — Christianity. I. Title.
  BV210.3.Y36   2006
  248.3'2 — dc22   2006009434

Permissions and credit lines for quoted material may be found in the back of the book under "Credits."

Any Internet addresses (websites, blogs, etc.) and telephone numbers printed in this book are offered as a resource. They are not intended in any way to be or imply an endorsement by Zondervan, nor does Zondervan vouch for the content of these sites and numbers for the life of this book.

Cover design: Cindy Davis
Cover photo of desert: Allen Birmback, Masterfile
Interior design: Beth Shagene

Printed in the United States of America

14 15 /DCI/ 25 24 23 22 21 20 19 18 17 16 15 14 13 12 11 10

The reason why we pray
is simply that we cannot help praying.

WILLIAM JAMES

CONTENTS

PART 1

KEEPING COMPANY WITH GOD

For prayer exists, no question about that.
It is the peculiarly human response to the fact
of this endless mystery of bliss and brutality,
impersonal might and lyric intimacy that composes
our experience of life.

PATRICIA HAMPL

CHAPTER 1

OUR DEEPEST LONGING

When a doctoral student at Princeton asked, "What is there left in the world for original dissertation research?" Albert Einstein replied, "Find out about prayer. Somebody must find out about prayer."

I chose the wrong time to visit St. Petersburg, Russia. I went in November of 2002 just as the city was reconstructing itself to prepare for its three-hundredth birthday the following year. Scaffolding covered every building of note and rubble littered the quaint cobblestone streets, which turned my morning jogging routine into an adventure. I ran in darkness (the sun rose mid-morning at that latitude) with my head down, dodging the workmen's piles of brick and sand while glancing ahead for the dim gloss that betrayed the presence of ice.

I must have lost concentration one morning, for suddenly I found myself facedown on the street, dazed and shivering. I sat up. I could remember jerking my head sideways as I fell, to avoid a piece of steel rebar protruding from the curb at a wicked angle. I removed my gloves, reached for my right eye, and felt blood. The entire right side of my face was wet with blood. I got up, dusted dirt and flecks of snow from my running suit, and felt for more damage. I walked slowly, testing my throbbing knees and elbows. I tasted blood, and a couple of blocks away I realized a front tooth was missing. I returned to search for it in the dark, in vain.

When I reached Nevsky Prospekt, a busy boulevard, I noticed that people were staring at me. Russians rarely look strangers in the eye, so I must have been a sight. I limped to the hotel and talked my way past dubious security guards to get to my room. I knocked on the door and said, "Janet, let me in — I'm hurt."

11

We had both heard horror stories about medical care in Russia, where you can go in with a surface wound and come out with AIDS or hepatitis. I decided on self-treatment. After raiding the minibar for tiny bottles of vodka, we started cleaning the scrapes on my face. My upper lip was split in two. I gritted my teeth, poured the alcohol over the cuts, and scrubbed my face with a packaged refresher-cloth left over from the Lufthansa flight. We taped the lip together tightly with a Band-Aid, hoping it would heal straight. By now the area around my eye had swollen and turned a spectacular purple, but fortunately my sight seemed unimpaired.

I took a few aspirin and rested awhile. Then I went back out to Nevsky Prospekt and looked for an Internet café. I climbed three flights of stairs, used sign language to negotiate the price in rubles, and settled in at a computer terminal. My fingers rested on a strange keyboard and I faced the Cyrillic alphabet onscreen. After ten minutes of false starts, I finally found my way to an AOL screen in English. Ah, connected at last. I typed a note to a prayer group at my home church in Colorado and to a few friends and family members. The wireless network kept cutting on and off, and each time I had to find AOL again and retype the message.

The message was simple: a few background details, then "We need help. Please pray." I didn't know the extent of my injuries. The next few days I was supposed to speak at a booksellers' convention in St. Petersburg, then go on to Moscow for more speaking assignments. The news banner on AOL was telling me that armed Chechen rebels had just seized a theater full of patrons and Moscow was under military lockdown. I finished my message and pressed "Send" just as a warning popped up informing me my time was running out.

Is this how prayer works? I wondered as I walked back to the hotel. We send signals from a visible world to an invisible one, in hope that Someone receives them. And how will we know?

Still, for the first time that day I felt the lump of fear and anxiety in my stomach begin to loosen. In a few hours my friends and family, people who cared, would turn on their computers, read my message, and pray on my behalf. I was not alone.*

---

*Everything healed fine. And the request for prayer had one very practical benefit. The wife of my dentist, who was on the prayer team and received the message, immediately reserved an appointment for me so that the day after my return from Russia I had a root canal procedure!

A Universal Cry

Every faith has some form of prayer. Remote tribes present offerings and then pray for everyday things such as health, food, rain, children, and victory in battles. Incas and Aztecs went so far as to sacrifice humans in order to attract the gods' attention. Five times a day modern Muslims stop whatever they are doing—driving, having a coffee break, playing soccer—when the summons comes to pray.

Even atheists find ways to pray. During the heady days of Communism in Russia, party stalwarts kept a "red corner," placing a portrait of Lenin where Christians used to keep their icons. Caught up in the fervor, *Pravda* ran this advice to its readers in 1950:

> If you meet with difficulties in your work, or suddenly doubt your abilities, think of him—of Stalin—and you will find the confidence you need. If you feel tired in an hour when you should not, think of him—of Stalin—and your work will go well. If you are seeking a correct decision, think of him—of Stalin—and you will find that decision.*

We pray because we want to thank someone or something for the beauties and glories of life, and also because we feel small and helpless and sometimes afraid. We pray for forgiveness, for strength, for contact with the One who is, for assurance that we are not alone. Millions in AA groups pray daily to a Higher Power, begging for help in controlling their addictions. We pray because we can't help it. The very word *prayer* comes from the Latin root *precarius*—a linguistic cousin to *precarious*. In St. Petersburg, Russia, I prayed out of desperation. I had nowhere else to turn.

Prayer is universal because it speaks to some basic human need. As Thomas Merton put it, "Prayer is an expression of who we are.... We are a living incompleteness. We are a gap, an emptiness that calls for fulfillment." In prayer we break silence, and sometimes those words flow out of our deepest parts. I remember in the days after September 11, 2001, saying over and over the prayer, "God, bless America." "Save America" is what I meant. Save us. Let us live. Give us another chance.

According to Gallup polls, more Americans will pray this week than will exercise, drive a car, have sex, or go to work. Nine in ten of us pray regularly,

---

*Quotations from other sources, including the Bible, are referenced at the back of the book.

and three out of four claim to pray every day. To get some idea of the interest in prayer, type "prayer" or "pray" in an Internet search engine like Google and see how many millions of links pop up. Yet behind those impressive numbers lies a conundrum.

When I started exploring the subject of Christian prayer, I first went to libraries and read accounts of some of the great pray-ers in history. George Müller began each day with several hours of prayer, imploring God to meet the practical needs of his orphanage. Bishop Lancelot Andrewes allotted five hours per day to prayer and Charles Simeon rose at 4:00 a.m. to begin his four-hour regimen. Nuns in an order known as "The Sleepless Ones" still pray in shifts through every hour of the day and night. Susannah Wesley, a busy mother with no privacy, would sit in a rocking chair with an apron over her head praying for John and Charles and the rest of her brood. Martin Luther, who devoted two to three hours daily to prayer, said we should do it as naturally as a shoemaker makes a shoe and a tailor makes a coat. Jonathan Edwards wrote of the "sweet hours" on the banks of the Hudson River, "rapt and swallowed up in God."

In the next step I interviewed ordinary people about prayer. Typically, the results went like this: Is prayer important to you? *Oh, yes.* How often do you pray? *Every day.* Approximately how long? *Five minutes—well, maybe seven.* Do you find prayer satisfying? *Not really.* Do you sense the presence of God when you pray? *Occasionally, not often.* Many of those I talked to experienced prayer more as a burden than as a pleasure. They regarded it as important, even paramount, and felt guilty about their failure, blaming themselves.

A Modern Struggle

When I listened to public prayers in evangelical churches, I heard people telling God what to do, combined with thinly veiled hints on how others should behave. When I listened to prayers in more liberal churches, I heard calls to action, as if prayer were something to get past so we can do the real work of God's kingdom. Hans Küng's theological tome *On Being A Christian*, 702 pages long, did not include a chapter or even an index entry on prayer. When asked later, Küng said he regretted the oversight. He was feeling so harassed by Vatican censors and by his publisher's deadlines that he simply forgot about prayer.

Why does prayer rank so high on surveys of theoretical importance and so low on surveys of actual satisfaction? What accounts for the disparity between Luther and Simeon on their knees for several hours and the modern pray-er fidgeting in a chair after ten minutes?

Everywhere, I encountered the gap between prayer in theory and prayer in practice. In theory prayer is the essential human act, a priceless point of contact with the God of the universe. In practice prayer is often confusing and fraught with frustration. My publisher conducted a website poll, and of the 678 respondents only 23 felt satisfied with the time they were spending in prayer. That very discrepancy made me want to write this book.

Advances in science and technology no doubt contribute to our confusion about prayer. In former days farmers lifted their heads and appealed to brazen heavens for an end to drought. Now we study low-pressure fronts, dig irrigation canals, and seed clouds with metallic particles. In former days when a child fell ill the parents cried out to God; now they call for an ambulance or phone the doctor.

In much of the world, modern skepticism taints prayer. We breathe in an atmosphere of doubt. Why does God let history lurch on without intervening? What good will prayer do against a nuclear threat, against terrorism and hurricanes and global climate change? To some people prayer seems, as George Buttrick put it, "a spasm of words lost in a cosmic indifference"—and he wrote those words in 1942.

Prosperity may dilute prayer too. In my travels I have noticed that Christians in developing countries spend less time pondering the effectiveness of prayer and more time actually praying. The wealthy rely on talent and resources to solve immediate problems, and insurance policies and retirement plans to secure the future. We can hardly pray with sincerity, "Give us this day our daily bread" when the pantry is stocked with a month's supply of provisions.

Increasingly, time pressures crowd out the leisurely pace that prayer seems to require. Communication with other people keeps getting shorter and more cryptic: text messages, email, instant messaging. We have less and less time for conversation, let alone contemplation. We have the constant sensation of *not enough*: not enough time, not enough rest, not enough exercise, not enough leisure. Where does God fit into a life that already seems behind schedule?

If we do choose to look inward and bare our souls, therapists and support groups now offer outlets that were once reserved for God alone. Praying to

15

an invisible God does not bring forth the same feedback you would get from a counselor or from friends who at least nod their heads in sympathy. Is anyone really listening? As Ernestine, the nasal-voiced telephone operator played by comedienne Lily Tomlin, used to ask, "Have I reached the party to whom I am speaking?"

Prayer is to the skeptic a delusion, a waste of time. To the believer it represents perhaps the most important use of time. As a Christian, I believe the latter. Why, then, is prayer so problematic? The British pastor Martyn Lloyd-Jones summed up the confusion: "Of all the activities in which the Christian engages, and which are part of the Christian life, there is surely none which causes so much perplexity, and raises so many problems, as the activity which we call prayer."

Pilgrim Quest

I write about prayer as a pilgrim, not an expert. I have the same questions that occur to almost everyone at some point. Is God listening? Why should God care about me? If God knows everything, what's the point of prayer? Why do answers to prayer seem so inconsistent, even capricious? Does a person with many praying friends stand a better chance of physical healing than one who also has cancer but with only a few people praying for her? Why does God sometimes seem close and sometimes faraway? Does prayer change God or change me?

Before beginning this book I mostly avoided the topic of prayer out of guilt and a sense of inferiority. I'm embarrassed to admit that I do not keep a journal, do not see a spiritual director, and do not belong to a regular prayer group. And I readily confess that I tend to view prayer through a skeptic's lens, obsessing more about unanswered prayers than rejoicing over answered ones. In short, my main qualification for writing about prayer is that I feel unqualified — and genuinely want to learn.

More than anything else in life, I want to know God. The psychiatrist Gerald C. May observed, "After twenty years of listening to the yearnings of people's hearts, I am convinced that human beings have an inborn desire for God. Whether we are consciously religious or not, this desire is our deepest longing and most precious treasure." Surely, if we are made in God's own image, God will find a way to fulfill that deepest longing. Prayer is that way.

By journalistic instinct, I asked many other people about prayer: my neighbors, other authors, fellow church members, spiritual mentors, ordinary people. I have included some of their reflections in drop-in boxes scattered throughout the book, as examples of actual down-to-earth encounters with prayer and also as a reminder to myself not to stray far from their questions. I use mostly first names, though some of them are well-known in Christian circles, to avoid any kind of hierarchy. When it comes to prayer we are all beginners.

I have not attempted a guide book that details techniques such as fasting, prayer retreats, and spiritual direction. I investigate the topic of prayer as a pilgrim, strolling about, staring at the monuments, asking questions, mulling things over, testing the waters. I admit to an imbalance, an overreaction to time spent among Christians who promised too much and pondered too little, and as a result I try to err on the side of honesty and not pretense.

In the process of writing, however, I have come to see prayer as a privilege, not a duty. Like all good things, prayer requires some discipline. Yet I believe that life with God should seem more like friendship than duty. Prayer includes moments of ecstasy and also dullness, mindless distraction and acute concentration, flashes of joy and bouts of irritation. In other words, prayer has features in common with all relationships that matter.

If prayer stands as the place where God and human beings meet, then I must learn about prayer. Most of my struggles in the Christian life circle around the same two themes: why God doesn't act the way we want God to, and why I don't act the way God wants me to. Prayer is the precise point where those themes converge.

CHAPTER 2

VIEW FROM ABOVE

We must stop setting our sights by the light of each passing ship;
instead we must set our course by the stars.
GEORGE MARSHALL

To climb a 14,000-foot mountain in Colorado you need an early start—as
in four o'clock in the morning early—but you need to limit coffee intake
in order to avoid dehydration. You drive on chassis-slapping rutted roads in
the dark, always alert for wildlife, gaining elevation to somewhere between
9,000 and 10,000 feet, where the hiking trail begins. Then you begin the
hike by wending your way through a forest of blue spruce, lodgepole pine,
and Douglas fir on a trail that feels spongy underfoot from fallen needles.
The ground gives off a pungent smell of decay and earth. You walk beside
a tumbling creek, silvery white in the predawn moonlight, its burbling the
only sound until the birds awake.

Around 11,000 feet the trees thin, giving way to lush meadows carpeted
in wildflowers. The sun is rising now, first casting a reddish alpenglow on
the mountain tops, then dropping its rays into the basins. Bright clumps of
lupine, fireweed, columbine, and Indian paintbrush dapple the open spaces,
while plants with more exotic names—monkshood, elephant head, bishop's
cap, chiming bell, marsh marigold—cluster near the water's edge.

You follow the creek up the basin, skirting cliff banks, until a climber's
trail veers off to zigzag up the grassy shoulder of the peak you have chosen to
climb. By now your heart is racing like a sprinter's, and despite the morning
chill you feel sweat under your backpack. You take a water break, then head
up the steep trail, forcing yourself to gut it out. The dawn chorus of birds has
begun, and you are startled by a flash of indigo, bright as neon, as a flock of
Western bluebirds suddenly catches the sun's rays.

The high-altitude wildflowers have shrunken into miniature versions of themselves; to really see them, you must stoop to their level, practicing what the locals call "belly botany." Marmots, the alpine cousins of woodchucks, waddle to their lookout posts and whistle reports of your progress to their colleagues higher up.

Soon you leave dirt and grass and begin stepping across a boulder field. Chunks of granite the size of wheelbarrows are decorated by lichen in shades of orange, lime-green, and yellow. You keep your head down, testing each rock for stability before shifting weight to it. Finally, after an hour of rock-hopping you reach the ridge, a narrow line of ascent you hope will lead you all the way to the summit. You sling the backpack off and stop to catch your breath. You drink more water, eat a snack. The rush of blood pounding in your ears overwhelms all other sounds. Looking back over your route, you feel accomplished. You'll make the summit, you feel certain.

Down below you see something, a tiny dot just at the edge of timberline. No, two dots. Animals or merely rocks? One spot moves — can't be a rock. A marmot? Size is so hard to judge up here. The second dot looks red. Could they be hikers? You glance skyward, searching for signs of the thunderstorms that roll in before noon. If they are hikers, they're flirting with danger, starting their climb at least three hours late. You watch the ant-crawl progress as the tiny dots edge up the trail.

Then it hits you: from this vantage point, three hours ago you too were a dot like that, a speck of human life on a huge, hulking, weather-creating mountain that has little regard for it. (As a famous climber said, "Mountains don't kill people. They just sit there.") You feel appropriately small, almost insignificant. You get a tiny, fractional glimpse of what God must see all the time.

One of the psalms describes thunder as the voice of the Lord, who strikes the earth with flashes of lightning. We know, of course, that lightning occurs when a positively charged streamer rushes up from the ground to meet a negative charge at the bottom of a cloud. A hundred times a second lightning strikes somewhere on earth, and I for one do not believe God personally programs each course. I have, however, been caught in terrifying storms near the summit of a mountain. With my ice axe humming and my scalp tingling, squatting with feet close together so the charge won't circuit through my body, spaced far enough from my partner to lessen the odds of us both dying, counting the seconds between bolts ("two seconds ... half a mile") — then, too, I get a glimmer of my true state, a helpless two-legged creature perched on the skin of a molten planet.

I live in daily hope of getting my life under control. At home I left a desk covered with to-do lists: study the manual for my balky printer, unclog pine needles in the gutter, unstick the toilet, change snow tires, check on my sick neighbor. Maybe if I take a day off, I'll have time … On the mountain one bolt of lightning, splitting a rock on a nearby peak and exploding against my eardrums, exposes any illusion that I am ever in control. I can count on the moment before me, nothing more.

"Let me know how fleeting is my life," prayed one psalmist. A mountain storm thunderously answers that prayer. The priorities of my life crack apart and slide into a new place.

View from Below

I have had hints of another vantage point that even dwarfs the scale of mountains. One night in 1997 I drove to a lake near my home to watch a lunar eclipse. To the east, hanging just over the mountain peaks, the Hale-Bopp comet lit the sky, brighter far than any star. To judge its size I held my two fists at arm's length, barely covering its luminous, streaming tail. Then I gazed through binoculars at this object that had traveled the breadth of the solar system.

In another corner of the sky, the crescent shadow of earth began crossing the moon, dimming it to an unnatural orangish hue. Mars, closer to earth than it had been in centuries, glowed red above the moon. As the eclipse progressed, all the stars in the sky brightened as if on a rheostat. The Milky Way spilled across the expanse directly above, a broad river of diamond dust. I stood gazing so long that my craned neck grew stiff, and I left only as clouds gathered and snow began to fall, blotting out the celestial view.

I felt appropriately small that night too. To appreciate the scale, consider that if the Milky Way galaxy were the size of the entire continent of North America, our solar system would fit in a coffee cup. Even now two Voyager spacecrafts are hurtling toward the edge of the solar system at a rate of 100,000 miles per hour. For almost three decades they have been speeding away from earth, approaching a distance of 9 billion miles. When engineers beam a command to the spacecraft at the speed of light, it takes thirteen hours to arrive. Yet this vast neighborhood of our sun — in truth the size of a coffee cup — fits along with several hundred billion other stars and their minions in the Milky Way, one of perhaps 100 billion such galaxies in the universe. To send a light-speed message to the edge of that universe would take 15 billion years.

"When I consider your heavens, the work of your fingers, the moon and the stars, which you have set in place, what is man that you are mindful of him?" asked the psalmist. An excellent question, as well as a reminder of a point of view I easily forget. We are, we humans, a mere pinch of dust scattered across the surface of a nondescript planet. At the heart of all reality is God, an unimaginable source of both power and love. In the face of such reality we can grovel in humanoid humility or we can, like the psalmist, look up instead of down, to conclude, "O Lord, our Lord, how majestic is your name in all the earth!"

To explore the mystery of prayer I begin here, recalling the vantage I get from the summit of a mountain looking down or from an observatory looking up. Each provides a mere sliver of a glimpse of reality as God must see it. Like a flash of lightning, prayer exposes for a nanosecond what I would prefer to ignore: my own true state of fragile dependence. The undone tasks accumulating at home, my family and every other relation, temptations, health, plans for the future — all these I bring into that larger reality, God's sphere, where I find them curiously upended.

Prayer helps correct myopia, calling to mind a perspective I daily forget. I keep reversing roles, thinking of ways in which God should serve me, rather than vice versa. As God fiercely reminded Job, the Lord of the universe has

The Peace of Wild Things

WENDELL BERRY, *COLLECTED POEMS*

When despair grows in me
and I wake in the middle of the night at the least sound
in fear of what my life and my children's lives may be,
I go and lie down where the wood drake
rests in his beauty on the water,
and the great heron feeds. I come into the peace of wild things
who do not tax their lives with forethought
of grief. I come into the presence of still water.
And I feel above me the day-blind stars
waiting with their light. For a time
I rest in the grace of the world, and am free.

many things to manage, and in the midst of my self-pity I would do well to contemplate for a moment God's own point of view.

Where were you when I laid the earth's foundation?
Tell me, if you understand.
Who marked off its dimensions? Surely you know!

Prayer raises my sight beyond the petty—or, as in Job's case, dire—circumstances of daily life to afford a glimpse of that lofty perspective. I realize my tininess and God's vastness, and the true relation of the two. In God's presence I feel small because I am small.

When, after shrugging aside all his caustic theological queries, God enlightened hapless Job, the poor man crumbled. *I'm sorry*, Job said, in effect. *I had no idea what I was asking.* Job did not receive a single answer to his probing questions, a fact that no longer seemed to matter.

'Who is this that obscures my counsel without knowledge?' [God asked]
Surely I spoke of things I did not understand,
    things too wonderful for me to know.

Kicking and screaming all the way, I am still learning the lesson of Job. God needs no reminding of the nature of reality, but I do.

The third rock from the sun, our planet, has spun off its theological axis. There was a time, Genesis informs us, when God and Adam walked together in the garden and conversed as friends. Nothing seemed more natural for Adam than to commune with the One who had made him, who gave him creative work, who granted his desire for a companion with the lovely gift of Eve. Then, prayer was as natural as conversation with a colleague, or a lover. At the moment of the fall, for Adam and for all who succeeded him, God's presence grew more remote, easier to doubt and even deny.

Every day my vision clouds over so that I perceive nothing but a world of matter. It requires a daily act of will to remember what Paul told the sophisticated crowd in Athens: "[God] is not far from each one of us. For in him we live and move and have our being." For this reason prayer may seem strange, even embarrassing. (How odd, that prayer seems foolish to some people who base their lives on media trends, superstition, instinct, hormones, social propriety, or even astrology.)

For most of us, much of the time, prayer brings no certain confirmation we have been heard. We pray in faith that our words somehow cross a bridge between visible and invisible worlds, penetrating a reality of which we have no proof. We enter God's milieu, the realm of spirit, which seems much less real to us than it did to Adam.

Joining the Stream

Jane, a character in Thornton Wilder's play *Our Town*, got a letter addressed to her farm, town, county, state, and then, the envelope continued, "the United States of America; Continent of North America; Western Hemisphere; the Earth; the Solar System; the Universe; the Mind of God." Perhaps the Christian should reverse the order. If I started with the mind and will of God, viewing the rest of my life from that point of view, other details would fall into place—or at least fall into a different place.

My home sits in a canyon in the shadow of a large mountain along a stream named Bear Creek. During the spring snowmelt and after heavy rains the stream swells, tumbles frothily over rocks, and acts more like a river than a creek. People have drowned in it. Once I traced the origin of Bear Creek to its very source, atop the mountain. I stood on a snowfield marked by "sun cups," the bowl-shaped indentations that form as snow melts. Underneath I could hear a soft gurgling sound, and at the edge of the snow, runnels of water leaked out. These collected into a pool, then a small alpine pond, then spilled over to begin the long journey down the mountain, joining other rivulets to take shape as the creek below my house.

It occurs to me, thinking about prayer, that most of the time I get the direction wrong. I start downstream with my own concerns and bring them to God. I inform God, as if God did not already know. I plead with God, as if hoping to change God's mind and overcome divine reluctance. Instead, I should start upstream where the flow begins.

When I shift direction, I realize that God already cares about my concerns —my uncle's cancer, world peace, a broken family, a rebellious teenager— more than I do. Grace, like water, descends to the lowest part. Streams of mercy flow. I begin with God, who bears primary responsibility for what happens on earth, and ask what part I can play in God's work on earth. "Let justice roll on like a river, righteousness like a never-failing stream!" cried the prophet. Will I stand by the bank or jump in the stream?

With this new starting point for prayer, my perceptions change. I look at nature and see not only wildflowers and golden aspen trees but the signature of a grand artist. I look at human beings and see not only a "poor,

23

bare, forked animal" but a person of eternal destiny made in God's image. Thanksgiving and praise surge up as a natural response, not an obligation.

I need the corrective vision of prayer because all day long I will lose sight of God's perspective. I turn on the television and face a barrage of advertisements assuring me that success and achievement are measured by possessions and physical appearance. Driving downtown, I see a grizzled panhandler holding up a "God bless. Can you help?" sign by the express-way off-ramp, and I avert my eyes. I hear a news report on a dictator in Africa who has just bulldozed entire neighborhoods of squatter homes in an Operation to Drive Out the Trash, leaving 700,000 people homeless. The world obscures the view from above.

Prayer, and only prayer, restores my vision to one that more resembles God's. I awake from blindness to see that wealth lurks as a terrible danger, not a goal worth striving for; that value depends not on race or status but on the image of God every person bears; that no amount of effort to improve physical beauty has much relevance for the world beyond.

Alexander Schmemann, the late priest who led a reform movement in Russian Orthodoxy, tells of a time when he was traveling on the subway in Paris, France, with his fiancée. At one stop an old and ugly woman dressed in the uniform of the Salvation Army got on and found a seat nearby. The two lovers whispered to each other in Russian about how repulsive she looked. A few stops later the woman stood to exit. As she passed them she said in perfect Russian, "I wasn't always ugly." That woman was an angel of God, Schmemann used to tell his students. She opened his eyes, searing his vision in a way he would never forget.

A Habit of Attention

"Be still and know that I am God." I read in this familiar verse from Psalms two commands of equal importance. First, I must be still, something that modern life conspires against. Ten years ago I responded to letters within a couple of weeks and kept my correspondents happy. Five years ago I faxed a response in a couple of days and they seemed content. Now they want email responses the same day and berate me for not using instant messaging or a mobile phone.*

---

*When a journalist asked Thomas Merton to diagnose the leading spiritual disease of our time, the monk gave a curious one-word answer: efficiency. Why? "From the monastery to the Pentagon, the plant has to run ... and there is little time or energy left over after that to do anything else."

Mystery, awareness of another world, an emphasis on being rather than doing, even a few moments of quiet do not come naturally to me in this hectic, buzzing world. I must carve out time and allow God to nourish my inner life.

On a walking pilgrimage to Assisi in Italy, the writer Patricia Hampl began to make a list in answer to the question, What is prayer? She wrote down a few words. Praise. Gratitude. Begging/pleading/cutting deals. Fruitless whining and puling. Focus. And then the list broke off, for she discovered that prayer only seems like an act of language: "Fundamentally it is a position, a placement of oneself." She went on to discover that "prayer as focus is not a way of limiting what can be seen; it is a habit of attention brought to bear on all that is."

Ah, a habit of attention. Be still. In that focus, all else comes into focus. In that rift in my routine, the universe falls into alignment.

Stillness prepares me for the second command: "know that I am God; I will be exalted among the nations, I will be exalted in the earth." Only through prayer can I believe that truth in the midst of a world that colludes to suppress, not exalt, God.

In testimony given before the Truth and Reconciliation Commission hearings in South Africa, one black man told of crying out to God as the white officers attached electrodes to his body after beating him with truncheons. They laughed in his face: "We are God here," jeered one of the guards. The Commission hearings bared the delusion of that brash claim, for the guards, stripped of all power, now sat in a defendants' box with heads bowed as their accusers paraded before them. They had been dethroned.

Psalm 2 depicts God laughing in the heavens, scoffing at the kings and rulers arrayed in revolt. For the South African prisoner, or a pastor harassed in China, or believers persecuted in North Korea, it requires a great leap to attain that sublime faith, to believe that God is indeed exalted among the nations.* I think of Paul *singing* in a Philippian jail and of Jesus correcting Pilate with the plain truth, "You would have no power over me if it were not given to you from above." Even at that moment of crisis, Jesus had the long view, the view from a time antedating the solar system.

---

* A seventeenth-century prayer from the British House of Commons gets the right perspective, in words that sound eerily foreign in today's political climate: "Almighty God, by whom alone Kings reign, and Princes decree justice; and from whom alone cometh all counsel, wisdom and understanding; We thine unworthy servants, here gathered together in thy Name, do most humbly beseech thee to send down thy heavenly wisdom from above, to direct and guide us in all our consultations; And grant that we, having thy fear always before our eyes, and laying aside all private interests, prejudices, and partial affections, the result of all our counsels, may be the glory of thy blessed name."

"Be still and know that *I* am God": the Latin imperative for "be still" is *vacate*. As Simon Tugwell explains, "God invites us to take a holiday [*vacation*], to stop being God for a while, and let him be God." Too often we think of prayer as a serious chore, something that must be scheduled around other appointments, shoehorned in among other pressing activities. We miss the point, says Tugwell: "God is inviting us to take a break, to play truant. We can stop doing all those important things we have to do in our capacity as God, and leave it to him to be God." Prayer allows me to admit my failures, weaknesses, and limitations to One who responds to human vulnerability with infinite mercy.

To let God be God, of course, means climbing down from my own executive chair of control. I must uncreate the world I have so carefully fashioned to further my ends and advance my cause. Adam and Eve, the builders of

Bless You, Child

REINER

How well I remember my first real prayer. A youth leader was explaining to my friend Udo how to become a Christian. "Let's kneel down right now," he said. "What about you, Reiner? Do you want to become a Christian too?" Without thinking I said yes, and prayed as he instructed us. It was an unforgettable experience that changed me forever. I looked up at the stars in the sky and felt connected to the universe. At age twelve, I had found my place, a whole new identity.

A few minutes later I came back down to earth as my mother yelled at me for coming home so late. I tried to explain, but she could not understand. For her, prayers were the formal recitations you heard at church, nothing so personal. For three days I did not eat. "All you do is think about God," Mother complained. She was right.

Shy and introverted, I learned to pray aloud by listening to others, learning their phrases, figuring out when to jump in and when to stay silent. Prayer seemed a kind of social skill. Oddly enough, it came easier when I traveled from Germany to the U.S.A. to study. Praying in my new language, English, forced me to be more aware and authentic. I couldn't fall back on old patterns and familiar phrases.

Babel, Nebuchadnezzar, the South African guards, not to mention all who struggle with addictions or even ego, know well what is at stake. If original sin traces back to two people striving to become like God, the first step in prayer is to acknowledge or "remember" God—to restore the truth of the universe. "That Man may know he dwells not in his own," said Milton.

Aliens

For several years I have tried to help a Japanese family, the Yokotas, in their desperate search for justice. In 1977 their thirteen-year-old daughter Megumi vanished on her way home from badminton practice after school. Police dogs tracked her scent to a nearby beach, but the distraught Yokotas had no clues that might explain their daughter's sudden disappearance.

Eventually I became a pastor. As I listened to people pour out their heartaches and human problems, I would try to respond with comfort. Sometimes I had the feeling that the words I spoke to them at such a moment became a prayer. I realized that more than two of us were present.

I also became a father, with a daughter and a son. As they slept, I would step into their rooms, make the sign of the cross over them, and pray for their future. A parent has such little control. You have to fall back on God.

My son has epilepsy. His first grand mal seizure terrified me. We called for an ambulance, and I held him in my arms as his head shook from side to side, stroking his forehead, trying to say calming words while inside I felt the opposite of calm. Consciously I tried to pour my spirit into his, to take on his pain. I doubt I've ever felt closer to my son than during that first seizure when I held him—both of us so helpless, so afraid.

Prayer for me has become a form of blessing. Bless you, I would say to the parishioners who laid bare their stories. Bless you, child, I would say over my daughter's crib. Bless you, I would say while holding my convulsing son. I want to be a conduit of God's blessing to others. I want to feel that blessing for myself, in prayer.

Sometimes I rest, relaxed in God's love. Sometimes I thrash and tremble, like my son during a seizure.

Sixteen years later, long after the Yokotas had resigned themselves to Megumi's death, a North Korean defector made a stunning claim: a Japanese woman named Megumi, who played badminton, was living in North Korea at a training institute for intelligence agents. Scores of Japanese, he said, had been kidnapped and forced to teach Korean spies the Japanese language and culture. He provided heartrending details of Megumi's abduction: agents had seized her, wrapped her in a straw mat, and rowed her to a waiting spy ship, where she had spent the night scratching against the hold with bloody fingers, crying "Mother!"

For years North Korea dismissed all such reports as fabrications. But in the face of mounting pressure, Kim Jong-il himself, the "Dear Leader" of North Korea, at long last admitted to the abduction of thirteen Japanese, including Megumi. Five returned to Japan, but North Koreans insisted the other eight had died, including Megumi who, they said, in 1993 had used a kimono to hang herself. Much information supplied by North Korea proved false, however, and the Yokotas refused to believe the reports of their daughter's death. All over Japan, prayer groups sprang up to support the abductees. Mrs. Yokota traveled across the globe in her quest for justice, becoming in the process one of the most familiar faces on Japanese media. Eventually she visited the Oval Office and told her story in person to President George W. Bush, who took up her cause.

In 2004, twenty-seven years after the abduction, the North Koreans gave Megumi's parents three photos of their daughter. The most poignant, taken just after her capture, shows her at age thirteen still in her Japanese schoolgirl's uniform, looking unbearably forlorn. "We couldn't help crying when we saw the picture," her mother tearfully told reporters. Two other photos showed her as an adult, a woman in her thirties standing outdoors in a winter coat.

The Yokotas fondled the photos over and over, finding some solace in the fact that the later photos showed their daughter looking healthy and reasonably well-cared-for. They tried to imagine Megumi's life. Had she met with other abductees and conversed with them to keep from forgetting her mother tongue? What had helped her remember who she was: not an immigrant to North Korea but a Japanese taken captive against her will? Had she tried to sneak a message back to them? Attempted an escape? What memories did she retain of her life in Japan, life as their daughter? How many times had Megumi looked toward the island of Japan and scoured newspapers in search of clues of her former home?

On a trip to Asia in 2004, I was asked to speak to the combined prayer groups in Tokyo. I agonized over what I might say to bring comfort to the family and concerned friends. I turned to the Bible in search of anything that might relate to the Yokotas' predicament, and made a list of characters who had served God in foreign lands: Abram departing for a new homeland that included Sodom and Gomorrah; Joseph abducted, presumed dead, then rising to prominence in Egypt; Daniel and other prophets serving enemy administrations in Babylon (Iraq) and then Persia (Iran); Esther risking her life to preserve her compatriots in Persia; Paul taking the gospel to Rome in chains, forerunner of a host of missionaries who would encounter resistance from foreign cultures, including many early martyrs in Japan itself.

All these, like Megumi, must have struggled to retain a memory of who they were: aliens swept into a new and strange culture. The prophet Daniel defied a tyrant's orders by opening his window and praying three times a day toward his home city of Jerusalem. For him, for the other believers living in foreign lands, and perhaps for Megumi as well, prayer was the main reminder of a reality contradicted by all surroundings. A channel of faith, it served to restore the truth belied by everything around them.

For us, too, prayer can be that channel. We live on a broken planet, fallen far from God's original intent. It takes effort to remember who we are, God's creation, and faith to imagine what we someday will be, God's triumph.

Why pray? I have asked this question almost every day of my Christian life, especially when God's presence seems far away and I wonder if prayer is a pious form of talking to myself. I have asked it when I read theology, wondering what use there may be in repeating what God must surely know. My conclusions will unfold only gradually, but I begin here because prayer has become for me much more than a shopping list of requests to present to God. It has become a realignment of everything. I pray to restore the truth of the universe, to gain a glimpse of the world, and of me, through the eyes of God.

In prayer I shift my point of view away from my own selfishness. I climb above timberline and look down at the speck that is myself. I gaze at the stars and recall what role I or any of us play in a universe beyond comprehension. Prayer is the act of seeing reality from God's point of view.

CHAPTER 3

JUST AS WE ARE

The prayer preceding all prayers is
"May it be the real I who speaks.
May it be the real Thou that I speak to."

C. S. LEWIS

Sometimes I wonder if the words I use are the least important part of prayer. Who am I? And who is God? If I can answer those two questions, the words I pray recede. Prayer invites me to lower defenses and present the self that no other person fully knows to a God who already knows.

A few years ago I received a letter from a reader I'll call Mark. He began,

I have suffered from a very serious emotional condition all of my adult life — borderline personality disorder — with the attendant depression, extreme anxiety, and debilitating physical symptoms. In way of explanation, and not blame, during the first years of my life I was the subject of very serious sexual and emotional abuse at the hands of my mother. Enough said on that.

He went on to say that accounts in my books of inspiring people only made him feel worse about himself.

I suppose my question is: what is the heavenly reward for those of us who are *not* laboring in God's fields in the inner city? Or who struggle daily with pornography, where a major breakthrough is a day not on the Internet. Or who at the height of our recovery may have maybe 10 percent of the moral character of the average unbeliever. Does one have to be a healthy Christian servant to receive God's grace?

The gospel offers sure comfort to a troubled person like Mark. I replied to him that God's grace flows like water, steadily downward to the lowest part. Indeed, how could we experience grace at all except through our defects? In Jesus' day tax collectors, prostitutes, and unclean persons reached out their hands to receive God's grace while religious professionals closed theirs into tight fists. In receiving a free gift, having open hands is the only requirement.

Long after my reply, however, Mark's letter kept coming to mind. I had quoted to him King David's words, "a broken and contrite heart, O God, you will not despise," and there are certainly times when I fall back on that assurance. Not everyone suffers from borderline personality disorder, however; not everyone lives with chronic self-doubt. Must we always wallow in failure before God? What is the natural state we all share in approaching God? And how can we assure that "the real I" is praying?

Guilty

Advice books on prayer emphasize the act of confession. Some people come readily to the point of self-abasement, feeling what one author called "a desire to lay my personality at someone's feet as a puppy deposits a slobbery ball." I meet people like Mark who yearn for the healing balm of grace. With delight I point them to the tender mercies of Jesus, who turned away no one, who embraced the hungry and thirsty and those who mourn — in other words, the desperate.

Other people, and I stand at the head of this line, find it a painful process to be stripped of illusion, to let the searing light of God's truth reveal who we really are. What makes confession so necessary?

For perspective I recall the view from the mountain ridge looking down at the tiny specks far below, let alone the view of planet earth from the other side of Andromeda. I begin with confession not in order to feel miserable, rather to call to mind a reality I often ignore. When I acknowledge where I stand before a perfect God, it restores the true state of the universe. Confession simply establishes the proper ground rules of creatures relating to their creator. The well-known pastor Haddon Robinson begins almost every sermon with the same brief confession: "God, if these people knew about me what you know about me, they wouldn't listen to a word I said."

Besides being good theology, confession makes for good psychology.*
Prayer, after all, is the currency of a relationship. Like many husbands, I had
to learn in my marriage that repressed issues do not go away. Just the opposite. I would bring up a minor hurt or misunderstanding that had occurred
several weeks or even months before, only to find it was no longer minor. In
relationships, as in the physical body, a thorn close to the surface may work
itself out, but an internal infection buried deep and disregarded will threaten
health and even life.

When Jesus cut through the carapace of the Pharisees, some of the most
religious people of his day, they wanted to do away with him. Truth hurts.
Yet I cannot receive healing unless I accept God's diagnosis of my wounded
state. God already knows who we are; we are the ones who must find a way
to come to terms with our true selves. Psalm 139 cries out, "Search me, O
God. . . . See if there is any offensive way in me." In order to overcome self-
deception, I need God's all-knowing help in rooting out hidden offenses like
selfishness, pride, deceit, lack of compassion.

Whenever I get depressed by a lack of spiritual progress, I realize that my
very dismay is a sign of progress. I have the sense of slipping further from
God mainly because I have a clearer idea of what God desires and how far
short I fall. And that is why I could reply to Mark with words of hope. Like
a recovering alcoholic, out of weakness and near-despair he had stumbled
into the very state most amenable to God's grace and healing. Mark need
not go through the painful stages required in humbling himself, for the circumstances of his life had already accomplished just that.

Walter Wangerin Jr. tells of a time early in his marriage when he had
committed some wrong against his wife, Thanne. Even though he was studying in seminary in hopes of becoming a pastor, he had always avoided praying aloud with her. It seemed too intimate, too personal an act. This time,
with a riptide of guilt sweeping away his shyness, he agreed. They lay for a
while side by side in bed, each waiting for the other to start. Walt began
with a hymn-like, formal prayer in the style he had learned in seminary.

---

* As Frederick Buechner notes, God asked Adam and Eve two penetrating questions after their first
act of disobedience: "Where are you?" and "What is this you have done?" Therapists, he remarks,
have been asking the same questions ever since. "Where are you?" exposes the present reality. They
are hiding, naked, ravaged by never-before-known feelings of guilt and shame. "What is this that you
have done?" exposes the past. In his encounter with Adam and Eve, God sets forth the consequences
of their behavior and then provides clothing to equip them for the new state they have brought about.
"They can't go back, but they can go forward clothed in a new way," says Buechner—the result any
good therapist hopes to accomplish.

After a silence, he heard Thanne's simple, clear voice speaking humbly and conversationally to God about him, her husband. Listening to her, he began to weep. The guilt dissolved, and he learned that the humbling was no end in itself, but a necessary step to the healing.

Jesus warned his disciples not to pray like hypocrites, who love to perform in public; instead, they should go into a closet and pray to the Father, who alone sees what is done in secret. His instructions have puzzled some commentators, who note that the one-room houses of Jesus' day, probably including his own, had no closets. Jesus must have been using a figure of speech, suggesting that we construct an imaginary room, a sanctuary of the soul, that fosters complete honesty before God. Though I need not find a literal closet, somehow I must ensure that my prayers are heartfelt and not a performance. That happens most conveniently in a closed room, but it may happen also in a church full of other people, or sitting with an elderly parent in a nursing home, or lying next to a spouse in bed.

Helpless

Norwegian theologian Ole Hallesby settled on the single word *helplessness* as the best summary of the heart attitude that God accepts as prayer. "Whether it takes the form of words or not, does not mean anything to God, only to ourselves," he adds. "Only he who is helpless can truly pray."

What a stumbling block! Almost from birth we aspire to self-reliance. Adults celebrate it as a triumph whenever children learn to do something on their own: go to the bathroom, get dressed, brush teeth, tie shoelaces, ride a bike, walk to school. When the child stubbornly insists, "I do it myself!" the parent takes secret pride in that independent spirit even when the child proceeds to make a mess of the task.

As adults we like to pay our own way, live in our own houses, make our own decisions, rely on no outside help. We look down upon those who live off welfare or charity. Faced with an unexpected challenge, we seek out "self-help" books. All the while we are systematically sealing off the heart attitude most desirable to God and most descriptive of our true state in the universe. "Apart from me you can do nothing," Jesus told his disciples, a plain fact that we conspire to deny.

The truth, of course, is that I am not self-reliant. As a first-grade student I hated having the teacher stand over me to correct my reading miscues; I wanted to "do it myself!" But had the teacher not assumed her proper role, I may never have learned to read books, much less write them. As an adult I rely on public utilities to bring me electricity and fuel, vehicle manufacturers to provide me transportation, ranchers and farmers to feed me, pastors and mentors to nourish me spiritually. I live in a web of dependence, at the center of which is God in whom all things hold together.

Prayer forces me to catch sight of this my true state. In Henri Nouwen's words, "To pray is to walk in the full light of God, and to say simply, without holding back, 'I am human and you are God.' At that moment, conversion occurs, the restoration of the true relationship. A human being is not some-

Bearing Secrets

JOHN

I've been working around street people, mostly homeless, for twenty-five years now. I help run a coffeehouse where they can drop in, and then on Sunday we hold a small urban church service upstairs. We never know what will happen there. Some of the people smell bad, disturbed people pray too long, and visitors wander in and out of the service. The other week one person prayed, "Thank you, Lord, for Metamusil," and another chimed in, "That's a 10-4, God."

I was surprised to learn how many street people are fundamentalists, at least those who claim any kind of faith. No wonder: the missions they go to preach a steady diet of hellfire and brimstone, and many street people carry around some notion of a mean God from their childhood. There is plenty of shame and worthlessness to go around.

I have a theory that both street people and fundamentalists suffer from attachment disorders. Somehow in childhood they never learned to bond with parents and never learned to bond with God either. How can you trust another *person* with who you are, much less God?

My friends in AA tell us we're as sick as our secrets. I know many folks with dark secrets, and nowhere to take them. Sometimes they go crazy, literally insane, because they can't stand being alone with their dark thoughts and secrets. Or they get loaded, or get high.

An acquaintance of mine ran a street ministry just a few blocks away. He had secrets about failures in his past and financial pressures in his

one who once in a while makes a mistake, and God is not someone who now and then forgives. No, human beings *are* sinners and God *is* love."

Most parents feel a pang when the child outgrows dependence, even while knowing the growth to be healthy and normal. With God, the rules change. I never outgrow dependence, and to the extent I think I do, I delude myself. Asking for help lies at the root of prayer: the Lord's Prayer itself consists of a string of such requests. Prayer is a declaration of dependence upon God.

A character in one of Henry Adams's novels cries out in frustration, "Why must the church always appeal to my weakness and never to my

---

present that he never told anyone. They bottled up inside him. One day his wife walked in the front door and found his body swaying from a rope. I cannot tell you what a blow that was for the people he ministered to. They barely hang on to life themselves, and then to have their pastor commit suicide ...

We all bear secrets. Those of us fortunate enough to have a spouse, a friend, or someone we can trust, have someone to share our secrets with. If not, at least we have God, who knows our secrets before we spill them. The fact that we're still alive shows that God has more tolerance for whatever those secrets represent than we may give God credit for.

If I'm right about attachment disorders, the best ministry I can offer is a long-term relationship. I tell people that I hang with the poor all day, and that sums it up. I hope that over the years and decades they learn to trust me as someone who can handle their secrets. I hope that trust will gradually spill over to God. And I tell people who encounter the homeless on the streets and are confused about how to respond, that eye contact and a listening ear may be more important than food or money or Bible verses. They need to connect in some small way with another human being.

A German poet wrote a poem about the poor. It's really a prayer:

> Make it so the poor are no longer
> despised and thrown away.
>
> Look at them standing about—
> like wildflowers, which have nowhere else to grow.

strength!" I can think of several reasons. In a world that glorifies success, an admission of weakness disarms pride at the same time that it prepares us to receive grace. Meanwhile, the very weakness that drives us to pray becomes an invitation for God to respond with compassion and power.

> The Lord upholds all those who fall
> and lifts up all who are bowed down.

In the presence of the Great Physician, my most appropriate contribution may be my wounds.

Humble

In words that apply directly to prayer, Peter says, "'God opposes the proud but gives grace to the humble.' Humble yourselves, therefore, under God's mighty hand, that he may lift you up in due time. Cast all your anxiety on him because he cares for you." Note the progression: humility, the step down, makes possible God's lifting us up. By trying to be strong, I may even block God's power.

Jesus' story of the Pharisee and the tax collector draws a sharp contrast between a prayer of pious superiority, which God rejects, and a prayer of desperation — "God, have mercy on me, a sinner" — which God welcomes. Jesus drew this conclusion to his story: "For everyone who exalts himself will be humbled, and he who humbles himself will be exalted."

For a time I did not appreciate humility, which I confused with negative self-image. Humble Christians seemed to grovel, parrying compliments with an "It's not me, it's the Lord" attitude. Since then, however, I have seen true humility at work in the people I most admire. For them humility is an ongoing choice to credit God, not themselves, for their natural gifts and then to use those gifts in God's service.

My first employer, Harold Myra, showed humility in the kind and patient way he treated me, a young writer still wet behind the ears. He never made an editorial change without painstakingly convincing me that the change would actually improve my work. He saw as his mission not just to improve words but to improve writers, and he could do so only by walking me through the steps that led to the editing he proposed.

Other heroes of mine exercised humility by finding a group overlooked and underserved. I think of Dr. Paul Brand, a promising young physician who volunteered in India as the first orthopedic surgeon to work with leprosy patients, many of them from the untouchable caste. Or of Henri Nouwen, professor at Yale and Harvard, who left those schools to become a chaplain among people having a fraction of the Ivy League students' IQs: the mentally handicapped at l'Arche homes in France and Canada. As I got to know both of these men, they demonstrated how downward mobility can lead to the success that matters most.

All of America watched how President Jimmy Carter handled the humiliation of losing an election and the subsequent shunning by his own party. Once the most powerful person in the world, he decided against golf and the talk-show circuit and devoted his retirement to such causes as helping the poor in Africa and building houses for Habitat for Humanity.

The cultures of ancient Greece and Rome did not favor humility, admiring instead the values of accomplishment and self-reliance. Likewise today, a modern celebrity culture shines the spotlight on a billionaire who takes delight in firing people, as well as on supermodels, strutting rap musicians, and boastful athletes. As theologian Daniel Hawk puts it, "The basic human problem is that everyone believes that there is a God and I am it." We need a strong corrective, and for me prayer offers that very corrective.

Why value humility in our approach to God? Because it accurately reflects the truth. Most of what I am — my nationality and mother tongue, my race, my looks and body shape, my intelligence, the century in which I was born, the fact that I am still alive and relatively healthy — I had little or no control over. On a larger scale, I cannot affect the rotation of planet earth, or the orbit that maintains a proper distance from the sun so that we neither freeze nor roast, or the gravitational forces that somehow keep our spinning galaxy in exquisite balance. There is a God and I am not it.

Humility does not mean I grovel before God, like the Asian court officials who used to wriggle along the ground like worms in the presence of their emperor. It means, rather, that in the presence of God I gain a glimpse of my true state in the universe, which exposes my smallness at the same time it reveals God's greatness.

Doubting

In one of his briefest parables Jesus described a man searching for treasure in a field. All too often I focus on the hiddenness of the treasure and the work required to dig it out. Much of Christian belief seems obscured: God hidden in a baby in a manger, and also in sacred words composed mainly by Jews throughout their tortured history, and then most improbably in the church, an institution no more holy or supernatural than, well, myself.

I keep digging, searching for ways to explain a doctrine like the Trinity so that Jewish and Muslim friends can even comprehend it. I question the cost of God's slow plan of redemption and re-creation: can it really be worth all that pain, including God's own? Why would God mount a rescue plan for the human species but not the fallen angels? And will my few decades' sojourn on this planet truly determine how I will spend eternity?

On a trip to Japan I found myself late at night in a pastor's study in one of the largest churches in Tokyo (which isn't saying much, since the average congregation numbers thirty in a nation where Christians claim only 1 percent of the population). I had flown in that morning and had already endured a rigorous day of meetings. I wanted to check into my hotel room and go to sleep, but Japanese hospitality required this courtesy visit.

Ich bete wieder, du Erlauchter

RAINER MARIA RILKE, FROM *RILKE'S BOOK OF HOURS: LOVE POEMS TO GOD*

I am praying again, Awesome One.
You hear me again, as words
from the depths of me
rush toward you in the wind.

I've been scattered in pieces,
torn by conflict,
mocked by laughter,
washed down in drink.

In alleyways I sweep myself up
out of garbage and broken glass.
With my half-mouth I stammer you,
who are eternal in your symmetry.
I lift to you my half-hands
in wordless beseeching, that I may find again
the eyes with which I once beheld you.

The pastor pulled out a sheaf of papers and, through an interpreter, told me that during his entire career he had worried over this one issue but was afraid of speaking to anyone about it. Would I listen? I nodded for him to continue and reached for a mug, breaking my rule against late-night coffee.

For the next twenty minutes without interruption the pastor poured out the agony he felt over the 99 percent of Japanese who had not accepted Jesus. Would they all burn in hell because of their ignorance? He had heard of theologians who believed in people having a second chance after death and knew the mysterious passage in 1 Peter about Jesus preaching to those in Hades. Some theologians he had read seemed to believe in universal salvation although certain passages in the Bible indicated otherwise. Could I offer him any hope?

Thinking aloud, I mentioned that God causes the sun to rise on the just and unjust and has no desire that anyone should perish. God's Son on earth

I am a house gutted by fire
where only the guilty sometimes sleep
before the punishment that devours them
hounds them out into the open.

I am a city by the sea
sinking into a toxic tide.
I am strange to myself, as though someone unknown
had poisoned my mother as she carried me.

It's here in all the pieces of my shame
that now I find myself again.
I yearn to belong to something, to be contained
in an all-embracing mind that sees me
as a single thing.
I yearn to be held
in the great hands of your heart —
oh let them take me now.
Into them I place these fragments, my life,
and you, God — spend them however you want.

spent his last strength praying for his enemies. We discussed the view of hell presented in C. S. Lewis's intriguing fantasy, *The Great Divorce*, which shows people like Napoleon who have a second chance after death but opt against it. "*Thy* will be done," says God reluctantly to those who make a final rejection.

"I do not know the answer to your questions," I said at last. "But I believe strongly that at the end of time no one will be able to stand before God and say 'You were unfair!' However history settles out, it will settle on the side of justice tempered by mercy."

Like Job, I reached that conclusion not through observation or argument but through encounter. "Surely God will be able to understand my doubts in a world like this, won't He?" asked the Dutch prisoner Etty Hillesum from a Nazi concentration camp. I believe God will, in part because God's revelation to us includes eloquent expressions of those very doubts.

I challenge skeptics to find a single argument used against God by the great agnostics — Voltaire, David Hume, Bertrand Russell — that is not already included in such biblical books as Habakkuk, the Psalms, Ecclesiastes, Lamentations, and, yes, Job. These strong passages from the Bible express the anguish of dislocation: of hurt and betrayal, of life that doesn't make sense, of God who seems not to care or even exist. Most important, these accusations contained in the Bible itself are framed as prayers.

Prayer allows a place for me to bring my doubts and complaints — in sum, my ignorance — and subject them to the blinding light of a reality I cannot comprehend but can haltingly learn to trust. Prayer is personal, and my doubts take on a different cast as I get to know the Person to whom I bring them.

For many years I missed the point of Jesus' parable. The man may have labored to find treasure hidden in a field, but "then in his joy went and sold all he had and bought that field." After that discovery, I doubt he dwelt much on the effort involved in digging.

Honest

I was teaching a class at a church in Chicago when a young woman raised her hand with a question. I knew her as a shy, conscientious student who attended faithfully but never spoke. The rest of the class seemed surprised as well and listened attentively. "I'm not always sincere when I pray," she began. "Sometime it seems forced, more like a ritual. I'm just repeating words. Does

God hear those prayers? Should I keep going even though I have no confidence that I'm doing it right?"

I let the silence hang in the room for a moment before attempting an answer. "Do you notice how quiet it is in here?" I said. "We all sense your honesty. It took courage for you to be vulnerable, and you touched a nerve with others of us in the room. You seem sincere, unlike a salesman, say, who gets paid to give a spiel. We're tuned in, listening, respectful, because you are being authentic. And I imagine it's the same with God. More than anything else, God wants your authentic self."

The Japanese, famous for their inscrutability, have two words that hint at the divided self. There is the *tatemae* (pronounced *tah-teh-mah-eh*), the part of myself I let people see on the outside, and the *hon ne* (pronounced *hon[g] neh*), what takes place on the inside where no one can see. Perhaps we need three words: one for the image of ourselves that we project to colleagues at work, clerks at the supermarket, and other casual acquaintances; one for the more vulnerable parts we make visible to select family members and best friends; and a third for the secret places we never make known.

That third place is what God invites us to lay open in prayer. Prayer makes room for the unspeakable, those secret compartments of shame and regret that we seal away from the outside world. In vain I sometimes build barriers to keep God out, stubbornly disregarding the fact that God looks on the heart, penetrating beyond the *tatemae* and *hon ne* to where no person can see. As God informed the prophet Samuel, "The Lord does not look at the things man looks at. Man looks at the outward appearance, but the Lord looks at the heart."

In truth, what I think and feel as I pray, rather than the words I speak, may be the real prayer, for God "hears" that too. My every thought occurs in God's presence. (Psalm 139:4, 7–8: "Before a word is on my tongue you know it completely, O Lord.... Where can I flee from your presence? If I go up to the heavens, you are there; if I make my bed in the depths, you are there.") And as I learn to give voice to those secrets, mysteriously the power they hold over me melts away.

I know what happens in human relationships when I remain at a shallow level. With casual friends I discuss the weather, sports, upcoming concerts and movies, all the while steering clear of what matters more: a suppressed hurt, hidden jealousy, resentment of their children's rude behavior, concern for their spiritual welfare. As a result, the relationship goes nowhere. On the other hand, relationships deepen as I trust my friends with secrets.

Likewise, unless I level with God—about bitterness over an unanswered prayer, grief over loss, guilt over an unforgiving spirit, a baffling sense of God's absence—that relationship, too, will go nowhere. I may continue going to church, singing hymns and praise choruses, even addressing God politely in formal prayers, but I will never break through the intimacy barrier. "We must lay before Him what is in us, not what ought to be in us," wrote C. S. Lewis. To put it another way, we must trust God with what God already knows.

A friend from Canada wrote me that for much of her life she shamed herself for having negative emotions such as sadness, fear, and anger. She tried to suppress them but realized that any false attempt to change negative emotions into more positive ones would mean pretending not to feel things that she was actually feeling. She concluded,

> And to do that before God is a waste of time. So I'm trying, instead of shaming or pretending, to come to terms with my emotions, and bring them before God honestly. I have come to realize that I'm never going to stop having emotions, and probably strong emotions, because that is the way I'm wired. I'm emotionally rich—I have a large emotional bank account from which to make withdrawals. I must, however, learn to live rightly in the midst of my fluctuating emotions, and I believe that God can teach me to do this.

Exposed

It occurred to me one day that though I often worry about whether or not I sense the presence of God, I give little thought to whether God senses the presence of *me*. When I come to God in prayer, do I bare the deepest, most hidden parts of myself? Only when I do so will I discover myself as I truly am, for nothing short of God's light can reveal that. I feel stripped before that light, seeing a person far different from the image I cultivate for myself and for everyone around me.

God alone knows the selfish motives behind my every act, the vipers' tangle of lust and ambition, the unhealed wounds that paradoxically drive me to appear whole. Prayer invites me to bring my whole life into God's presence for cleansing and restoration. Self-exposure is never easy, but when I do it I learn that underneath the layers of grime lies a damaged work of art that God longs to repair.

"We cannot make Him visible to us, but we can make ourselves visible to Him," said Abraham Joshua Heschel. I make the attempt with hesitation, shame, and fear, but when I do so I feel those constraints dissolving. My fear of rejection yields to God's embrace. Somehow, in a way I can only trust and not understand, presenting to God the intimate details of my life gives God pleasure.

> "Can a mother forget the baby at her breast
>   and have no compassion on the child she has borne?
> Though she may forget,
>   I will not forget you!
> See, I have engraved you on the palms of my hands."

I think of the way mothers dote on their infants, who offer so little in return. Every sneeze, every turn of the head and dart of the eyes, every whimper and smile the mother scrutinizes as if studying for a test on infantile behavior. If a human mother responds with such absorbing love, how much more so God.

We humans represent the only species on earth with whom God can hold a conversation. Only we can articulate praise or lament. Only we can form words in response to the miracle, and also the tragedy, of life. We dare not devalue this our unique role in the cosmos, to give words to existence, words addressed to our creator. God eagerly bends an ear toward those words.*

David Ford, a professor at Cambridge, asked a Catholic priest the most common problem he encountered in twenty years of hearing confession. With no hesitation the priest replied, "God." Very few of the parishioners he meets in confession behave as if God is a God of love, forgiveness, gentleness, and compassion. They see God as someone to cower before, not as someone like Jesus, worthy of our trust. Ford comments, "This is perhaps the hardest truth of any to grasp. Do we wake up every morning amazed that

---

*In John Milton's *Paradise Lost*, a fallen Adam and Eve wander the earth disconsolate, wondering at their deeds that have seemed to knock the entire planet off its axis, wondering whether God will ever again incline toward them. Then Adam sees a ray of hope:

> For, since I sought
> By prayer the offended Deity to appease,
> Kneeled and before him humbled all my heart,
> Methought I saw him placable and mild,
> Bending his ear; persuasion in me grew
> That I was heard with favour; peace returned
> Home to my breast.

we are loved by God?... Do we allow our day to be shaped by God's desire to relate to us?"

Reading Ford's questions, I realize that my image of God, more than anything else, determines my degree of honesty in prayer. Do I trust God with my naked self? Foolishly, I hide myself in fear that God will be displeased, though in fact the hiding may be what displeases God most. From my side, the wall seems like self-protection; from God's side it looks like lack of trust. In either case, the wall will keep us apart until I acknowledge my need and God's surpassing desire to meet it. When I finally approach God, in fear and trembling, I find not a tyrant but a lover.

The apostle Paul prayed "that you, being rooted and established in love, may have power, together with all the saints, to grasp how wide and long and high and deep is the love of Christ." I doubt Paul prayed this prayer once only; for my part, I have to pray it every day. The most important purpose of prayer may be to let our true selves be loved by God.

> [God] does not treat us as our sins deserve
>> or repay us according to our iniquities.
> For as high as the heavens are above the earth,
>> so great is his love for those who fear him;
> as far as the east is from the west,
>> so far has he removed our transgressions from us.
> As a father has compassion on his children,
>> so the Lord has compassion on those who fear him;
> for he knows how we are formed,
>> he remembers that we are dust.
>
> PSALM 103:10–14

CHAPTER 4

THE GOD WHO IS

Who one believes God to be is most accurately revealed
not in any credo but in the way one speaks to God
when no one else is listening.
NANCY MAIRS

On a visit to Nepal I bought a prayer wheel. Shaped like a rolling pin and inlaid with colorful stones, it has a handle attached to a weighted cylinder which spins around and around by centrifugal force as I rotate my wrist. Unscrew the top, and inside you find an elaborate prayer written out in spidery Nepali script. Devout Buddhists in Nepal believe that each rotation of the wheel sends a prayer up to heaven. Outside their gold-domed temples, priests turn giant versions of these wheels all day long. (Tech-savvy Buddhists download prayers onto their computer hard drives, which spin around at 5400 revolutions per minute.)

In Japan I have watched well-dressed men and women visit a Shinto shrine. The collector accepts Visa and American Express cards, an important convenience since worshipers must pay a minimum of fifty dollars to have a priest offer prayers. First the priest bangs a drum to get the gods' attention, then says the prayer. To the side stand large barrels of sake liquor, or rice wine, set aside for the gods. Before leaving, the pilgrims attach their written requests to "prayer trees" which surround the shrine, the white slips of paper rustling in the breeze like cherry blossoms.

In Taiwan, walking along the side of a mountain road, I picked up what I thought was litter. It turned out to be "ghost money" tossed out the window by truck drivers to appease the road ghosts and protect against accidents. Taoist temples sell this money, printed on cheap paper like Monopoly money, and worshipers at the temple burn it by the bundle in large incinerators. Such money may keep an underworld ghost from pestering you, or perhaps please a departed relative who needs cash in heaven. The temples also sell model cars and motorbikes, so that the departed may have transport in heaven, as well as a smorgasbord of food for the gods.

Taiwan is a high-tech country that manufactures most of the world's notebook computers, and yet many Taiwanese treat their religion as a kind of good-luck charm. They view deity as an impersonal force that controls fate. Likewise, Hindus in India appease the gods with offerings of food, flowers, and animal sacrifices.

In truth, Christians often treat prayer the same way. If I do my duty, then God "owes me." Worship becomes a kind of transaction: I've given God something, so it's God's turn to reciprocate. Prayer as transaction rather than relationship can decline into a practice more duty than joy, an occasional and awkward exercise with little connection to life — not so different from the Buddhist monk spinning his prayer wheel or the Japanese businesswoman performing her temple ritual. A man may "say his prayers" at night or before meals, repeating words he learned in childhood. His wife prays more conversationally, in bits and snatches during the day, but she too views God as distant and unapproachable, off in heaven somewhere. Neither has much sense of a loving God who wants an intimate involvement in their lives.

Jonathan Aitken, a former Member of Parliament in Great Britain, compares his early relationship with God to that with a bank manager: "I spoke to him politely, visited his premises intermittently, occasionally asked him for a small favour or overdraft to get myself out of difficulty, thanked him condescendingly for his assistance, kept up the appearance of being one of his reasonably reliable customers, and maintained superficial contact with him on the grounds that one of these days he might come in useful." When convicted of perjury and sentenced to prison, Aitken decided to pursue a more personal relationship.

Afterimages

As Aitken soon discovered, those who desire to communicate directly with God face unique challenges. A letter I received from a reader in Cornwall, England, abruptly reminded me of that fact.

> I was brought up in a loving Christian home and worshiped in a small country chapel. Many of the services were times of great joy and encouragement and quite emotional. However, similar to your upbringing, I was

brought up to believe in a God who was very strict and I grew up to live in fear of His judgement rather than in gratitude for His love. I became very depressed and began to question my faith and to ask myself what I did believe.... What I do miss is that close relationship, the emotional assurance that I knew before my doubts and questioning arose. One of our hymns has the words "Where is the blessedness I knew when first I saw the Lord?" I no longer have that cosy, simple, close relationship that I had from childhood.

Everyone approaches God with a set of preconceptions gleaned from many sources: church, Sunday school lessons, books, movies, sermons by television evangelists, stray comments by believers and skeptics alike. These tend to linger, as afterimages burned into the mind. Much like the man in Cornwall, I used to conceive of God as a glowering, cosmic Supercop, a God to be feared more than loved.

A woman I know cringes every time she hears someone address God as Father in prayer because her earthly father's abuse forever spoiled that word for her.* Another friend grew up with the image of a white male God up there, with a huge white beard and large hands, an autocrat who kept track of all her defects. Years later she described that image of God to a spiritual mentor. After a long, empathetic pause the mentor suggested, "Why don't you just consider firing that God?" So she did.

I did not grow up with such a visual image of God, probably because the church warned so severely against "graven images" and kept its concrete block walls free of religious artwork. Instead, I would hear about God's roles—as creator or judge, for example—and think of God primarily within that role. I found it as difficult to imagine a real Person behind that role as it was for me in the first grade to imagine a real person behind the teacher or principal.

As an adult, I still relate to people by virtue of their roles: the clerk at Starbucks, the car wash attendant, the software support person on a phone line from India. When I choose friends, though, people I want to know on a more intimate level, I push past the externals to the real person underneath. I spend time with my closest friends not because of what they can do for me but for the pleasure of their company. How can I do that with God?

---

*George MacDonald gave this advice to those for whom the positive image of "father" has been stained: "You must interpret the word by all that you have missed in life." The fatherhood of God represents an ideal which for many people has been badly marred.

A Vast Difference

All my friends have some similarities to me and some differences. One shares a background in Southern fundamentalism but thinks it bizarre that I read the sports pages; another enjoys many of the same authors I read but thinks me an old fogey for listening to classical music. Every relationship spawns a kind of dance between the self and the other. How much more so with a holy, ineffable God who lives in a realm of spirit.

I am overwhelmed by the vastness of God, the imbalance of any creature's relationship to such a being. "Since it is God we are speaking of, you do not understand it. If you could understand it, it would not be God," said Saint Augustine. We who barely comprehend ourselves are approaching a God we cannot possibly comprehend. No wonder some Christians through the centuries have felt more comfortable praying to saints or relying on intermediaries.

As a journalist, I have had occasion to spend time with famous people who make me feel very small. I have interviewed two presidents of the United States, members of the rock band U2, Nobel laureates, television stars, and Olympic athletes. Although I prepare my questions thoroughly in advance, I rarely sleep well the night before and have to fight a case of nerves. I hardly think of these people as mutual friends. I wonder what I would do if seated at a banquet next to, say, Albert Einstein or Mozart. Would I chitchat? Would I make a fool of myself?

In prayer I am approaching the creator of all that is, Someone who makes me feel immeasurably small. How can I do anything but fall silent in such presence? More, how can I believe that whatever I say matters to God? If I step back and look at the big picture, I even wonder why such a magnificent, incomprehensible God would bother with a paltry experiment like planet earth.*

The Bible sometimes emphasizes the distance between humans and God (subjects of a king, defendants before a judge, servants of a master) and sometimes emphasizes the closeness (bride of a bridegroom, sheep of a shepherd, God's offspring). Without question, though, Jesus himself taught us to

---

*Reynolds Price suggests an answer by analogy: "From the range of emotions that might inspire you or me, or another rational human, to create a universe, love seems the one most likely to cause such a mammoth and long-lasting enterprise." We understand God's motive only by weak comparisons. For example, why do parents endure the effort, expense, and sacrifice involved in raising children? For love. And that, in fact, is the very motivation described by Jesus: "For God so *loved* the world that he gave his only Son ..." In creating human beings, God wanted someone to love as well as someone capable of returning that love, no matter how feebly.

count on the closeness. In his own prayers he used the word *Abba*, an informal word of address that Jews before him had not used in prayer. A new way of praying was born, says the German scholar Joachim Jeremias: "Jesus talks to his Father as naturally, as intimately and with the same sense of security as a child talks to his father."

The early churches adopted Jesus' style of intimate prayer. "Because you are sons, God sent the Spirit of his Son into our hearts, the Spirit who calls out, 'Abba, Father,'" Paul assured them. Elsewhere he takes the intimacy one step further: "We do not know what we ought to pray for, but the Spirit himself intercedes for us with groans that words cannot express."

In one hand I hold the truth of God's vastness, and in the other hand I hold the truth of God's desire for intimacy. Dante spoke of "the love that moves the sun and other stars." I gaze at the stars and marvel at the apparent insignificance of the entire human experiment; then I read a biblical passage about God rejoicing over us with singing. Only lately have I understood that the vast difference between God and us allows this very capacity. God operates by different rules of time and space. And God's infinite greatness, which we would expect to diminish us, actually makes possible the very closeness that we desire.

A God unbound by our rules of time has the ability to invest in every person on earth. God has, quite literally, all the time in the world for each one of us. The psalmist exclaimed that "a thousand years in your sight are like a day that has just gone by," and the reverse also applies: to God, one day is like a thousand years.* The common question, "How can God listen

---

*Modern physics helps us conceive of the relative nature of time. According to Einstein's theory of relativity, a person traveling at the speed of light would see the entire history of the universe pass by in a single instant. On the other hand, a God who encompasses the entire universe can "view" what happens on earth and what happened fifteen thousand or billion years ago simultaneously (a word that doesn't really apply to a timeless God). We see the stars as they used to be, receiving light on Earth that they generated millions of years ago. As the Dutch novelist Harry Mulisch speculates in his fantasy *The Discovery of Heaven*, if we had the technology to place a mirror on a celestial object forty light-years away, beamed images from earth to that mirror, then gazed at it through a very powerful telescope, we would see right now reflections of what took place on earth eighty years ago—forty years for Earth's light to reach the distant planet, and forty years for the reflection to reach Earth. Past and present merge. An omnipresent Being large enough to coexist on the Andromeda galaxy and also on Earth would experience time in a completely different way, experiencing at once both the history of earth and the billion-year-old history of the galaxy, as well as all years in between. If a star explodes in Andromeda, this Being takes note of it immediately, yet will also "see" it from the viewpoint of an observer on earth many years later *as if it has just happened*. God is *outside* time, say the theologians, in a way that we are only beginning to imagine. Time, like everything else in creation, ultimately serves the creator.

to millions of prayers at once?" betrays an inability to think outside time. I cannot imagine a being who can hear billions of prayers in thousands of languages because I am stunted by my humanity. Trapped in time, I cannot conceive of infinity. The distance between God and humanity — a distance that no one can grasp — is, ironically, what allows the intimacy.

Jesus, who accepted the constraints of time while living on this planet, understood better than anyone the vast difference between God and human beings. Obviously, he knew of the Father's greatness and at times reflected nostalgically on the big picture, "the glory I had with you before the world began." Yet Jesus did not question the personal concern of God who watches over sparrows and counts the hairs on our heads.

More to the point, Jesus valued prayer enough to spend many hours at the task. If I had to answer the question "Why pray?" in one sentence, it would be, "Because Jesus did." He bridged the chasm between God and human beings. While on earth he became vulnerable, as we are vulnerable; rejected, as we are rejected; and tested, as we are tested. In every case his response was prayer.

Unpredictable Presence

Besides the disproportion between us, relating to God presents another major challenge: invisibility. Although we "live and move and have our being" in God, as Paul said, my awareness of God's presence may be as fickle as the weather. I think back to the letter-writer from Cornwall, who had lost the feeling of intimacy: "Where is the blessedness I once knew?"

These things feed my faith: epiphanies of beauty in nature, sunbursts of grace and forgiveness, the portrait of God I get in Jesus, stirring encounters with people who truly live out their faith. And these feed my doubts: God's baffling tolerance of history's atrocities, my unanswered prayers, sustained periods of God's seeming absence. Meetings with God may include ecstasy and joy, or withdrawal and silence; always they include mystery.

To come to terms with this unpredictability I tell myself that every friendship has a misty side, that all relationships sometimes reveal and sometimes conceal. When I wonder why God doesn't simply "show up," I recall that when God did, especially in Old Testament days, the appearance hardly enhanced communication: usually the person fell to the ground, flattened by blinding light. In any event, I console myself, all relationships go through hot and cold spells. Sometimes communication is verbal, sometimes silent, sometimes close, sometimes distant. Usually, these lectures to myself fail to convince. I am left with the unsettling truth that God, not I, has ultimate control over the relationship.

Etty Hillesum, the young Jewish girl who kept a journal during her stay at Auschwitz, wrote of an "uninterrupted dialogue" with God. She had epiphanies even in that morally barren place. "Sometimes when I stand in some corner of the camp, my feet planted on Your earth, my eyes raised towards Your Heaven, tears sometimes run down my face, tears of deep emotion and gratitude." She knew the horror. "And I want to be there right in the thick of what people call horror and still be able to say: life is beautiful. Yes, I lie here in a corner, parched and dizzy and feverish and unable to do a thing. Yet I am also with the jasmine and the piece of sky beyond my window."

Hillesum concluded, "For once you have begun to walk with God, you need only keep on walking with God and all of life becomes one long stroll—a marvelous feeling." I read her words of defiant faith and wonder what I might have written in my private journal as I breathed in ashes from the ovens each day, burnt offerings of a race "chosen" by Hitler. Yes, walking with God makes life one long stroll—but for how many, and how often, is it a marvelous feeling?

Prayer is a subversive act performed in a world that constantly calls faith into question. I may have a sense of estrangement in the very act of prayer, yet by faith I continue to pray and to look for other signs of God's presence. If God were not present at some submolecular level in all of creation, I believe, the world would simply cease to exist. God is present in the beauties and oddities of creation, most of which go undetected by any human observer. God is present in his Son Jesus, who visited the planet and now serves as advocate for those left behind. God is present in the hungry, the homeless, the sick, and the imprisoned, as Jesus claimed in Matthew 25, and we serve God when we serve them. God is present in base communities in Latin America and in house churches that meet surreptitiously in barns in China, as well as in cathedrals and buildings constructed to God's glory. God is present in the Spirit, who groans wordlessly on our behalf and who speaks in a soft voice to all consciences attuned to him.

I have learned to see prayer not as my way of establishing God's presence, rather as my way of responding to God's presence that is a fact whether or not I can detect it. To quote Abraham Joshua Heschel, "Contact with Him is not our achievement. It is a gift, coming down to us from on high like a meteor, rather than rising up like a rocket. Before the words of prayer come to the lips, the mind must believe in God's willingness to draw near to us, and in our ability to clear the path for His approach. Such belief is the idea that leads us toward prayer."

My *feelings* of God's presence — or God's absence — are not the presence or the absence. Whenever I fixate on techniques, or sink into guilt over

---

Soul Listening

ANTHONY

As a forty-nine-year-old man stumbling through his midlife passage, I have been dealing with a divorce and trying to find closure in my father's death, among other challenges. It is because of these experiences, and what I have learned about myself, that I realize the importance of leading a more spiritual life. Trying to live up to the honor code of traditional masculinity (not asking for help, no crying, staying logical, being in control, etc.) has only led to unhealthy and destructive behaviors.

I have begun to make time to help me be more open to God. I make time for prayer and reflection, long walks, spiritual readings. In fact, I ask myself a series of questions each day that help me focus on the spiritual instead of relying on the material parts of my life.

Questions like,

> How can I slow down?
> How can I simplify things?
> How can I bring silence into my life?
> How can I savor this moment?
> How can I speak up? (Tell the truth)
> How can I settle in? (Establish roots and rituals)
> How can I shed my armor and masks?
> How can I soften my approach to life?
> How can I serve the community?

These questions help me to touch my soul, listen to my soul, and bring me closer to God. As J. Heinrich Arnold said, "Christian discipleship is not a question of our own doing, it is a matter of making room for God so that he can live in us."

my inadequate prayers, or turn away in disappointment when a prayer goes unanswered, I remind myself that prayer means keeping company with God who is already present.*

A friend of mine, an attractive young woman of mixed race, goes each day to visit the most violent prison in South Africa. Her efforts there have shown remarkable results in calming the violence, twice prompting the BBC to produce a documentary on her. In trying to explain those results, Joanna said to me, "Well, of course, Philip, God was already present in the prison. I just had to make him visible." I have come to see prayer along the same lines. God is already present in my life and all around me; prayer offers the chance to attend and respond to that presence.

Hearing God

The author Brennan Manning, who leads spiritual retreats several times each year, once told me that not one person who has followed his regimen of a silent retreat has failed to hear from God. Intrigued and a bit skeptical, I signed up for one of his retreats, this one extending over five days. Each attendee met for an hour each day with Brennan, who would give us assignments for meditation and spiritual work. We also met for a daily worship time during which only Brennan talked. Otherwise we were free to spend our time as we wished, with one requirement: two hours of prayer per day.

I doubt I had devoted more than thirty minutes to prayer at any one session in my life. The first day I wandered to the edge of a meadow and sat down with my back against a tree. I had brought along Brennan's assignment for the day and a notebook in which to record my thoughts. *How long will I stay awake?* I wondered.

To my great fortune, a herd of 147 elk (I had plenty of time to count them) wandered into the very field where I was sitting. To see one elk is exciting; to watch 147 elk in their natural habitat is enthralling. Yet, as I soon learned, to watch 147 elk for two hours is, to put it mildly, boring. They lowered their heads and chewed grass. They raised their heads in unison and looked at a raspy crow. They lowered their heads again and chewed grass. For two hours

---

* Austin Farrer gives an important reminder: "Prayer can seem dull or difficult; though if we give ourselves to it, commonly ends up less dull and less obstructed than it began. Only what is dull or dark or labored on our side is not so on the side of God, who rejoices in every least motion of our good will towards him; and where we see the merest vestige of his presence, there with cherubim and seraphim and all the host of heaven is he."

nothing else happened. No mountain lions attacked, no bulls charged each other and locked antlers. All the elk bent over and chewed grass.

After a while the very placidity of the scene began to affect me. The elk had not noticed my presence and I simply became a part of their environment, taking on their own rhythms. I no longer thought about the work I had left at home, the deadlines facing me, the reading that Brennan had assigned. My body relaxed. In the leaden silence, my mind fell quiet.

"The quieter the mind," said Meister Eckhart, "the more powerful, the worthier, the deeper, the more telling and more perfect the prayer is." An elk does not have to work at having a quiet mind; it feels content standing in a field all day with its fellow elk, chewing grass. A lover does not have to work at attending to the beloved. I prayed for, and in fleeting moments received, that kind of absorbed attention to God.

I said few words during my two-hour prayer time that day, but I learned an important lesson. Job and the Psalms make clear that God finds pleasure not only in human companions but in the manifold creatures on this planet. A scene from nature that stands out as a highlight for me, God "sees" every day. I had gained another glimpse of my place in the universe, and God's—the view from above.

I never saw the elk again, even though every afternoon I searched the fields and forest for them. Over the next few days I said many words to God. I was turning fifty that year, and I asked for guidance on how I should prepare my soul for the rest of life. I made lists, and many things came to mind that would not have come to mind had I not been sitting in a field for hours at a time. The week became a kind of spiritual checkup that pointed out paths for further growth. I realized how many afterimages of God I still bore from childhood, and how I responded to God with a certain reserve, perhaps even with distrust. I heard no audible voice, and yet at the end of the week I had to agree with Brennan that I had heard from God.

I became more convinced than ever that God finds ways to communicate to those who truly seek God, especially when we lower the volume of the surrounding static. I remembered reading the account of a spiritual seeker who interrupted a busy life to spend a few days in a monastery. "I hope your stay is a blessed one," said the monk who showed the visitor to his cell. "If you need anything, let us know and we'll teach you how to live without it."

We learn to pray by praying, and two concentrated hours a day taught me much. To begin, I need to think more about God than about myself when I am praying. Even the Lord's Prayer centers first in what God wants from us. "Hallowed be your name, your kingdom come, your will be done"—God wants us to desire these things, to orient our lives around them.

How often do I come to God not with consumer requests but simply a desire to spend time with God, to discern what God wants from me and not vice versa? When I did that in the elk meadow, I mysteriously found that the answers to my prayers for guidance were around me all along. Nothing changed but my receptors; through prayer I opened them to God. "For all things sing you," wrote the poet Rilke; "at times we just hear them more clearly."

Prayer that focuses on God, meditative prayer, can serve as a kind of self-forgetfulness. Some have called it a "useless" act because we do it not for the sake of getting something out of it, but spontaneously, as uselessly as a child at play. After an extended time with God, my urgent requests, which had seemed so significant, took on a new light. I began to ask them for God's sake, not my own. Though my needs may drive me to prayer, there I come face-to-face with my greatest need: an encounter with God's own self.

Prayer that is based on relationship and not transaction may be the most freedom-enhancing way of connecting to a God whose vantage point we can never achieve and can hardly imagine. Quoting a psalm, Peter assures us that "the eyes of the Lord are on the righteous and his ears are attentive to their prayer." We need not bang a drum or bring animal sacrifices to get God's full attention; we already have it.

CHAPTER 5

COMING TOGETHER

If man is not made for God, why is he only happy in God?
If man is made for God, why is he so opposed to God?
BLAISE PASCAL

The main purpose of prayer is not to make life easier, nor to gain magical powers, but to know God. I need God more than anything I might get from God. Yet when I seek to know God through prayer, certain problems rear up.

Years ago, when I was beginning a writing career at *Campus Life* magazine, I used to discuss these problems with my colleague Tim Stafford. He later wrote about them in his book *Knowing the Face of God*, and I will simply quote him:

> Silently gazing into a friend's eyes may seem purer, and certainly more romantic, than mere talk. But conversation, not silence, builds relationships. Though I will never minimize the effect of beautiful eyes, I expect to talk to the people I care about—and to hear them talk back. We do not build relationships on a sentence or two spoken every few years. Conversation between real friends is a constant stream.
>
> So I have a problem with God. I have never had a conversation with him; I have never heard his audible voice. Though I sometimes feel powerful religious emotions, I am cautious in interpreting my impulses and feelings as messages from God. I do not want to take the Lord's name in vain. I do not want to say, "The Lord told me," when in reality I heard a mental recording of my mother's voice. I have spent any number of hours talking to God, and he has not yet answered back in a voice that was undeniably his.

Tim adds that he continues to pray, making requests of God and offering praise and worship, but questions persist. Why praise God who, unlike friends, does not need a lift? Why inform God of needs that God already knows about? Why thank God, who hardly needs a pat on the back?

Some people say that we should pray not because God needs it, but because we need it. When we praise him, we remind ourselves of what is fundamentally important. When we thank him, we humbly remember our utter dependence on his care. When we pray for people, we are encouraged to then go out and do something to help them. From this perspective prayer is a self-help exercise.

No doubt prayer does these and other good things for me, but if they are the principal reasons for praying, my "personal relationship" is in trouble. Prayer that is only a useful exercise is not conversation. It is more like writing a diary, which is also good for you, but it is entirely private and one-sided.

Why pray? What makes this strange practice, so problematic for many, important to God?

Why Jesus Prayed

I look first to Jesus for clues to the mysteries of faith, and regarding prayer he did not seem to share some of my biggest struggles. He never wondered whether God exists, whether anyone is truly listening. He never questioned the importance of prayer; indeed, he would flee a crowd of needy people in order to spend time alone with God and sometimes devote all night to the task. The way Jesus talked, prayer made everything else possible.

Jesus seemed fully at ease with the Father and at unease with the world. For him, prayer provided a refreshing reminder of cosmic reality, the "view from above" so often obscured on planet earth. Sometimes Jesus reminisced about that hidden realm: praying at supper the night of his arrest he recalled "the glory I had with you before the world began." Occasionally he felt such frustration with conditions on earth that he would let loose with a sigh: "O unbelieving generation ... how long shall I put up with you?" Jesus came from a place where God's command met no opposition; he knew exactly what he was asking when he instructed us to pray: "your will be done on earth as it is in heaven."

Just as Jesus reminisced about his suspended identity, in a few rare instances the Father brought it tenderly to mind. "You are my Son, whom I love; with you I am well pleased," God said as Jesus emerged from the water at his baptism. He heard a similar word of reinforcement at the Mount of Transfiguration—a close encounter that left his disciples face-down on the ground, terrified—and yet another at a melancholy moment shortly before his death. Each time, bystanders heard the voice and were startled by the phenomenon. Jesus, a refugee from heaven, felt comfort, not astonishment.

From his thirty-something years on earth, we have only these three glimpses of a supernatural boost. The rest of the time, for spiritual nourishment Jesus relied on the very thing we rely on: prayer. Jesus counted on prayer as a source of strength that equipped him to carry out a partnership with God the Father on earth. Jesus freely admitted his dependence: "the Son can do nothing by himself; he can do only what he sees his Father doing."

In a telling comment Jesus also said, "Your Father knows what you need before you ask him." He could not mean that prayer is unnecessary, for his own life belied that. He could only mean that we need not strive to convince God to care; the Father already cares, more than we can know. Prayer is not a matter of giving God new information. Instead of presenting requests as if God may not know them, it might be more appropriate to say, "God, you know I need this!"

And that is how Tim Stafford found a sort of resolution to his questions about prayer:

> Here, I believe, is the key to understanding what is most personal in prayer. We do not pray to tell God what he does not know, nor to remind him of things he has forgotten. He already cares for the things we pray about.... He has simply been waiting for us to care about them with him. When we pray, we stand by God and look with him toward those people and problems. When we lift our eyes from them toward him, we do so with loving praise, just as we look toward our oldest and dearest friends and tell them how we care for them, though they already know it.... We speak to him as we speak to our most intimate friends—so that we can commune together in love.

Friendship

Tim's depiction of prayer as relationship strikes a chord with me because for a period of time we worked closely together as friends and colleagues. We attended the same prayer group, read many of the same books, edited each other's articles, and faced the same career challenges. Sitting by a tennis court waiting for a vacancy, we talked about trivial things like sports and the weather. At other times we talked about our futures, the women we loved, our families, our dreams and disappointments.

The analogy of friendship has biblical roots as well. The Bible speaks of Abraham and Moses as being friends of God, and of David as a man after God's own heart. "You are my friends if you do what I command," said Jesus, who then explained, "I no longer call you servants, because a servant does not know his master's business. Instead, I have called you friends, for everything that I learned from my Father I have made known to you." Having shared the knowledge, Jesus now asks us to take up the partnership of God's work on earth. As we do so, we can picture God as a friend, not merely a boss. Prayer is the currency of that friendship.

I am drawn to friends for different reasons. With some I share common values and interests, but I also enjoy eccentric friends who encourage me to see things unconventionally. In either case I look for someone who will reward my honesty and not punish it, who will push my introverted self to a deeper level of intimacy. I look for companions along the journey, people I would not hesitate to call upon if I fall sick, or if I want to spring a surprise party. I want someone I can count on and, if that fails, someone able to handle it when I express my feelings of hurt and betrayal.

I communicate with friends on different levels. I'll spend an afternoon playing golf with three buddies and that evening my wife will ask what we talked about. My mind goes blank. *Did you see where my ball went? Great shot! How'd you correct that slice?* Oh, we may speak of families or vacation plans or work, but in five-minute spurts as we walk from one ball to the next. More in-depth communication takes place over a snack in the clubhouse than in five hours on the course.

With certain friends I like to toss around ideas and opinions. *Who are you planning to vote for? Why? What do you think of the situation in the Middle East?* With others—and the field narrows sharply—I express emotions and vulnerability. We talk about our marriages, aging parents, children, major disappointments, struggles with lust and other temptations.

I can count on one hand my most intimate friends, those with whom I would share anything. I can hardly think of a boundary on our conversations. We reached that plane of relationship after long hours together and considerable risk. If a doctor informs me tomorrow that I have a terminal disease, they will be my first calls.

Most of my intimate friends live in other cities, and as a result I may see them only once a year. When we meet, though, we skip the chitchat and go right to the heart of what concerns us most. I don't worry about being judged or second-guessed or made the subject of gossip. With true friends, I feel safe.

Friendship with God encompasses each of these levels of communication. God cares about the ordinary and everyday as well as the peak experi-

---

Time with God

SARA

As a new Christian I attended a private Ivy League – type school, where the only real option for fellowship was a charismatic prayer group. Many times in that group I had a strong sense of God's presence — a sense that has come and gone in the years since.

I didn't grow up with the idea that God answers specific prayers, and I must say that whenever I heard of Christians praying for parking places and the like, it bugged me. But when my teenagers went away to college and got exposed to risky behaviors, I prayed very specific prayers of desperation in the early hours of the morning. As a parent, you read news reports of binge drinking and sex parties on campus, and you feel so helpless, wondering what your kids are doing. I sometimes think of mothers whose children have committed suicide. They prayed too....

I'm trying to pray less "parentally," in other words, telling God what to do. Rather, I try to look behind the symptom of rebellion or risky behavior and ask God to help my children find better ways of finding meaning and of handling the stress in their lives.

I have had other serious emotional struggles with God, sometimes over

ences. I bring to God my failures and sins (confession, repentance) as well as my triumphs and joys (praise, thanksgiving). I bring to God my worries and concerns (petition, intercession). The very attempt to hide something from God is folly, for God knows all of who I am: the *hon ne* as well as the *tatemae*, the genetics as well as the environment, the thoughts and motives as well as the actions. I can sit silent before God, and still we can communicate—sometimes even better.

I used to puzzle over Jesus' comment that "your Father knows what you need before you ask him." Why bother to pray, then? Through friendship I understand his insight into intimacy. The more I know someone, the less information I need to communicate. When I go to a new doctor I have to fill out elaborate forms on my entire medical history; when I visit my family physician, who knows all that, we focus on what's bothering me right now. Similarly, casual friends and I have to catch up on our lives when we see

personal issues like marriage, but also over politics, terrorist attacks, war, environmental destruction, those issues. The fact that God does not seem to answer the prayers of many people for peace and well-being probably ought to get us Christians way more upset.

I don't really pray according to a formula, and I've never taken a class on centering prayer or meditation techniques. But I do see a spiritual director every six weeks or so. That helps keep me accountable to a discipline, and it helps to have someone point out what may be God's movement in my life. Otherwise, I try to pray along with the flow of my life, reaching toward what seems usable, honest, meaningful, and even enjoyable. I assume that is what God wants prayer to be: useful, honest, enjoyable. Something that makes me want to spend time with God.

While studying for a graduate degree, I often wondered how to integrate the academic work with God. I found a quote from Abraham Joshua Heschel which I propped up on my desk: "The school is a sanctuary ... learning is a form of worship." I see prayer not as a separate act, but as something intimate with my life. I pray in interludes of the day: the three-minute walk to my friend's house, waiting in line, driving. Prayer is like exercise. I know it's good for me and I benefit from it. Yet, as with exercise, I wish I did it more often. I know I would profit more.

each other; my closest friends, who already know those details, move quickly to more personal "soul matters."

The psalms express all levels of friendship with God, One who is in some ways like us and in some ways not. They include trivia as well as profundity, outrage as well as praise. Apparently God is the kind of friend who rewards honesty, for why else would the Bible include the more plaintive psalms? Jesus himself turned to them at a moment when he felt betrayed. "My God, my God, why have you forsaken me?" he cried, quoting from Psalms to pour out his sense of abandonment even as he called on God by name.

We are completely known to God, said C. S. Lewis—known like earthworms, cabbages, and nebulae, as objects of divine knowledge. "That is our destiny whether we like it or not. But though this knowledge never varies, the quality of our being known can." We can assent with all our will to be so known; we can unveil before God; we can offer ourselves to view. We can invite God into our lives and ourselves into God's. When we do that, putting ourselves on a personal footing with God, so to speak, relationship heats up and a potential for extraordinary friendship stirs to life. For God is a Person, too, and though a person unlike ourselves, One who surely fulfills more of what that word means, not less.

Running Dialogue

I am writing away from home, sequestered in the mountains in the middle of winter. At the end of each day I talk with my wife, Janet, about the events of the day. I tell her how many words I wrote and what obstacles I met in the process, what Nordic ski or snowshoe trails I explored (exercise serves as either cure or surrender to writer's block), which prepackaged frozen food I ate for dinner. She tells me about the progress of her nagging cold, the mail that has been accumulating in my absence, the neighbors she has encountered walking their dogs to the mailboxes down the road. We discuss the weather, current events, news from relatives, upcoming social engagements. In essence we meditate on the day with each other, in the process bringing its details into a new light.

What I have just described bears a striking resemblance to prayer, too. Prayer, according to one ancient definition, is "keeping company with God." I like that notion. It encompasses the epiphanies that happen during my day: turning a corner on a ski trail and seeing a gray fox skitter away, watching the pink alpenglow on the mountains as the sun sets, meeting an old friend at the grocery store. By incorporating those experiences into my prayers, I prolong and savor them so that they do not fall too quickly into my memory bank, or out of it.

"To pray is to make the most of our moments of perception," says Alan Ecclestone. "You pause on the thing that has happened, you turn it over and over like a person examining a gift, you set it in the context of past and future, you mentally draw out its possibilities, you give the moment time to reveal what is embedded in it." Janet, after all, shared my experiences vicariously as I described them to her whereas God was present all along.

On the other hand, keeping company with God also includes expressing the times of trial and frustration. In *Fiddler on the Roof*, Tevye keeps up a running dialogue with God, giving credit for the good things but also lamenting all that goes wrong. In one scene he sits dejected by the side of the road with his lame horse. "I can understand it," he says to God, "when you punish *me* when I am bad; or my *wife* because she talks too much; or my *daughter* when she wants to go off and marry a Gentile, but ... *What have you got against my horse?!*"

Jesus set the pattern for prayer as a continuous mode of friendship. The Old Testament contains many beautiful and magnificent prayers, usually led by a king or a prophet, and the Jews tended to view prayers as formal recitations led by someone else. Even the psalms contain notations for use in group worship rather than private meditation. Some scholars suggest that Jesus virtually invented private prayer. No one in the Old Testament directly addressed God as "Father," whereas Jesus did so 170 times. The model prayer he gave deals with the stuff of daily life—God's will, food, debts, forgiveness, temptation—and his own prayers showed a spontaneous communion with the Father that had no precedent. His disciples, no novices at prayer themselves, marveled at the difference. "Teach us to pray," they asked.

As every follower of Jesus learns, however, prayer does not come as naturally to the rest of us as it did to the original prayer revolutionary. I find prayer hard work, not the rejuvenating refuge it meant to Jesus. I struggle to see prayer as a dialogue, not a monologue. How can I commune with a God who tends not to use audible words in response? When I review the day with my wife on the telephone, she responds with laughter and empathy. God does not, at least not in any measurable way.

As a training ground, I read the psalms. I read Jesus' prayers, and the prayers of his followers. In the process I learn some of God's mysterious ways: an odd preference for ornery and even rebellious characters (this gives me

63

comfort), a propensity for tests of faith, a baffling tolerance of human freedom, a slowness to act, a shyness. I learn that God and I have a different view of the use of power and a different time line. God has no need to prove anything.

In prayer I speak haltingly at first, "slow of speech and tongue" like Moses. I open my soul, exposing by will what God already knows by wisdom. The psalms tell of panting with an open mouth, of thirsting for the living God, of longing for God as parched earth longs for water. They sound like letters from a heartsick lover, and at the core that's what we seekers are. I tell myself that God is inclining an ear to my prayer, and over time I learn to believe it. I see that God, like most of us, cares mainly about being loved, believed, trusted, honored.

As I persist at prayer, I recognize an answering partner who takes up the other side of the dialogue, a kind of internal alter ego representing God's point of view. When I want revenge, this partner reminds me of forgiveness;

Still Waiting

JOANNE

If you had asked me as a young Christian whether I believed in prayer, I would have quickly said yes. I would have told you about the time I spun out in the snow and didn't get hurt, or the time I dropped a house key somewhere in my '74 Dodge Dart and couldn't find it for hours, until I prayed. Maybe God takes care of neophyte believers, I don't know. He doesn't seem to take care of old-timers, though.

I could list probably a hundred prayers that haven't been answered. I'm not speaking of selfish prayers, but important prayers: God, keep my kids safe, keep them away from the wrong crowd. All three ended up in trouble with the law, abusing drugs and alcohol.

I've got to say, Jesus' story of the persistent widow who keeps pestering the judge *sours*. Thousands of people pray for a Christian leader who has cancer, and he dies. What did Jesus mean by that parable — that we keep beating our heads against a wall?

I've been living at the edge of the abyss for several years now. Yes, I have had close times, have felt the presence of God, and these memories alone are

when obsessed with my own selfish needs, I am struck with the needs of others. Suddenly I realize I am not talking to myself in this inner dialogue. The Spirit of God is praying within me, communicating the will of the Father.

"My secret is a very simple one: I pray," wrote Mother Teresa of Calcutta, a modern master of the skill:

> Prayer is simply talking to God.
> He speaks to us: we listen.
> We speak to him: he listens.
> A two-way process:
> speaking and listening.

Learning to dialogue with God will never end because we are unequal partners, God and I. Admitting that, bowing before it, helps open my ears. Pursuing God despite the differences helps open my mouth, and then my heart.

---

what keep me from checking out. Two times, maybe three, I have heard from God. Once the voice almost seemed audible. I was driving to the hospital as a young woman just out of college, having learned that I had leukemia, when these words from Isaiah came sharply to mind, "Do not be dismayed, for I am your God. I will strengthen you and help you; I will uphold you with my righteous right hand." I cling to those few memories, and get nothing else, no new sign that God is listening.

I'd guess maybe 20 percent of my prayers get anything like the answer I want. Over time, I give up. I pray for those things I believe will happen. Or I just don't pray. I review my journal and see God doing less and less. I get mad. Like a child, I stop talking. I'm passive-aggressive with God. I put him off. Maybe later.

I went to a mentor and poured out my soul, describing in detail all I've been through in the past few years with my health and especially with my kids. "What do I do?" I asked.

He sat there for the longest time and said, "I don't know, Joanne." He sighed. I waited for words of wisdom. None came. That's how it is with prayer too.

Passionate Alliance

To call God and me unequal partners is a laughable understatement. And yet by inviting us to do kingdom work on earth, God has indeed set up a kind of odd-couple alliance. God delegates work to human beings so that we do history together, so to speak. Clearly, the partnership has one dominant partner—something like an alliance between the United States and Fiji, perhaps, or between Microsoft and a high school programmer.

We know well what happens when human beings form such unequal alliances: the dominant partner throws weight around and the subordinate mostly keeps quiet. God, who has no reason to be threatened by the likes of us, instead invites a steady and honest flow of communication.

I have sometimes wondered why God places such a high value on honesty, even to the extent of enduring unjust outbursts. As I review the prayers recorded in the Bible, I am startled to see how many have a tone of petulance: Jeremiah griping about unfairness; Job conceding, "What profit should we have, if we pray unto him?"; Habakkuk accusing God of deafness. The Bible schools us to pray with blistering honesty.

Walter Brueggemann suggests one obvious reason for candor in the book of Psalms: "because life is like that, and these poems are intended to speak to all of life, not just part of it." Brueggemann finds it jarring to visit upbeat evangelical churches and hear only happy songs, when half of the psalms are "songs of lament, protest, and complaint about the incoherence that is experienced in the world. At least it is clear that a church that goes on singing 'happy songs' in the face of raw reality is doing something very different from what the Bible itself does."

I once thought of Psalms as the kind of book designed to give comfort at funerals or a hospital bedside. Choose carefully, I have since learned. As Brueggemann points out, Psalms includes passages that are angry, whiny, petty, remorseful, explosive, loud, irreverent, and oh so human. They read like uninhibited private memos to the major partner. (The prophets give God's side of the equation.) God formed an alliance based on the world as it is, full of flaws, whereas prayer calls God to account for the world as it should be.

For a time my wife and I participated in a couples' group that studied Deborah Tannen's book *You Just Don't Understand*, which explores the difference between male and female styles of communication. Rather bravely, Tannen delved into a common stereotype of female conversation, one that usually goes by the name "bitching," for which Tannen substituted the much more respectable term "ritual lament." On this topic our group discussion ratcheted up in intensity, with taciturn Gregg becoming especially animated.

"Yeah, let's talk about this!" Gregg said. "I remember one ski trip where I met some of my buddies in Jackson Hole, Wyoming. We spent three days together, and then our wives joined us. We guys were having a great time. Suddenly, when the women showed up, everything changed. Nothing was right. The weather was too cold and the snow too crusty, the condo was drafty, the grocery store understocked, the hot tub dirty. Every night we heard them complain about sore muscles and raw spots where their ski boots rubbed. The thing is, we guys had been experiencing all that stuff for three days, but it never really got to us—we were thinking about skiing. It became a joke. We would listen to the women gripe, then just look at each other, roll our eyes, and say, 'The women are here!'"

Tannen's explanation for such behavior is that women tend to bond in suffering. Through complaining, through gossip, they reaffirm connections with each other, connections strengthened through the ritual of lament: "We join together in facing the harsh elements." Women don't necessarily want the problem solved—who can fix the weather, for instance?—they mainly want understanding and sympathy. Men, in contrast, instinctively want to respond to a complaint by fixing the problem that caused it. Otherwise, why complain?

One male member of our group had no appreciation for the female bonding ritual. "You all know the 'serenity prayer,' right?" he asked. "God grant me the courage to change the things I can, the serenity to accept what I can't change, and the wisdom to know the difference. Where does serenity come into the picture with this 'ritual lament'? The whole thing sounds like emotional pollution to me. You feel bad, so you spill all over me, making me feel bad too. I don't get it."

Because I happened to be teaching a course on the Bible at the time, I was struck by how much of its communication with God lacks serenity, to put it mildly. In prayer, God seems to encourage ritual lament. Jeremiah whined, complained, and filled an entire book with lamentations. Job, who gave the most irreverent speeches in the Bible, emerges as the hero in the end, the spiritual director for his censured friends. If I question the propriety of an outburst before God, I need look no further than God's Son Jesus, who prayed "with loud cries and tears" and who in Gethsemane fell to the ground in anguish, shedding sweat like drops of blood.

Deborah Tannen notes that women usually outlive men and wonders if their tendency to let emotions out, rather than harbor them inside, might contribute to longevity. The Bible, and the Jewish race, came out of an Eastern culture that values emotional outbursts and intense feelings. Even today in a Middle Eastern market you might spend ten minutes haggling loudly over the price of a sack of tomatoes. That kind of passionate style makes a sharp contrast to Greeks and Romans in the ancient world, who sought a golden mean of emotions, a stoical response of restrained passion.

That God allows, even encourages, such gusts of passion shows the strength of God's alliance with us. True friends and true partners hold each other accountable. The Old Testament partners appeal to God's reputation, even God's pride: "Don't let your enemies humiliate you!" They defend their role in the partnership: "Do those who are dead rise up and praise you?" They bring up previous acts of grace, recounting God's own words and promises. They point to their own contributions, their "righteousness." When all that fails, they appeal to God's pity: "Have mercy on me."

Reading these prayers gives me the freedom to complain that the world is not running according to what I believe about it. I believe in God's love and justice and instead see oppression and violence and poverty. Evil people prosper while bad things happen to good people. The Bible's laments darkly remind me of what I believe intellectually, and then bring to light what does not match up.

From the Bible's prayers I learn that God wants us to keep it in the alliance, to come in person with our complaints. If I march through life pretending to smile while inside I bleed, I dishonor the relationship.

The Hasidic Tales includes the story of Dovid Din of Jerusalem who was approached by a man suffering a crisis of belief. Whatever reply Reb Dovid attempted, the man dismissed. So Reb Dovid restrained himself and simply listened to the man's rant and rave. For hours he listened. Finally, he said, "Why are you so angry with God?"

> This question stunned the man, as he had said nothing at all about God. He grew very quiet and looked at Dovid Din and said: "All my life I have been so afraid to express my anger to God that I have always directed my anger at people who are connected with God. But until this moment I did not understand this."

Then Reb Dovid stood up and told the man to follow him. He led him to the Wailing Wall, away from the place where people pray, to the site of the ruins of the Temple. When they reached that place, Reb Dovid told him that it was time to express all the anger he felt toward God. Then, for more than an hour, the man struck the wall of the *Kotel* with his hands and screamed his heart out. After that he began to cry and could not stop crying, and little by little his cries became sobs that turned into prayers. And that is how Reb Dovid Din taught him how to pray.

PART 2

UNRAVELING THE MYSTERIES

Lord heare! *Shall he that made the eare,*
Not heare?

GEORGE HERBERT

CHAPTER 6

WHY PRAY?

Prayers like gravel
   flung at the sky's
window, hoping to attract
   the loved one's
attention . . .
   R. S. THOMAS

Does God really care about the details of our lives, such as getting a house sold or finding a lost cat? And if the answer is yes, then what about a hurricane that flattens a city or a tsunami that washes away a quarter million people? Why does God seem so capricious in deciding if and when to intervene on this chaotic planet?

Prayers of request tend to fall into one of two categories: trouble or trivia. As if by instinct we cry out to God when trouble strikes. A parent hovering over a sick child, a frightened airplane passenger, a sailor caught in a lightning storm—we call upon God when in danger, sometimes with an appeal no more articulate than "Oh, God!" At that moment, forget any lofty notion of keeping company with God. I want help from some Power greater than I. "There are no atheists in foxholes," Army chaplains like to say.

We also pray for trivial things. In Tolstoy's *War and Peace* a hunter prays earnestly that the hunted wolf might come in his direction. "Why not grant me this?" he asks God. "I know Thou art great and that it's wrong to pray about this; but for God's sake make the old wolf come my way and let Karay [a dog] spring at it—in front of 'Uncle' who is watching from over there—and fix his teeth in its throat and finish it off!"

In part to put behind him the bitter taste of divorce, a friend of mine traveled to South America and visited a national park. He prayed diligently, with all the right motives he assured me, to see some rare mammals and snakes. To increase the odds he stayed awake during the night and even spent twenty hours on a mosquito-ridden treetop platform. Others in the eco-tour group happened across rare mammals by chance, while time and again my friend just missed seeing them. He returned from the trip wondering if God ever intervenes: neither his urgent prayers against the divorce nor his worshipful prayers to appreciate the wonders of nature met an answer.

Of course, if our trivial prayers do get answered—if Tolstoy's wolf had walked toward Rostov and a menagerie of indigenous mammals had paraded before my friend's spotting tower—that raises other, serious problems. As one philosophy professor put it, "If God can influence the course of events, then a God who is willing to cure colds and provide parking spaces but is not willing to prevent Auschwitz and Hiroshima is morally repugnant. Since Hiroshima and Auschwitz did occur, one must infer that God cannot (or has a policy never to) influence the course of worldly events."

Even for one who rejects the professor's extreme conclusion, the haunting questions linger.

What Is the Point?

Not wanting to treat prayer as an abstraction, I opened a file drawer and read through letters I have received from readers of my books. They pose questions about prayer not in the abstract but personally, often poignantly.

A prisoner wrote from Indiana, "God's overall supervision of creation is scripturally clear, but does He concern himself at all, to the point of intervention, in our daily trivial lives? Or are His promises of help aimed only at our spiritual self, to help how we respond to events, not to affect events themselves?" He mentioned his own troubling circumstances—his incarceration, a sister in divorce proceedings, a girlfriend jilting him—and then told of an inner-city family he stays close to.

The teen son has endured chronic asthma, a touch of cerebral palsy, physical abuse by his father, shame for his various disabilities and, finally, the murder of his mother. Something's wrong when all that can happen to innocents like them, especially when Jesus spoke so poignantly about His protection for the meek and doing good to "the least of these." I keep going back to the scene where I drove that teen out to find his mother's grave site only to discover that his relatives hadn't been rich enough to buy a headstone. Begging God's intervention in *any* part of those sad people's lives would not be considered a request for frivolous magic but the merest mercy.

The prisoner had read about filmmaker Francis Ford Coppolla, who directed one of his movies entirely from a remote trailer, watching the proceedings on a bank of monitors and communicating with the actors and staff through a microphone and headsets. "Does God run the world like that?" he asked.

Another reader, from Idaho, described his struggles with prayer as middle-class whinings about such things as college debts, poor money management, marriage struggles, a failing business, an aging father. The tone of the letter quickened, though, when he mentioned his son, who because of a stroke at birth had grown up with a severely deformed foot and a useless hand. "We pray daily for his body to be healed," wrote the father. Does God care about such matters? Most of us have secret desires—if not for healing, then for success, happiness, security, peace. "Do we dare ask God for some of these things?... I'm looking for a road that I can walk on, and teach my son."

A woman, age forty-one, wrote first about her conversion as a Jewish believer in Jesus, and then of a daunting trial, breast cancer that had spread to lungs and liver. Sometimes she would pull away from God completely, but then "after sulking in silence for a period of days or weeks, I would come back to God slowly and reluctantly, a pout still on my face, but recognizing that I didn't know how to live apart from God." Throughout the long ordeal, she agonized over how to pray.

> What is the point of praying for something to happen? I can understand the point of praying as a means of simply trying to establish communion with God. But why should I pray for someone to be healed or for my husband to get a job or for my parents to come to salvation? I pray for others because I often feel helpless to do anything else, and I cling to hope that maybe, just maybe this time it will matter.
>
> My spiritual leaders are always admonishing our congregation to spend hours in prayer, interceding for those in need. Why, if God has plans and knows what we want and need and what's best for us, should I spend hours asking him to change his mind? And how do I pray with faith when it seems that the kind of prayer I am lifting up rarely gets answered?

She told of the hundreds of people who were praying for her healing from cancer, and wondered whether their prayers mattered. "Am I more likely to get healed than my friend who also has cancer but has only a handful of people regularly praying for her? I sometimes joke that God has got to heal me or he will have to answer to every one of those people who is praying for me." She teaches an elementary class in a Christian school and one day gave this assignment: If you met Jesus walking down the street, what would you ask him? Most of the students wrote questions of curiosity: "What is heaven like?" and "How was it when you were a kid?" One student wrote, "Why won't you heal my mom?" and "Why doesn't my dad find a job?" With a pang, she recognized the student's handwriting—her own son's.

The most disturbing letter spoke of the fresh wound of an unanswered prayer. For years two parents had prayed for protection for their emotionally troubled son. One day they got a call from their daughter, who had just found the young man, age twenty-two, dead of carbon monoxide poisoning. The letter recorded their simple response to God: "Lord, we prayed regularly for

---

Shaking My Fist

Dee

Prayer is an area where I desperately miss my elderly friend Paul. I used to steal glimpses of his face as he prayed. The last time I prayed with him, I opened my eyes and he had his hands folded on the kitchen table with his head resting on them. Bowed before his Maker. I always felt that when Paul prayed, God silenced heaven, leaned forward on his throne and said, "Be still, my faithful servant Paul is praying."

Now I treasure my Wednesday evening prayer times with Paul's widow, Margaret. I head over to her cottage soon after work. We share a meal and go to prayer meeting at her church, then afterwards we have our own time of prayer together. She too prays in a way that silences heaven. I'm wondering if living in prayer comes with age, if maybe by the time I'm eighty-something, I too will have simple, elegant, trusting faith.

Back in my dark ages my therapist, who had been laboring with me to forgive my father, suggested to me that, given the choice between forgiving my father for what he had done to me and going to hell, I'd choose hell. He was right. Hell—hands down.

At some point in the darkness, while still shaking my fist in God's face, I began to pray "He is not willing that any should perish but that all should come to repentance." I kept reminding God that "any" and "all" are inclusive

all three of our children—didn't You hear our prayers?" Then the mother wrote out some of her favorite verses from the Bible: "Ask whatever you wish and it will be given to you.... I will never leave you, I will never forsake you.... My grace is sufficient.... In all things God works for the good of those who love Him." How could she reconcile those verses with her son's suicide?

Jesus at Prayer

Although I replied to each of these letters, doing so left me with more questions than answers. All that follows—indeed the very existence of this book —flows out of my search for answers, and I will approach these questions

---

words, and therefore must include me. It was all I could pray.

Sitting in my cubicle at work one day, I was suddenly overwhelmed with the longing to be prayed for and I thought of Paul and Margaret. Miraculously, they were home and had no commitments. My pastor and his wife came too, and as we sat together in Paul and Margaret's living room I spilled out the sewer in my heart. Paul felt, in addition to praying for me, they should also pray for my father. I wasn't so sure. I clearly remember my pastor's first words in his prayer, "I don't want to pray for this man."

There really is not a word in the English language to describe how I felt at the conclusion of their prayer for me. The combination of all the emotions made me feel like I was going to disintegrate. In a very uncharacteristic move, I reached out and placed my hand on Paul's knee. He immediately picked up my hand and held it in his, tenderly stroking it. That prayer session was the initial assault on the stronghold of evil in my heart.

So many times when I pray I feel like I'm either shaking my fists in God's face (defiance) or pounding them on his chest (grief). Would that I could just place them on his knees, and have him hold my hands in his.

I saw a movie in which the lead actress is hurt and angry and pounds her fist on the hero's chest. As he very calmly takes her hands in his, the camera zooms in for a closeup on their hands—his holding hers. That image is a visual prayer of mine.

from different angles as I circle the mystery of prayer. What can I discover about prayer that might somehow offer consolation?

As a starting point I take the real-life stories of a prisoner, a middle-class man from Idaho, a forty-one-year-old breast cancer survivor, and a family devastated by suicide and look for insights from the first-century rabbi who changed the world. Surely Jesus must have known the potential as well as the limitations of prayer. I have said that the simplest answer to the question "Why pray?" is "Because Jesus did." What relevance might Jesus' prayers have for the people who wrote me letters?

The Gospels record just over a dozen specific prayers by Jesus, along with several parables and teachings on the subject. He followed the normal Jewish practice of visiting the synagogue, the "house of prayer," and of praying at least three times a day. We can safely assume that Jesus often prayed in private too, for when his disciples asked for instruction on prayer Jesus said they should seclude themselves. Such prayers made an impression on his followers: five times the Gospels mention Jesus' practice of praying alone.

Like most of us, Jesus turned to prayer in times of trouble. No doubt he prayed intensely as he fasted and meditated on the Bible during his time of wilderness tempting. He prayed aloud as the rendezvous with death approached, the words expressing his inner turmoil: "Now my heart is troubled, and what shall I say? 'Father, save me from this hour'? No, it was for this very reason I came to this hour." His prayers in the garden of Gethsemane pushed him to the edge of endurance, and three times he fell to the ground, overcome. Jesus' prayers held back nothing.

Two of the prayers in troubled times (the *Abba* in Gethsemane and *Eloi* from the cross) were so moving that words from the original Semitic language stuck in the minds of hearers. Of the seven cries from the cross, at least three were prayers. Hebrews reports that "he offered up prayers and petitions with loud cries and tears to the one who could save him from death"—but of course he was not saved from death. Like the people who wrote me letters, like all of us at times, Jesus knew the sensation of getting no answer to his pleas.

The other typical form of request, prayer for trivial things, apparently had little place in Jesus' practice. Common, everyday things, yes: the Lord's Prayer mentions daily bread, temptations, and broken relationships, but these requests are hardly trivial. Jesus' prayers, in fact, show a remarkable lack of concern about his own needs. "Take this cup from me" may represent the only time Jesus asked something for himself.

If he made few requests on his own behalf, Jesus often lifted up prayers for others. He prayed for children brought to him by their mothers, and for "the people standing here" at Lazarus's grave side, and for Simon Peter who faced a time of testing. In his final intercessory prayer, one last gasp of grace, he asked on behalf of his persecutors, "Father, forgive them, for they do not know what they are doing."

When alone, Jesus relied on prayer as a kind of spiritual recharging. After an exhausting day of ministry—recruiting disciples, preaching to crowds, healing the sick—he would withdraw to an isolated place to pray. The tempter had used the lure of popularity and acclaim to test him in the wilderness, and perhaps Jesus needed to escape the clamor in order to firm up his resistance and renew his sense of mission. "I have food to eat that you know nothing about," he reassured his disciples, who worried about his lack of nourishment at such times.

Jesus' prayers intensified around key events—his baptism, an all-night session before choosing his twelve disciples, on the Mount of Transfiguration—and especially as he prepared for his departure. Once, he burst into an exuberant prayer when a large group of his followers on a short-term mission returned with tales of spiritual triumph. He prayed for his disciples that the Holy Spirit would come as a "Counselor to be with you forever." In one long, magnificent prayer recorded in John 17, he prayed not only for the immediate disciples but for all of us throughout history who would believe in him because of their message.

Does Prayer Matter?

After surveying Jesus' practice of prayer, I realize that his example does answer one important question about prayer: Does it matter? When doubts creep in and I wonder whether prayer is a sanctified form of talking to myself, I remind myself that the Son of God, who had spoken worlds into being and sustains all that exists, felt a compelling need to pray. He prayed as if it made a difference, as if the time he devoted to prayer mattered every bit as much as the time he devoted to caring for people.

A physician friend of mine who learned I was investigating prayer told me I would have to start with three rather large assumptions: (1) God exists; (2) God is capable of hearing our prayers; and (3) God cares about our prayers. "None of these three can be proved or disproved," he said. "They must either be believed or disbelieved." He is right, of course, although for me the example of Jesus offers strong evidence in favor of that belief. To discount prayer, to conclude that it does not matter, means to view Jesus as deluded.

In keeping with his race, Jesus truly believed that prayer could change things. Romans of the time prayed to their gods as one would finger a good luck charm, not really expecting much. The skeptical Greeks derided prayer, their playwrights weaving foolish, ridiculous, and even obscene prayers into their plays to provoke the audience to uproarious laughter. Only the stubborn Jews, despite their tragic history of unanswered prayers, contended that a supreme and loving God ruled the earth, listened to their prayers, and would someday respond.

Jesus claimed to be part of that response, the fulfillment of the Jewish longing for Messiah. "Anyone who has seen me has seen the Father," he once said, and went about exhibiting the will of the Father by feeding the hungry, healing the sick, and liberating the captives. When I get letters from people with intractable problems, I tell them I cannot answer the "Why?" questions. I can, though, answer another question, and that is how God feels about their plight. We know how God feels, because Jesus gave us a face, one sometimes streaked with tears. We can follow Jesus through the Gospels and see how he responds to a widow who has lost her son, to an outcast woman whose bleeding won't stop, even to a Roman officer whose servant has fallen ill. In his tender mercy Jesus gave us a visible sign of how the Father must hear our prayers even now.

"Your will be done on earth as it is in heaven," Jesus taught us to pray, and he of all people knew the contrast between the two places. On earth Jesus daily confronted tokens of opposition to that will. Mothers thrust sick babies toward him, beggars called out, widows grieved, demons mocked him, enemies stalked him. In such an alien environment, he turned to prayer both as a refuge from mewling crowds and as a reminder of his true home, a place that had no room for evil, pain, and death.

Jesus clung to prayer as to a lifeline, for it gave him both the guidance and the energy to know and do the Father's will. To maintain belief in the "real" world from which he came, to nourish memory of eternal light, he had to work at it all night on occasion or rise before daybreak. Even then he sometimes grew exasperated with his earthly surroundings ("O unbelieving generation, how long shall I stay with you?"), sometimes fought temptation ("Do not put the Lord your God to the test"), and sometimes doubted ("My God, my God, why have you forsaken me?").

Skeptics raise questions about prayer's usefulness: If God knows best, what's the point? As one pastor asked me, "Should I just stop bothering him with my petty requests for myself and others, and let God get on with the business of running the universe while I do my best to take care of things down here?"* To such questions, I have no better answer than the example of Jesus, who knew above any of us the wisdom of the Father and yet who felt a strong need to flood the heavens with requests.

Although Jesus offered no metaphysical proofs of the effectiveness of prayer, the very fact that he did it establishes its worth. "Ask and you will receive," he said frankly, a rebuke to anyone who considers petition a primitive form of prayer. When his disciples failed in their attempts to heal an afflicted boy, Jesus had a simple explanation: lack of prayer.

Prayer Limits

And yet, it appears, prayer was no simple matter even for Jesus. I once wrote an article titled "Jesus' Unanswered Prayers," and it gave me wistful comfort to review the record of Jesus' prayers and find that in respect to prayer, too, he fully shared the human condition. Like the people who write me letters, Jesus knows the heartbreak of unanswered prayers. His longest prayer, after all, centers in a request for unity, "that all of them may be one, Father, just as you are in me and I am in you." The slightest acquaintance with church history (at recent count 34,000 distinct denominations and sects) shows how far that prayer remains from being answered.

I included in my list of problematic prayers the night when Jesus sought guidance for choosing the twelve disciples whom he would entrust with his mission. "Jesus went out to a mountainside to pray, and spent the night praying to God," Luke records. "When morning came, he called his disciples to him and chose twelve of them, whom he also designated apostles." Yet as I read the Gospels I marvel that this dodgy dozen could constitute the answer to any prayer. They included, Luke pointedly notes, "Judas Iscariot, who became a traitor," not to mention the ambitious Sons of Thunder and the hothead Simon, whom Jesus would soon rebuke as "Satan." When Jesus

---

* The philosopher Rousseau had a similar explanation for why he did not pray: "Why should I ask of him that he would change for me the course of things?—I who ought to love, above all, the order established by his wisdom and maintained by his Providence, shall I wish that order to be dissolved on my account?"

later sighed in exasperation over these twelve, "How long shall I put up with you?" I wonder if he momentarily questioned the Father's guidance back on the mountainside.

In his provocative book *The Gospel According to Judas*, theologian Ray Anderson ponders Jesus' selection of Judas as one of the twelve. Did Jesus foresee Judas's destiny the night he prayed? Did he remind the Father of that prayer as Judas left the Last Supper table to betray him? Anderson draws from the experience of Judas a key principle about prayer: "Prayer is not a means of removing the unknown and unpredictable elements in life, but rather a way of including the unknown and unpredictable in the outworking of the grace of God in our lives."

Jesus' own prayers for his disciples surely did not remove the "unknown and unpredictable elements." The twelve periodically surprised and disap-

---

Treasure Hunt

HAROLD

For as long as I can remember, prayer has been a presence in my life. For years I would take an hour-long prayer walk every day on an old railroad bed behind my home. I kept lists of answers to prayer. Other times I've simply stopped praying for a while, out of frustration and questions about its usefulness — but always I come back. As I read of people like Mother Teresa, Billy Graham, Henri Nouwen, I take encouragement in the fact that all of them struggled with prayer at some point.

Several days ago I woke up depressed, as I often do, and prayed, "Lord, I'm in an emotional pit. I need your help to climb out." By eleven that morning, it dawned on me that God had answered that prayer, and I paused to thank him. Through prayer I reconnect to God throughout the day. My body chemistry actually changes as I consciously release my problems to God and seek his help.

We truly live only one day at a time. It doesn't really help to worry about the future, which we can't control, or the past, which we can't change. So I ask God to help me maximize what he wants emphasized in my day. Each day is a kind of treasure hunt, looking for God's treasures, but it takes an intentional connection with God to awaken me, to make me aware.

pointed Jesus with their petty concerns and their inadequate faith. In the end, all twelve failed him at the hour of his deepest need. Eventually, however, eleven of the twelve underwent a slow but steady transformation, providing a kind of long-term answer to Jesus' original prayer. John, a Son of Thunder, softened into "the apostle of Love." Simon Peter, who earned Jesus' rebuke by recoiling from the idea of Messiah suffering, later showed how to "follow in his steps" by suffering as Christ did. The one exception, Judas, betrayed Jesus and yet that very act led to the cross and the salvation of the world. In strange and mysterious ways, prayer incorporates the unknown and unpredictable in the outworking of God's grace.

Although Jesus' prayers do not offer a foolproof formula, they do give clues as to how God works — and does not work — on this planet. Especially when trouble strikes, we want God to intervene more decisively, but Jesus'

For me, prayer is the key to making life an adventure. In the *Lord of the Rings* series by Tolkien, poor Frodo only gets enough direction for the next lap of the journey. As he looks back, it all works out, but most of the time he wanders around confused and helpless. Only occasionally, and in subtle ways, does Gandalf actively give assistance and guidance.

Like Frodo, we live in a world of opposition, one saturated with sex and full of evil, violence, and poverty. *This* is my Father's world? I come to God with my complaints and laments. I grapple with God, call him to account. And I believe God welcomes that dialogue. In the process, I learn who I am. Someone asked the Swiss counselor Paul Tournier, "What's your definition of a hypocrite?" and he replied, *C'est moi* — It is I. Prayer reminds me of that truth.

Prayer also straightens out my expectations. My son, small for his age, loves to play football. He practices faithfully, slogging through the mud, and during games he *expects* to get smashed by defensive players who outweigh him by a hundred pounds. He sees football as a kind of battle, and naturally it will include pain and conflict. I see the Christian's life on this planet as a battle, too. We try to follow God on a place in active rebellion against him. I don't expect prayer to make that any easier, any less problem-filled. I do expect it to give me the inner strength to keep fighting. Persistence is my way of demonstrating faith.

prayers underscore God's style of restraint out of respect for human freedom. Often God rules by overruling.

One scene in particular shows the built-in limitations of prayer. "Simon, Simon, Satan has asked to sift you as wheat," Jesus informed Peter, pointedly using his old name. "But I have prayed for you, Simon, that your faith may not fail." With characteristic bluster Peter insisted he would follow Jesus to prison and to death, and it was then Jesus revealed the ugly truth that actually Peter would deny him three times before the rooster crowed that same day. I cannot help wondering why Jesus didn't flat-out deny Satan's request to test Simon: "No, he's off limits. You can't touch him!" Or why didn't Jesus miraculously embolden Peter so that he could withstand the sifting? Instead he chose the more subtle tack of praying that Peter's faith not fail.

Of course, Peter's faith did fail, three times. Does this request belong in the list of Jesus' unanswered prayers? Or does it, rather, hint at the underlying pattern of how God operates on earth? The scene with Peter has fascinating parallels with the account of Judas. There too, a trusted disciple failed a test of faith, with consequences that seemed catastrophic. Luke, staggered by such treachery, reports simply, "Then Satan entered Judas." How else to explain such a deed?

Judas and Peter both got caught up in a drama of spiritual warfare that they could neither recognize nor fathom. Satan directly pursued both disciples, yet each bore a measure of personal responsibility, for Satan conquers no one without cooperation. Both men miserably failed their test of faith, betraying a master they had followed for three years. Nonetheless, even after their failure both faced the possibility of redemption. One realized his error and hung himself. The other realized his error, repented, and became a pillar of the church. Is it possible that Jesus' prayer for Peter kept him from becoming another Judas? And what might Jesus have prayed for Judas—he who taught us to pray for our persecutors and himself did so from the cross? Their last scene together has Jesus saying to Judas, "Friend, do what you came for."

Peter's testing faintly echoes the plot of Job: Satan asks permission to work mischief, God grants it and then, showing puzzling restraint, waits to see how the tested human will respond. Peter, like Job, like everyone, had the freedom to pass or fail the test. Jesus adds one more factor: his own fervent prayer on Peter's behalf. The working out of this plot, in people like Job, Judas, and Peter, throws light on the great puzzle of human history. Why does God "sit on his hands" while Satan works mischief, while evil tyrants oppress good people, while a traitor delivers God's own Son to the enemy?

The Bible draws a strong contrast between the freedom-crushing style of evil and the freedom-respecting style of good. In a vivid scene of possession by an evil spirit, Mark 9 shows a young boy foaming at the mouth, gnashing his teeth, and throwing himself into fire or water. In every way evil possession transforms the boy into a caricature of a human being, forcibly overwhelming human freedom. Contrast that scene with possession by the Holy Spirit. Paul warns, "Quench not the Spirit" and "grieve not the holy Spirit of God." The Lord of the universe becomes so small, so freedom-respecting as to put himself somehow at our mercy.

Words fail to capture the enormity of descent when a sovereign God takes up residence in a person and says, in effect, "Don't hurt me. Don't push me away." The poet John Donne prayed, "Batter my heart, three-person'd God." But God rarely does. God woos, and waits.

Jesus' prayers for Peter—and perhaps for Judas as well—express God's unfathomable respect for human freedom. Even when he senses his close friend will betray him, Jesus does not intervene with a freedom-crushing miracle. He allows history to take its course, at enormous personal cost, praying all the while that even betrayal and death may be redeemed as part of the outworking of the grace of God. For Peter's sake, for Judas's, and for the world's, that prayer found an answer.

Unprayed Prayers

I learn as much from the prayers Jesus did *not* pray as from those he did. These, too, underscore God's mysterious style of working on this planet. When his cousin John faced imprisonment and certain execution, Jesus did not pray for his release and miraculous delivery—just as he did not pray that Satan keep hands off Peter, nor that Judas change his mind.

And, in a tantalizing aside, Jesus reprimanded Peter for his violent resistance in Gethsemane: "Do you think I cannot call on my Father, and he will at once put at my disposal more than twelve legions of angels?" A Roman legion comprised 6,000 soldiers, which means Jesus chose not to pray for 72,000 celestial reinforcements at the moment of his arrest! Judas and Peter both heard the bold claim, but evidently neither believed it, Judas proceeding with his treachery and Peter fleeing into the darkness.

As a result of Jesus' unprayed prayer, instead of a *Starwars*–style movie depicting a sky full of warrior-angels and ferocious cosmic combat, we get Mel Gibson's movie of a solitary figure whose body is lashed into shreds of skin. What if Jesus had prayed that prayer? How would history have changed? Jesus could have put an end to evil—and to all human history, for that matter—by praying for heavenly rescue forces, but he elected not to. Instead of a triumphant victory by force, he opted for a much more arduous (for him and for the rest of us) path to redemption.

All who struggle with God can look back to that dark night when the Son of God himself struggled with the Father.

> "Abba, Father," he said, "everything is possible for you." *Ah, there is a way out. I need not endure the pain and humiliation after all. Everything is indeed possible. Legions of angels await my command.*
>
> "Take this cup from me." *There, I've said it. The unprayed prayer has passed my lips. I give in, give up. I cannot bear the future, cannot bear the present. There must be some other way. I beg you, Father, if there is any other way . . .*
>
> "Yet not what I will, but what you will." *More than anything, I will rescue and deliverance from the enemy. That is what you will also—only not just for me but for the world. We cannot have one without surrendering the other and that, of course, is why I came. Therefore I yield. Your greater, more costly will, Father, becomes mine.*

In that struggle, by all accounts an authentic one of sweat and blood and ardent appeals to heaven, Jesus' fate was sealed—by his own choice. Astonishingly, a spirit of tranquillity carried him through everything that followed: the trials before the Sanhedrin, Herod, and Pilate, the beatings, the torture, the crucifixion itself. Mel Gibson's *The Passion of the Christ* does not always depict it that way, but in the Gospels' accounts Jesus is the least intimidated, most composed character on the scene. When he volunteers himself to the arresting guards, they draw back and fall to the ground. Jesus is calling the shots, as he reminds Pilate: "You would have no power over me if it were not given to you from above."

For most of us prayer serves as a resource to help in a time of testing or conflict. For Jesus, it was the battle itself. Once the Gethsemane prayers had aligned him with the Father's will, what happened next was merely the means to fulfill it. Prayer mattered that much. In the words of Haddon Robinson,

> Where was it that Jesus sweat great drops of blood? Not in Pilate's Hall, nor on his way to Golgotha. It was in the Garden of Gethsemane. There he "offered up prayers and petitions with loud cries and tears to the One

who could save him from death" (Hebrews 5:7). Had I been there and witnessed that struggle, I would have worried about the future. "If he is so broken up when all he is doing is praying," I might have said, "what will he do when he faces a real crisis? Why can't he approach this ordeal with the calm confidence of his three sleeping friends?" Yet, when the test came, Jesus walked to the cross with courage, and his three friends fell apart and fell away.

Parental Pain

In the end, what can I learn from Jesus' example about how prayer works? More to the point, what can I tell the people whose letters I quoted early in this chapter? I wish I could tell them that the Lord's Prayer would find a speedier answer—that God's will shall soon be done on this earth as it is in heaven. I believe in miracles, but I also believe they are *miracles*, meaning rare exceptions to the normal laws that govern the planet. I cannot, nor can anyone, promise that prayer will solve all problems and eliminate all suffering. At the same time, I also know that Jesus commanded his followers to pray, certain that it makes a difference in a world full of opposition to God's will.

For whatever reason, God now tolerates a world in which fathers abuse their physically disabled sons, children live with congenital birth defects, breast cancers metastasize, and distressed young people commit suicide. Why does God so rarely step in and bring miraculous intervention to our prayer requests? Why is suffering distributed so randomly and unfairly? No one knows the complete answer to those questions. For a time, God has chosen to operate on this broken planet mostly from the bottom up rather than from the top down—a pattern God's own Son subjected himself to while on earth. Partly out of respect for human freedom, God often allows things to play out "naturally."

Even so, God surely feels the same compassion for human suffering that Jesus demonstrated as he walked among us. When Jesus looked out over the city of Jerusalem, knowing what its leaders had in store for him, he cried out, "O Jerusalem, Jerusalem, you who kill the prophets and stone those sent to you, how often I have longed to gather your children together, as a hen gathers her chicks under her wings, but you were not willing." Though not a parent, he knew well the helpless state of loving parents who watch their children make self-destructive choices. As I pray, I keep before me the compassionate face of Jesus.

Jesus knew, too, the cost of divine restraint, the deeply personal cost of letting the world have its way with him. He understood that redemption comes from passing through the pain, not avoiding it: "for the joy set before him [he] endured the cross." Somehow redeemed suffering is better than no suffering at all, Easter better than skipping Good Friday altogether. Although Jesus knew the redemptive pattern in advance—he had revealed it to his disciples—how remote it must have seemed to him in the garden and on the *via dolorosa*. How remote it seems to all of us in the midst of our trials.

Jesus' prayer for Peter shows the same pattern in sharp relief. Satan partially got his way with Peter, sifting him like wheat. But in answer to Jesus' prayer, the sifting rid Peter of his least attractive qualities: blustery self-confidence, a chip on his shoulder, a propensity to violence. The Gospels show Peter urging Jesus to avoid the cross, cowering in the darkness the night of Jesus' trial, and denying with an oath that he knows him. In the book of 1 Peter a transformed apostle uses words like *humble* and *submit*, and welcomes suffering as a badge of honor.

God has not leashed the forces of evil, not yet anyway,* but has provided resources beyond our awareness, including the personal concern of the Son, to counter and even transform evil. We know that prayer matters because after leaving earth Jesus made it one of his primary tasks: "Therefore he is able to save completely those who come to God through him, because he always lives to intercede for them." As Jesus once prayed for Peter, now he prays for us, including all those whose letters I quoted. In fact, the New Testament's only glimpse of what Jesus is doing right now depicts him at the right hand of God "interceding for us." In three years of active ministry, Jesus changed the moral landscape of the planet. For nearly two thousand years since, he has been using another tactic: prayer.

When I betray the love and grace God has shown me, I fall back on the promise that Jesus prays for me—as he did for Peter—not that I would never face testing, nor ever fail, but that in the end I will allow God to use the testing and failure to mold me into someone more useful to the kingdom, someone more like Jesus.

---

*The Bible promises that this style of working is temporary. Contrast Jesus' prayer for Peter with this prediction of how Jesus will handle evil in the future: "And then the lawless one will be revealed, whom the Lord Jesus will overthrow with the breath of his mouth and destroy by the splendor of his coming."

CHAPTER 7

WRESTLING MATCH

Biblical prayer is impertinent,
persistent, shameless, indecorous.
It is more like haggling in an outdoor bazaar
than the polite monologues of the church.
WALTER WINK

The church I attend reserves a brief time in which people in the pews can voice aloud their prayers. Over the years I have heard hundreds of these prayers, and with very few exceptions the word *polite* indeed applies. One, however, stands out in my memory because of its raw emotion.

In a clear but wavering voice a young woman began with the words, "God, I hated you after the rape! How could you let this happen to me?" The congregation abruptly fell silent. No more rustling of papers or shifting in the seats. "And I hated the people in this church who tried to comfort me. I didn't want comfort. I wanted revenge. I wanted to hurt back. I thank you, God, that you didn't give up on me, and neither did some of these people. You kept after me, and I come back to you now and ask that you heal the scars in my soul."

Of all the prayers I have heard in church, that one most resembles the style of prayers I find replete in the Bible, especially those from God's favorites such as Abraham and Moses.

In Nelson Mandela's autobiography I came across another prayer typical of the Bible's style:

The opening prayer of one of the ministers has stayed with me over these many years and was a source of strength at a difficult time. He thanked the Lord for His bounty and goodness, for His mercy and His concern for all men. But then he took the liberty of reminding the Lord that some of His subjects were more downtrodden than others, and that it sometimes seemed as though He was not paying attention. The minister then said that if the Lord did not show a little more initiative in leading the black man to salvation, the black man would have to take matters into his own two hands. Amen.

A century before Mandela, the ex-slave Sojourner Truth, a leader in both abolitionism and the woman's suffrage movement, had no qualms about praying exactly what was on her mind. When her son fell ill she prayed, "Oh, God, you know how much I am distressed, for I have told you again and again. Now, God, help me get my son. If you were in trouble, as I am, and I could help you, as you can me, think I wouldn't do it? Yes, God, you *know* I would do it." When she fell on hard times financially, she prayed "Oh, God, you know I have no money, but you can make the people do for me, and you must make the people do for me. I will never give you peace till you do, God."

Each of these testy prayers from successive centuries follows the track laid down in the Bible long ago.

The Bargainer

Abraham, a man rightly celebrated for his faith, heard from God in visions, in one-on-one conversations, and even in a personal visit to his tent. God dangled before him glowing promises, one of which stuck in his craw: the assurance that he would father a great nation. Abraham was seventy-five when he first heard that promise, and over the next few years God upped the ante with hints of offspring as bountiful as dust on the earth and stars in the sky.

Meanwhile nature took its course, and at an age when he should be patting the heads of great-grandchildren Abraham remained childless. He knew he had few years of fertility left, if any. On one of God's visitations, Abraham made a veiled threat to produce an heir through a liaison with one of his household servants. At the age of eighty-six, following his barren wife Sarah's suggestion, he did just that.

The next time God visited, that offspring, a son named Ishmael, was a teenage outcast wandering the desert, a victim of Sarah's jealousy. Abraham laughed aloud at God's reiterated promise, and by now sarcasm was creeping into his response: "Will a son be born to a man a hundred years old? Will Sarah bear a child at the age of ninety?" Sarah shared the bitter joke, muttering, "After I am worn out and my master is old, will I now have this pleasure?"

God responded with a message that to Abraham's ears must have sounded like good news and bad news both. He would indeed father a child, but only after performing minor surgery on the part of his body necessary for the deed. Abraham thus becomes the father of circumcision as well as Isaac.

That pattern of feint and thrust, of Abraham standing up to God only to get knocked down again, forms the background for a remarkable prayer, actually an extended dialogue between God and Abraham. "Shall I hide from Abraham what I am about to do?" God begins, as if recognizing that a valid partnership requires consultation before any major decision. Next, God unveils a plan to destroy the cities of Sodom and Gomorrah, notorious for their wickedness and moral pollutants of Abraham's extended family.

By now Abraham has learned his own role in the partnership and he makes no attempt to conceal his outrage. "Far be it from you to do such a thing—to kill the righteous with the wicked, treating the righteous and the wicked alike. Far be it from you! Will not the Judge of all the earth do right?"

Then ensues a bargaining session much like what occurs in any Middle Eastern bazaar. *What if there are fifty righteous persons in the city, will you spare it?* All right, if I can find fifty righteous, I'll spare the whole place. With a jolt Abraham remembers who he's bargaining with—*Now that I have been so bold as to speak to the Lord, though I am nothing but dust and ashes*—but proceeds to lower his request to forty-five persons.

Forty-five? No problem. *May the Lord not be angry . . . Now that I have been so bold*—Abraham bows and scrapes, then continues to press. *Forty? Thirty? Twenty? Ten?* Each time God concedes without an argument, concluding, "For the sake of ten, I will not destroy it."

Although ten righteous people could not be found to save Sodom and Gomorrah, Abraham got what he really wanted, deliverance for his nephew and grand-nieces. And we readers are left with the tantalizing fact that Abraham quit asking before God quit granting. What if Abraham had bargained even harder and asked that the cities be spared for the sake of one righteous person, his nephew Lot? Was God, so quick to concede each point, actually looking for an advocate, a human being bold enough to express God's own deepest instinct of mercy?

As Abraham learned, when we appeal to God's grace and compassion the fearsome God soon disappears. "The Lord is slow to anger, abounding in love and forgiving sin and rebellion." God is more merciful than we can imagine and welcomes appeals to that mercy.

Arguing with God

Skip forward half a millennium when another master bargainer appears on the scene. God, who has "remembered his covenant with Abraham," hand-picks a man with the perfect résumé for a crucial assignment. Moses has spent half his life learning leadership skills from the ruling empire of the day and half his life learning wilderness survival skills while fleeing a murder rap. Who better to lead a tribe of freed slaves through the wilderness to the Promised Land?

So as to leave no room for doubt, God introduces himself via an unnatural phenomenon: a fiery bush that does not burn up. Appropriately, Moses hides his face, afraid to look, as God announces the mission: "The cry of the

---

More than Enough?

JENNY

My father drank way too much, and still does. Mom spent most of my childhood depressed, and so I grew up with an emptiness deep in my belly. I wanted somebody to protect me, nurture me, and want me around. I wanted somebody to love me, and it wasn't going to happen at my house. So I went to church with a hope that maybe something was there. My dad would take us to church — the one time when he was never drinking. And I soon found it was more than just a sober Dad that I was encountering in church.

One Saturday afternoon I stood in the back of the church and looked up at the cross and it dawned on me that if Jesus died for me then he must love me. My life began to change at ten years old when I found God and he found me.

Now my continuing struggle is that I am single and don't really want to be. Singleness is an awkward thing to talk about, especially in a culture like the church that's always promoting family and marriage. What's wrong with her? people think. Is she gay? Is she too picky? Maybe she's afraid of commitment. Oh, the poor thing.

Israelites has reached me, and I have seen the way the Egyptians are oppressing them. So now, go. I am sending you to Pharaoh to bring my people the Israelites out of Egypt."

Unlike Abraham, Moses turns argumentative from the very first meeting. He tries false humility: *Who am I, that I should go to Pharaoh?* When that fails, he marshals other objections: *I don't know your name . . . and what if the Israelites don't believe me . . . I have never been eloquent.* God answers each one, orchestrating a few miracles to establish credibility. Still Moses begs off: *O Lord, please send someone else to do it.* Patience runs out and God's anger flares, but even so God suggests a compromise, a shared role with Moses' brother Aaron. The famous exodus from Egypt thus gets under way only after an extended bargaining session.

Moses puts that knack for negotiation, that chutzpah, to a supreme test sometime later when God's patience with the tribe truly has run out. After watching ten plagues descend on Egypt, after walking away from slavery

---

The song "Enough" by Chris Tomlin is cast as a prayer: "All of you is more than enough for all of me. You satisfy every thirst and every need. Jesus, you are more than enough." The Scriptures agree, promising that Christ fills everything in every way: "My God will supply all your needs, according to his riches in Christ Jesus." God and I have an ongoing argument about those passages. After all, if you're not married, you have to find someone to fight with!

The fight goes like this: "God, if you are really more than enough, then why don't you just take care of my problem?" God doesn't answer, and the fight goes on. "Okay, if you're really enough, then why is it harder today than it was twelve months ago to be single? Why does it get harder and not easier?" And God still doesn't answer, and the fight goes on and on.

The truth is, 49 percent of the time God isn't enough. It hurts. It is hard to drive home alone all the time. But 51 percent of the time God is enough. Especially when I rely on others in the body of Christ — and the loving families who have "adopted" me — to fill that emptiness deep inside me. Meanwhile, we keep fighting, God and I.

scot-free and burdened down by plunder, after seeing a pharaoh's state-of-the-art army swept underwater, after following a cloud by day and a pillar of fire by night, after receiving miraculous supplies of water and food (some of it digesting in their bellies at that very moment) — after all that, the Israelites grow afraid, or bored, or "stiff-necked" in God's diagnosis, and reject it all in favor of a golden idol made for them by Moses' sidekick brother, the very Aaron God had recruited by way of compromise.

God has had quite enough. "Let me alone, so that I may destroy them and blot out their name from under heaven. And I will make you into a nation stronger and more numerous than they." Moses knows well the destructive power God can unleash for he has seen it firsthand in Egypt. *Let me alone,* God says! Moses hears that remark less as a command than as the sigh of a beleaguered parent who has reached the end of a tether yet somehow wants to be pulled back — in other words, an opening stance for negotiation.

Moses rolls out the arguments. *Look at all you went through delivering them from Egypt. What about your reputation? Think of how the Egyptians will gloat! Don't forget your promises to Abraham.* Moses flings down a sack of God's own promises.* For forty days and forty nights he lies prostrate before the Lord, refusing food and drink. At last God yields: "Go up to the land flowing with milk and honey. But I will not go with you, because you are a stiff-necked people and I might destroy you on the way." Moses proceeds to win that argument, too, as God reluctantly agrees to accompany the Israelites the rest of the way.

Sometime later, the tables have turned. This time Moses is the one ready to resign. "Did I conceive all these people? Did I give them birth? Why do you tell me to carry them in my arms, as a nurse carries an infant, to the land you promised on oath to their forefathers?" And this time it is God who responds with compassion, calming Moses, sympathizing with his complaints, and designating seventy elders to share the burden.

Moses did not win every argument with God. Notably, he failed to persuade God to let him enter the Promised Land in person (though that request, too, was granted many years later on the Mount of Transfiguration).

---

*Martin Luther suggests this image: "Our Lord God could not but hear me; I threw the sack down before his door. I rubbed God's ear with all his promises about hearing prayer." Elsewhere, he writes of his struggle with God over the healing of his friend Philipp Melanchthon: "This time I besought the Almighty with great vigor. I attacked him with his own weapons, quoting from Scripture all the promises that I could remember, that prayers should be granted, and said that he must grant my prayer, if I was henceforth to put faith in his promises."

But his example, like Abraham's, proves that God invites argument and struggle, and often yields, especially when the point of contention is God's mercy. In the very process of arguing, we may in fact take on God's own qualities.

"Prayer is not overcoming God's reluctance," writes Archbishop Trench; "it is laying hold of his highest willingness."

A Strange Intimacy

Were Abraham and Moses the only biblical examples of standing toe-to-toe with God, I would hesitate to see in their grappling encounters any kind of model for prayer. They rank, however, as two prime representatives of a style that recurs throughout the Bible. (Perhaps this very trait explains why God chose them for such important tasks?)

The arguments of those two giants of faith seem tame compared to the rants of Job. His three friends speak in platitudes and pious formulas, using the demure language often heard in public prayers at church. They defend God, try to soothe Job's outbursts, and reason their way to accepting the world as it is. Job will have none of it. He bitterly objects to being the victim of a cruel God. Job speaks to God directly from the heart—a deeply wounded heart. He nearly abandons prayer because, as he tells his mortified friends, "What would we gain by praying to him?" Yet in the ironic twist at the end of Job, God comes down squarely on the side of Job's bare-all approach, dismissing the friends' verbiage with a blast of contempt.

The psalmists likewise complain of God's absence and apparent injustice. One attributed to David captures the spirit:

> I am worn out calling for help;
> > my throat is parched.
> My eyes fail,
> > looking for my God.

A litany of protests in Psalms and in the Prophets remind God that the world is askew, that many promises remain unfulfilled, that justice and mercy do not rule the earth.

The two most prolific prophets respond to God's call much as Moses did. Isaiah gives this initial reaction: "Woe to me! I am ruined! For I am a man of unclean lips, and I live among a people of unclean lips." Jeremiah musters an immediate excuse—"I do not know how to speak; I am only a child"—and balks at God's assignments throughout his long career. He pulls no punches: "Ah, Sovereign Lord, how completely you have deceived this people and Jerusalem by saying, 'You will have peace,' when the sword is at our throats."

Abraham Heschel, the great Jewish student of the Prophets, underscores their spirit of protest. "The refusal to accept the harshness of God's ways in the name of his love was an authentic form of prayer. Indeed, the ancient Prophets of Israel were not in the habit of consenting to God's harsh judgment and did not simply nod, saying 'Thy will be done.' They often challenged him, as if to say, 'Thy will be changed.'" Heschel adds, "Man should never capitulate, even to the Lord."

I have already spoken of the wrestling match that occurred in the garden of Gethsemane, of Jesus struggling with God's will and accepting it only as a last resort since there was no other way. Later, when God chose the least likely person (a notorious human-rights abuser named Saul of Tarsus) to carry his message to Gentiles, a church leader voiced dissent: "I have heard

---

Prayer after Tsunami

ISAAC (FROM SINGAPORE)

God, we cry for the victims, even more so for those who do not believe in your name. Have mercy on us all. Surely, it pains our hearts to see people suffer greatly in this tsunami catastrophe. Sometimes it makes us wonder if you care at all. I know you did not punish us because of our sins, for you came to save the sinners. We know you love us, for you came to die on our behalf. But why do you choose to be silent now?

Why was the world made imperfect with so many fault lines lying underneath? It could not be our doing that caused the fault lines, could it? Does it pain your heart to see families separated, young lives taken and wasted?

We know a pot cannot question a potter, we know you have the truth, and who can we turn to but you? But we cannot help but think that if a man can forgive and love his enemy, how can the author of our love let those who do not believe in him perish? Forgive us for questioning your love—we question because we believe you are love and we seek explanations for the bad that happened. We know our questions will not be answered on earth, we just pray that you will continue to keep our faith in you alive. Amen.

many reports about this man and all the harm he has done to your saints in Jerusalem." God cut this particular argument short: "Go! This man is my chosen instrument ..." Several years later the same man, now named Paul, was himself bargaining with God, praying repeatedly for the removal of a physical ailment.

Why would God, the all-powerful ruler of the universe, resort to a style of relating to humans that seems like negotiation—or haggling, to put it crudely? Does God require the exercise as part of our spiritual training regimen? Or is it possible that God, if I may use such language, relies on our outbursts as a window onto the world, or as an alarm that might trigger intervention? It was the cry of the Israelites, after all, that prompted God's call of Moses.

I best understand what God wants from us in prayer by analogy to the people closest to me. I think of my brother, who alone knows secrets of shame and pain from our childhood. I think of my wife, who knows more about me than any person on earth, and with whom I negotiate everything from what to order at a restaurant to what state we live in. Or my editor, who holds my hand through each angst-ridden stage of producing a book. With each of these people, my intimate partners, I act in a way reminiscent of the bargaining scenes with God. I make suggestions, back off, accommodate their point of view, reach a compromise, and come away changed.

Like Abraham, I approach God at first in fear and trembling, only to learn that God wants me to stop groveling and start arguing. I dare not meekly accept the state of the world, with all its injustice and unfairness. I must call God to account for God's own promises, God's own character.

Robert Duvall's movie *The Apostle* includes a scene in which Sonny, a preacher with a hot temper and a criminal record, stomps around in an upstairs room kicking furniture and yelling. A neighbor calls to complain about the noise: "Sounds like you have a madman over there." Sonny's mom smiles and explains that's just Sonny. "Ever since he's been a little-bitty boy my son's been talking to the Lord. Sometimes he talks to the Lord and sometimes he yells at the Lord, and tonight he just happens to be yelling at the Lord."

God-Wrestlers

I used to worry about my deficiency of faith. In my prayers I expect little and seem satisfied with less. Faith feels like a gift that a person either has or lacks, not something that can be developed by exercise, like a muscle. My attitude is changing, though, as I begin to understand faith as a form of *engagement* with God. I may not be able to summon up much belief in miracles, or dream big dreams, but I can indeed exercise my faith by engaging with God in prayer.

I recall a scene from very early in my marriage. We were visiting friends out West who had arranged for us to stay at a four-bedroom guest house that had no other occupants at the time. Over dinner, some comment hit one of us the wrong way, and before long a marital spat had escalated. We sat up late trying to talk it through, but instead of bringing us together the conversation only moved us further apart. Aware that I had a business meeting the next day, I stormed off from our bedroom to another one in search of peace and sleep.

A few minutes went by, the door opened, and Janet appeared with a new set of arguments supporting her side. I fled to another bedroom. The same thing happened. She would not let me alone! The scene became almost comical: a sulking, introverted husband running away from an insistent, extroverted wife. By the next day (not before), we could both laugh. I learned an important lesson, that not communicating is worse than fighting. In a wrestling match, at least both parties stay engaged.

That image of wrestling evokes one last scene from the Bible, the prototype of struggle with God. Abraham's grandson Jacob has gotten through life by trickery and deceit, and now he must face the consequences in the person of his hot-tempered brother, whom he cheated out of family birthrights. Ridden by fear and guilt, Jacob sends his family and all his possessions on ahead across a river, with elaborate peace offerings to mollify Esau. For twenty years he has lived in exile. Will Esau greet him with a sword or an embrace? He shivers alone in the dark, waiting.

Someone bumps him — a man? an angel? — and Jacob does what he has always done. He fights as if his life depends on it. All night the two wrestle, neither gaining the advantage, until at last the first gleam of daybreak brightens the horizon. "Let me go," the figure says, reaching down with a touch so potent it wrenches Jacob's hip socket.

Staggering, overpowered, scared out of his wits, Jacob still manages to hang on. "I will not let you go unless you bless me," he tells the figure. Instead of wrenching his neck with another touch, the figure tenderly bestows on Jacob a new name, Israel, which means "God-wrestler." At last Jacob learns the identity of his opponent.

A little later, Jacob sees his brother Esau approaching with four hundred men and limps forward to meet him. Their own wrestling match began before birth, a tussle in utero. And now the moment of truth has arrived. God-wrestler holds out his arms.

A contemporary Jewish author, Arthur Waskow, came across this ancient story in the midst of a long feud with his own brother, with whom he was seeking reconciliation. Once they met in a cabin in Maryland, sealed in by falling snow, and talked in depth as adults for the first time ever. Another time they met on a crisp fall day in Oregon and the brother stared at him coldly and said he might have to kill him someday after all. After these experiences Arthur wrote a book, *Godwrestling*, about the two brothers with a father named Waskow and the two with a father named Isaac.

"Wrestling feels a lot like making love," he wrote, recalling how in childhood he and his brother used to scuffle in bed at night, throwing their bodies against each other only to fall back, spent.

> *But Esau*
> *struggled to*
> *his feet from*
> *his own*
> *Wrestle,*
> *And gasped across the river to his brother:*
> *It also*
> *Feels*
> *A lot*
> *Like*
> *Making*
> *War.*

Jacob felt some of each, making love and making war, with the elusive figure in the night and with hairy Esau in the day. From a distance, it's hard to distinguish a stranglehold from a hug.

God does not give in easily. Yet at the same time God seems to welcome the persistence that keeps on fighting long after the match has been decided. Perhaps Jacob learned for the first time, that long night by the riverside, how to transform struggle into love. "To see your face is like seeing the face of God," Jacob told his brother, words unimaginable had he not met God face-to-face the night before.

Although Jacob did many things wrong in life, he became the eponym for a tribe and a nation as well as for all of us who wrestle with God. We are all children of *Israel*, implied Paul, all of us God-wrestlers who cling to God in the dark, who chase God from room to room, who declare "I will not let you go." To us belong the blessing, the birthright, the kingdom.

The Opposite of Indifference

"Prayer in its highest form and grandest success assumes the attitude of a wrestler with God," concluded E. M. Bounds, who wrote eight books on prayer. Our no-holds-barred outbursts hardly threaten God, and sometimes they even seem to change God. As the touch on Jacob's hip socket proved, God could have ended the match at any point during that long night in the desert. Instead the elusive figure lingered, as eager to be held as Jacob was to hold.

I am privileged to be associated with a group in England called St. Colomba's Fellowship. Its members consist of hospice staff, nurses and others who work among those who are dying. My wife and I are sometimes invited to speak at the fellowship's conferences.

At one of these conferences, we heard a hospice chaplain tell of a patient who asked to see him because he was in great emotional distress. He was in the last stages of cancer and was feeling very guilty because he had spent the previous night ranting, raving and swearing at God. The following morning he felt dreadful. He imagined that his chance of eternal life had now been lost forever, and that God would never forgive one who had so cursed and abused him.

The chaplain asked the patient, "What do you think is the opposite of love?"

The man replied, "Hate."

Very wisely, the chaplain replied, "No, the opposite of love is indifference. You have not been indifferent to God, or you would never have spent the night talking to him, honestly telling him what was in your heart and mind. Do you know the Christian word that describes what you have been doing? The word is 'prayer.' You have spent the night praying."

ROY LAWRENCE

CHAPTER 8

PARTNERSHIP

The universe is done. The greater masterpiece, still undone,
still in the process of being created, is history. For accomplishing
His grand design God needs the help of man.

ABRAHAM JOSHUA HESCHEL

History is the story of God giving away power. After entrusting the human species with the gift of free choice, God invited its representatives to act as partners, even to argue and wrestle with the One who created them. Yet virtually everyone God picked to lead a new venture—Adam, Abraham, Moses, David—proved disappointing in part. Apparently God committed to work with human partners no matter how inept.

Jesus stayed on earth barely long enough to assemble a dozen followers (no less flawed), to whom he handed the keys of the kingdom of God. Against all odds the movement took off, and the human partnership has not stopped since. We are "God's fellow workers," the apostle Paul said. We collaborate with God's actions in the world.* And as God's coworkers we are encouraged to submit our requests, our desires, our petitions in prayer.

Even as I write these words, however, warning bells go off. Something has changed since biblical days. Adam carried on conversations with God, Abraham bargained like an auctioneer, Moses saw a burning bush, Samuel heard God's audible voice, the disciples spoke to Jesus in the flesh. God irrupted in human history. Does that still happen today?

If one partner has such striking powers, why not use them more often on the other's behalf? Every college student seeking God's will, every parent

---

*In her fourteenth-century language, Julian of Norwich identified prayer as the main channel in which God continues the partnership today. "Prayer oneth the soul to God.... For He beholdeth us in love and would make us partners of His good deed, and therefore He stirreth us to pray for that which it pleaseth him to do."

nursing a sick child, every persecuted Christian living under a hostile regime wonders.

Some years ago I wrote a book (*Disappointment with God*) in an attempt to understand what lay behind these irruptions and why they seem so sporadic. The ten plagues orchestrated through Moses, for example, followed four centuries of God's silence. The prophet Samuel's call came at a time when "the word of the Lord was rare; there were not many visions." In search of a pattern I studied every miracle reported in the Bible, every appearance by God, every word that God spoke.

I concluded that much of our current disappointment comes from an expectation that God will act in the same spectacular ways today. We too want to hear God's voice from a bush ablaze, to have our diseases healed and our relatives resurrected. We read the rousing stories from the Bible, hear stirring sermons about them, pray in faith—and don't get the same results.

Looking closer, I detected an Old Testament pattern of God as the reluctant intervener in history. God waits, chooses a partner, moves with agonizing slowness, does a few miracles, then waits some more. In the Gospels supernatural activity again bursts out, with power radiating from Jesus. Yet Jesus, too, intervened selectively, performing miracles not as a cure-all but as *signs* of God's rule.

A Change Underway

Jesus also announced a major change. In those days Jews traveled to the temple to worship God, believing God's presence rested there. But when questioned by a Samaritan woman about the proper place for worship, Jesus replied: "A time is coming and has now come when the true worshipers will worship the Father *in spirit and truth*, for they are the kind of worshipers the Father seeks." He dislocated God's presence from its traditional place in a building (which he predicted would soon be destroyed) and relocated it in a most unlikely place: ordinary people like the Samaritan woman herself.

As the apostle Paul would later explain, Jesus repaired the rupture between God and human beings. We no longer have to approach God through a priest who requires ritual sacrifices. We ourselves are God's temple, the Spirit's home. God lives inside us. And that is the decisive reason Jesus gave in explaining why he must depart: "Unless I go away, the Counselor will not come to you; but if I go, I will send him to you."

God did not design this planet as an arena in which to demonstrate natural law – bending skills, much as we humans may crave that at times. Mainly, God wants to relate to creatures personally, to love and be loved. Restoring such a relationship has been painfully slow, fraught with error, and punctuated by fits and starts. Compared to Old Testament stories of miracle and triumph, it often seems like regression. To the contrary, the New Testament presents a long but steady advance in intimacy with God.

I know Christians who yearn for God's older style of a power-worker who topples pharaohs, flattens Jericho's walls, and scorches the priests of Baal. I do not. I believe the kingdom now advances through grace and freedom, God's goal all along. I accept Jesus' assurance that his departure from earth represents progress, by opening a door for the Counselor to enter. We know how counselors work: not by giving orders and imposing changes through external force. A good counselor works on the inside, bringing to the surface dormant health. For a relationship between such unequal partners, prayer provides an ideal medium.

Prayer is cooperation with God, a consent that opens the way for grace to work. Most of the time the Counselor communicates subtly: feeding ideas into my mind, bringing to awareness a caustic comment I just made, inspiring me to choose better than I would have done otherwise, shedding light on the hidden dangers of temptation, sensitizing me to another's needs. God's Spirit whispers rather than shouts, and brings peace not turmoil. Although such a partnership with God may lack the drama of the bargaining sessions with Abraham and Moses, the advance in intimacy is striking. Listen to the apostle Paul as he tries to explain matters:

> Work out your salvation with fear and trembling, for it is God who works in you to will and to act according to his good purpose.

> I worked harder than all of them — yet not I, but the grace of God that was with me.

> I no longer live, but Christ lives in me.

> For we are God's workmanship, created in Christ Jesus to do good works, which God prepared in advance for us to do.

The partnership binds so tight that it becomes hard to distinguish who is doing what, God or the human partner. God has come that close.

God-Incidents

Because we live in a world of matter, most of the ways we encounter God—nature, the Bible, the Word made flesh, the sacraments, other people, the church—include materiality. God's own state, though, God's preferred milieu if you will, is the realm of spirit. Prayer reflects that difference between us. Although we may ask God to intervene directly, it should not surprise us if God responds in a more hidden way in cooperation with a person's own choice. An alcoholic prays, "Lord, keep me from drink today." The answer to that prayer will likely come from the inside, from a stiffening resolve or a cry of help to a loyal friend, rather than from some marvel like the magical disappearance of liquor bottles from a cabinet.

In the normal course of providence, God works through and in creation, not despite it. For this reason, most answers to prayer are difficult to prove with any certainty. In C. S. Lewis's *The Screwtape Letters*, a senior devil gives this advice on prayer to a young recruit:

> Worry him with the haunting suspicion that the practice is absurd and can have no objective result. Don't forget to use the "Heads I win, tails you lose" argument. If the thing he prays for doesn't happen, then that is one more proof that petitionary prayers don't work; if it does happen, he will, of course, be able to see some of the physical causes which led up to it, and "therefore it would have happened anyway," and thus granted prayer becomes just as good a proof as a denied one that prayers are ineffective.

The point made satirically in *Screwtape*, Lewis explored more philosophically in *Miracles*:

> This impossibility of empirical proof is a spiritual necessity. A man who knew empirically that an event had been caused by his prayer would feel like a magician. His head would turn and his heart would be corrupted. The Christian is not to ask whether this or that event happened because of a prayer. He is rather to believe that all events without exception are *answers* to prayer in the sense that whether they are grantings or refusals the prayers of all concerned and their needs have all been taken into account. All prayers are heard, though not all prayers are granted.

"Only faith vouches for the connection," Lewis concludes. "No empirical proof could establish it." We believe a prayer has been answered not because of any scientific criteria proving cause and effect, but because we have faith. Trusting God's character, we can see in the relation between our prayer and an event more than a coincidence. We see a true partnership, intimate and intertwined.

Twelve-step groups sometimes toss around the saying, "Coincidence is God's way of protecting his anonymity." Yes, and perhaps faith is our way of acknowledging God's background activity. As I think through answers to prayer, I must agree with Lewis that almost all of them admit to other explanations.

A month ago I was standing, frantic, in downtown Budapest, Hungary, after a ten-hour flight. On my laptop computer I had notes to prepare for a series of speeches, and upon checking into my hotel I realized I had left the AC power cord in an airport lounge somewhere in transit. Stores were closing in an hour, the next day was Sunday, and I had no clue where I might find computer parts in that foreign city, much less navigate the public transportation to get there. I breathed a quick prayer and started searching for anyone who spoke English. No success. Just as I was feeling desperate, a

---

A Franciscan Benediction

May God bless you with discomfort
At easy answers, half-truths, and superficial relationships
So that you may live deep within your heart.

May God bless you with anger
At injustice, oppression, and exploitation of people,
So that you may work for justice, freedom and peace.

May God bless you with tears
To shed for those who suffer pain, rejection, hunger and war,
So that you may reach out your hand to comfort them and
To turn their pain into joy.

And may God bless you with enough foolishness
To believe that you can make a difference in the world,
So that you can do what others claim cannot be done
To bring justice and kindness to all our children and the poor.

Amen

young man and his mother came up to me and said, "Can we help you?" The young man, a student, had just completed his English proficiency exam and the two were heading toward a train station adjacent to a mall that included a computer store — one of two stores in Budapest, it turned out, that carried the particular part I needed. Was that coincidence?

A year ago I attended a conference of 1,200 people and had one meal on my own. I entered the dining hall, walked past a long line of tables, and chose a seat at random. As conversation unfolded, I learned that all five other guests at the table were members of the same family. The father, back home in Michigan, was living through the final stages of esophageal cancer, days from death, and at the last minute two in-laws had made arrangements to stay with him. The daughters had driven twenty hours, through the night, from another state. For six months the mother had not left her husband alone. She came to the conference hoping to talk to me about the topic of suffering because she knew that my wife had worked as a hospice chaplain. She had brought along a list of questions, in faint hope of spending some time discussing them. Would I mind?

"When I pray, coincidences happen," said Archbishop William Temple; "when I don't, they don't." Rather than dissecting such incidents, I try to use them as building blocks of faith, to see them as "God-incidents" instead of coincidences. If I remember (and I blush at how often I forget), I can commit to God in advance a difficult letter I must answer, a thorny problem I must deal with in my writing, a nagging physical ailment, a phone call to a needy relative, a social engagement I dread. The very process of presenting these requests to God puts me in a different frame of mind before the event. And if I remember to pause afterward and reflect on what happened, often the traces of God appear, seen not by proof but by faith.

A rabbi taught that experiences of God can never be planned or achieved. "They are spontaneous moments of grace, almost accidental." His student asked, "Rabbi, if God-realization is just accidental, why do we work so hard doing all these spiritual practices?" The rabbi replied, "To be as accident-prone as possible."

Stages of Prayer

I hesitate to use the word *stages* for fear of setting up a false ranking of novice and advanced prayers. I am not describing a set of skills or competency at prayer, rather a progressive maturity in our partnership with God. From my own experience I can identify at least three such stages.

The first stage is a simple childlike request for something I desire. Several times friends have sent their unaccompanied children to visit us in Colorado. Having no experience as a parent, I am amazed at the one-way relationship between a child and adult. Kids automatically assume you'll wake them up, clean the room behind them, feed them, transport them to fun places, and pay for everything along the way. They may offer an occasional "Thank you," but they give little feedback and rarely initiate conversation. Adults, they assume, exist to satisfy their every need. Kids are, in a word, immature, and I sometimes remind myself of that word when I besiege God with a series of demands, wanting God to solve my problems and satisfy my desires.

Still, I cannot discount such childlike requests because they impressed Jesus, especially when they came from an unlikely source: a foreign woman, a Roman centurion, the friends of a paralyzed man breaking through a roof. Most of the spectacular answers to prayer I know about personally have come to young Christians who "don't know any better" than to pray for exactly what they want. I marvel at their childlike trust. Martin Luther said we should first open wide our aprons and boldly ask what we want to receive from our Father.

A Japanese Christian told me that on his first trip to the United States he was shocked by the directness of our prayers. The American pray-er, he said, resembles a person who goes to Burger King and orders "a Whopper well-done, but hold the pickle and lettuce—with extra ketchup, please." The Japanese is more like the tourist who walks into a foreign restaurant unable to read the menu. He finally communicates, with gestures and reference to a phrase book, that he would like the house specialty. That Eastern approach to prayer, suggests my friend, involves more trust, as well as more suspense and adventure. You never know what you will get, for the host determines it. Both cultures have something to learn from each other about making requests in prayer.

The second stage of prayer (and again, I do not use the word *stage* to imply a higher value) involves a kind of meditation, what I have called keeping company with God. The mystics suggest that we should progress beyond prayer requests and instead make meditation our primary goal. I cannot agree with their dismissal of petition for the simple reason that when Jesus taught about prayer he emphasized requests. Is not the Lord's Prayer itself a series of requests?

Over time, however, I have come to appreciate how meditation can transform my requests. Ultimately, I want to pray for what God wants, and if God doesn't want something for me, I shouldn't want it either. Spending time in meditative prayer, getting to know God, helps align my desires with God's. I can never completely align with God's will because I do not have the capacity for fully knowing it. What I do know, though, informs my prayers.* As one well-known pastor used to say, "Nothing lies beyond the reach of prayer except that which lies outside the will of God." Of course, we don't fully know God's will, which explains why we pray.

Jesus prayed "Your will be done" at the *end* of his struggle with God in Gethsemane, as a resolution to all that had gone before, including a clear request for another way out. I have become convinced that the phrase "Your will be done" belongs at the end of my prayers, not at the beginning. If I begin with that qualifier I am tempted to edit my prayers, to suppress my desires, to resign myself to whatever happens. I thus cut short what God wants from me: that I make known my requests, and in so doing make known my self.

I have discovered that God wisely answers prayer in a different way than I envision. I pray that my book will win a prize and instead find I need to improve my writing. I pray to get rich and instead find that money would be a curse distracting me from more important things. After enough of these lessons, I adjust my immature prayers in the light of what I have learned from knowing God through meditation.

Nowadays health clubs offer courses in "meditation," which tend to emphasize relaxation and self-improvement. We risk losing the true meaning of meditation, which puts the emphasis not on me the pray-er but on God the object of my prayers. If I seek God more than anything else, I will eventually seek more of what God wants for me, and be content with that. The author Patricia Hampl says that prayer only looks like an act of language. Mainly, we need to place ourselves in the correct position to God. "Focus. Get there, and all that's left to say is the words."

The book of Daniel gives a fine illustration of faith that encompasses both a personal desire for deliverance and also acceptance of God's will no matter what. Three young men, explaining to the king why they would

---

*The theologian Terrance Tiessen writes, "On many occasions we find ourselves unsure of the specific action that God would wish to do in the situation that confronts us, and so we present our requests, but we qualify them with the condition 'if it is your will.' This is not a lack of faith; it is a lack of knowledge. We believe that God will do what is best, but we are uncertain what that is and so we ask according to our best wisdom." Søren Kierkgaard put it this way: "The true relation in prayer is not when God hears what is prayed for, but when the person praying continues to pray until he is the one who hears, who hears what God wills."

not worship him despite his threat of a fiery furnace, announced, "If we are thrown into the blazing furnace, the God we serve is able to save us from it, and he will rescue us from your hand, O king. *But even if he does not,* we want you to know, O king, that we will not serve your gods or worship the image of gold you have set up."

The italicized phrase suggests the third stage of prayer, the stage of submission that Jesus reached after a long night of struggle: "Not my will but yours be done." In the end, I learn that God has ordained prayer as a means of getting God's will done on earth, not ours. Yes, God hears and responds to my requests. Yes, God somehow incorporates those requests into a plan of action on earth. But as many martyrs have learned, including God's own Son as well as Christians in the persecuted church today, we do not always get what we earnestly desire.

"Be slow to pray," cautions Eugene Peterson. "Praying puts us at risk of getting involved with God's conditions.... Praying most often doesn't get us what we want but what God wants, something quite at variance with what we conceive to be in our best interests. And when we realize what is going on, it is often too late to go back."

Kingdom Partners

Sometimes when I am puzzled by the way the world operates I let my mind roam over alternatives. Presumably God could have set up creation with very different rules. God could have decided to act with more frequent and spectacular interventions (although this approach did not seem to make much difference to the Israelites in the wilderness). On the other hand, God could have withdrawn even further, as the deists presume: a watchmaker who sets things in motion and then departs (in which case prayer becomes irrelevant).

Instead, from the very beginning God has relied on human partners to advance the process of creation. After equipping Adam to cultivate the land and supervise the animals, God left the work of the garden in his hands. All through history, the pattern has continued. Though the earth provides seeds and soil and rain, food crops only grow with cultivation. Abundant materials exist for technology, but human beings themselves must figure out how to use them. When God wanted a dwelling place on earth, a tabernacle and temple did not descend from the sky like a spaceship; thousands of artists and craftsmen worked to fashion them.

"I will build my church," Jesus announced, proclaiming the new reign of God's kingdom on earth. That, too, has taken shape gradually and fitfully over twenty centuries, with many embarrassing setbacks to go along with the advances. I think of the profound grief God must feel over some chapters of church history. Yet, as Paul put it in an astonishing metaphor, "the head cannot say to the feet, 'I don't need you!'" God has made the work of the kingdom dependent on the notoriously unreliable human species.

One busy day, after resurrecting a dead girl and healing a sick woman, then restoring sight to two blind men and voice to a mute, Jesus seemed overwhelmed by the unfinished task. Crowds had gathered, and he felt a surge of compassion "because they were harassed and helpless, like sheep without a shepherd." In the face of such endless human need, Jesus gave

---

Justice Partners

GARY

Fresh out of college I worked with Bishop Desmond Tutu in South Africa confronting the crimes of apartheid, and later became a lawyer investigating genocide in Rwanda and police abuse in the United States. I became convinced that Christians need to serve on the front lines of justice, so I founded an organization (International Justice Mission) that focuses the light of God's truth — as well as legal pressure and powerful publicity — on specific cases of injustice. We operate in twelve countries, specializing in cases of human trafficking, slavery, illegal detention, and torture, as well as assisting widows and orphans.

From the very beginning, I believed we needed reminders that the work of justice is God's work, and that God is on our side in the battle for justice. Otherwise, we might get overwhelmed by the enormity of the evil we confront. I feared a slide toward what I call "prayerless striving." So every day our entire staff begins with thirty minutes of silence, in which we encourage prayer and meditation. We don't talk, we don't work. We sit at our desks and pray. In addition, every day we get together at eleven o'clock and spend thirty minutes praying for each other and the cases we're involved in. Our staff members often report this is the most meaningful part of their day.

We also rely on more than five thousand prayer partners who have agreed

one of the few direct commands on what to pray for. "Ask the Lord of the harvest, therefore, to send out workers into his harvest field."

What a strange request! If Jesus sensed the need for more workers, why not simply recruit more? Or ask the Lord of the harvest himself?

That scene as much as any shows the role Jesus had in mind for himself. Yes, he made a lasting impact on a small corner of Palestine, but he would need partners to carry the good news of the kingdom to Rome and to continents beyond. Already Jesus himself had appealed to the Lord of the harvest, in an all-night ordeal that resulted in the twelve disciples standing before him. Now he called on those twelve to pray for more workers because he knew the Father would listen to their prayers. He was welcoming them as partners of the kingdom.

---

to pray for our work. Once a year we invite them all to a weekend prayer conference in which we update them and pray together. Somebody asked me whether anything would change if we had fifty thousand people on that list rather than five thousand. I don't know. What I do know is that God cares about justice in the world, that God is pleased when more of his people are involved in these issues, and that the Bible teaches us that God is moved by our prayers. As a side benefit, the more people who are engaged, the more partners God has in his kingdom work on earth.

In our prayers we appeal to God's own desires: "You're the one who loves this child in slavery in Thailand." And I could tell you many stories of apparently miraculous answers to prayer: for example, of victims who were pleading to God for help just before one of our lawyers or social workers showed up.

Sometimes our faith gets tested. This morning we continued to pray for the release of nine women being held in prison in Southeast Asia. Almost nine months ago we organized a major raid on a brothel, freeing over ninety women from sexual slavery. What joy! However, many of these women had been trafficked across international borders and had no documents. The host country, which had cooperated reluctantly with our raid, put the undocumented women into prison. Month by month, we've been working to free them and to reunite them with their families back home. We'll pray for them tomorrow, and the next day, until they all get freed. In the meantime, we'll work as hard as we can to accomplish just that.

In the late nineteenth century William Carey felt a call to travel to India as one of those workers in the harvest. Pastors around him scoffed at his idea: "Young man, if God had wanted to save the heathen in India, he could certainly do it without the likes of you or us." They missed the point of partnership. God does very little on earth without the likes of you and us.

As partners in God's work on earth, we insist that God's will be done while at the same time committing ourselves to whatever that may require of us. "Your kingdom come, your will be done," Jesus taught us to pray. These words are not placid invocations but demands, expressed in the imperative mood. Give us justice! Set the world aright! God has called out partners on earth to serve as heralds of a world on the way to healing and redemption.

We have different roles to play, we and God. As God made clear to Job, we humans lack the capacity to figure out providence and cosmic justice and answers to the "Why?" questions. It is our role, rather, to follow in Jesus' steps by doing the work of the kingdom both by our deeds and by our prayers. What is God doing in the world? The answer is another question: What are God's people doing? We are Christ's body on earth, to borrow Paul's metaphor. We are "in Christ," a phrase the New Testament repeats 164 times. Those we minister to, Christ ministers to; those we forgive, Christ forgives. When we extend mercy to the broken, we reach out with the hands of Christ himself.

More to the point, those we pray for, Christ prays for. Paul said, "Because you are sons, God sent *the Spirit of his Son* into our hearts, the Spirit who calls out, 'Abba, Father.'" Even when we do not know what we ought to pray for, or how to pray, that Spirit intercedes for us: "And he who searches our hearts knows the mind of the Spirit, because the Spirit intercedes for the saints in accordance with God's will."

Christ's Spirit is praying within us even when we lack both the wisdom and the words for prayer. Although we may not know God's will on a given issue, the Spirit within us surely does. In other words, our most immature prayers have an inbuilt self-corrective. Though we feel ignorant in our prayers, the Spirit does not. Though we feel exhausted and confused, the Spirit does not. Though we feel lacking in faith, the Spirit does not. God is not so far off that we need to raise our voices to be heard. We need only groan.

Double Agency

Some people worry that prayer may lead to passivity, that we will retreat to prayer as a substitute for action. Jesus saw no contradiction between the two: he spent long hours in prayer and then long hours meeting human needs. The church in Acts did likewise, acting out a true partnership. They prayed for guidance about caring for widows, then appointed deacons in order to free up other leaders for the vital act of prayer. Stop praying, and they just might stop caring about widows. They prayed together about the cultural controversies between Jews and Gentiles, then convened a council to hammer out a compromise.

The apostle Paul prayed diligently for the early churches, but also wrote and visited them. He prayed and worked with equal abandon. On a sea voyage, after being convinced as a result of his prayers that all passengers would survive an impending shipwreck, he proceeded to take charge of the 276 on board, giving orders and organizing the salvage efforts.

The accounts in Acts present a double agency that makes it impossible to distinguish God's work from the Christians' work—the point, exactly. Recall Paul's paradoxical command to the Philippians: "Continue to work out your salvation with fear and trembling, for it is God who works in you to will and to act according to his good purpose."

In my own frustrations with prayer, I used to focus on the lack of God's intervention. Why won't God do what I ask? My perspective has changed as I understand prayer as partnership, a subtle interplay of human and divine that accomplishes God's work on earth.* God asks me to make myself known to him in prayer and then works my prayers into a master plan for my life—a plan which I can only faintly grasp.

Eugene Peterson, translator of *The Message*, points out the elusive "middle voice" in Greek grammar, a tone halfway between the active and passive voices.

> My grammar book said, "The middle voice is that use of the verb which describes the subjects as participating in the results of the action." I read that now, and it reads like a description of Christian prayer—"the

---

* Irish playwright Sean O'Casey has one of his characters say, "The two o' them, 'ud give you a pain in your face, listenin' to them; Jerry believin' in nothin', an' Bentham believin' in everythin'. One says that all is God an' no man; an' th' other that says all is man an' no God!"

113

subject as participating in the results of the action." I do not control the action; that is a pagan concept of prayer, putting the gods to work by my incantations or rituals. I am not controlled by the action; that is a Hindu concept of prayer in which I slump passively into the impersonal and fated will of gods and goddesses. I enter into the action begun by another, my creating and saving Lord, and find myself participating in the results of the action. I neither do it, nor have it done to me; I will to participate in what is willed.

My pastor spent a day of hard labor installing stone steps in his backyard. The individual stones weighed between a hundred and two hundred pounds, and it took all of Peter's strength and a few tools to maneuver them into place. His five-year-old daughter begged to help. When he suggested she just sing, to encourage him in his work, she said no. She wanted to *help*. Carefully, when it would not endanger her, he let her place her hands on the rocks and push as he moved them.

Peter admitted later that Becky's assistance actually complicated the task. He could have built the steps in less time without her "help." At the end of the day, though, he had not only new steps but a daughter bursting with pride and a sense of accomplishment. "Me and Dad made steps," she announced at dinner that night. And he would be the first to agree.

CHAPTER 9

WHAT DIFFERENCE
DOES IT MAKE?

Earth gapes, hell burns, fiends roar, saints pray . . .
SHAKESPEARE, *RICHARD III*

"Electricity will replace God. The peasants should pray to it; in any case they will feel its effects long before they feel any effect from on high," wrote Vladimir Lenin in the heady days of the Russian Revolution. Some years later, when President Roosevelt suggested consulting the pope on European policies, Lenin's successor Stalin sneered, "The pope! How many divisions has he got?"

Does prayer have any real impact in the outer world or is it merely a private conversation with God? I ask that as a serious, not rhetorical, question. In Russia I visited large cathedrals that for fifty years were forced to house museums of atheism: Lenin and his cronies shut down 98 percent of the churches in the Soviet Union even as priests and parishioners were praying to keep them open. Hitler murdered six million Jews and several million Christians, their prayers for deliverance evaporating in the ovens along with their bodies.

Attempts to track the footsteps of God in history invariably founder. Tolstoy failed to make any theological sense of Napoleon's ruinous misadventures in Russia. To declare the modern state of Israel an answer to the prayers of European Jews rings hollow to Palestinian Christians chased from their homes. Was "the miracle of Dunkirk" an answer to prayer? What about Hiroshima?

Like the Old Testament prophets who could not fathom God making use of the pagan nations Babylon and Assyria, we can only circle the questions and shake our heads at the mystery. Surveys show that Europeans' sharp decline in faith traces back to the despair that settled in after two devastating world wars on the continent. How could such things happen in Christian Europe?

Even for the faithful, prayers about current events—the war on terrorism, nuclear proliferation, environmental catastrophe—may seem futile. Richard Mouw tells a story about a tourist who observes a devout Jewish man praying at the Western ("Wailing") Wall in Jerusalem. The Jew rocks back and forth with closed eyes, beating his breast, sometimes raising his hands. When he finishes, the tourist asks, "What do you pray for?"

The Jew responds, "I pray for righteousness. I pray for the health of my family. I pray for peace in the world, especially in Jerusalem."

"Are these prayers effective?" the tourist asks.

"It's like talking to a wall."

Our Strongest Weapon

Shortly after the reelection of George W. Bush in 2004, *Time* magazine ran a cover story on the twenty-five most influential evangelicals in the United States. The media were scrambling to understand this newly powerful voting bloc. President Bush certainly understood their strategic importance, for every week the White House arranged a video conference call with leading evangelicals. Indeed, *Time* seemed to rank the influence of evangelicals by their proximity to the inner circle of the White House. Did she get invited to breakfast there? Does his name make the conference call list?

I know some of the evangelical leaders profiled in *Time*, and I know too the seduction of power. I know what it is like to return from a White House meeting loaded down with briefing books and souvenirs, inflated with a sense of self-importance, and then enter my prayer closet and try to regain Jesus' perspective on the world. After all, Jesus never got invited to Rome, the seat of power then, and the only time he visited a provincial palace he came at the end of a rope, his hands tied behind his back. Despite his apparent powerlessness, Jesus predicted a kingdom that would survive the mightiest empire of his day, that would span the world, that would prove larger and more lasting—into eternity, even—than all kingdoms constructed of stone and mortar.

When I pray, especially after brushing the skirts of power, I must remember that God's kingdom is not an adjunct to U.S. politics, not a mere voting bloc; nor is it an international fellowship, a genteel and moral version of the United Nations useful for such tasks as feeding orphans and drilling wells. God's rule encompasses all human institutions and all history. "The globe itself lives and is upheld as by Atlas arms through the prayers of those whose love has not grown cold. The world lives by these uplifted hands, and by nothing else!" thundered Helmut Thielicke. He spoke not as an otherworldly monk but as a pastor who lived through Hitler's idolatrous reign in Germany and endured the Allies' fire-bombing of Stuttgart.

My travels have taken me to places like Myanmar (Burma) and China, where governments are more likely to summon Christian leaders to prison than to the seat of power. I have heard appalling stories of persecution, of twenty years in a frigid cell without a blanket, of beatings and torture and intimidation. I interviewed a Chinese pastor who spent two decades in prison; even so, annually he leads several hundred converts in a prayer of commitment on the banks of a river, everyone present knowing that the act of baptism may well lead to their own arrest and imprisonment. "What can Christians in the rest of the world do for you?" I ask, and every time without exception I get the same answer. "You can pray. Please tell the church to pray for us."

The first few times I heard that answer, I wanted to say, "Yes, of course, but we honestly do want to help. What else can we do?" I have since learned that Christians who have no access to earthly power truly believe prayer gives them access to a greater power. They see prayer, in fact, as our strongest weapon against invisible forces. They believe the apostle Paul's words: "For our struggle is not against flesh and blood, but against the rulers, against the authorities, against the powers of this dark world and against the spiritual forces of evil in the heavenly realms."

When the prophet Daniel got no answer to his prayer, he withdrew for three weeks of fasting and spiritual discipline, puzzled by the silence of God. Finally a creature with a countenance dazzling as lightning arrived to explain the delay: "But the prince of the Persian kingdom resisted me twenty-one days. Then Michael, one of the chief princes, came to help me, because I was detained there with the king of Persia." What seemed to Daniel like one more case of unanswered prayer had, in ways hidden to him, sparked a battle among unseen combatants in the spiritual realm.

The question that obsesses modern thinkers, "Why do bad things happen?" gets little systematic treatment in the Bible because Bible writers believed they knew why bad things happen: we live on a planet ruled by powers intent on blocking and perverting the will of God. The New

Testament openly describes Satan as "the god of this age" and "the ruler of the kingdom of the air, the spirit who is now at work in those who are disobedient." Of course bad things happen! On a planet ruled by the Evil One we should expect to see violence, deception, disease, and all manner of opposition to the reign of God.

We pray because against such forces we have no more powerful way to bring together the two worlds, visible and invisible. I present my world, whatever its circumstances, to God and ask for God's help in equipping me to counter the forces of evil. The persecuted church, much like Daniel, confronts those forces in the form of hostile governments and violent opposition. The European church confronts them as cynicism and indifference. The U.S. church faces a seduction to rely on power, wealth, and political influence. The developing world faces disease, poverty, and political corruption.

Karl Barth wrote, "To clasp the hands in prayer is the beginning of an uprising against the disorder of the world." The prophet Daniel would surely agree. As he clasped his hands in prayer three times a day he acted in civil disobedience against a tyrannical regime that had outlawed such prayer.

Free at Last

SERGEY

Those of us who lived under Communism know well the power of prayer. My father worked on Soviet rockets in Siberia, and I grew up under the propaganda of atheism and Communism. We were constantly told that our system was better than the West, even though we all knew the opposite. No one could even imagine that Communism would someday fall and that the Soviet Union would break up. Even today, few give credit to what I believe was the real force: the power of prayer.

All over Eastern Europe, the church organized peace marches with "people power" marching in the streets and holding candles. No one fought a war, and very few shots were fired, yet the mighty Soviet empire came crashing down. By that time, my family had settled in the Ukraine, and since then we have seen our own Orange Revolution bring down a corrupt government. That revolution, in 2004, spread mainly through text messages on cell phones.

Since then, we Christians have organized a national prayer time at ten

What followed, after his arrest and confinement in a den of lions, proved who had the real power.

Scenes of Uprising

Our own time has witnessed uprisings led by prayer.

In the 1980s, a pastor named Laszlo Tokes took over a small Reformed church to minister to his fellow Hungarians, an oppressed minority living inside the borders of Romania. His predecessor had openly supported the communist Romanian government, even to the extent of wearing a red star on his clerical robes. In contrast, Tokes spoke out against injustice and protested government actions. Soon the sanctuary began filling each Sunday, bringing together worshipers and dissidents of both Romanian and Hungarian descent. Membership grew from forty persons to five thousand.

The courageous new pastor attracted the attention of special agents as well. They threatened Tokes many times with violence, and one evening the police were dispatched to evict him. Word spread quickly and hundreds of

---

o'clock every night, to pray for our country. We have organized in groups of three, "triplets," to teach one another to pray. You see, most of us have only known the long, formal, boring prayers we hear in churches. We are just now discovering the privilege of talking to God as to a friend!

I have heard incredible stories of faith from Ukraine and from its neighbors. One friend of mine from Moldova used to tell his atheist parents that he was heading to the outdoor bathroom, then jump over the fence and pray with his neighbor. Sometimes Christians got baptized in frozen lakes, after chopping through the ice. Foreign visitors smuggled in books and Bibles, which we distributed according to an elaborate secret system. Many, many pastors spent time in prison for their work with the church.

Now that we are free, we are in danger of growing complacent, of not treasuring the freedom to worship. In fact, Christians in parts of the former Soviet Union have actually voted for the Communists to return to power because the church was so much more pure in those days. It seems we handle persecution better than prosperity. I, for one, pray we never have to return to those days. I pray that we will learn to praise God for what we have, rather than have to plead for it.

Christians—Baptist, Orthodox, Reformed, and Catholic alike—poured out of their homes to surround Tokes's house as a wall of protection. They stood through day and night, singing hymns and holding candles.

A few days later, police broke through the protestors to seize Tokes. Rather than dispersing and filing home, the protestors decided to march downtown to the police station. As the procession moved noisily through the streets, more and more people joined in. Eventually the crowd in the town square swelled to 200,000, nearly the entire population of that area. The Romanian army sent in troops, who in one bloody incident opened fire on the crowd, killing a hundred and wounding many more. Still the people held their ground, refusing to disperse.

A local pastor stood to address the protestors in an attempt to calm the rising anger and prevent a full-scale riot. He began with three words, "Let us pray." In one spontaneous motion that giant mass of farmers, teachers, students, doctors, and ordinary working people fell to their knees and recited the Lord's Prayer—a corporate act of civil disobedience. Within days the protest spread to the capital city of Bucharest, and a short time later the government that had ruled Romania with an iron fist toppled to the ground.

During the darkest days of Communist rule the Poles used to joke there were two solutions to their political crisis, a realistic solution and a miraculous one. In the realistic solution, Our Lady of Czestochowa would appear in the heavens, scaring the Russians into leaving. In the miraculous solution, the Russians would simply pack up and leave on their own. To no one's prediction, exactly that miracle transpired. How many divisions has the pope? Quite a few, as it happened. Several million Poles welcomed Pope John Paul II to his homeland by shouting, in defiance of their Communist leaders, "We want God! We want God!" The chant went on for more than thirteen minutes, and historians trace the beginnings of the Polish Resistance and Solidarity to that dramatic day.

The city of Leipzig in East Germany had been the scene of a violent protest against Communist rule in 1953, only to have it crushed by force. In four decades violence changed nothing behind the Iron Curtain. But in 1989 Christians meeting in a church where Johann Sebastian Bach used to play the organ began a practice of candlelight prayer marches. Ten thousand, thirty thousand, fifty thousand, then half a million joined the marches in Leipzig, and a million more in Berlin, until finally one night the Berlin Wall itself, the reviled symbol of that Iron Curtain, yielded to a different kind of power and splintered into a million pieces.

"He will strike the earth with the rod of his mouth," said the prophet Isaiah of the coming Messiah; "with the breath of his lips he will slay the wicked." The nouns—*mouth, breath, lips*—seem oxymoronic when paired with such fierce verbs. I think of Eastern Europeans marching through cobblestone streets, cupping tiny candles in their hands against the wind and singing hymns, with snipers watching nervously from the rooftops. I think of the museums in places like Leipzig and Budapest where tourists now shuffle through the very interrogation rooms that once kept entire nations in the grip of fear. I think of one frosty morning when I went jogging in Moscow and came across a park in which lay giant statues of Lenin, Stalin, and Marx, icons once elevated to the status of gods now piled like cordwood on a vacant lot.

Disarming Prayer

Does prayer make a difference in world events? Switch scenes to South Africa. In the early 1990s everyone knew South Africa's racist government would have to change, but most observers expected massive bloodshed to accompany that change. I know a man there named Ray McCauley, a Pentecostal preacher with a fascinating life story and an imposing physical presence (he competed against Arnold Schwarzenegger in the Mr. Universe contest). In the final days of the apartheid regime, the emerging black leadership of Nelson Mandela and Bishop Desmond Tutu courted Ray, no doubt because his weekly television audience represented a large constituency.

One day Mandela called on Ray for help. Forty-five black people had been murdered in a township, and Ray went with Bishop Tutu to visit and comfort the families. A week later the two returned to attend the funeral service at a sports ground filled with 15,000 people. As the service came to an end, anger surged through the crowd like a current of electricity. Impromptu speakers called for them to march together en masse and get their revenge. Ray noticed with some nervousness that he was the only white person present in that volatile crowd. Bishop Tutu turned to him and said, "Ray, don't worry, I'll take care of these marchers."

Ray recalls, "I then saw one of the most moving scenes of my life. Desmond Tutu stood before the crowd of 15,000, motioned for silence, and in his high-pitched, melodic voice he began to speak. 'I am your bishop, appointed by God.' *Yes. That's right! Preach it!* 'I have been awarded the Nobel Peace Prize.' *You got it! Yes, yes. Amen.* 'And yet do you see that police dog over there? That dog can go on beaches in South Africa that would not tolerate my presence!'

"The crowd exploded. They were cheering and stomping and waving handkerchiefs. Tutu kept building momentum. He had them eating out of his hand. Then the most extraordinary thing happened. In the next thirty minutes, using nothing but words ['the rod of his mouth'], this great man of God silenced the crowd, brought peace to that powder keg scene, and closed in prayer. And 15,000 demonstrators, many of whom were out for blood, simply turned around and walked home."

A few months later Tutu and McCauley stood before an even larger crowd, this one 100,000 strong. Earlier, black Africans had marched on one of the homelands, an area like a reservation set aside for native Africans. The homeland's leader callously ordered army troops to fire on the marchers, killing twenty-eight and wounding two hundred. Now a huge mob was assembling at the border. Once again Tutu flew with a group of church leaders to try to defuse the scene.

"When is it all going to stop?" Tutu asked the crowd. "We have a country that is on the verge of exploding. We keep having to be wiping tears from people's eyes." Behind him, armored vehicles blocked the road and soldiers aimed weapons at the crowd.

Ray, a well-known preacher but a political neophyte, found himself in the midst of perhaps the tensest drama to face the new nation striving to be born. "I didn't know what to do," Ray said. "Once again Bishop Tutu told me, 'I'll take care of the marchers.' But he added, 'You'd better calm down those soldiers over there.'

"I went to them, nervous young boys crouching by their machine guns, backed up by tanks. You could see the fear in their eyes. They were, after all, facing 100,000 chanting black protestors. Most of the white boys, I knew, were church-going Calvinists. I asked if we could pray, and they all respectfully removed their caps and helmets. I put everything I had into that prayer, and I meant every word. We spent the entire day there, a whole group of church leaders, and I truly believe that our prayers with both groups helped defuse what could have been a scene of great violence."

Two years later, on the eve of the changeover in South Africa, McCauley found himself before the king of the Zulus. Nelson Mandela had felt angry and betrayed when he learned that the white South African government with whom he had been negotiating was secretly paying Zulu warriors to carry out killings in black townships in order to spread discord. Meanwhile the Zulu king was favoring a boycott of the nation's first open elections, which would undermine their legitimacy. The nation's future hung in the balance, and emissaries and diplomats were scrambling to keep the fragile transition plan from unraveling. Prayer groups sprang up all over the country, imploring God for a miracle that would somehow allow the stubborn white leaders of the country and the former terrorist Mandela to work out a compromise.

McCauley arranged a charter flight with Bishop Tutu just twelve days before the elections were due to take place. The pastors spent six hours with the Zulu king. Ray remembers, "He sat on a kind of portable throne covered by leopard-skin robes, surrounded by warriors with spears. Even now I can't believe what I did, but at the time I felt a prompting of the Spirit. I said, 'Oh, king, you are a great king, but surely even you would wish to kneel before the King of Kings.' He hesitated a moment, then got off his throne and kneeled. I prayed for peace that day, and the next days our country faced. I prayed against violence. I prayed for unity. I prayed for the kingdom of God."

After the meeting the king made an urgent appeal to the Zulu people to stop fighting and to remain calm and peaceful. The elections went ahead on schedule, with no violence. "I'll never doubt the power of prayer again," said Ray. "Go figure—each one of those groups thought God was on their side. And yet in the midst of crisis, each one was willing to bow down, to yield before the God they thought they served."

Angle of Repose

After the changeover in South Africa, Bishop Desmond Tutu found that his work had just begun. He accepted the arduous assignment of presiding over the Truth and Reconciliation Commission hearings of South Africa. The horror stories knew no end. He heard gruesome accounts of beatings, and electric shock torture, and the abuse of pregnant women, and "necklacing" with burning tires. Day after day for nearly two years he listened to stories of deeds from hell acted out in his own country. In the midst of that time a reporter asked him, "Why do you pray?"

> If your day starts off wrong, it stays skewed. What I've found is that getting up a little earlier and trying to have an hour of quiet in the presence of God, mulling over some Scripture, supports me. I try to have two, three hours of quiet per day and even when I exercise, when I go on the treadmill for thirty minutes, I use that time for intercession. I try to have a map in my mind of the world and I go around the world, continent by continent—only Africa I try to do in a little more detail—and offer all of that to God.

Then he would put on his judicial robes and take his seat before a commission that tried to bring truth and reconciliation to a morally stained land. The musician Bono once asked Tutu how he managed to find time for prayer and meditation. Tutu replied, "What are you talking about? Do you think we'd be able to do this stuff if we didn't?"

In prayer we stand before God to plead our condition as well as the conditions around us. In the process, the act of prayer emboldens me to join the work of transforming the world into a place where the Father's will is indeed done as it is in heaven. We are Christ's body on earth, after all; he has no hands but ours. And yet to act as Christ's body we need an unbroken connection to the Head. We pray in order to see the world with God's eyes, and then to join the stream of power as it breaks loose.

In the mountains where I live, geologists and miners use the elegant term "angle of repose" to describe the precise angle at which a boulder will rest on the side of a hill, rather than tumble downward. I think of that image as the point at which prayer and action meet. Every so often one of those boulders breaks loose, releasing the potential energy in a crashing rockslide that permanently alters the landscape. Something similar happens in an avalanche, when an accumulation of tiny, almost weightless snowflakes breaks loose.

Dietrich Bonhoeffer's secret, said one German theologian, was the creative way in which he combined prayer and earthiness, forging a spirituality that made room for piety as well as activism. While sequestered in a monastery and awaiting orders from the German resistance movement, Bonhoeffer wrote, "A day without morning and evening prayers and personal intercessions is actually a day without meaning or importance." A pastor, he continued to observe regular prayer times even after he went to prison for participating in a plot against Hitler.

Bonhoeffer grasped the nature of prayer as partnership with God's activity on earth. He scolded German Christians who retreated into piety while resigning themselves to the evil around them ("That's just the way things are"). We cannot simply pray and then wait for God to do the rest. At the same time, Bonhoeffer cautioned against an activism that opposed the forces of evil without drawing on the power of prayer. The battle against evil requires both prayer and prayerful action.

During the 1960s and 1970s prayer almost vanished from the campuses of mainline Protestant seminaries, which emphasized the social gospel. Talk about a private life of prayer made a person suspect and might even provoke a lecture on the dangers of pietism. As a result many Protestants began visiting monasteries in search of spiritual direction. They learned from activists such as Dorothy Day and Thomas Merton that social action unsupported by prayer may well lead to exhaustion and despair.

In my travels overseas I have seen the clear results of prayerful action. Christians have a strong belief in a powerful and good God and an equally strong calling to live out the qualities of that God on a damaged and rebellious planet. For this reason, wherever Christian missionaries have traveled they have left behind a trail of hospitals, clinics, orphanages, and schools. To preach God without the kingdom is no better than to preach the kingdom without God.

We will not all find ourselves in the kind of dramatic circumstances that faced Bonhoeffer in Germany or Tutu in South Africa. But each of us in our own way will feel the tension between prayer and activism, between action and contemplation. I receive a newsletter from "The Center for Action and Contemplation" and together those two words encompass most of what we are called to do in following Jesus. The founder of the center says, "I have often told folks that the most important word in our title is not 'action' nor even 'contemplation,' but 'and.'"

A Spur to Action

Critics view prayer as a waste of time, an escapist way of dealing with problems. Charles Dickens drew that caricature of prayer through a character with a most appropriate name, Mr. Pecksniff. Saying grace before a bountiful meal, Pecksniff committed "all persons who had nothing to eat to the care of Providence, whose business (so said the grace, in effect) it clearly was, to look after them."

James answers the complaint raised by Dickens in language equally pointed:

> Suppose a brother or sister is without clothes and daily food. If one of you says to him, "Go, I wish you well; keep warm and well fed," but does nothing about his physical needs, what good is it? In the same way, faith by itself, if it is not accompanied by action, is dead.

I would add, "If one says 'I'll pray for you' but does nothing else, what good is it?" I was right to ask the Christians in China and Myanmar, "What else can we do?" but only if I emphasized the word *else*. "The things, good Lord, that we pray for, give us the grace to labour for," as Sir Thomas More expressed it.

Praying can be a risky enterprise, I have found, as the Spirit often convicts me of the very thing I am praying about. "Lord, help my neighbor, a single mother, in her hard life." Hmm, have I offered to take her son skiing lately? "Father, I pray for Brandon and Lisa's troubled marriage." What am I doing to support them, keep them together, hold them accountable? The inner voice of prayer expresses itself naturally in action, just as the inner voice of my brain guides all my bodily actions.

Esther had the Jews in Persia fast and pray for three days, and then worked all her charm as she approached the king. The early church prayed for Paul's

---

Patient in Adversity

NEIL

I currently serve as the U.S. national director of OMF International, the organization that grew out of China Inland Mission. From the very beginning our founder, Hudson Taylor, set up a vital dependence on God through prayer. For example, the mission never asks for money; we simply make our needs known and then pray.

Our faith has been tested many times, never so severely as in 1949 when the Maoist government ordered all foreign missionaries to leave China. We had more than nine hundred workers in the country, all of whom believed God had called them to China. How could they square that with the cold political reality of eviction?

Mission leaders met to discuss options for the future, and for the first two days they prayed. Some suggested they shut down the mission. Had not God led Hudson Taylor and the rest to China and nowhere else? Others proposed that missionaries relocate to other countries in Asia — the option that was ultimately agreed upon.

Today OMF has personnel in closed or security-risk countries whom we cannot talk about publicly. We would feel helpless in offering them support — helpless, that is, without prayer. I believe God built into the design of history the potential for being affected by our prayers, for accomplishing things not possible through mere human cleverness. Sometimes we hear of great breakthroughs, such as the spiritual revivals in South Korea and in China. Think of the irony in China: after all missionaries are kicked out and

safety and then lowered him over the city wall in a basket to aid his escape. Paul himself used the full extent of the Roman legal system as a way to protect his rights and ultimately to fulfill his heartfelt prayer to carry the gospel to Rome.

Sometimes, like the boy who asks his parents to solve a math problem while he plays video games, we ask God for things we should be doing ourselves. Israel cried to God for yet another rescue, "Awake, awake! Clothe yourself with strength, O arm of the Lord; awake, as in days gone by, as in generations of old." In the next chapter comes the response, "Awake, awake, O Zion, *clothe yourself* with strength."

---

the government passes restrictive legislation against religion, the greatest numerical revival in world history breaks out!

Yet sometimes we hear of great defeats, of stubborn opposition, of missionaries persecuted and even martyred (we lost seventy-nine missionaries and children in the Boxer Rebellion of 1900). We continue to pray, and let God sort it all out. We cannot force our will on others, just as we cannot force people to support our work financially, or to volunteer with our mission — nor would we want to. We present our requests and pray, as the Heidelberg Catechism puts it, to be patient in adversity and thankful in prosperity.

Before joining the U.S. office I worked as a missionary surgeon in Thailand. For me, medical missions provide a fine example of partnership. God has given us the honor of doing his will on earth, which includes bringing health and comfort where there is injury and distress. Our surgical team prayed with patients before administering the anesthetic. At the same time, I did everything in my power to apply my skills on their behalf. Many times I would pause during an operation, stumped, overwhelmed, and lift my head to stare out the window and pray. "I am at the end of my knowledge, God," I would pray. "I need your help, your guidance."

In the old days development tended to follow evangelism. First we would proclaim the gospel, then minister to physical needs by providing help with water, agriculture, and health needs. Now it's often the reverse: development work provides an entrée into restricted countries, and conversions flow out of our compassionate ministry. In that way, too, we are partners with God. We strive to do God's will on earth as it is in heaven so that God's name will be known, even hallowed, among every people.

Prayer may seem at first like disengagement, a reflective time to consider God's point of view. But that vantage presses us back to accomplish God's will, the work of the kingdom. We are God's fellow workers, and as such we turn to prayer to equip us for the partnership. Karl Barth, living in the crisis days of Nazi rule, declared prayer to be "the true and proper work of the Christian," and observed that "the most active workers and thinkers and fighters in the divine service in this world have at the same time, and manifestly, been the most active in prayer."

In modern-day Los Angeles, at the Catholic Worker soup kitchen, the day's work begins with this prayer: "Make us worthy, Lord, to serve our brothers and sisters who live and die in poverty and hunger. Give to them through our hands this day their daily bread and, by our understanding love, give peace and joy."

One volunteer reports that often this initial prayer does not suffice:

No sooner are these words out of our mouths than the vigorous chopping of vegetables for the soup and salad begins, as we prepare for the thousand-plus meals we will serve in a few hours. As a result, sometimes I get all caught up in the heavy responsibility of our task, and I have to take a step back to repeat the words of the prayer again. And then I remember, "Oh yes, I'm not in charge. God is. Somehow, there will be enough food; somehow, there will be enough time to prepare it; and somehow, there will be enough volunteers to serve it. Somehow, we will get through this day."

During the food preparation, one person volunteers to go off and pray for an hour. The crew insists on this practice even though the extra pair of hands could be chopping vegetables or making coffee. They want it to be God's work, not theirs. And by eliminating the time for prayer they would be yielding to the workaholism of our culture. In addition, one morning a week the entire community gathers for a half hour of meditative prayer. For activists on the front lines, prayer serves as part oasis and part emergency room.

Disciplines for Emergency Workers

After the deadly Christmas 2004 tsunami hit countries in Asia, I turned on National Public Radio and heard a Buddhist, Muslim, and Christian give their perspectives on the tragedy. The Buddhist explained that he does not really believe in a personal god and sees natural disasters as an inevitable part of fate, though he and many other Buddhists were extending aid to the victims. The Muslim had a more pointed diagnosis: perhaps the tsunami had come as a punishment, or at least a warning, to Muslims in the area who had not been taking their religion seriously.

The commentator reminded listeners that most of the tsunami victims were either Buddhist or Muslim before he turned the microphone over to the Christian, a representative of an international aid organization. "I have no good explanation for why such a thing happens, and cannot pretend to guess at God's involvement," he said. "We are there on the ground because we follow a man who defined love by telling the story of a Good Samaritan reaching out to a person who was his ethnic and religious opponent. Jesus showed that same love, and we believe that by following Jesus we are doing God's will on earth."

A few days later I received an email from an acquaintance, Ajith Fernando, who was helping to organize the relief work in Sri Lanka. "Disciplines for Emergency Workers," he titled it—a good title for anyone involved in God's kingdom work. Ajith mentioned that during times of disaster we tend to push ourselves beyond what is healthy. He then gave practical advice to other relief workers. Get enough sleep. Don't neglect your family. Tend to your emotional needs. In order to help others, you have to be strong yourself.

Finally, Ajith turned to spiritual disciplines.

> People like Mother Teresa have shown us that anyone who wants to do crisis ministry long term must have a healthy devotional life. God has built into our systems a rhythm of life which we must not violate: output and input; work and rest; service and worship; community activity, family activity and solitude. Yet it is so easy at a time like this to neglect some of the less active disciplines in this list.... Every time I sit down to pray or read my Bible there seem to be so many other urgent demands that call for my attention.

I live far away from the devastation caused by the tsunami. I prayed for Ajith and the other workers in the area, some of whom I know, and I gave money to support them. It seemed a frail thread, I must admit, to pray for people who had dropped everything to help their countries recover. And yet Ajith would be the first to say, "No, the prayer is essential. I live on the prayers. They alone can strengthen me to fight despair and fatigue."

I know a man in Chicago who camps in abandoned buildings for a week at a time, consecrating the building, praying for a way to convert it to serve the homeless. Then he goes out to raise money and recruit volunteers to rehab the buildings. Several hundred homeless people now have a place to live because of that man's efforts.

I know a couple in New Jersey who saw signs on their street and announcements in the paper notifying the neighborhood that a registered sex offender had just been released from prison and had moved into the area. The couple started praying for the man pictured on the posters, and occasionally they would see him on the street. Neighbors made a wide berth around the home he was living in, sometimes wrote graffiti on it, and warned their children against the occupant. After praying, this couple visited him and then opened their home to a weekly breakfast for ex-offenders like him. For twenty-one years they have been hosting that breakfast. The most despised men in the area have one place to go where they feel welcome and are treated like human beings.

What would happen if we followed literally Jesus' command to love our enemies and pray for those who persecute us? How would it affect the reputation of Christians in the United States if we became known not for our access to the White House but for our access to heaven on behalf of those who strenuously, even violently, disagree with us?

In a scene recorded in the book of Revelation the apostle John foresees a direct linkage between the visible and invisible worlds. At a climactic moment in history, heaven is quiet. Seven angels stand with seven trumpets, waiting, for about the space of half an hour. Silence reigns, as if all heaven is listening on tiptoe. And then an angel collects the prayers of God's people on earth—all the accumulated prayers of outrage, praise, lament, abandonment, despair, petition—mixes them with incense, and presents them before the throne of God. The silence finally breaks when the fragrant prayers are hurled down to earth: "and there came peals of thunder, rumblings, flashes of lightning and an earthquake."

"The message is clear," comments Walter Wink about that scene, "history belongs to the intercessors, who believe the future into being." The pray-ers are essential agents in the final victory over evil, suffering, and death.

CHAPTER 10

DOES PRAYER CHANGE GOD?

Prayer is the power by which that comes to pass
which otherwise would not take place.
ANDREW MURRAY

"I the Lord do not change" (Malachi 3:6).

"My heart is changed within me; all my compassion is aroused" (Hosea 11:8).

Those two statements, both recorded in the Bible as the words of God, frame a mystery. I could marshal other verses describing a changeless God and balance them with more passages that show God changing his mind. Truth to tell, we want some of both: a dependable God we can count on and yet an attentive God whom we can affect.

Not everyone worries about the philosophical underpinnings of prayer. For those of us who do, however, what we conclude about this issue may well determine how we view the utility — or futility — of prayer.

Origen was the first Christian writer known to mull over the paradox of praying to a God who does not change: "First, if God foreknows what will come to be and if it must happen, then prayer is in vain. Second, if everything happens according to God's will and if what He wills is fixed and none of the things He wills can be changed, then prayer is in vain." Origen came down solidly on the side of a changeless God, arguing that from the moment of creation God could foresee all that we would freely choose, including the contents of our prayers. Many philosophers followed the same track: Immanuel Kant, for example, called it "an absurd and presumptuous delusion" to think that one person's prayer might deflect God's plans.

Calvinism, with its emphasis on God's absolute sovereignty, shifted the focus of prayer from its effect on God to its effect on the person praying. The

131

devout Jonathan Edwards questioned petitionary prayer. He wrote, "It is not to be thought that God is properly moved or made willing by our prayers"; instead, God bestows mercy "*as though* he were prevailed upon by prayer." (John Calvin himself, I should note, had no such doubts about prayer. He urged people to pray and included a chapter on it in the *Institutes* next to his chapter on predestination. About his more extreme followers he said, "It is very absurd, therefore, to dissuade men from prayer, by pretending that Divine Providence, which is always watching over the government of the universe, is in vain importuned by our supplications.")

As discoveries in science explained away phenomena that people had always considered part of providence, sons and daughters of the Enlightenment saw less reason for prayer. The natural cycle of storms and droughts became more predictable, apparently less subject to the whims of God or those who prayed to God. Thomas Hardy described God as "the dreaming, dark, dumb Thing that turns the handle of this idle Show." In the modern novel *Slaughterhouse-Five* Kurt Vonnegut mocks prayer in a scene where the main character, Billy Pilgrim, puzzles over the well-known Serenity Prayer:

> GOD GRANT ME THE SERENITY TO ACCEPT
> THE THINGS I CANNOT CHANGE,
> COURAGE TO CHANGE THE THINGS I CAN,
> AND WISDOM ALWAYS TO TELL THE DIFFERENCE.

Among the things Billy Pilgrim could not change were the past, the present, and the future.

Vonnegut had no need to point out the obvious conclusion: What good is prayer in such a predetermined world?

The Bible's View

Turn to the Bible's view of history, however, and you see a picture of God as a personal Being who alertly listens to prayers and then responds. Jesus filled in that portrait, and the disciples took up praying right where Jesus left off, making specific and personal requests for God to act.

The most famous prayer, the Lord's Prayer (or, the Our Father), Jesus gave spontaneously in answer to his disciples' request for help. Introducing this model prayer, Jesus acknowledged that God already knows our needs in advance:

And when you pray, do not keep on babbling like pagans, for they think they will be heard because of their many words. Do not be like them, for *your Father knows what you need before you ask him.* This, then, is how you should pray ...

Some see God's omniscience as a disincentive to prayer: Why pray if God already knows? In contrast, Jesus treated God's knowledge not as a deterrent but as a positive motivation to pray. We do not have to work to gain God's attention through long words and ostentatious displays. We don't have to convince God of our sincerity or our needs. We already have the Father's ear, as it were. God knows everything about us and still listens. We can get right to the point.

"Prayer holds together the shattered fragments of the creation. It makes history possible," wrote Jacques Ellul, a modern French thinker who could not avoid the Bible's direct statements that God acts in response to prayer. Indeed, the great events of the Old Testament — Abraham's family, Joseph's rebound in Egypt, the exodus, the wilderness wanderings, the victories of Joshua and King David, deliverance from Assyria and Babylon, the rebuilding of the temple, the coming of Messiah — took place only after God's people had cried out in prayer.

Throughout, the Bible depicts God as being deeply affected by people, both positively and negatively. God "delights in those who fear him, who put their hope in his unfailing love." Yet, as the prophets tell, at times God also feels wearied by disobedience and eventually God's patience reaches an end point: "For a long time I have kept silent, I have been quiet and held myself back. But now, like a woman in childbirth, I cry out, I gasp and pant."

The New Testament presses home that our prayers make a difference to God and to the world:

Ask and it will be given to you.

And the prayer offered in faith will make the sick person well....
    The prayer of a righteous man is powerful and effective.

The eyes of the Lord are on the righteous and his ears are attentive
    to their prayer.

You do not have, because you do not ask God.

Underscoring these lavish promises, the Bible tells of prophets and apostles praying for physical healings and even the resuscitation of dead bodies; Sarah, Rebekah, Rachel, Hannah, and Elizabeth praying against their infertility; Daniel praying in a den of lions even as his three friends had prayed in the midst of fire. When God sent the prophet Isaiah, the most God-connected person of his day, to inform King Hezekiah of his imminent death, Hezekiah prayed for more time. Before Isaiah had left the palace grounds, God changed his mind, granting Hezekiah fifteen more years of life.

In a sort of negative proof of the power of prayer, three times God commanded Jeremiah to *stop* praying; God wanted no alteration in his plans to punish a rebellious nation. Prayer had, after all, softened God's resolve before. "Forty more days and Nineveh will be overturned," the prophet Jonah proclaimed to a heathen city, but "when God saw what they did and how they turned from their evil ways, he had compassion and did not bring upon them the destruction he had threatened." Four times the Old Testament reports that God "relented" or "changed his mind" in response to a request, and each shift forestalled a promised punishment.

A Work in Process

How do we reconcile the changeless God described in the Bible with the responsive God also described in the Bible? The revivalist Charles Finney, who moved away from the strict Calvinism of his youth, grounded his belief in the power of prayer, ironically, in God's unchanging character: "If you ask why he ever answers prayer at all, the answer must be, Because he is unchangeable." To give an example, a God bound by unchanging qualities of love and mercy must forgive a sinner who prays repentantly. God changes course in response to the sinner's change in course, and does so because of those eternal qualities.

The contemporary theologian Clark Pinnock follows a similar line of logic. Since God's nature is love, he says, God must be impressionable and sympathetic: "Because God's love *never* changes, God's experience *must* change." Pinnock contrasts two models of God's sovereignty. We can picture God as an aloof monarch, removed from the details of the world. Or we can picture God as a caring parent with traits of love, generosity, and sensitivity—an infinite Being who personally interacts with and responds to creation. Accordingly, God considers prayers much as a wise parent might consider requests from a child.

Andrew Murray, himself a Calvinist, concluded that "God does indeed allow Himself to be decided by prayer to do what He otherwise would not

Written Proof

Gail

If I ever doubt that God hears and responds to our prayers, I pull out my prayer journal. These days my "altar" is a computer desk. I sit there each day with an open Bible and record my spiritual journal on the computer. I need that kind of focus to help me meditate.

I ask God what I should do that day, and one by one names pop into mind. By the end of the time, I usually have three or four hours of work ahead of me, because I believe God often relies on us to help answer the very requests we make of him.

Each day I print out my journal and refer back to it, reminding myself of what I learned. Then, once a year I condense and compile the entire thing. I divide my notes into categories: insights, poetry, family highlights, repentance, fun times, sorrows—and answers to prayer. The synthesis of last year's journal took up fifty-six pages in a footnote-sized type. Reading it over, I'm simply amazed at how God worked in response to my prayers. I see a softening in my niece's husband, an agnostic. I see transformation in the members of my small group, and spiritual awakenings in my neighbors. I see growth in my own marriage.

I used to think that if I worked hard to be good enough, God would answer my prayers in the way that I wanted. Now I've learned to bow low. I'm just a steward, a pawn, with no real concept of what's best for me. The hard times I've gone through—and there are many—have taught me that God can use anything for his purposes. Sometimes my husband and I have longed for a particular result, only to realize later that it would have been disastrous for us. I've learned humility in prayer. God is the boss, not me. Whatever makes me bow lower is good for me because it seems God takes great delight in raising us up.

I'm blessed to have a husband who prays with me. Why is it so many men have difficulty praying with their wives (and vice versa) when they may well participate in prayer groups with near strangers? Perhaps it's because we can spot any superficiality in our spouses' prayers. We can't pretend. That, too, is a way of keeping me humble.

135

have done." Murray points to the Trinity for a clue into how God's mind might change. We have seen how Jesus on earth relied on prayer to commune with the Father and to make requests—some of which, notably, were not granted. Now Jesus as our advocate represents human interests within the Godhead. The apostle Paul affirms that the Holy Spirit also has an intimate role in prayer: "We do not know what we ought to pray for, but the Spirit himself intercedes for us with groans that words cannot express." In one of the few verses that mention all persons of the Trinity, Paul brings the three together: "For through him [Christ] we both have access to the Father by one Spirit." The Father, Son, and Holy Spirit conduct a kind of inner conversation, showing that God welcomes debate and counsel.

C. S. Lewis seemed fascinated by the questions posed by prayer, especially how a sovereign God might listen and respond to our prayers. As a young Christian in England, he had felt embarrassed about praying for his brother Warren overseas when he heard of a Japanese attack on Shanghai. What difference might one puny prayer make against the inevitability of fate or providence? He went on to explore the topic in several of his books and many of his essays and letters.

Lewis once presented the problem in the voice of a skeptic akin to Kurt Vonnegut:

> I don't think it at all likely that God requires the ill-informed (and contradictory) advice of us humans as to how to run the world. If He is all-wise, as you say He is, doesn't He know already what is best? And if He is all-good won't He do it whether we pray or not?

In reply, Lewis said that you could use the same argument against *any* human activity, not just prayer. "Why wash your hands? If God intends them to be clean, they'll come clean without your washing them.... Why ask for the salt? Why put on your boots? Why do anything?" God could have arranged things so that our bodies nourished themselves miraculously without food, knowledge entered our brains without studying, umbrellas magically appeared to protect us from rainstorms. God chose a different style of governing the world, a partnership which relies on human agency and choice. God granted the favored human species the "dignity of causality," to borrow a phrase from Pascal.

The skeptic, then, is objecting not merely to prayer but to the basic rules of creation. God created matter in such a way that we can manipulate it, by cutting down trees to build houses and damming rivers to form reservoirs.

God granted such an expanse of human freedom that we can oppress each other, rebel against our Creator, even murder God's own Son. Lewis suggests that we best imagine the world not as a state governed by a potentate but as a work of art, something like a play, in the process of being created. The playwright allows his characters to affect the play itself, then incorporates all their actions into the final result.

In this view, prayer as a means of advancing God's kingdom is no stranger than any other means. Go into all nations and preach the gospel, Jesus told his disciples, thus launching the missionary movement with its harrowing history; would not a large banner in the sky have served God's purpose just as well? Heal the sick, visit prisoners, feed the hungry, house strangers—Jesus also commanded these activities, delegating them into our hands rather than enlarging his own Galilean ministry to global scale. Consistently, God chooses the course of action in which human partners can contribute most.

Lewis sums up the drama of human history as one "in which the scene and the general outline of the story is fixed by the author, but certain minor details are left for the actors to improvise. It may be a mystery why He should have allowed us to cause real events at all; but it is no odder that He should allow us to cause them by praying than by any other method." Prayer is a designated instrument of God's power, as real and as "natural" as any other power God may use.

Timeless Complexity

I envy, truly I envy, those people who pray in simple faith without fretting about how prayer works and how God governs this planet. For some reason I cannot avoid pondering these imponderables. At the same time, a little reading in modern physics and cosmology has convinced me that creatures bound by time and space may never gain more than an inkling of the rule upholding the universe.

For example, physicist Stephen Hawking cites with approval Augustine's notion that any God must exist outside of time. We humans are confined to a space-time universe that began at a moment of time, but God is not. Experiments on relativity have proved that, strange as it seems, time itself is no constant. As a person's velocity approaches the speed of light, time "slows down" for that person, so that an astronaut launched at high speed into space will return measurably younger than her twin brother left at home.

Cosmologists seriously speculate about a reverse arrow of time that might allow us to travel backwards in time; popular movies like *The Time Machine* and *Back to the Future* depict adventures the traveler might have, tempted to change the details of history even before they occur.

How does God's timelessness affect prayer? C. S. Lewis decided it altogether reasonable to pray at noon for a medical consultation that might have been conducted at ten o'clock as long as we do not know the final result before we pray. "The event certainly has been decided—in a sense it was decided 'before all worlds.' But one of the things taken into account in deciding it, and therefore one of the things that really cause it to happen, may be this very prayer that we are now offering." Lewis notes such a notion would be less shocking to modern scientists than to nonscientists.

Older models of physics also established a clear trail of cause and effect. One billiard ball strikes another, energy gets transferred, and both balls move along a predictable and determined path. New models, though, deal with complexity theory and information theory. In a complex system—such as a single cell in the human body, much less an entire body, much less a community comprising many persons all of whom exercise free will—simple rules of cause and effect do not apply. Each step up the ladder, from matter to mind to many minds, introduces staggering new levels of uncertainty and complexity. We need a model far more sophisticated and, yes, mysterious than anything Isaac Newton might have dreamed up to figure out why things happen and whether prayer might enter in.

Scientists insist that measuring the spin of one particle may affect the spin of another particle billions of miles away. Some even suggest, in a theory called "the butterfly effect," that the flapping of a single insect's wings may contribute to the great causal chain that eventuates in a hurricane in the Gulf of Mexico or a tornado in Texas. Who can say with confidence what *causes* any single event, in nature or in a human being?*

What caused the hurricanes that ravaged Florida in 2004 and New Orleans in 2005? Or if a teenager decides to get drunk one weekend, what role do genes, brain chemistry, parental nurturing, and stubborn free will

---

*The conversations of modern cosmologists bring to mind arcane discussions from the Middle Ages. In the sixteenth century, in an attempt to reconcile sovereignty and free will, the Spanish Jesuit Luis de Molina proposed a "middle knowledge" of God: the ability to project in advance what every possible creature would do as well as how those free choices might affect each possible world. Stephen Hawking and several Nobel laureates endorse a many-worlds theory in which any choice I make may have an effect in some alternate universe, although I only perceive the one present to my consciousness. (String theory proposes at least eight additional dimensions of reality undetectable by us.)

play in the decision? What role does God play in natural events like weather anomalies and birth defects? Does prayer ever influence those events? Why must people suffer natural calamities? Why are pain and pleasure distributed so randomly and unfairly?

When the Old Testament character Job posed his anguished version of such questions, God erupted with a science lesson of his own. Poor Job repented in dust and ashes, shamed into silence by his ignorance in the face of God's own "complexity theory." (In an intriguing aside to the story, God informed Job's friends, who thought they had cause and effect all figured out, that he would deal with them not according to their "folly" but according to Job's *prayer* for them!)

At various times, according to the biblical record, God has indeed played a direct role in manipulating natural events: causing a drought or a plague of locusts, reversing the course of disease and disability, even restoring life to a corpse. Apart from these rare events called miracles, however, the Bible emphasizes an ongoing providence, of God's will being done through the common course of nature and ordinary human activity: rain falling and seeds sprouting, farmers planting and harvesting, the strong caring for the weak, the haves giving to the have-nots, the healthy ministering to the sick. We tend to place God's activity in a different category from natural or human activity; the Bible tends to draw them together. Somehow God works in all of creation, all of history, to bring about ultimate goals.

The act of prayer brings together Creator and creature, eternity and time, in all the fathomless mystery implied by that convergence. I can view prayer as a way of asking a timeless God to intervene more directly in our time-bound life on earth. (Indeed, I do so all the time, praying for the sick, for the victims of tragedy, for the safety of the persecuted church.) In a process I am only learning, I can also view prayer from the other side, as a way of entering into the rhythms of eternity and aligning myself with God's "view from above," a way to harmonize my own desires with God's and then to help effect, while on earth, what God has willed for all eternity.

In prayer I ask for, and gradually gain, trust in God's love and justice and mercy and holiness, despite all that might call those traits into question. I immerse myself in the changeless qualities of God and then return to do my part in acting out those qualities on earth: "Your will be done on earth as it is in heaven."

So many times I turn to prayer feeling besieged. The news from CNN reminds me of poverty and injustice, of human cruelty and terrorism and nuclear threats and a hundred things that foster anxiety. My distress spirals inward as I think of family, friends, and neighbors, so many of them battling illness, divorce, financial burdens, children in trouble. To my shame, petty interruptions in my own life often crowd out these concerns: a balky computer, a series of car and home repairs, a to-do list that never gets done. I confess to God my sins and realize they are the same sins I confessed yesterday, and last week, and the week before. Will nothing ever change? Will I?

Go into your closet and shut the door, Jesus advised. I envision doing just that: entering a closet with my pressing, time-bound burdens and asking God to renew, refresh, remind—in other words, to pour some eternity into me. I try to get my mind off myself, to empty it.

I think of Mother Teresa's nuns kneeling in their chapel long before daybreak, asking for the energy and the purity to go forth this day and ease the destitute of Calcutta toward a merciful death. I think of hospice workers and Army chaplains and so many of God's servants who daily face mountains before which my own worries shrink into molehills. I think of Jesus himself,

---

Losing Control

JIM

Although I was raised in the church, for many years I simply tuned God out. I never doubted he was there, but I guess I held a grudge against God for some of the things that had happened to me. I came back to God during a Promise Keepers rally in a football stadium. As thousands of men sang the old hymns I sat there and wept, realizing that for selfish reasons I had kept myself and my whole family away from church for at least two decades.

For a time I was insatiable. I read every Christian book I could get my hands on. An insomniac, I'd wake up in the middle of the night and read for several hours. During those days, I brought God a list of requests and complaints. Truth be told, I spent a lot of time whining to God.

Then I went on a silent retreat. For a week I just listened. God spoke to me, and I kept a spiritual journal for the first time in my life. I developed a taste for intimacy with God, a tiny sample of what it must mean to "pray without ceasing." Paul talks about the Spirit groaning inside us, and I finally began to understand what that means.

facing the darkest day in human history, pausing to pray the longest prayer recorded in the Gospels, the prayer of John 17.

Timeless Love

The scene of Jesus huddled in a locked room with a dozen friends, one of them a traitor, while outside temple guards and Roman legionnaires buckle on their swords and whips and torture devices, preparing for another dreary night's work, stands as a tableau of human history. A hushed moment of foreboding, a heartfelt prayer, a subdued connection with eternity, while just outside invisible forces of evil mobilize in opposition.

Anticipating his death, Jesus prays to the Father for his disciples: "I am coming to you now, but I say these things while I am still in the world.... They are not of the world any more than I am of the world." As if to underscore the point he repeats himself: "My prayer is not that you take them out of the world but that you protect them from the evil one. They are not of the

Nowadays I don't spend time worrying, "Is God there or not?" I assume God's presence. I don't spend much time asking God for things either. Specific requests are almost a joke to me. Mainly, I want reassurance that God loves me, and that he understands what I'm concerned about.

I've learned to trust God. When I do that, everything else slides down in importance. I used to test God, praying things like, "If you're really listening, have a deer walk past in the next ten minutes." Sometimes that actually happened! But I began to see how shallow were those prayers. I was trying to control God. The same with my specific requests: I'd ask God to arrange for my kids to act in ways I wanted them to act.

I don't do that any more. I've learned that the things I grasp and pursue often turn out disappointing and sour. The best things in life are unexpected gifts dropped on me—"grace notes," as a friend of mine calls them. Prayer works the same way. Don't be anxious, but pray about everything, Paul tells the Philippians. That's the key to God's peace. I treasure the time I spend with God more than the requests I want him to fulfill.

world, even as I am not of it." He, too, must see the group gathered around the table as a tableau of the conflict he is setting loose in the world.

For thirty-three years Jesus has stripped himself of the prerogatives of God, including omniscience and a timelessness that sees all history in a flash. (He once admitted he did not know the time of final judgment and healing of the earth, though the Father did.) In this prayer, however, he bridges time and eternity, recalling for a moment his stunning existence before volunteering for this violent planet: "And now, Father, glorify me in your presence with the glory I had with you before the world began."

Jesus is reminiscing about life before planet Earth, eternity before time. In this lengthy, luminous prayer he gives the ultimate answer to the "Why?" questions. Why creation? Why free will? Why human history and the onslaught of time? From the beginning, before the beginning, God willed to share with other creatures the love and fellowship—the *life*—enjoyed in the godhead before creation, now, and forever. Despite all that has happened and is about to happen, God is committed to restoring creation to its original design, to regaining perfect intimacy and love with human beings. Jesus' prayer renews the vision, for himself and for us.

In a few other places the New Testament gives hints of God choosing us "before the creation of the world." God's grace, claims Paul, "was given us in Christ Jesus before the beginning of time," with Jesus "chosen before the creation of the world but revealed in these last times for your sake." Our eternal life was promised "before the beginning of time." Thus the essentials of hope—God's love, heaven, grace, resurrection—the Bible specifically grounds outside of time and creation. Long before Einstein's theory of the relativity of time and space, long before any notion of a Big Bang origin of the universe, the New Testament writers established these truths as, quite literally, timeless.

Our sun, now middle-aged, will burn itself out in four or five billion years. Eventually the universe itself may collapse. Yet in the words of the Creator we have assurance that we will be reunited. The universe is not such a sad, lonely place. The prodigals have a home after all.

Of all that Jesus said that night in the candlelit room in the warrens of Jerusalem, one comment must have puzzled the disciples more than any other. Jesus knew the melancholy effect of his words about impending death: "Because I have said these things, you are filled with grief." As if to cheer them up, he added, "But I tell you the truth: *It is for your good* that I am going away."

142

Those words puzzle me as well. I cannot help thinking of all the ways God could have accomplished the divine will in the world: by providing enough manna to solve the world's hunger; by eradicating each new strain of virus and bacteria as it mutates into dangerous form; by narrowing the margins of human freedom to eliminate tyrants like Hitler and Pol Pot. Instead, God sent his Son to live in a remote corner of the earth for a few years. He delivered in person the message he wanted to convey and then he left, claiming it to be somehow for our good.

Soon the disciples who were accustomed to presenting their questions, complaints, and requests to Jesus in person would have to fall back on a different approach: prayer. Of all the means God could have used, prayer seems the weakest, slipperiest, and easiest to ignore. So it is, unless Jesus was right in that most baffling claim. He went away for our sakes, as a form of power sharing, to invite us into direct communion with God and to give us a crucial role in the struggle against the forces of evil.

Making Requests Known

Karl Barth, the twentieth-century theologian who pounded home the theme of God's sovereignty, saw no contradiction in a God who chooses to be affected by prayers. "He is not deaf, he listens; more than that, he acts. He does not act in the same way whether we pray or not. Prayer exerts an influence upon God's action, even upon his existence. That is what the word 'answer' means." Barth continues, "The fact that God yields to man's petitions, changing his intentions in response to man's prayer, is not a sign of weakness. He himself, in the glory of his majesty and power, has so willed it."

Why pray? Evidently, God likes to be asked. God certainly does not need our wisdom or our knowledge, nor even the information contained in our prayers ("your Father knows what you need before you ask him"). But by inviting us into the partnership of creation, God also invites us into relationship. God is love, said the apostle John. God does not merely have love or feel love. God *is* love and cannot *not* love. As such, God yearns for relationship with the creatures made in his image.

"Do not be anxious about anything, but in everything, by prayer and petition, with thanksgiving, present your requests to God," Paul instructs. The King James Version speaks of "making known" our requests. How can we make known a request to a God who already knows? Relationship is the key.

143

Occasionally in the mail I get a request for help from a stranger, often a prisoner or someone in a foreign country. Sometimes I give in response, sometimes I check the facts with a local person, sometimes I refrain from getting involved for fear of encouraging a flood of similar requests. When my neighbor has a need though, or my nephew, or someone *known* to me, I do everything I can to meet the need. Relationship ups the urgency of any information — it's the difference between watching news reports of a tragedy overseas and watching those same reports when your son or your fiancée is there.

Consider again the act of repentance. Confessing my sins before God communicates something God already knows. Yet somehow the act of confession binds the relationship and allows a closeness that could not otherwise exist. I make myself vulnerable and dependent, bringing God and me together. The same kind of intimacy happens when (all too rarely) I apologize to my wife for something we both know about. I do not bring her information, I bring her my heart, my humbled self.

I will never figure out the precise role of prayer in events like the path of a hurricane or the downfall of Communism. None of us time-bound humans has that capacity. I go to God with my concerns, though, as a child goes to a loving Father. I admit my dependence and make known my requests, fully aware that God and not I will make the final decision. In the time I spend with God, I may come away with a different view of the world or at least a new appreciation of my limited point of view. In exchange God gets my attention, my engagement, my soul.

By using prayer rather than other, more direct means, God once again chooses the most freedom-enhancing style of acting in the world. God waits to be asked, in some inscrutable way making God's activity on earth contingent on us. Does the kingdom, or "God's will," advance more slowly because of that choice?* Yes, in the same way parents slow their pace when the youngest child is learning to walk. Their goal is to equip someone else, not themselves.

---

*C. S. Lewis writes, "For He seems to do nothing of Himself which He can possibly delegate to His creatures. He commands us to do slowly and blunderingly what He could do perfectly in the twinkling of an eye. He allows us to neglect what He would have us do, or to fail. Perhaps we do not fully realize the problem, so to call it, of enabling finite free wills to co-exist with Omnipotence. It seems to involve at every moment almost a sort of divine abdication." Lewis adds in another book, "Creation seems to be delegation through and through. He will do nothing simply of Himself which can be done by creatures. I suppose this is because He is a giver."

CHAPTER 11

ASK, SEEK, KNOCK

... And if by prayer
Incessant I could hope to change the will
Of Him who all things can, I would not cease
To weary him with my assiduous cries.

JOHN MILTON

Jesus' story about village neighbors must have provoked smiles and chuckles in his first-century audience. A man opens his door to an unexpected guest late one night—not uncommon in a desert climate that encourages travel after sunset—only to find his pantry bare. In a region renowned for hospitality, no decent person would turn away a weary traveler or put him to bed without nourishment, so the host strikes out to a friend's house to ask for bread.

Kenneth Bailey, a Presbyterian missionary who lived in Lebanon forty years, illuminates some of the cultural nuances behind the story. Palestinians use bread as Westerners use silverware: they break off bite-sized pieces, dip into a common dish of meat and vegetables, and eat the entire sop. The man with empty cupboards was likely asking his friend for a main course as well as loaves of bread, and even that was typical. Villagers frequently borrowed from each other in hospitality emergencies. Bailey recalls one instance: "While living in primitive Middle Eastern villages, we discovered to our amazement that this custom of rounding up from the neighbors something adequate for the guest extended even to us when we were the guests. We would accept an invitation to a meal clear across the village, and arrive to eat from our own dishes which the villagers had borrowed quietly from our cook."

In Jesus' story, though, the neighbor stubbornly refuses the request (see Luke 11). He has already gone to bed, stretched out with his family on a mat in the one-room house—and, besides, the door is bolted shut. "Don't bother me," he calls to his neighbor outside. "I can't get up and give you anything."

145

A Middle Eastern audience would have laughed out loud at this lame excuse. Can you imagine such a neighbor? Jesus was asking. *Certainly not! No one in my village would act so rudely. If he did, the entire village would know about it by morning!*

Then Jesus delivers the punch line: "I tell you, though he will not get up and give him the bread because he is his friend, yet because of the man's boldness [his *persistence*, his *shamelessness*] he will get up and give him as much as he needs." The application to prayer follows immediately: "So I say to you: Ask and it will be given to you; seek and you will find; knock and the door will be opened to you."

Luke positions this story right after Jesus' teaching on the Lord's Prayer, drawing a sharp contrast between the reluctant neighbor and God the Father. If a cranky neighbor who has turned in for the night, who wishes more than anything you would go away, who does his best to ignore you—if such a neighbor eventually rouses to give what you want, how much more will God respond to your bold persistence in prayer! After all, what earthly father would sneak a snake under his son's pillow when he asks for a fish, or drop a scorpion on his daughter's breakfast plate instead of an egg?

The Lord's Prayer, often reduced to a mumbled ritual, an incantation, takes on new light in this story abutting it. We should pray like a salesman with his foot wedged in the door opening, like a wrestler who has his opponent in a headlock and won't let go.

The God "who watches over you will not slumber," promises a psalm of comfort. Even so, sometimes when we pray it feels as if God has indeed nodded off. Raise your voice, Jesus' story implies. Strive on, like the shameless neighbor in the middle of the night. Keep pounding the door.

Battering the Gates

A few chapters later Luke records another charming story, this time featuring a nagging widow as the unlikely heroine. Some of Jesus' parables left his disciples scratching their heads, but this one came with an unmistakable point: "to show them that they should always pray and not give up." The story takes the even riskier step of comparing God to a callous, corrupt judge who has to listen to the widow's loud grievance.

Today, many cities have a free legal aid clinic to help poor and underserved clients negotiate a confusing system of courts and depositions. To illustrate the very different situation in Jesus' day, Kenneth Bailey cites a scene witnessed by a Western traveler in nineteenth-century Iraq:

> On a slightly raised dais ... sat the *Kadi*, or judge, half buried in cushions. Round him squatted various secretaries and other notables. The populace crowded into the rest of the hall, a dozen voices clamoring at once, each claiming that his cause should be the first heard. The more prudent litigants joined not the fray, but held whispered communications with the secretaries, passing bribes, euphemistically called fees, into the hands of one or another. When the greed of the underlings was satisfied, one of them would whisper to the *Kadi*, who would promptly call such and such a case. It seemed to be ordinarily taken for granted that judgment would go for the litigant who had bribed highest. But meantime a poor woman on the skirts of the crowd perpetually interrupted the proceedings with loud cries for justice. She was sternly bidden to be silent, and reproachfully told that she came there every day. "And so I will," she cried out, "till the *Kadi* hears me." At length, at the end of a suit, the judge impatiently demanded, "What does that woman want?" Her story was soon told. Her only son had been taken for a soldier, and she was alone, and could not till her piece of ground; yet the tax-gatherer had forced her to pay the impost, from which as a lone widow she could be exempt. The judge asked a few questions, and said, "Let her be exempt." Thus her perseverance was rewarded. Had she had money to fee a clerk, she might have been excused long before.

Jesus' story has fewer details and only two characters but otherwise reflects a nearly identical setting. The judge finally yields to the plaintiff's pleas: "Even though I don't fear God or care about men, yet because this widow keeps bothering me, I will see that she gets justice, so that she won't eventually wear me out with her coming!" (The phrase "wear me out" actually translates a boxer's term for a repeated blow under the eye.)

Once again Jesus is presenting a parable of contrasts. In our prayers we may sometimes feel like the widow: alone, powerless, a victim of unfairness, disregarded, the least and last person in line. The truth, though, is the opposite. We have both an advocate and a direct line to a loving Father who has nothing in common with the insensitive judge in the story. When God seems slow to respond, we may suspect a lack of concern. Jesus corrects the misconception, pointing beyond how we may feel to an assurance of God's mercy. If even this widow gets justice from a heartless judge, how much more will "God bring about justice for his chosen ones, who cry out to him day and night."

And then, just as the audience settles back in comfortable reassurance, comes the sting in the tail: "However, when the Son of Man comes, will he find faith on the earth?" The disciples would have known exactly what Jesus meant, for he had just been talking about his eventual return, the second coming. Justice will surely reign one day. Appearing this time in power and great glory, the Son of Man has pledged to turn the tables on this violent planet, righting every wrong and restoring the world to what God intended: a world without unjust judges and neglected widows; without any poverty, or death, suffering, or rebellion. Until that future day, some will be tempted to doubt, to disbelieve in God completely or to see God as a merciless judge.

Years after hearing this parable in person, the apostle Peter wrote that in the last days some will scoff at such prophecies: "Where is this 'coming' he promised? Ever since our fathers died, everything goes on as it has since the beginning of creation." And after twenty more centuries of waiting, the conditions of this unredeemed planet further tempt us to give up, to lose faith in a powerful, loving God. Jesus told the story of the nagging widow to teach us to "always pray and not give up." History is a test of faith, and the correct response to that test is persistent prayer.

Older versions of the Bible apply the little-used word "importunate" to the widow and the borrower in Jesus' stories. Sometimes our requests will seem annoying, as that word implies. I think of William Wilberforce submitting the same bill, year after year, before the British Parliament as he argued importunately for the abolition of slavery. Or of Senator William Proxmire giving a speech every day on the floor of the Senate—3211 speeches delivered over nineteen years—until his colleagues finally passed a bill outlawing genocide. I think of Sister Helen Prejean, portrayed in the movie *Dead Man Walking*, who tirelessly crosses the United States pleading against the death penalty. And of Martin Luther King Jr. as he addressed the bloodied Selma marchers from the steps of Alabama's state capitol, voicing again and again their question about justice: "How long?... How long?... How long will it take?"

Activists who take up a cause—third world debt, AIDS in Africa, homelessness, abortion, sexual trafficking, racism, hate crimes, drunk driving, health care, unjust wars, the environment, pornography, prison reform, terrorism, human rights, and a hundred others—will doubtless grow weary and may be tempted to give up the fight. To them, God must resemble the callous judge or the crotchety neighbor in Jesus' stories. Jesus insists otherwise. Unlike the judge and the neighbor, God has infinite tolerance for our requests and demands, especially those supporting the cause of God's own kingdom. Why else would the Bible include so many importuning psalms, so many prophetic laments?

In his sermon "The Parable of the Importunate Widow," Helmut Thielicke notes that "God is doing nothing less than offering to his praying church a part in his government of the world." The giants of history, Thielicke says (thinking of his contemporaries Hitler and Stalin), stride across the stage under the delusion that they are directing the drama of the world, whereas

---

Someone to Talk to

SUSAN

All relationships take work—marriage, parenthood, friendship. We shouldn't be surprised that a relationship with God takes effort too. When I struggle, I turn back to the image Jesus uses, of God as Father.

My husband flew to China to pick up our adopted daughter. I felt helpless as I stayed home and prayed for that little person who would change our lives so dramatically. When he came back, he told me of crying on the bus on the way to pick her up in the orphanage. Already he had felt himself bonding with her, knitting our family together, even though he had only a photograph to go by. If we humans have that kind of bond, imagine God . . .

I learned to pray with my husband, late at night. We were going through a rough patch of marriage and didn't know where else to turn. I felt so inarticulate at first. I had never prayed aloud in group prayer meetings. They terrified me. But with my husband beside me I could simply let God know my needs. I thought of all the people in twelve-step groups like Alcoholics Anonymous. They pray simple prayers, something like, "Keep me sober!" with no real concept of God. Yet God seems to answer those prayers.

Often I pray myself to sleep. I try to calm down, thinking to myself, *I've gotta sleep, I've gotta sleep.* Of course, nothing happens. Now when I can't sleep, I have someone to talk to. I don't have to manage life on my own. God can help keep my heart from jumping out of my throat.

I used to worry about falling asleep during prayer. Now, as a parent, I understand. What parent wouldn't want her child to fall asleep in her arms?

in reality they are only bit players permitted onstage for a moment. Real power rests in those who perceive history as God's own drama, who tap into a power accessible only to those who ask and seek and knock. Prayer sets God loose. As we revolt against the world's disorder in our actions and in our prayers, refusing to resign ourselves to evil, we demonstrate that there remains, in Jesus' phrase, "faith on the earth."

Generations may pass before persistent prayer receives its answer. How many soldiers died before Thielicke's own prayers for peace and justice in his homeland Germany were answered? How many Jews died praying for a future at a time when it seemed the entire race was being incinerated? Filipinos prayed importunately for relief before People Power brought down a corrupt regime. Millions languished in prison camps before the Iron Curtain fell to the ranks of peaceful protestors. How many Chinese Christians still suffer imprisonment and torture while outside the prison walls an unprecedented spiritual revival continues to gather steam?

On a more personal level, how many abuse victims plead for healing and still wake up every day feeling wounded and ashamed? Addicts pray for deliverance and then rise each day to fight the same relentless battles. Parents grieve in prayer over children who seem determined to live self-destructively.

I will always remember an alcoholic friend who expressed to me his frustration at praying daily for God to remove his desire for drink, only to find each morning his thoughts turning to Jack Daniel's whiskey. Was God even listening? Later, it dawned on him that the desire for alcohol was the main reason he prayed so diligently. Persistent temptation had compelled persistent prayer.

Evil looms like a great iron gate—"the gates of hell" in Jesus' image—and prayers hit against it like hammer strokes. Gates don't threaten or even advance. They just stand there, awaiting the onslaught. Our prayers may seem as tinny as the sound a hammer makes when it bounces off a sheet of metal, but we have Jesus' strong promise that the gates of hell will not prevail. They will surely fall, shattering into pieces like the Berlin Wall that once divided Germany, like the Iron Curtain that once divided Europe.

Once Is Not Enough

Author Jerry Sittser sees persistence through the eyes of a parent. "My kids have asked me for many things over the years—a CD player, bicycle, boat, car, house, exotic vacations ... You name it, they have asked it. I ignore them most of the time. I am as hardhearted as they come, a parent made of granite. My ears perk up, however, when they persist, because persistence usually means they are serious about something."

Unlike a human parent, God knows my true motive, whether pure or impure, noble or selfish, from the moment of the original request. As I ponder Jesus' stories, I cannot help wondering why God places such a premium on persistence. If I find it tedious to repeat the same requests over and over, surely God tires of hearing them. Why must I pound on the door or elbow my way into the courtroom? Why won't a single sincere request suffice?

In search of clues, I turn first to the account of Jesus' life, and in several scenes I can see the value of persistence. After Lazarus died, his two sisters, the industrious Martha and meditative Mary, both accused Jesus: "Lord, if you had been here, my brother would not have died." They vented their accumulated grief and frustration, so much so that Jesus, too, sank into sorrow — before granting their deepest wish in one of his greatest miracles.

In another scene, a Canaanite woman pestered Jesus about her afflicted daughter. "Send her away, for she keeps crying out after us," urged the disciples, reminiscent of the hard-hearted villains in Jesus' parables. Even Jesus brushed her off, first ignoring her request and then challenging her right to make it. The foreign woman persisted and Jesus, impressed, granted her wish and then held her up as a model of faith.

Beside a well in Samaria, Jesus parried with a woman about her lifestyle and her religious beliefs. On the way to Jerusalem, he engaged a rich young man in a discussion on the dangers of wealth. The woman persisted and found her life transformed; the rich man gave up and turned away sad.

From these scenes I learn about God's interest in the process I go through. Always respectful of human freedom, God does not twist arms. God views my persistence as a sign of genuine desire for change, the one prerequisite for spiritual growth. When I really want something, I strive and persist. Whether it's climbing Colorado's mountains, chasing the woodpeckers away from my roof, or getting a high-speed Internet connection for my home, I'll do whatever it takes. Do I show the same spirit in prayer?

"Prayer does not change God, but it changes him who prays." Søren Kierkegaard may have first made that remark, but I have seen it repeated in a dozen books and articles. For reasons discussed in the previous chapter (mainly the Bible's own testimony), I cannot fully agree with the first half of the formula. God wants us to bring our requests boldly and without reservation. By failing to do so I will likely miss out on some delightful surprises. What if the ten with leprosy by the side of the road had not shouted out to Jesus for healing or if the Canaanite woman had shyly abandoned the request for her daughter?

All too often pray-ers use God's presumed changelessness as an excuse not to pray: "If God has already decided the future, why bother?" That very fatalism, ironically, defeats the second half of the formula, for we do indeed change in the very process of storming heaven with our prayers. If I stop believing that God listens to my requests—the emphatic point of Jesus' two parables—I will likely stop praying, thus closing off God's primary mode of relationship with me.

Persistent prayer keeps bringing God and me together, with several important benefits. As I pour out my soul to God, I get it off my chest, so to speak, unloading some of my burden to One who can handle it better. Little by little, as I get to know God I learn that God has nothing in common with an unjust judge or a stingy neighbor, though at times it may seem so. What I learn from spending time with God then better equips me to discern what God wants to do on earth, as well as my role in that plan.

Cicero gave a blunt assessment of the purpose of pagan prayer: "We do not pray to Jupiter to make us good, but to give us material benefits." For the Christian, something like the reverse applies. We may approach God with some material benefit in mind, and sometimes, blessedly, we receive it. But in the very act of praying we also open up a channel that God can use in transforming us, in making us good. Persistent prayer changes me by helping me see the world, and my life, through God's eyes. As the relationship progresses I realize that God has a clearer picture of what I need than I do.

When I persistently pursue another person, I am usually trying to persuade that person to adopt my point of view. I want the car salesman to match my price, the neighbor to vote for my candidate. I may, especially in the early stages of prayer, approach God the same way, but inevitably I find that God is the wise and senior partner in the relationship. I find, in fact, that God has been asking, seeking, knocking too, in the subtle ways I so easily ignore.

"A God that should fail to hear, receive, attend to one single prayer, the feeblest or worst, I cannot believe in; but a God that would grant every request of every man or every company of men, would be an evil God—that is no God, but a demon," said George MacDonald. Prayer is not a monologue but a true dialogue in which both parties accommodate to the other.

Although I bring my honest concerns to God, over time I may come away with an entirely different set of concerns. When Peter went on a roof to pray (Acts 10), he was mainly thinking about food. Little did he know that he would descend from the roof convicted of racism and legalism. In persistent prayer, my own desires and plans gradually harmonize with God's.

Winning by Losing

"Why should I spend an hour in prayer when I do nothing during that time but think about people I am angry with, people who are angry with me, books I should read and books I should write, and thousands of other silly things that happen to grab my mind for a moment?" Henri Nouwen posed that question in different forms, toying with different answers. Sometimes he fell back on the need for spiritual discipline, for being faithful even with no apparent reward: "We must pray not first of all because it feels good or helps, but because God loves us and wants our attention."

In the end, Nouwen concluded that "sitting in the presence of God for one hour each morning—day after day, week after week, and month after month, in total confusion and with a myriad of distractions—radically changes my life." He learned humility and dependence, and after hours of persistent prayer with no obvious sign of fruitfulness, he realized that a small, gentle voice had indeed been speaking all the while.

"Prayer does not change God, but changes him who prays"? Perhaps, sometimes, the internal changes wrought through prayer make possible the answers that we have long been seeking—the "change" in God if you will. Persistent prayer leads us into a new spiritual state for God to deal with. Perhaps that is why Abraham, Moses, Jacob, and the others found themselves wrestling so fiercely: the apparent struggle against God was developing in them the Godlike qualities that God wanted all along.

"Isn't it the greatest possible disaster, when you are wrestling with God, not to be beaten?" asked Simone Weil. To put it another way, what feels like a defeat at the time may emerge as an enduring victory. Jacob the cheat walked cockily on two good legs; Israel limped into history as the father of nations. The real value of persistent prayer is not so much that we get what we want as that we become the person we should be.

Whether climbing a mountain or writing a book, I have a goal-oriented, accomplish-the-mission attitude toward life, and prayer stops me in my tracks. I learn that I cannot "fix" the people I am praying for. I cannot get everything I want in the time frame I want. I must slow down and wait. I have to present my requests in a manner that seems at first like surrender. I "give them up" to God, and through that act of submission God can at last begin to grow in me the qualities, or "fruit," that I needed all along: peace, patience, kindness, goodness, faithfulness, gentleness, self-control.

A person prays, said Augustine, "that he himself may be constructed, not that God may be instructed." I examine my own erratic prayer life and see it as a time when God has indeed worked to lop off the protuberances and smooth the rough edges. I see defeats and victories both. Like a child who quits badgering a parent, I have sometimes found that I get an answer to my persistent request after I have learned to do without it. The answer then comes as a surprise, an unexpected gift of grace. I seek the gift, find instead the Giver, and eventually come away with the gift I no longer seek.

Luke's version of the parable of the crotchety neighbor ends with these words: "If you then, though you are evil, know how to give good gifts to your children, how much more will your Father in heaven give the *Holy Spirit* to those who ask him!" Matthew repeats the same saying, with one change: "If you, then, though you are evil, know how to give good gifts to your children, how much more will your Father in heaven give *good gifts* to those who ask him!"

In prayer we present requests, sometimes repeatedly, and then put ourselves in a state to receive the result. We pray for what God wants to give us, which may turn out to be good gifts or it may be the Holy Spirit. (From God's viewpoint there is no better response to persistent prayer than the gift of the Holy Spirit, God's own self.) Like Peter, we may pray for food and get a lesson in racism; like Paul we may pray for healing and get humility. We may ask for relief from trials and instead get patience to bear them. We may pray for release from prison and instead get strength to redeem the time while there. Asking, seeking, and knocking does have an effect on God, as Jesus insists, but it also has a lasting effect on the asker-seeker-knocker.

"For we are God's workmanship, created in Christ Jesus to do good works," Paul wrote the Ephesians. *Workmanship* conveys rather clumsily the meaning of the Greek word *poiema*, origin of the English word *poem*. We are God's work of art, Paul is saying. Of all people, Paul with his history of beatings, prison, shipwreck, and riots, knew the travail involved in the fashioning of that art—and the role that prayer played. Prayer offers an opportunity for God to remodel us, to chisel marble like a sculptor, touch up colors like an artist, edit words like a writer. The work continues until death, never perfected in this life.

PART 3

THE LANGUAGE
OF PRAYER

You beg. You whimper. You load God down with empty praise.
You tell him sins that he already knows full well.
You seek to change his changeless will. . . .
And sometimes, by God's grace, a prayer is heard.

FREDERICK BUECHNER

CHAPTER 12

YEARNING FOR FLUENCY

*The paradox of prayer is that it asks for a serious effort
while it can only be received as a gift.
We cannot plan, organize or manipulate God;
but without a careful discipline, we cannot receive him either.*
HENRI NOUWEN

I cannot remember a time without prayer. As a child I recited prayers before falling asleep and bowed my head before every meal. I faithfully attended Wednesday night prayer meetings and New Year's Eve watch night services, both of which sorely taxed a child's ability to stay awake. I prayed with childlike trust, so much so that friends of the family who lost a wedding ring or a family pet would phone to ask for my prayers, often calling back later to report a happy result. (Meanwhile my own family pets would get run over, die of distemper, or get attacked by neighbors' dogs despite my pleas for their protection.)

For several years I attended a Bible college that enforced praying with the rigor of a military academy. A bell rang at 6:00 a.m. and by 6:30 every student was required to begin a half-hour "quiet time" of Bible reading and prayer. Deans sometimes made surprise checks in the dorms, and stories abounded of a dean opening a door and switching on a light to find one student kneeling by the side of his bed while his roommate sat on the bed with an open Bible, both sound asleep in total darkness.

The school also scheduled periodic "prayer days." Instead of going to classes we prayed privately and in groups most of the day until gathering for a triumphant service of prayer and testimony in the evening. Students reported on answers to prayer, such as the timely financial gifts that allowed them to stay in school. At one of these services I heard my roommate tearfully confess a series of wild escapades that I knew he was embellishing. Like prisoners bragging about their crimes, young sinners gained inverted prestige through dramatic public repentance. Another student asked prayer for his girlfriend, critically injured in an auto accident while driving to see him. This sad, lonely boy from my hometown in fact had no girlfriend, was gay, and would eventually die of AIDS; he had made up the story to attract attention and sympathy.

In the years since, while working with Christian organizations and serving on various church committees, I have sat through many group prayer sessions. Some moved me deeply and bonded the group together. Others seemed an exercise in positioning, and I too felt the temptation to gain status by praying impressively, my words addressed as much to those around me as to God.

I have experienced times when prayer made little sense. Questions I have already mentioned (Why tell God what God already knows? Why ask God to be merciful if God is by nature merciful? Why pray at all?) muzzled me. For a solid year I could come up with no authentic prayers of my own and simply read from prayers in a *Liturgy of the Hours*, asking God to take those written words and accept them as my prayers whether I felt them sincerely or not. Then one day the cloud lifted and I wondered what had been my problem all that time.

I have not since experienced such a time of blockage or desolation, yet I have never stopped struggling with the act of prayer. When I hear of people who spend an hour a day meditating, I wonder how they do it. I strain to spend fifteen minutes, and anything longer tends to degenerate into distraction and lapses of concentration. Typically, I have the sense that my cluttered world of tasks undone and letters unanswered imposes on an ordered time with God. I am learning, though, to dismantle the barriers separating the act of prayer from the rest of life and instead to invite God to "impose" on my tightly ordered life.

Adjusting Expectations

Even when prayer seems a duty, like a homework assignment, we sustain the hope that it could grow into something more. A hidden treasure lies inside, if only we can quarry it. A new country awaits us, if only we can find the language in which to converse. We babble like infants, yearning for fluency. "I was less a man praying than a man *being* a man praying," recalls Frederick Buechner about a phase when his prayers seemed self-conscious and stagy.

Some who attempt prayer never have the sense of anyone listening on the other end. They blame themselves for doing it wrong, feeling ever a failure. An Australian wrote me about his concern for those who feel *autistic* in prayer: not only the depressed and those with borderline personality disorders, but also ordinary, timid people in the pews who feel undeserving of God's attention.

Another friend of mine who knew I was investigating prayer wrote that in her experience few people find prayer fulfilling, easy, or rewarding. She added,

> I think prayer is analogous to sex. (People's ears always perk up when I say that.) Most people would complain about their sex lives; a few do really well. Sex and prayer are intimate and over-glamorized relationships. We all are led to believe that we should be in the stratosphere in sex and in prayer. It sets up a false expectation. And breaks down intimacy.

This woman spent several months in Africa, which forced her to adopt a slower pace. There she found the silence to pray in a new way. "Again, similar to sex, when we are so busy and filled with the cacophony of life, it is hard to relax, be quiet and communicate."

As I thought about her unlikely analogy, it occurred to me that reading a book about prayer has some parallels to reading a sex manual. What sounds so thrilling on paper bears little resemblance to how sex usually plays out between two vulnerable people who approach it with very different expectations. Like sex, prayer centers in relationship more than in technique, and the differences between the two parties in prayer are far more profound than the differences between two lovers. Should it surprise us that problems arise?

A media-saturated culture conditions us to expect a quick fix to every problem. Relationship problems, however, rarely lend themselves to quick and easy solutions. I have not seen, for instance, that shelves of books on "how to save your marriage" have had any discernible effect on divorce rates. If relating to another person proves so resistant to formulaic advice, how much more does relating to God? The secret to keeping company with God will likely not be found in a new set of tapes, another book, a different preacher, a weekend seminar.

After reading scores of books and interviewing scores of people about prayer, I would expect a more noticeable improvement in my own prayer life. If I invested the same energy in, say, golf or learning a foreign language,

I would likely see results. Still I find that prayer involves an effort of will. Sometimes it proves rewarding, sometimes not, at least not in ways I can detect at the time. Prayer requires the faith to believe that God listens, though I have no hard evidence, and that my prayers matter. Neither belief comes easily to me.

When I enter another culture, I have to communicate by their rules, not mine. In South India I learned that shaking the head from side to side means yes, not no. When I got married, I learned that men are from Mars and women are from Venus; after thirty-five years I am still discovering ways in which we differ. And when I seek to know God, I must learn a new way of communicating. I am seeking company with an invisible God, after all.

I recently heard from a missionary doctor who has spent the past three years in Ecuador. His letter recounted some of the frustrations involved in

---

Digging a Small Shaft

KARL RAHNER, FROM *THE NEED AND THE BLESSING OF PRAYER*

Oh everyday prayer! You are poor and a little tattered and the worse for wear like the everyday itself. August thoughts and exalted feelings are difficult for you. You are not an exalted symphony in a great cathedral, but more like a devout song, well-intended and coming from the heart, a little monotonous and naive. But, prayer of the everyday, you are the prayer of loyalty and reliability, the prayer of selfless, unrewarded service to the divine majesty, you are the dedication which makes the gray hours light and the trivial moments great. You don't ask about the experience of the one praying, but about the honor of God. You don't want to experience something, but to believe. Your gait may sometimes be weary, but you still walk. Sometimes you may appear to come just from the lips and not from the heart. But isn't it better that at least the lips are blessing God than when the entire human being becomes mute? And isn't there more hope then that the sound from the lips will find an echo in the heart than when everything in man remains mute? And in our prayer-poor times, what one chides oneself or others for as lip-prayer is most often in reality the prayer of a poor but loyal heart that laboriously and honestly, in spite of all the weakness, weariness, and inner discontent, is at least continuing to dig a small shaft through which a small ray of the eternal light falls into our heart that is buried by the everyday.

learning a language. Even after three years he makes childish mistakes in grammar, looks foolish in front of the native-speakers, and can express only haltingly what his brain processes fluently. Speaking Spanish has been a continuing lesson in humility, he said. He makes progress, yes, but every day he realizes that he has failed to communicate fully and has missed nuances of meaning.

Reading his letter, I drew the parallel to prayer. If I want fluency in a foreign language, I must set aside time, no doubt giving up something else in the process. I must keep working at it, persisting despite the awkward feelings of a beginner. I persevere only because I value the final result. Nearly everything worthwhile — learning a sport, mastering the guitar, improving computer skills — involves the same process.

Prayer remains a struggle for me. On the other hand, so does forgiving someone who has wronged me. So does loving my neighbor. So does caring for the needy. I persist because I am fulfilling God's command, and also because I believe I am doing what is best for me whether or not I feel like it at the time. Moreover, I believe that my perseverance, in some unfathomable way, brings pleasure to God. We should always pray and not give up, Jesus taught.

I take dark encouragement in the fact that after following Jesus around for months, the disciples still had no clue and had to ask, "Teach us to pray." I take encouragement from Christians far advanced in spiritual disciplines who have similar struggles. (If you doubt that, read some accounts of Trappist monks, who spend all day pursuing life with God and who confront the same obstacles that stump us part-timers.) How do we learn to pray? Mother Teresa answers, "By praying.... If you want to pray better, you must pray more."

The great English preacher Leslie Weatherhead's experience echoes that of many others:

> I have always found prayer difficult. So often it seems like a fruitless game of hide and seek in which we seek and God hides. I know God is very patient with me. Without that patience I should be lost. But frankly I have to be patient with him. With no other friend would I go on seeking with such scant, conscious response. Yet I cannot leave prayer alone for long. My need drives me to him. And I have a feeling that he has his own reasons for hiding himself, and that finally my seeking will prove infinitely worthwhile.... I long for more satisfaction, but I cannot cease

from questing. Jesus sometimes found prayer difficult. Some of his most agonized prayers were not answered. But he did not give up his praying. I frankly have little to show for all my prayers, but I cannot give up, for "my soul longeth for God," and I know that outside God there is nothing at all but death.

Choosing a Routine

In the midst of a hectic, confusing period of his life, Henri Nouwen took a sabbatical from his professorship at Yale and spent seven months at a Trappist monastery in upstate New York. He asked a mentor there for advice on how to develop a deeper prayer life in the midst of his busyness. When he tried to pray, he said, his mind drifted to the many things he had to do, most of which seemed more urgent and important than prayer. The mentor recommended that Nouwen set a prayer schedule that he would stick to at all costs. He suggested an hour in the morning before work and a half hour before going to bed, a schedule far more lenient than the monks' own.

Nouwen decided on a more realistic prayer regimen of half an hour each day. At first his thoughts ran wild, like untamed animals. He kept at it, telling himself, "Since I am here for this half hour anyhow, I might just as well pray." The sense of awkwardness gradually faded, and in time he felt his soul settling down to a more calming rhythm. It may seem that nothing happens when you pray, he observed. But when you stay with a routine, over time you realize that something indeed has happened.

Along with Nouwen, I too appreciate prayer mostly in retrospect. The process itself feels like work. I look for ways to avoid it and keep glancing at the clock as I'm praying. During the day, however, thoughts and impressions come to mind that stem directly from my prayers. I am far more likely to view events that occur and people I encounter from God's point of view. Like a lingering scent, prayer carries over into the rest of the day.

I must admit that when I read the masters of prayer I feel myself tensing against their advice to make prayer a discipline. Mother Teresa prescribed a full hour of contemplation for each of the sisters in her order. (They rise at 4:30 a.m. and take a cold-water bath before morning prayers.) Some medieval authors recommended pausing before every prayer to tell yourself you might die at the end of your prayer, in order to focus its intensity. When I read such advice, I have an allergic reaction that probably traces back to that six o'clock bell in the Bible college.

Yet I remind myself that in some areas I willingly show discipline, somehow finding time for what matters to me. I check email without fail. I exercise faithfully. I keep doctor's appointments. I sit at my desk and work whether I feel in the mood or not. And if I travel away from my wife, I think about her during the day and call her in the evening.

Don Postema says, "I used to write in my daily calendar '7–7:30 a.m.: Prayer.' But many times I passed that up. It was one more thing to pass by that day. Now I write '7–7:30 a.m.: God.' Somehow that's a little harder to neglect." I have found that my reluctance to pray increases when I regard it as a necessary discipline and decreases when I see it as a time to keep company with God.

True prayer comes from within, from the longing of the heart. A woman named Judy Morford expressed this well:

> My own prayer life has been through many changes over the years. As a young mother, I had a five-year-old, a three-year-old, and a one-year-old, and I found the only time I could really pray was literally in the middle of the night. If I woke up then, I would pray. As the kids grew older, I began to get up at 4:30 in the morning to pray. I still don't have ideal conditions for regular prayer. As a mother of three teenagers and working full time, I sometimes get too tired to pray. But most days I'm able to work in some time for quiet prayer.
>
> Because of my changing schedule over the years, I've asked myself, *Just what does God expect of me in my prayer life?* The answer I come up with is he wants a love relationship. He doesn't want a hired servant; he wants a bride. A true love will always find a way. It may not always be the same way, or the prescribed way, but it will be a way that reflects love. That's what God wants from me.

The routine of prayer for Judy Morford bears little resemblance to that of Henri Nouwen, not to mention his Trappist adviser. I must find my own way to pray, not someone else's. And as life changes, my prayer practice will no doubt change with it. A person battling chronic illness will pray differently than a college student who mainly worries about final exams and a noisy roommate. Taking a mission trip, getting married, managing a houseful of kids, giving care to an aging parent — every major life change will have its effect on prayer, both its practice and its content. The only fatal mistake is to stop praying and not begin again.

Showing Up

Life today conspires against a regular, satisfying prayer time. Reading the classic devotional literature, I am struck by how much of it came from the pens of people who lived in communities organized for that purpose (such as convents and monasteries) or from those who had servants to handle the time-consuming chores (they say nothing of the servants' prayer lives). I find scant advice on prayer written by a mother of three teenagers or an executive who puts in seventy-hour weeks at the office.

Add to modern hindrances the barrage of "noise" in an information society — chat rooms, mobile phones, television, text messaging, iPods, BlackBerry Internet devices — and prayer simply gets drowned out. In airports I see business people walking around with Bluetooth earpieces permanently attached to their ears, waiting for the next interruption. Of course, all the electronic devices have an on/off switch, but somehow their offerings seem more productive or enticing than sitting quietly in conversation with God.

Let's be honest: by most standards they *are* more productive and enticing than prayer. Some manuals on prayer imply that time spent with God will rank as the high point of a day and that prayer flowing spontaneously from anointed lips will usher in miraculous answers. Instead, the pray-er finds herself battling boredom, fatigue, and a nagging feeling that she's wasting time. *What went wrong?* she wonders.

Daniel Yankelovich, an astute observer of social trends, points to a cultural shift that occurred in the West in the 1970s. Before then, society valued self-denial or "deferred gratification." Spouses sacrificed, even if it meant holding two jobs and accepting transfers to other cities, in pursuit of long-term goals. Parents trapped in an unsatisfying marriage stayed together for the sake of the children. In the 1970s the rules changed: the self-denial ethic morphed into a self-fulfillment ethic. We listen to our emotional needs and want them fulfilled now, without sacrifice, without waiting. We buy whatever we want on credit and jettison anything that proves complicated or irksome (like a troublesome marriage, for instance).

Under the new rules prayer loses out. It requires discipline, involves persevering through periods of darkness and dryness, and its results are difficult to measure. Rarely does it satisfy emotional cravings right away.

Indeed, the New Testament presents prayer as a weapon in a prolonged struggle. Jesus' parables on prayer show a widow pestering a judge and a man pounding on his neighbor's door. After painting a picture of the Christian as a soldier outfitted with the "full armor of God," Paul gives four direct commands to pray. Elsewhere, Paul urges his protégé Timothy to endure hardship like a soldier, to toil like a farmer, to compete like an athlete.

I have neither farmed nor served in the military but for thirty years I have been a runner, often entering charity races. I remember well how it all started. I met a young man named Peter Jenkins at a writers' conference as he was working on the book A Walk Across America, which later became a national bestseller. As he recounted some of his adventures on a long walk across the country, he said, "I get tired of these reporters flying down from New York, renting a car, then driving out to meet me. They hit the electric window button of their air-conditioned car, lean out, and ask, 'So, Peter, what's it like to walk across America?' I'd like a reporter to walk with me for a while!" Without thinking, I volunteered.

As our agreed-upon time approached, I realized that if I planned to walk through Texas in July with a sixty-pound pack on my back, I had better get into shape. I bought some cheap running shoes, stepped out the door, and sprinted down the driveway, expecting to run a few miles. At the end of the block I pulled up, gasping and wheezing, with an abrupt lesson in physical fitness. Lay off exercise for a decade or more, and the body no longer responds.

I ran as far as I could that day—one block—then walked a block, ran another block, and limped home humiliated. The next day I ran two blocks, kept walking, and ran some more. Within six weeks, just in time for my Texas assignment, I was running seven miles without stopping. That began a routine of aerobic exercise that continues to this day. My body has become so accustomed to the regimen that if I have to skip a few days because of injury or illness I feel edgy and restless.

I learned early on never to ask myself, "Do you feel like running today?" I just do it. Why? I can think of many reasons. Regular exercise allows me to eat what I want without worrying about weight gain. It does long-term good for my heart and lungs. It allows me to do other activities, such as skiing and mountain climbing. All these benefits represent the kind of "deferred gratification" Daniel Yankelovich referred to.

As with physical exercise, much of the benefit of prayer comes as a result of consistency, the simple act of showing up. The writer Nancy Mairs says she attends church in the same spirit in which a writer goes to her desk every morning, so that if an idea comes along she'll be there to receive it. I approach prayer the same way. Many days I would be hard-pressed to describe a direct benefit. I keep on, though, whether it feels like I am profit-ing or not. I show up in hopes of getting to know God better, and perhaps hearing from God in ways accessible only through quiet and solitude.

For years I resisted a regular routine of prayer, believing that commu-nication with God should be spontaneous and free. As a result I prayed infrequently and with little satisfaction. Eventually I learned that spontane-ity often flows from discipline. Leonardo da Vinci spent ten years drawing ears, elbows, hands, and other parts of the body in many different aspects. Then one day he set aside the exercises and painted what he saw. Likewise, athletes and musicians never become great without regular practice. I found that I needed the discipline of regularity to make possible those exceptional times of free communication with God.

The English word *meditate* derives from a Latin word which means "to rehearse." Virgil speaks of a shepherd boy "meditating" on his flute. Often my prayers seem like a kind of rehearsal. I go over basic notes (the Lord's Prayer), practice familiar pieces (the Psalms), and try out a few new tunes. Mainly, I show up.

Two Worlds

In medieval times, and still today in monasteries, the chiming of a church bell would cause all who heard it to stop and say the prescribed prayer. It forced them to remember God. Living in a place where church bells do not ring, I must make a deliberate effort to remember. Otherwise my mind fills with different content: images from the television screen, details of pending trips, a pile of laundry, anxiety over a sick friend.

When I pray, it may seem that I am narrowing my world, retreating from the real world into a prayer closet in Jesus' metaphor. Actually I am entering another world, just as real but invisible, a world that has power to change both me and the world I seem to be retreating from. Regular prayer helps me to protect inner space, to prevent the outer world from taking over. "Blessed are the pure in heart, for they will see God," Jesus said. When I think of how long a single image crafted by Hollywood lust-masters can live on in my mind, I understand his saying. So often I fill my mind with images that crowd out all room for God. Prayer involves a "renewing of the mind," a two-stage process of purging out what displeases God and damages me (the same, it turns out) and allowing God to fill my mind with what matters far more.

Contact with God doesn't just provide a moment of spiritual ecstasy; it equips me for the rest of life. I corral a few minutes of calm in the morning in hopes that I can carry some part of that calm into the rest of the day. If I pray consistently I feel free and strong, able to meet the challenges and temptations of the day. As the book of Psalms demonstrates so well, prayer does not mean retreating away from life, but rather bringing the stuff of our world—the rhythms of nature, harassing problems, disturbed emotions, personality conflicts—before God, then asking for a new perspective and new energy to take back to that world.

In short, prayer invites God into my world and ushers me into God's. Jesus himself, who spent many hours in solitary prayer, invariably returned to a busy world of weddings, dinners, and crowds of sick and needy people. He rejected Peter's suggestion to build a tent on a mountaintop and returned instead to the masses below. Following that pattern, I look for ways to bring the two worlds together, God's and mine, to let them become one.

Praying in Snatches

DEBRA RIENSTRA, FROM *SO MUCH MORE*

I received a request recently from a writer who wanted to put together an article on prayer for a Christian magazine, an article she was calling "Giving God the First Fruits." She explained enthusiastically how she herself had changed her daily prayer time from evening to morning and found that she suddenly started to grow spiritually and felt her life transformed. She was looking for similar stories to fill out this piece on putting prayer first in your day. I tried to reply to her request; but I could only observe that since I started managing a job, three young children, and a husband who works evenings, if anything my prayer life had gone downhill. I pray for a few moments in the morning; I pray when I first get to my desk at the office for a few minutes as I wait for the electric kettle to boil water for tea; I pray in snatches while driving or stirring supper on the stove or waiting for programs to load on the computer; and sometimes on a good day, I pray for a few brief moments before I crawl into bed. I finally gave up trying to put an inspirational twist on this tale. Reports on prayer struggles were not what this person was after. She wanted triumphs and turnarounds.

The morning offers a chance to plot out the day in advance, to bring before God every scheduled appointment and phone call as well as to ask God to keep me mindful of any sacred interruptions. None of us knows what any day will bring, of course, and I find it helps to request in advance a sensitivity to whatever might transpire. I need to tune in to God's work behind the scenes. As my pastor in Chicago used to pray, "God, show me what you are doing today, and how I can be a part of it." Amazingly, when I preview my day in prayer, priorities will tend to rearrange themselves during the course of the day. An unexpected phone call may take on more significance than the scheduled task of finishing my income tax forms.

On the other hand, prayer in the evening provides a natural coda to the day. I can review all that happened, reflect on what I learned, repent of how I failed, and deliver into God's hands all that remains unresolved and troubling. Many times I go to bed confused about a computer error or some problem in my writing and awake the next day with a fresh idea on how to solve it. Regardless, if I do not schedule such times in the morning or evening, they do not happen of their own accord. I have to make time, just as I make time for physical exercise, for watching the news, for eating.

Like many people, I have found that a regular place helps settle me into a spirit of prayer. President Jimmy Carter reserved a room next to the Oval Office as a private place to pray. I know a woman who has constructed a "prayer closet" in her oversized bathroom. She hangs artwork in that corner, lights candles, and retreats there several times a day for the sole purpose of prayer.

When he was on the faculty at Yale, Henri Nouwen converted a walk-in clothes closet into a prayer closet. "The simple fact that I'm in the closet means I'm praying," he said. "I might have a thousand things to think about while I'm in there, but the fact that I'm sitting in this physical place means I'm praying. I force myself to stay there for fifteen minutes. I do my best to center my mind and clear it of distracting thoughts and get down to prayer, but if after fifteen minutes I haven't been entirely successful, I say, 'Lord this was my prayer, even all this confusion. Now I'm going back to the world.'"

I begin each day in a solarium that looks out over a copse of trees. Early-rising birds flit to the birdfeeder and heated birdbath. Squirrels stretch themselves awake and scurry down to the spilled birdseed. The first rays of sun shoot over the surrounding hills. I have the sense that God has already been at work that day and through the night, and my own petty problems take on a different light in the rhythms of the larger world, and of eternity.

Ben Patterson, currently chaplain at Westmont College, California, tells of a time when he ruptured a disc and the doctor prescribed six weeks of total bed rest. Heavily medicated and lying flat on his back, he found that reading was virtually impossible. In that incapacitated state, he learned an important lesson about prayer.

> I was helpless.
>
> I was also terrified. What was this all going to mean? How was I to take care of my family? What about the church? I was the only pastor it had, and I could do nothing for it. Out of sheer desperation I decided to pray for the church. I opened the church directory and prayed for each member of the congregation, daily. It took nearly two hours, but since there was nothing else I could do for the church, I figured I might as well pray for it. It was not piety that made me do it, it was boredom and frustration. But over the weeks the prayer times grew sweet. One day near the end of my convalescence, I was praying and I told the Lord, "You know, it's been wonderful, these prolonged times we've spent together. It's too bad I don't have time to do this when I'm well."
>
> God's answer came swift and blunt. He said to me, "Ben, you have just as much time when you're well as when you're sick. It's the same twenty-four hours in either case. The trouble with you is that when you're well, you think you're in charge. When you're sick, you know you're not."

CHAPTER 13

PRAYER GRAMMAR

Not my preacher, not my teacher, but it's me, O Lord,
standin' in the need of prayer.
Gospel song

We learn to speak not by studying vocabulary and grammar but by babbling, forcing the mouth and supple tongue to form sounds that mimic those we hear. Most children speak first in single words—*No! Wawa. More! Daddy. Bye-bye*—and then progress to the kind of simple sentences spoken by a foreigner: "I go play."

Amazingly, even deaf children babble, but with no aural feedback their ability dwindles. To talk, we need others' help. A child cannot learn language in isolation, as proved by the horrific cases of children locked for years in attics and closets.

We need help learning to read, too. I remember staring at an oversized children's book, then dragging it to my mother, bent over an ironing board, and asking repeatedly, "What's that?" She taught me letters, then phonetic combinations of letters, and helped me link the words to pictures of cats and dogs on the page. I learned to recognize more letters and more word patterns, then finally I gained the skill to fit the words into a sentence that had meaning. Later, in school, I learned rules of grammar that govern how the words are used. Now I read without even noticing individual letters, oblivious to the subconscious process my brain goes through to assemble meaning from black marks on a page.

Learning to pray, like learning to talk, read, or walk, takes time and involves trial and error. The process will doubtless include feelings of awkwardness and failure. Like grammar, the "rules" of prayer have the ultimate goal of making it a natural act. Fortunately, we have many mentors in the process and many resources to draw from. People have been praying for a very long time.

Prayers of the Bible

With high hopes you decide to begin a regular practice of prayer. You set aside time one morning and locate a Bible to read as an aid. Shouldn't God's Word help clear a channel of communication? You open it at random and read a few verses. That won't do — it's a long list of tribes being counted in a kind of census. You turn elsewhere, to one of the big books of prophets. So many foreign names! Scanning, a few pages later you come across descriptions of massacres and starvation. Any meditative feelings slip away, replaced by agitation and confusion. What are you doing wrong?

A newcomer to the Bible will likely find a rather low proportion of passages that stimulate a sense of prayer and worship. A gap of several millennia separates our world from that of the writers, vastly reducing the odds of a meeting of the minds. Until you become familiar with the Bible's scheme, the random method will yield random results. For this reason it's best to begin with passages that focus specifically on prayer. The Bible includes around 650 prayers, some short and some long, reflecting many different circumstances and moods. Taken together, they provide an excellent guide for anyone seeking to learn to pray.

The Lord's Prayer

Consider first the Lord's Prayer, or the "Our Father." Jesus taught it to his disciples, who were already well-trained in the Jewish prayers of their day. Yet they recognized a new approach in Jesus' style of praying and asked for help. In response, he gave this model prayer.

Like most churchgoers I have prayed the Lord's Prayer hundreds of times, so that I say it without even thinking. It helps me to slow down, reflect on each phrase, and even add my own personal application.

Our Father, who art in heaven

I begin with an endearing term of relationship, "Father." Remind me today that you live and reign, not in heaven only but all around me and in my life. Make me aware of your active presence all day, in all my undertakings and in the people I meet.

Hallowed be your name

How can I recognize you—in the splendor of nature, in the odd mix of people I meet, in the still voice that calls me to be more like you? May I "hallow" what lies before me, by consciously referring it to you, and also honor your perfection, your holiness, by seeking to become more like you.

Your kingdom come

Yes, and allow me to be an agent of that kingdom by bringing peace to the anxious, grace to the needy, and your love to all whom I touch. May people believe in your reign of goodness because of how I live today.

Your will be done on earth as it is in heaven

I see that will most clearly in Jesus, who healed the sick and comforted the grieving, who lifted up the downtrodden, who stood always for life and not death, for hope and not despair, for freedom and not bondage. He lived out heaven's will on earth. Help me be like Jesus.

Give us today our daily bread

We have no guarantee of a day beyond this one. May I trust you for what I need today, nourishment for both body and soul, and not worry about future needs and wants. May I also be ever responsive to those who lack bread today.

Forgive us our debts, as we also have forgiven our debtors

Remind me of my true state, as a debtor who can never buy my way into your favor. Thank God, I do not have to. Grant me the same attitude of forgiving grace toward those who owe me, and who have wronged me, that you show toward me.

And lead us not into temptation, but deliver us from the evil one

Let me not slide mindlessly toward evil today. Make me alert to its temptations and strong to resist it, with neither fear nor regret.

The Psalms

The book of Psalms offers a practicum in how to pray. "It is my custom to call this book *An Anatomy of All the Parts of the Soul*," wrote John Calvin, "since there is no emotion anyone will experience whose image is not reflected in this mirror." Fear, praise, anxiety, anger, love, sorrow, despair, gratitude, grief, doubt, suffering, joy, vengeance, repentance—every human emotion and experience surges to the surface in the prayer-poems of Psalms.

From its earliest days the Christian church adopted these Jewish prayers into worship, singing psalms together in prayer to God. After all, Jesus himself had sung a psalm with his disciples at the Last Supper and had quoted psalms as he hung dying. When Hitler's Reich Board for the Regulation of Literature tried to fine Dietrich Bonhoeffer for publishing a book on Psalms—a part of the *Jewish* Old Testament, they charged—Bonhoeffer successfully appealed by arguing that Psalms was the prayer book of Jesus.

Today Christians and Jews still use this prayer book, and in some places Muslims do as well. The prayers bare the human soul before God in a way that strikes a universal chord. "Whatever can stimulate us when we are about to pray to God, this book teaches," said Calvin.

Ordinary life prompts many of the psalmists' compositions: a view of stars, sheep on a hillside, family problems, wars and rumors of wars, depression or an emotional high. Read straight through the psalms and you will rail against God, praise God for his faithfulness, wish yourself dead, exult in the beauties of nature, bargain for a better life, and spit curses against your enemies.*

Psalms keeps me honest by furnishing words to prayers I would not pray apart from their prompting. I have learned to pray more *humanly* by reading the psalms and making them my prayers. As I read psalms of anger and

---

*Because the cursing psalms create such a problem to many readers, I will briefly summarize some of the thoughts I detailed in another book, *The Bible Jesus Read*:

As Dorothy Sayers once remarked, we all have diabolical thoughts, but there's a world of difference in how we act on those thoughts, whether, say, we write a murder mystery or commit murder. If a person wrongs me unjustly, I have several options. I can seek personal revenge, a response condemned by the Bible. I can deny or suppress my feelings of hurt and anger. Or, I can take those feelings to God, entrusting God with the task of retributive justice. The cursing psalms are vivid examples of that last option. The authors are expressing their outrage to God, not to the enemy.

Instinctively, we want to clean up our feelings in our prayers, but perhaps we have it all backwards. Perhaps we should strive to take all our worst feelings to God. After all, what would be gossip when addressed to anyone else is petition when addressed to God. What is a vengeful curse when spoken about someone ("Damn those people!") is a plea of helpless dependence when spoken directly to God ("It's up to you to damn those people—only you are a just judge").

I see the cursing psalms as an important model for how to deal with evil and injustice. I should not try to suppress my reaction of horror and outrage at evil. Nor should I try to take justice in my own hands. Rather, I should deliver those feelings, stripped bare, to God. As the books of Job, Jeremiah, and Habakkuk clearly show, God has a high threshold of tolerance for what is appropriate to say in a prayer. God can "handle" my unsuppressed rage. I may well find that my vindictive feelings need God's correction—but only by taking those feelings to God will I have that opportunity for correction and healing.

revenge, I have to face the same tendencies in myself. The psalms expose to the light resentments and wounds long hidden. I find it liberating that God welcomes, even encourages, me to face into my dark side in my prayers. I can trust God with my secrets.

For example, after repeated failure I sometimes turn to Psalm 51, that great prayer written by David at a time of public humiliation after his moral failures became known to the nation. (Think of the period when lurid details of President Bill Clinton's dalliance with Monica Lewinsky were coming out.) The king's behavior was on everyone's lips in the form of jokes and gossip, then suddenly this psalm appeared.

In the psalm, David traces the devastating effects of sin. Guilt dominates his thoughts: "my sin is always before me." He has lost all sense of God's presence. He feels like hiding from God—but where can he go? Even though his crimes have brought tragedy to many other people, David knows that ultimately "against you, you only, have I sinned." He has broken the last five

---

Living with Lust

JUANITA

I moved to Brazil to study medicine after failing to get into medical school in my native Spain. Living away from home, the rigors of study, and the language barrier all combined to make this a very difficult year. I found myself seeking solace in lust. Brazil is a very sex-saturated culture, and I used that as an outlet.

Lust nearly destroyed my spiritual life. I felt like a misfit in Brazil, a complete failure, and every approach to God seemed blocked. I thought that I was no longer pure on the inside and no longer worthy even to come before God. I felt a tattered remnant of the person I once was. Finally I spoke my problem out loud to a Christian friend. He was kind and nonjudgmental, assuring me that I was not the only one who struggled with lust. He suggested reading Psalm 51 as a guide to healing and forgiveness.

Psalm 51 is indeed the best psalm I could have read. The psalmist asked God to hide his face from the sins, not from himself. The first time I read Psalm 51, I cried, I was so ashamed. I didn't think God would see *anything* but my sins. I felt like I was one big mistake, so ugly that God wouldn't be

of God's ten commandments. Unless he can somehow restore a relationship with God, he will never recover the joy and strength he once knew.

When I fail, I go through each stage that David describes in this psalm. I cling to the truth that brought solace to a king who committed adultery and murder:

> The sacrifices of God are a broken spirit;
> a broken and contrite heart,
> O God, you will not despise.

Psalm 51 sets out the pattern of guilt, repentance, and restoration that I must follow when I fail God. Its words have become my words.

Once, I took a sequence of ten psalms (35–44) and listed other principles of prayer I had learned from them. I found that the psalms broadened my notion of prayer by taking more risks, demanding more of the relationship, expressing more passion. In short, they exposed the shallowness of my own

---

able to look at me let alone accept me into his arms.

Then I came to the verse which says "Save me from bloodguilt, O God, the God who saves me." I began reading the psalm as a prayer, making it my prayer. *Wash away my sins, blot out my iniquity.* I've tried to read it every day, in my quiet time, as a plea to God.

I've cut off the things that encouraged my lustful thinking. I have asked God for friends, and I am starting a Bible study with a local group of Brazilians. One of them prayed over me and hugged me. She told me that she loved me ... It's amazing what a *real* hug can do. Looking back, I think loneliness was the core problem, and lust just a symptom.

Though I don't think I will ever be completely free of lust, I know I am free of the actual habit and lustful lifestyle. At first I was terrified of the loneliness that I thought would threaten me if I were to stop depending on lust. I've found that was a lie, and the truth is that I am less lonely now than before. Even better, I no longer live with constant guilt. Yet I sense that as I get toward the top of a hill, that is when I am most likely to be hit by an unsuspected falling rock. Old lies have a way of creeping back. I feel very helpless — and that's why I pray for help.

prayers and challenged me to engage with God at a deeper level. Here is some of what I learned:

- Work out animosity toward enemies not by gossip or hostility, but by informing God of their injustice and asking God to set things right.
- It's all right to express impatience to God, asking for a speeded-up answer to prayer—and even to spell out God's own interests in achieving the desired results.
- Prayer sometimes involves talking to yourself ("Do not fret ... Trust in the Lord ... Be still"), saying aloud what you know to be healthy but have a hard time putting into practice.
- Focus not just on the unfairness and problems of life, but also on all that does turn out well. Review the good things of the past, and don't forget in the darkness what you learned in the light.
- Project yourself into the future as a changed person. Behavioral psychologists would call this the "Act as if" principle.

Beyond these principles, I learned from Psalms to converse with God as I would converse with my employer, my friend, my wife—in short, to treat God as a Person in every sense of the word. I had seen prayer as a kind of duty, not as a safe outlet for whatever I was thinking or feeling. Psalms freed me to go deeper.

Many people have found it a fruitful exercise to rewrite psalms in their own words, substituting particulars of thanks or anguish or petition for the original words. After Eugene Peterson paraphrased a few psalms in modern language and published them in a magazine, an outpouring of reader response encouraged him to translate the entire Bible (*The Message*). For him, the psalms decisively answer the question of how to pray. Composed by passionate and all-too-human people who nonetheless saw God as the center of their lives, they supply words that encompass all human experience:

That's it: open our Bibles to the book of Psalms and pray them—sequentially, regularly, faithfully across a lifetime. This is how most Christians for most of the Christian centuries have matured in prayer. Nothing fancy. Just do it.

The Prayers of Paul

Of Paul's letters, all but Titus contain at least one prayer. He prays for an increase of love among the Thessalonians, for more mature behavior by the Corinthians, for strength and obedience and unity in his readers even as they learn to resist evil. His prayer for the Philippians sums up his desire, that "he who began a good work in you will carry it on to completion until the day of Christ Jesus."

I have found it a useful exercise to work through these prayers too, because they help me move beyond my egocentric requests. Paul raises my sights to a cosmic level. The experience on Damascus Road convinced him in a flash that Jesus Christ is the center of the universe and that we should ally with his forces on earth. Our struggle is "against the powers of this dark world and against the spiritual forces of evil in the heavenly realms," Paul told the Ephesians, and he prayed as though he believed it.

Often Paul opens with a prayer of thanksgiving for the growth he has observed in his intended readers. He prays as if it matters, truly *matters* whether they are maturing in the faith. I get the sense, reading Paul's prayers, that he cares more for others' well-being than for his own. Do I have that same passion for the spiritual welfare of my friends and family? The prayers of Paul expose by contrast the immature prayers I often hear at church meetings—and my own prayers—which tend to revolve around physical and financial well-being.

Yet Paul prays for practical matters too: sick friends, travel plans, requests for boldness and safety. Sometimes in the middle of a dense prose paragraph his thoughts will spontaneously lift into prayer. God is never far from Paul's thoughts, and thanksgiving and praise come to mind whenever something good happens. He practices the presence of God by giving credit to God, not himself.

Paul's prayers, like the psalms, give me a template for my own. I may insert the name of a college student struggling with doubts into the sequence of Paul's prayer for the Ephesians. Or, when I read his exalted prayers for favorite churches and his stern prayers of warning for wayward believers, I turn those prayers like a searchlight on myself. Is my love abounding more and more in knowledge and depth of insight, as Paul prayed for the Philippians? Am I comforting those in trouble, as he prayed for the Corinthians?

From Paul's prayers I learn to dethrone myself by first considering a cosmic point of view and then looking at my friends and family, my life, the church, and indeed all history from that vantage.

Other Prayers in the Bible

While working on *The Student Bible* my colleague and I made a selection of great prayers of the Bible, which can be read in a two-week period, one prayer a day. Some are intimate and private while others were delivered in a very public setting. Each gives an actual example of a person talking to God about an important matter and teaches something unique about prayer:

> Genesis 18: Abraham's plea for Sodom.
>
> Exodus 15: Moses' song to the Lord.
>
> Exodus 33: Moses meets with God.
>
> 2 Samuel 7: David's response to God's promises.
>
> 1 Kings 8: Solomon's dedication of the temple.
>
> 2 Chronicles 20: Jehoshaphat prays for victory.
>
> Ezra 9: Ezra's prayer for the people's sins.
>
> Psalm 22: A cry to God for help.
>
> Psalm 104: A prayer of praise.
>
> Daniel 9: Daniel's prayer for the salvation of Jerusalem.
>
> Habakkuk 3: A prophet's prayer of acceptance.
>
> Matthew 6: The Lord's prayer.
>
> John 17: Jesus' prayer for his disciples.
>
> Colossians 1: Paul's prayer of thanksgiving.

Besides teaching the "grammar" of prayer, studying the Bible affords a glimpse of the broad sweep of God's actions in history. It gets my own life off center stage. I learn the wisdom of reviewing the big picture, of placing my own small story in the context of God's story. I learn that I am not the only one who has wrestled with God or who has endured a time of wilderness and testing. I learn how to adore God, something that does not come naturally to me. Prayers based on the Bible help me recognize God's voice.

Others recommend taking a further step beyond simply reading the Bible's prayers: memorize them, so that they can be recalled at any moment. Debra Rienstra calls the process "stocking up" on words of the Bible, "giving the Spirit a bigger repertoire to work with in speaking to you — more Post-its on the bulletin board." One friend memorized relevant psalms as she rode a subway to nursing school each day, and found they helped relieve anxiety over the crushing workload. Ben Patterson adds about memorization:

Paul's prayers are especially good for this. Take, for example, his prayer for the Ephesians, that "the eyes of your heart may be enlightened in order that you may know the hope to which he has called you, the riches of his glorious inheritance in the saints." Or, "that you may be filled to the measure of all the fullness of God." The thought of memorizing prayers seems an artificial and stilted way to restore something as vital as spiritual hunger. But consider what Rabbi Abraham Heschel said to the members of his synagogue who complained that the words of the liturgy did not express what they felt. He told them that it was not that the liturgy should express what they feel, but that they should learn to feel what the liturgy expressed. Recited faithfully, great thoughts put into great words can do that for us.... Memorization can be to our hunger for God what practicing a musical instrument is for performance. It can be the singing of the scales of the soul.

Written and Spoken Prayers

The church I grew up in considered written prayers downright unspiritual. How could a prayer be sincere and heartfelt if someone read it from a piece of paper? That instinctive reaction probably traces all the way back to low-church rebellion against the Church of England. For centuries Christians had relied on carefully crafted prayers. Yet the Puritan John Milton scorned the majestic prayers of the Anglican prayer book as "cuckoo-notes." John Bunyan and George Fox likewise warned against printed prayers, and the Independents in England even disdained use of the Lord's Prayer in public worship.

Over time, Protestant overreaction tempered. C. S. Lewis preferred fixed prayers for his private devotions because they kept the focus on permanent things rather than contemporary problems. (For this reason, Lewis opposed revising the Prayer Book: "the more 'up to date' the Book is, the sooner it will be dated.") He also felt uncomfortable with the casual, extemporaneous prayers common in evangelical churches. How can we mentally join in a prayer until we've heard it? he asked. The prayer may contain actual heresy. He preferred fixed prayers, the theology of which had been honed by the church.

Written prayers serve an especially useful purpose, I have found, during periods of spiritual dryness, when spontaneous prayer seems an impossible chore. I borrow the words, if not the faith, of others when my own words fail.

179

At such a time I have two options. I can stop praying completely, which only serves to distance me further from God. Or I can keep going, asking God to see me through this difficult period, meanwhile leaning on the prayers of others.

As I have mentioned, for a year I relied on prayers from a *Liturgy of the Hours*. I have also used *The Book of Common Prayer*; both of these collections are readily available in inexpensive editions. Because they are designed for group worship, under the guidance of a leader, they may not seem user-friendly at first. Yet they have the advantage of being compiled by people sensitive to both spiritual and literary concerns, and they have stood the test of time.

I must admit, however, that apart from exceptional times I tend not to rely on fixed prayers — not out of aversion but because as a writer I find them distracting. I start attending to the words and images, and my editing instinct kicks in: *Hmm, what if she had broken the line here, and not there, or used a metaphor rather than the flat statement* . . . In my profession I am always looking for new ways to express thoughts, and I find it difficult to read familiar words over and over. I consider this tendency a defect, and hope with time it will fade.

Oddly enough, I never have these editorial thoughts while reading the Bible, at least in a good translation, and if I stick to truly great writers, such as John Donne or George Herbert, the temptation to edit never occurs. Reflective poetry lends itself to meditative prayer. Already language is compressed; in meditation I plumb the metaphors and unpack the meaning, just as I do with the Bible. Well-written hymns and praise music can serve the same purpose.

For those who prefer extemporaneous prayers, practical advice abounds. Many popular guides recommend a formula based on the acronym ACTS, for Adoration, Confession, Thanksgiving, and Supplication. Rosalind Rinker made the formula even simpler, attaching a New Testament reference to each stage:

1. Jesus is here (Matthew 18:19–20)
2. Help me, Lord (James 5:13–16)
3. Thank you, Lord (Philippians 4:4–7)
4. Help my brother (Mark 11:22–25)

The Catholic masters of prayer, most of whom spent several hours daily at the task, have proposed a dizzying array of steps to prayer. Ignatius spelled out nine stages for preparation alone. Francis de Sales adapted that method into a pattern of meditation that has proved helpful to Catholics and Protestants alike. De Sales's method consists of four main stages:

Step 1: *Preparation*. Let the imagination roam, placing yourself in the presence of God, affirming that since God is everywhere, he is here now. Think of Christ as standing at your side, sharing your experience. Offer a prayer of confession and request guidance in the meditation to follow.

Step 2: *Consideration*. Propose a subject, perhaps suggested by a Bible passage you just read, and focus your mind on that subject. Act "like the bees, who do not leave a flower so long as they find any honey there to gather."

Step 3: *Resolution*. Involve your feelings and your will. How should your life change as a result of what you have considered? Resolve to make those changes accordingly, with God's help.

Step 4: *Conclusion*. As if you have been walking in a garden, choose a few flowers to take with you the rest of the day. Offer a prayer of thanksgiving for what you have learned, of consecration for what you intend to change, of petition for grace and strength to fulfill the resolution.

I have sampled various methods from time to time and find them useful as long as I think of them as a supporting structure, a sort of scaffolding, rather than a rigid formula I must follow. The goal is to spend time with God, not to follow a legalistic procedure. If a system helps achieve that goal, fine. If not, I move on. Moods change, life goes through seasons, personalities differ. Each person who prays will need to find a rhythm or method that fits, for each of us has a unique privilege of offering love and attention to the One who made and sustains us.

There are a variety of ways to learn the grammar of prayer, and in seasons of strength and seasons of weakness I have tried many. In the process, I have learned to trust that through the Spirit who makes intercession, God will hear our prayers, no matter how eloquent or prosaic.

Prayer Reminders

Jesus lived before the invention of clocks and watches, and bells from the Roman forum tolled divisions in the day—at 6:00 a.m., 9:00 a.m., noon, 3:00 p.m., and 6:00 p.m. Devout Jews adopted this schedule for their daily prayers, and early Christians continued the practice. The book of Acts shows

Peter and John healing a man on the steps of the temple on their way to observe afternoon prayers, and Peter receiving a vision on the rooftop while saying noon prayers.

Over the years, Christian communities formalized the "Prayer of the Hours" based on fixed-hour prayers. It was for this reason that the church produced such collections as the *Liturgy of the Hours* and *The Book of Common Prayer*, spelling out prayers and Bible readings for the appropriate hours of each day. In recent years, Christians acquainted mainly with free-form, spontaneous prayers have discovered rich rewards in following the Divine Hours at set times during the day, praying the collected wisdom of a hundred generations of believers as a kind of passing of the spiritual torch.

Phyllis Tickle speaks of the satisfaction of belonging to such a communion of prayer, knowing that the words she speaks to God were spoken an hour before in the time zone to the east and will be spoken again by fellow Christians to the west, until the very same prayer encircles the globe. In a trilogy of books, Tickle streamlined the practice into morning, midday, and evening prayers, while retaining the older prayer books' emphasis on the Bible and classical sources. "They are the songs of the fathers and mothers since the calling of Abraham; and by joining that chorus, each man or woman who prays slips joyfully into the long ribbon of life that is the vertical communion of the saints across the ages."

Tickle adds that fixed prayers do not supplant the need for prayers about her own personal concerns. She combines the two, often following the time-honored ACTS formula for spontaneous prayers. As one advocate of the Divine Hours puts it, "I think a lot of evangelicals have exhausted the individualized approach and find relief in the liturgical; people raised in cold liturgical traditions find relief in the warmth and informality of evangelical prayer." Phyllis Tickle suggests that a combination of the individual and liturgical can keep us refreshed.

Not all schedules lend themselves to breaks at fixed hours in the day. Not all personalities will find such a structure useful. The common danger we face, though, is getting so absorbed in daily life that we simply fail to show up. Any visitor to a Muslim country can see the difference. Five times a day, when the call to prayer goes out, all work and commerce stops, buses and trains empty, and faithful Muslims roll out prayer rugs, bowing low to say their prayers. Christians have no such ritual to stop and remember God. It's up to us.

In Victor Hugo's novel *Les Miserables*, convent chapel bells sound every hour, causing everyone in the convent—prioress, mothers, sisters, novices, postulants—to interrupt what they are doing or saying and turn their thoughts to God. For a time I tried something similar by setting my watch to chime softly each hour, a reminder to turn my thoughts to God. (I kept forgetting to turn it off, and halted the practice after irritating people in meetings and waking myself up at night.) It takes effort simply to *remember*.

A pious Jew, expected to pronounce a blessing more than a hundred times a day, remains always on the lookout for something deserving of a *barakhà*. Jews and Christians both, following the example of Nehemiah, shoot "arrow prayers" toward heaven, messages as brief as "Give me strength" or "Help, Lord!" Those who struggle with addictions may fire off an arrow prayer every time they pass a bar, see someone smoking, or log on to the Internet. The writer Anne Lamott says her favorite prayers are "Thank you, thank you, thank you," and "Help me, help me, help me."

I have sometimes chosen a phrase from a biblical prayer to repeat throughout the day, not as a talisman but as a needed reminder. When I have failed, I'll pray over and over, "Create in me a pure heart, O God"; when spiritually depressed, "Restore to me the joy of your salvation." The very repetition of the words throughout the day works its effect on my downcast soul. I ask God to help me believe the words I am praying.

For me, the words of prayer are less important than the act of remembering. I look for the spaces, the interstices, in my life. Lying awake at night, insomnious. Soaking in a bathtub. Driving. Biding time while my computer reboots. Sitting in a ski lift. Standing in line at a check-out counter. Waiting for someone who is late. Riding on a public bus or train. Exercising. Lengthy church services, I find, offer prime opportunities for prayer. Instead of fidgeting or staring at my watch during a lull, I pray.

If I remember, I try to turn those otherwise wasted moments into prayers, sometimes with startling results. I find myself more aware of the old woman in front of me fumbling through her change purse. I pray for the people inside as I pass a neighbor's house, a church, a bar, an AIDS clinic, a university. I pray while watching the news, or during commercials (Think how much an advertiser pays for fifteen seconds of my time).

"The wind blows wherever it pleases," Jesus said to Nicodemus. "You hear its sound, but you cannot tell where it comes from or where it is going." And so I have found, as I look for God in the everydayness of life. "Aha" moments catch me by surprise: a surge of gratitude, a pang of compassion. But they catch me, I have learned, only when I am looking for them.

CHAPTER 14

TONGUE-TIED

He that prays and does not faint will come to recognize
that to talk with God is more than to have all prayers granted —
that it is the end of all prayer.

GEORGE MACDONALD

It happens so often that I am tempted to think it diabolical. I sit down to pray and the phone rings. *Who on earth is calling at this hour of the morning?* Or I hear a toilet running in the bathroom and jump up to jiggle the handle. Half an hour later I'm elbow-deep in the tank, replacing seals, tightening nuts, making a general mess of things, my day ruined.

The next day, uninterrupted this time, I start to pray and find that my thoughts scatter like dust, taking me every direction but here. I think of an awkward conversation with my brother last night, and of a CNN report on Victoria's Secret lingerie, and of an article I'm supposed to turn in tomorrow — anything but God.

One of the masters of prayer, Teresa of Avila, admits to shaking the sand in her sixteenth-century hourglass to make the hour go faster. Martin Luther knew the prayer doldrums too:

> When I would speak and pray to God by myself, a hundred thousand hindrances at once intervene before I get at it. Then the devil can throw all sorts of reasons for delay in my path; he can block and hinder me on all sides; as a result, I go my way and never think of it again. Let him who has not experienced this only try it. Resolve to pray earnestly, and no doubt you will see how large an assortment of your own thoughts will rush in on you and distract you, so that you cannot begin aright.

Unworthiness

One hindrance in particular tied Luther's tongue: feeling unworthy. Like a person abused in childhood, he could not rid himself of a sense of shame. As a young monk, some days he would spend hours trying to identify every stray thought and sin. No matter how thorough his confession, as he knelt to pray he felt himself rejected by a righteous God. His great breakthrough came when he realized that Jesus had revealed God's character by offering grace and forgiveness to the foulest of sinners, the *least* worthy. From then on, whenever feelings of unworthiness plagued him, Luther would view them as the work of the devil and roar back in opposition.

I am convinced the main requirement in prayer is honesty, approaching God "just as we are." Nonetheless, many pray-ers labor under a Luther-like pall of inferiority. We feel guilty, or unfocused, or irritable, and assume those negative feelings will disqualify us from God's attention, as if God only listens to good people. Until we come to terms with an ornery classmate, we think—or straighten out a bad marriage, or stop yelling at the kids, or conquer the addiction that fetters us like a ball and chain—we don't deserve to pray. Consequently we turn away from the only source of forgiveness and potential healing.

As if in direct rebuttal, the Bible gives a detailed record of God listening to prayers from decidedly unworthy people: from short-fused Moses to puerile Samson to the rough sailors who threw Jonah overboard, let alone the sulky prophet himself. God responded to King David's prayers of repentance after the sins of murder and adultery, as well as the desperation prayer of wicked King Manasseh. Jesus commended the prayer of an unworthy tax collector above that of an upright Pharisee.

A sense of unworthiness hardly disqualifies me from prayer; rather, it serves as a necessary starting point. Apart from feeling unworthy, why call on God in the first place? Unworthiness establishes the ground rules, setting the proper alignment between broken human beings and a perfect God. I now consider it a motivation for prayer, not a hindrance.

A fourteenth-century Englishman, his name unknown, wrote a classic book about communicating with God called *The Cloud of Unknowing*. Before penetrating the cloud of unknowing above us, he said, we may need to imagine a "cloud of forgetting" beneath us. Forget past failures, forget recurring sins, forget feelings of inferiority, and instead open your mind to God, who cannot fill what has not been emptied.

Distractions

Pray with any regularity, and soon other distractions will interfere. The UPS truck shows up. The baby throws cereal all over the carpet. The washing machine overruns. An outdoor sprinkler starts spraying the neighbor's yard. The dog dashes through the house with muddy paws. Against all mathematical odds, these interruptions seem to multiply during prayer times.

Thomas à Kempis, celebrated author of *The Imitation of Christ*, reports that when he tried to focus on heavenly things a rout of carnal temptations would rush upon him. In the seventeenth century, before most mechanical distractions existed, John Donne described another set of interruptions:

> I throw my selfe downe in my Chamber, and I call in, and invite God, and his Angels thither, and when they are there, I neglect God and his Angels, for the noise of a Flie, for the rattling of a Coach, for the whining of a doore.... A memory of yesterdays pleasures, a feare of tomorrows dangers, a straw under my knee, a noise in mine eare, a light in mine eye, an any thing, a nothing, a fancy, a Chimera in my braine, troubles me in my prayer.

For as long as I can remember, I have battled insomnia. I have tried various remedies — relaxing my body, emptying my mind, playing a noise machine — but none has worked for me. The more I concentrate on stopping my thoughts, the more they flood in like a swarm of bees. Trying to relax makes me tense. Listening to the recorded sound of waterfalls and summer rain makes me want to go to the bathroom. And something similar happens when I pray.

Prayer consists in the "lifting up of the mind to God," said St. John Damascene. He may as well have said that prayer consists of closing the mind to all but God. As I focus on a passage of Scripture or meditate on a story from the Gospels, I suddenly think of a workman I forgot to call yesterday — *oops, I had best do that before he takes on another job*. Ten minutes later, my prayer time is in shambles.

I have heard suggestions on coping with distractions in prayer, but most prove about as effective as the suggestions on insomnia. Treat them like dreams, says one spiritual director: notice them as they dart in and out of your mind, but don't give them inordinate attention. Easier said than done. Treat them like restless children — ignore them! — suggests another. Children who cannot appreciate an important adult conversation will be constantly running through the room, seeking attention; don't let them drag you down to their level. Yes, well and good, but sometimes those children run into the coffee table, shattering the glass top. What then?

I have found only a few techniques that actually help me deal with distractions. First, I suppress all interference from electronic devices. I go to a computerless room and let an answering machine cope with any phone calls. Then, I keep a piece of note paper and a pen at my side. When a stray thought enters my mind—*call the contractor, get the oil changed*—I simply write it down and relegate it to a pile I'll take care of later. Sometimes one or two such thoughts come, and sometimes seven or eight. By writing them down, I capture them and keep them from nagging.

Finally, if appropriate, I try to incorporate the distractions into my prayer. If I watched the news during breakfast and images of a devastating earthquake linger in my mind, I focus on the families affected by the disaster and the relief workers headed to the scene. Last week I was nursing hurt feelings provoked by two letters, one from a hyper-Calvinist in my church who took me to task for implying that God does not directly cause all suffering, and one from an angry right-winger questioning my loyalty to my country. I brought those comments into my prayers, considering my responses, examining my motives, trying to learn from the criticisms.

In many cases, the distractions become my prayer. When I am with my wife or a close friend, naturally I talk about whatever is on my mind and do not follow a formal agenda. Likewise, apparent distractions may become the substance of my encounter with God. Prayer expresses a relationship between two persons, one of whom happens to be God. Reality, not flawless technique, is the goal.

Whenever I struggle against distractions, I try to remember the advice of British theologian Herbert McCabe:

> People often complain of "distractions" during prayer. Their mind goes wandering off on to other things. This is nearly always due to praying for something you do not really much want; you just think it would be proper and respectable and "religious" to want it. So you pray high-mindedly for big but distant things like peace in Northern Ireland or you pray that your aunt will get better from the flu—when in fact you do not much care about these things; perhaps you ought to, but you don't. And so your prayer is rapidly invaded by distractions arising from what you really do want—promotion at work, let us say. Distractions are nearly always your real wants breaking in on your prayer for edifying but bogus wants. If you are distracted, trace your distraction back to the real desires

it comes from and pray about these. When you are praying for what you really want you will not be distracted. People on sinking ships do not complain of distractions during their prayer.

Doing It Right

Newcomers to prayer often worry that they are not doing it right. Perhaps they have heard eloquent prayers from the pulpit or read them in books. They would never pray out loud in a group, and even shy away from private prayers for fear of saying the wrong thing, of offending a perfect God. Meeting a celebrity sends most of us into a tongue-tied state; what can we possibly say that would merit God's time and attention?

Staying in Touch

RON

As director of an international prison ministry, I have visited some 110 countries, and in the process I've heard just about every kind of prayer. Many of the church groups in prisons have a charismatic bent, and the repetition and sheer decibel level of prayers in those services used to drive me crazy. My Anglican tradition has a more reserved, formal style.

Yet the most phenomenal prayer experience I've ever had took place among 20,000 Catholic charismatics in Italy. They prayed as a group, the fluid Italian sounds rising in a kind of musical crescendo, then falling back again. Many were speaking in tongues, and in their worshipful midst I could not help feeling that the Spirit was in this.

I've also visited a Community of Beatitudes in France where Christians minister to street people and prostitutes. They pray, then do their work, then pray over their work—half a day praying, half a day working. And I have a friend in Toronto who reserves a sacred space, a "prayer tower," he calls it, for business executives to use. He makes available beautifully crafted prayers about life and work.

My wife and I often rely on written prayers. We've been reading a series of books with titles like *Praying with Hildegard of Bingen*, *Praying with Mother Teresa*, *Praying with C. S. Lewis*, twenty-four in the series in all (from St. Mary's Press). I often find that written prayers articulate what I want to

I have one word of advice: Relax.

From the sheer variety of prayers, it would be difficult to devise a formula for "doing it right." I have heard the adoration of a pious soul and the raves of a victim of injustice, the desperate pleas of the persecuted church and the soaring liturgy of a state church, the mechanical repetition of a formula everyone knows and a private prayer language that no one knows, a monotone delivery and a passionate outcry, ecstatic praise and humble repentance, prayers both serene and agitated, pleas for victory and laments of defeat, tender forgiveness and bitter revenge, words to flatter a distant King and words to please a loving Father.

We all differ, by personality and by life circumstances, and some will find their best prayer times while commuting to work and others while feeding

---

say to God better than I do. I may pray the Lord's Prayer ten times in a row, trying to focus.

I believe prayer is effective, but I don't really know how, why, or when. I had a personal experience of healing when a nun in Australia prayed over my ankle that had refused to heal despite surgery and much treatment. I got a letter from her saying she had prayed — the letter took ten days to reach me — and on the very day she had prayed, my ankle spontaneously healed. It has caused me no pain since.

I do know it helps to pray through one of my trips in advance: each of the appointments I'll have, the plane connections I'll make. If I neglect that, something always goes wrong. On one trip a doctor came with me and simply prayed each day for everything as it unfolded. I have never felt so free. That was one of the most productive trips I've taken.

I've built prayer into my daily routine. I write in a journal longhand, recording things I thank God for, examining myself, then praying for family and friends and moving on to our ministry and to global issues. The rector at my church suggested that when you pray for someone, envision taking that person by the hand and presenting them to the Lord. Imagine! I try to do that in my prayers of intercession.

I follow the routine whether I feel like it or not. With a discipline, you usually feel good afterwards, if not during. If I miss a day, I don't notice much difference. If I miss several days, I definitely do. I'm the one who loses out.

the baby. Some will preview the day while lying half-awake as it dawns, and others will take a break at noon to discuss with God what has just passed and what lies ahead. Prayer is not a comparison contest. The least educated and least notable soul has as much opportunity—and sometimes more—to become a master at prayer as do church professionals.

Martin Luther, who averaged two hours a day in prayer, counseled others, "The fewer the words, the better the prayer." Indeed, two of the Bible's shortest prayers, from a tax collector and a crucified thief, proved most effective. Luther reacted against the formal, showy prayers of his time, which tended to produce hypocrites. Pray from the heart, he said. Think of the God you are addressing, and not of others who may be listening.

"I'll never pray like Martin Luther.... I'll never have the spirit of Mother Teresa." Agreed. We are not called to duplicate someone else on earth but to realize our authentic selves. Thomas Merton made a distinction between the false self we project to the world and the true self that God knows. "For me to be a saint means for me to be myself," said Merton.

I learned long ago that I could never match my wife's instinctive skills as a social worker or hospice chaplain. When I meet someone in dire straits, I start to interview them, taking mental notes. When my wife meets them, she immediately tunes in to their concerns. Our prayer practices reflect another difference: I tend to pray in scheduled, ordered times while she prays in spurts throughout the day.

Apart from the requirement that we be authentic before God, there is no prescribed way to pray. Each of us presents a unique mix of personality, outlook, training, gifts, and weaknesses, as well as a unique history with church and with God. As Roberta Bondi says, "If you are praying, you are already 'doing it right.'"

Over the years the church has repeatedly shifted its emphasis in prayer. Early Christians, a tiny minority huddled against a hostile empire, prayed together for strength and courage. As Christianity became socially accepted the state church composed majestic prayers, while spiritual dissidents moved out into the desert in order to purify themselves. The Middle Ages, a harsh time of plague and poverty, stressed penitence and a plea for mercy. Later, Anselm and Bernard of Clairvaux led a rediscovery of the love and mercy of God, and St. Francis called forth a carefree joy that harked back to Jesus. Meister Eckhart, Teresa of Avila, and the Quaker George Fox explored the interior, mystical silence of the heart while Brother Lawrence practiced God's presence in the midst of mundane work. Luther steered away from mysticism toward practical devotion, even as Calvin emphasized the majesty of God.

The diversity continues today. I have stood in a Russian Orthodox cathedral and watched grandmothers weep uncontrollably though they understood barely a word of the prayers being chanted in Old Slavonic. I have listened as Korean Presbyterians in Chicago sang hymns and prayed loudly through the night. In some African-American churches, you can barely hear the prayer for all the cries of "Amen!" and "Now listen, Lord!" In Japan, when the pastor announces congregational prayer, everyone prays at once, aloud. Members of a Chinese house church in Germany continue the stringent practices of the mother country, sometimes praying three days straight while fasting. In Ukraine worshipers stand to pray; in Africa they dance.

Jesus taught a model prayer, the Lord's Prayer, but otherwise gave few rules. His teaching reduces down to three general principles: Keep it honest, keep it simple, and keep it up. Mainly, Jesus pressed home that we come as beloved children to a Father who loves us in advance and cares deeply about our lives. Ask young parents what is the correct way for their toddlers to approach them and you will probably get a puzzled look. Correct way? Being a parent means you do your best to remain available to your children and responsive to their needs. As Jesus said, if a human parent responds with compassion and not hostility, how much more will God.

"Let us then approach the throne of grace *with confidence*," urged the author of Hebrews, "so that we may receive mercy and find grace to help us in our time of need."

Prayer and Personality

Some pray-ers feel constrained by the body language of praying. Should we kneel? Close our eyes? Use a formal or casual approach? What is the appropriate prayer *style?**

The Bible itself includes a multitude of styles. Peter knelt, Jeremiah stood, Nehemiah sat down, Abraham prostrated himself, and Elijah put his face between his knees. In Jesus' day most Jews stood, lifting their open eyes to

---

*Theologian Jürgen Moltmann observes that the prostrate position in prayer is reminiscent of the vassal before an absolute Asiatic despot. "The vassal threw himself on his face before the ruler, presenting his unprotected neck for execution or pardon, and making himself as small as possible." Likewise, kneeling expresses helplessness and humility, and folding hands shows they are unarmed. Before God such posture may be appropriate. Yet early Christians stood upright, with heads raised and eyes open, an attitude of expectation and readiness to receive. They are free men and women. Moltmann notes that Jesus raised up whoever came to him humiliated, bent down, crippled. They looked him in the eyes, they walked, they could love again. He adds, "Healing only begins when we stand up completely, breathe deeply, raise our hands above our head, and experience with open eyes the coming of the life-giving Spirit."

heaven. The Virgin Mary prayed in poetry; Paul interspersed his prayers with singing.

In general, the early church preferred that worshipers use written rather than spontaneous prayers, which allowed for control over doctrine during a time when heresies abounded. Centuries passed before silent, private prayers — the norm today in many quarters — became widespread. Until the thirteenth century, most people both prayed and read aloud, even in private. (Augustine marveled at the ability of Bishop Ambrose to hold a book in silence with his eyes running over the page: Was he trying to save his voice?) When the skill of reading silently became widespread it also led to a surge in individual, private prayer; until then believers viewed both prayer and reading as group activities, guided by professionals.

Only recently has anyone attempted to look at prayer styles in light of personality differences. In one project, researchers studied the individual prayer preferences of people who had been tested for their personality profile using the Myers-Briggs Type Indicator test (MBTI). To no one's surprise, prayer retreats — and the research project itself — tended to attract a particular profile, namely the intuitive/feeling type of personality. Researchers also saw a sharp division between people who prefer order and discipline and those who prefer spontaneity and an unstructured approach.

The project's directors drew the reasonable conclusion that we should choose the prayer form that seems natural, that fits our personality type. A free spirit need not feel guilty when she finds that a highly structured system simply does not work for her. A multitasker may learn that long periods of meditation tax, rather than nurture, spiritual resources. As Evelyn Underhill, herself an expert on mysticism, wrote, "Persons whose natural expression is verbal, and who need the support of concrete image, make violent efforts to 'go into the silence' because some wretched little book has told them to do so."

Prayer is a way of relating to God, not a skill set like double-entry bookkeeping. We relate to other people not according to any rule book but freely, as individuals who possess a face, body, intelligence, and emotional makeup shared by no one else on earth. Far more than any person, God knows who we are, and why. It should hardly surprise God that we respond in a way that reflects our true self.

> O Lord, you have searched me and you know me.... You perceive my thoughts from afar.... You are familiar with all my ways. Before a word is on my tongue you know it completely, O Lord.

Helpers

If all else fails, and even if words fail, the apostle Paul promises that "the Spirit himself intercedes for us with groans that words cannot express." Speaking overseas, I must depend on translators in order to communicate to audiences. A poor translator can turn my best efforts into gibberish; with a sinking feeling I read the confusion on the faces of my listeners. On the contrary, a good translator can turn my most bumbling attempts into a triumph of communication. Paul holds out the strong promise that in prayer we have the perfect translator, so that even our wordlessness finds its way to the source of all grace.

In addition to a translator, we have an advocate to represent our interests to God. In that private gathering known as the Last Supper, four times Jesus promised his disciples that the Father would do anything they asked "in my name." Jesus came to earth as dramatic proof of God's desire to keep company with us. Having lived among us, he understands the human condition and now represents us to the Father. By praying in his name we rely on his good auspices to do for us what we could not do for ourselves.

In this era of identity theft, we know well the value of a name. As part of a crime ring, a clerk at the Department of Motor Vehicles in Chicago copied my wife's driver's license and Social Security number and produced a fake ID using the name Janet Yancey. The photo on the fake license, a woman of a different skin color with dyed, spiky hair, looked nothing like my wife, but through the use of Janet's name that woman was able to buy seven video recorders in one afternoon.

As a journalist, too, I know the value of a name. I once secured an interview with Bill Clinton during his first term as president. I was instructed to attend a political rally at a local junior high school and afterwards to hand the letter with his signature to one of the Secret Service agents. After the rally I stood with a pack of other journalists behind a police rope. Most of them were holding microphones and yelling questions: "Mr. President, Mr. President, do you have anything to say about ..."

Clinton smiled and waved, ignoring the questions, then climbed into the limousine. I shouldered to the front of the pack to find a Secret Service agent. When he saw the name at the bottom of the letter, he lifted the rope and escorted me to the limousine, leaving the other journalists to wonder, "Hey, what's he got that we don't have?" I had the president's name on a letter, and for that reason alone his staff treated me deferentially.

We use another person's name if that person has some clout with whomever we're petitioning. Given the proper name, credit mysteriously becomes available and limousine doors fly open. When it comes to prayer, Jesus promises, we have the right to use his own name in approaching the Father. We have access to his authority, his reputation, his *leverage*. My leverage with the White House ended ninety minutes later. We have the extravagant right to use the name of Jesus in perpetuity, for whatever we ask.

A Gymnasium for the Soul

I have called the book of Psalms a virtual practicum in prayer. When I am feeling inarticulate before God, I turn to that ready-made prayer book. There I can find prayers to fit any mood, 150 psalms arranged with no apparent

---

Prayer and Temperament

KATHY CALLAHAN-HOWELL, FROM *LEADERSHIP*

Is there a way to sit at Jesus' feet that works with, and not against, the personality and temperament God gave me?

That question led me to select Chester Michael and Marie Norrisey's book *Prayer and Temperament* for my sabbatical reading list. In it I found four forms of prayer and meditation. Each form is designed to accommodate one of four temperaments (based on the Myers-Briggs Type Indicator).

- The first meditation style, designed for "intuitive *feelers*" like myself, stresses creative exercises involving imagination, imagery, and journaling.

  One exercise is addressing Scripture passages to yourself. To bring this to life, just insert your name into a passage and meditate on it with the personal application. For example, Jesus says, "Come to me, Kathy, and I will give you rest." Stirring the heart with the recognition that the promises and commands of Scripture are meant for me personally opens a depth of feeling that is too often buried under the busywork of ministry.

- Scientifically minded folks, labeled "intuitive *thinkers*," may benefit from taking a Scripture passage and asking basic investigative

concern over jarring juxtapositions. Psalm 23, one of the brightest and most soothing, follows hard on the heels of Psalm 22, which includes the words of desolation Jesus quoted from the cross. Psalm 138, full of tranquil praise, follows a psalm of outrage and vengeance.

I have visited a Trappist monastery in which the monks recite together all 150 psalms in a two-week period, meaning they cover on average eleven psalms each day. (In some monasteries, skilled reciters chant through the entire book of Psalms in a single twenty-four hour period.) After years of repetition, they know them all by heart, as most people know their national anthem. Yet individual facial responses project as if on a screen which psalms speak to the true self at that moment.

The fat, bearded monk in the front row comes alive during the words of praise and thanksgiving. His austere neighbor with the surprisingly high

---

questions: who, what, when, where, why, and how. Going beyond those questions, you may ask yourself, "What area of my life will this help with?" This investigative type of meditation can help draw us into truth and discover how it applies to our lives.

- For those driven by duty, "sensory *judges*," a concrete, orderly system of meditation appeals to the spirit more than abstract notions of peace, grace, and joy. Using the senses to see, hear, and smell the scenes of Scripture as though actually there brings ancient truth to modern application.

  During Holy Week this year, I used this form of meditation to focus on Christ's passion. I imagined the two thieves and Jesus with a sign over his head, "King of the Jews." I imagined the jeers of the crowd, the weight of sin, and the sting of sweat and blood. Then I imagined a sign over my head saying "Beloved Child of God," and I realized anew how much it cost him to give me that title.

- The fourth form of meditation engages action in prayer. Fishing, hiking, and swimming can all be meditation-enhancing activities. And while outdoor enthusiasts may enjoy this kind of prayer, the key for "sensory *perceivers*" is not just being outside, but moving and working while they pray. Like Brother Lawrence, my friend Kim likes to pray while washing the dishes. What a Martha way to be Mary! Do the work and sit at Jesus' feet at the same time!

voice chimes in more intently during the psalms of turmoil. Power struggles? Illness? Death in the family? Doubts about the faith? Worries over the order's financial future? Whatever might be going on inside the walls of the monastery, chances are one of the psalms of the day evokes and speaks to it. St. Ambrose described the psalms as "a sort of gymnasium for the use of all souls." I like that image, of an emotional exercise room equipped with machines to fit any aspiring athlete of prayer.

Martin Marty, a Lutheran theology professor, began the practice of reading through Psalms with his wife during her long ordeal with terminal cancer. She had to wake up at midnight and take medication to combat the nausea caused by chemotherapy. It took a while for both of them to go back to sleep, and during that period her husband read the psalms aloud. One night she caught him skipping from Psalm 87 to 91. Marty had skimmed the words of 88 ("... my life draws near the grave, I am counted among those who go down to the pit ...") and moved ahead to a more consoling image: "He will cover you with his feathers, and under his wings you will find refuge."

"Why did you skip those psalms?" his wife demanded. Marty told her he wasn't sure she could take Psalm 88 that night. "Go back. Read it," she said. "If I don't deal with the darkness, the others won't shine out."

Martin Marty later wrote a book about that difficult time (*A Cry of Absence*) in which he estimated that, in this classic text of Christian devotion, half the psalms are *wintry* in tone, and only a third have the bright atmosphere of summer about them. They help to "domesticate terror and grief" in circumstances such as his wife faced, he said. He latched on to the words of others when he found himself wordless.

Marty confesses that throughout his life of faith, despite repeated efforts, he has rarely had the sensation of contacting God directly; the sense of "immediacy" has hit him only a handful of times. In communicating with God he has learned to rely on a secondary means of approach, such as the psalms, akin to how lovers write letters and maintain contact even during a period of absence.

Everyone who keeps company with God goes through stages encompassing bright, joyful times as well as dark, wintry times. Terry Muck draws an analogy from two contrasting outlooks, farmers and city dwellers. He quotes an old farmer who also works in a factory in town:

> The biggest difference I can see is that city people always think that this year has got to be better than last year. If they don't get a raise, acquire

196

something new, or find themselves somehow better off, they think they're failures. Farm folks look at things a bit differently. We know there are going to be good years and bad years. We can't control the weather. We can't prevent a bad crop. We can't control sickness. So you learn just to work hard and make up your mind to take what comes.*

I think through a mental chart of my own spiritual life, especially as reflected in prayer. As a child and adolescent, I believed whatever the church told me and got institutional reinforcement for praying, having a personal quiet time, and practicing the spiritual disciplines. In Bible college, as I sat in chapel on "prayer days" and tried to sort through the genuineness and the posturing, I found myself doubting all spiritual experience. The monastery-like atmosphere of campus seemed disconnected from the turbulent reality of society in the late 1960s outside its boundaries. I felt I was the only one not "getting it."

Since then, like a farmer I have known good years and bad years with prayer, seasons of contentment and gratitude and seasons of anguish and dereliction. I expected a straight-line vector of growth, something like the Wall Street charts of mutual funds that steadily gain in value every year. Instead, the line veers up and down erratically like that on a heart monitor. Only later, in retrospect, can I see that the darkest times solidified my faith and that somehow the words I wrote in those times God used to speak to others.

Many a pastor knows the experience of returning home Sunday afternoon feeling like a washed-out failure, only to hear from a parishioner that the day's sermon spoke to him more than any other. Perhaps God views our prayers the same way. As C. S. Lewis wrote, "I have a notion that what seem our worst prayers may really be, in God's eyes, our best. Those, I mean, which are least supported by devotional feeling and contend with the greatest disinclination. For these, perhaps, being nearly all will, come from a deeper level than feeling."

---

*Muck also quotes Martyn Lloyd-Jones on how the book of Psalms gives a good model for combating spiritual depression. The central cause of spiritual depression, he said, "is due to the fact that you are listening to yourself instead of talking to yourself." Lloyd-Jones points to Psalm 42 in which the poet says to himself: "Why are you downcast, O my soul? Why so disturbed within me?" After holding such an inner conversation, Muck concludes, "At some point we must take hold of ourselves and act."

CHAPTER 15

THE SOUND OF SILENCE

At that moment I needed prayer as much as I needed air
to draw my breath or oxygen to fill my blood. . . .
A void was behind me. And in front a wall, a wall of darkness.

GEORGES BERNANOS

Sooner or later most pray-ers hit the wall, to borrow a term from marathon running. Feelings go numb, words fail, confusion chases away clear thought. The act of prayer suddenly seems silly, even preposterous. You mumble alone in a room: Isn't talking to yourself a sign of a disturbed person?

A sense of betrayal steals in. What sort of trick is God playing? Is all prayer self-delusion? Words fall to the floor, bounce off the ceiling, and finally they die in the mouth unformed. God has withdrawn, leaving you desolate.

Not far from my home lives a retired lieutenant colonel from the Air Force who serves as a chaplain in a long-term care home. He used to work out regularly in an attempt to keep up with the young, physically fit recruits. Now he rolls his wheelchair down the hallways visiting senior citizens, some bed-bound, some broken by dementia. Every thirty minutes an alarm goes off and he lifts himself up by arm strength alone, then sets his motionless lower half down in a different position, to prevent pressure sores. I visited Karl at work and later in his home, and both times our conversation reverted to the topic of God's silence.

On our first meeting Karl gave me the background to his condition. "It goes back to one day when I was bicycling down a road in New Mexico. I saw a storm drain too late to avoid it, and as my front tire hit the grate I went flying headfirst over the handlebars. A little later I woke up to a man yelling, 'Don't move! Don't move!' and holding his orange hat to shield me from the New Mexico sun. Soon emergency technicians arrived and strapped me to a backboard. I had landed on my helmet, crushing vertebrae and damaging

198

the spinal cord. Since then I've been paralyzed from the chest down. My Air Force career ended, physical therapy replaced my workout routine, and I'm still coming to terms with my new identity as a 'disabled' person."

We talked about the adjustments he faced: moving into an accessible home, losing his military career, living with no bladder or bowel control, fighting muscle spasms and internal infections, having steel rods implanted along his spinal column. After listening to him describe these hardships in detail, I was stunned to hear what Karl said next: "I must say, though, there has been one change more difficult than any of those adjustments, even more difficult than the 'Why?' questions that I can't help asking. God's presence has withdrawn. Just when I need God most, I can no longer sense him. I keep on praying, and believing, but it's as if I'm praying to the ceiling. I get no response."

Later I visited Karl in his home, custom-constructed with wide doorways and halls, bare hardwood floors, and counter surfaces set to his wheelchair height. Walls and cabinets displayed mementoes he had collected while stationed with the Air Force in the U.S. and Europe. Karl told me he had felt the presence of God most strongly when he visited the Taizé community in France. Twice he spent a week there in silence, attending community worship but mostly meditating and praying. "I have never had such a powerful spiritual experience. The community is organized around God, and God's presence seems to permeate the place. Perhaps God gave me that experience to anchor me for what was to follow.

"I was trained as a Calvinist. What do I do with all that has happened to me? I don't lay the accident at God's feet — I don't believe God micromanages the planet. I believe God is present in the midst of our brokenness. I just wish I could feel that presence."

Touching the Void

Since the accident, Karl said, he has turned for comfort to portions of the Bible he had previously overlooked. When life was going well, he had paid little attention to the psalms of lament. Now he lives there. They give him permission to speak his own laments.

> How long, O Lord? Will you forget me forever?
>   How long will you hide your face from me?
> How long must I wrestle with my thoughts
>   and every day have sorrow in my heart?

But if I go to the east, he is not there;
if I go to the west, I do not find him.
When he is at work in the north, I do not see him;
when he turns to the south, I catch no glimpse of him.

O my God, I cry out by day, but you do not answer,
by night, and am not silent.

... my foes taunt me,
saying to me all day long,
"Where is your God?"

I spread out my hands to you;
my soul thirsts for you like a parched land.

After meeting with Karl, I too began paying more attention to those psalms. It struck me that these plaintive cries are *prayers*, addressed to a God who seems either deaf or wholly absent. Even more striking, the prayers occur in the Bible, somehow meriting inclusion in sacred Scripture. Evidently a season of dryness or depression or spiritual aridity—a state of God-forsakenness—is normal, to be expected.

Indeed, one of the prayers ("O my God, I cry out by day ...") simply extends the psalm Jesus quoted from the cross: "My God, my God, why have you forsaken me?" Not even God's own Son was exempt from the sensation of God's absence. I came to appreciate the somber tone of these psalms. At such a time, words of encouragement would have the effect of a bromide. Imagine the disciple Peter, present at the foot of the cross, attempting to comfort Jesus at that darkest of all moments: "No, no, don't say that. God has not abandoned you—it merely feels that way. Remember all you taught us about the Father's faithful love?"

For some, like Karl, the dark night begins with a terrible accident that changes everything, or with an illness that ravages the body as prayers go mockingly unanswered. For others the cloud descends as a marriage gets worse, not better, despite all prayers, or hovers over the wasteland that follows a divorce. Sometimes it descends with no apparent reason, a freak storm on a bright summer day. Why would God hide?

Instinctively we blame ourselves, assuming we have done something to offend God. A voice inside whispers that I am unworthy of God's presence, that God would not possibly respond to someone whose mind has been filled with such impure thoughts. I counter that voice with the reality that I am praying *because* of the pollution of my mind. I am praying for cleansing, for help.

I know a woman who did not pray for more than a year, benumbed by the fear that she must have committed the unpardonable sin. Thomas Green, a wise spiritual director, dispels that fear. We judge as immature, he says, a friend who pulls away wounded but refuses to reveal what we might have done to hurt him or her. Surely the God of love as revealed in Jesus does not act in such a childish way. Green recommends the following prayer:

> Lord, you care for me more than I care for myself. I cannot believe that you are playing guessing games with me. If the dryness I experience is due to some failing of mine, you make it clear to me and I will try to remedy it. But I will not entertain vague doubts; unless and until you make my failing clear to me, I will assume that is not the reason for the dryness.

I take some comfort in the fact that virtually all the masters of spirituality recount a dark night of the soul. Sometimes it passes quickly and sometimes it persists for months, even years. I have yet to find a single witness, though, who does not tell of going through a dry period. Teresa of Avila spent twenty years in a nearly prayerless state before breaking through to emerge as a master of prayer. William Cowper had prayer times in which he thought he would die from excess of joy; but later he described himself as "banished to a remoteness from God's presence, in comparison with which the distance from the East to the West is vicinity."

The seventeenth-century poet George Herbert, who wrote of the intimate sense of God's presence, wrote just as eloquently of the sense of God's absence:

> My knees pierce th' earth, mine eies the skie;
>   And yet the sphere
> And centre both to me denie
>   That thou art there...
> Where is my God? What hidden place
>   Conceals thee still?

Religious radio and television, as well as certain books and magazines, say little of God's silence. By their accounts God seems to speak volubly, commanding this minister to build a new sanctuary and that housewife to launch a new Web-based company. God represents success, good feelings, a sense of peace, a warm glow. To an audience regaled by such inspiring stories, an encounter with the silence of God hits like a shocking exception and stirs up feelings of inadequacy.

The exception, in fact, is the cheery optimism of modern consumer-oriented faith. For centuries Christians learned what to expect on the spiritual journey from the bumbling pilgrim in *Pilgrim's Progress*, from John of the Cross's *Dark Night of the Soul*, from Thomas à Kempis's challenging *Imitation of Christ*. The one mentor who wrote most openly about the presence of God, Brother Lawrence, composed his thoughts while washing dishes and cleaning toilets.

If I suffer a time of spiritual aridity, of darkness and blankness, should I stop praying until new life enters my prayer? Every one of the spiritual masters insists, No. If I stop praying, how will I know when prayer does become alive again? And, as many Christians have discovered, the habit of not praying is far more difficult to break than the habit of praying.

Survival Strategies

I have never had to deal with the shattering kind of test that blindsided Karl, the paraplegic chaplain. But I have experienced the silence of God often enough in smaller doses to develop a series of coping strategies.

I first run through a checklist of what might be blocking communication. Have I caused the blockage itself through my deliberate sin or callous inattention to God? If the blockage seems obvious, I must clear the channel through confession.

As part of the checklist, I also examine my motives in prayer. Perhaps I have been seeking misty devotional feelings: God on my terms and not God's. Dietrich Bonhoeffer asks, "May it not be that God Himself sends us these hours of reproof and dryness that we may be brought again to expect everything from His Word?" Instead of looking for a new revelation of God's presence, perhaps I should focus instead on the revelation God has already given: in creation, in the Bible, in Jesus, in the church. Bonhoeffer cautions against the vanity of relying on exceptional spiritual experiences as if we have some entitlement. "'Seek God, not happiness'—this is the fundamental rule of all meditation," he said, then added, "If you seek God alone, you will gain happiness: that is its promise."

I often find that during a season of dryness in prayer the rest of my life comes alive. I listen more attentively to friends; ideas leap out to me from books; nature speaks to me more deeply. Keeping company with God includes far more than the time I devote to prayer each day. God is alive all day, living both around me and inside me, speaking in a still, small voice and in other ways I may not even recognize. God is not really silent, we are deaf, says Teresa of Avila. My job is to remain vigilant like a sentry on duty, straining to hear the sounds of the night as well as the first signs of dawn.

Continuing with the checklist, I ask myself whether I have been primarily pursuing results from my prayer rather than companionship with God. When Paul prayed for removal of the "thorn in my flesh," at first he seemed puzzled by the lack of response. Wasn't God listening? Then he got a valuable spiritual insight: the affliction would force him continually to rely on God. He made an immediate adjustment, because Paul valued a close dependence on God more than physical health.

If I find no self-evident reason for God's silence in my checklist, I move on. I look on periods of blankness in prayer much as I look on suffering. It does little good, I have found, to spend much time dwelling on the "Why?" questions. The Bible itself moves the emphasis from past to future: not "Why did this happen?" but, "Now that it has happened, what can I learn from it and how should I respond?" Thus the major New Testament passages on suffering all focus on the productive value of suffering, the good that it can produce in us (perseverance, character, patience, hope, and so on).

In the same vein, I ask God to use the time of spiritual dryness to prepare me for future growth. Jesus hints at such a process in his analogy of the vine: "Every branch that does bear fruit he prunes so that it will be even more fruitful." As any vintner or rose-grower knows, the act of lopping off lush branches, which at first seems cruel and destructive, actually causes the pruned shoots to

Forgive the Silence

MARK JARMAN, FROM "FIVE PSALMS"
IN *TO THE GREEN MAN*

First forgive the silence
  That answers prayer,
Then forgive the prayer
  That stains the silence.

Excuse the absence
  That feels like presence,
Then excuse the feeling
  That insists on presence.

Pardon the delay
  Of revelation,
Then ask pardon for revealing
  Your impatience.

Forgive God
  For being only a word,
Then ask God to forgive
  The betrayal of language.

grow back more productive than ever. A vintner explained to me that he refuses to irrigate his vines because the stress caused by occasional drought produces the best, most tasty grapes. Seasons of dryness make the roots run deep, strengthening the vine for whatever the future holds.

In the words of Henry Blackaby, "You can respond to the silence of God in two ways. One response is for you to go into depression, a sense of guilt, and self-condemnation. The other response is for you to have an expectation that God is about to bring you to a deeper knowledge of Himself. These responses are as different as night and day."

The Questions Beneath

Lynn

Unfortunately, my parents' professed faith did not translate into their family life. About the age of eight I was molested by a relative, and I was emotionally and psychologically abused and neglected by both parents for as long as I can remember. I chose to cope by being a good girl, disappearing into the woodwork and performing perfectly, never acknowledging that I was in pain.

Then at age nineteen I was involved in a horrible auto accident which took the life of my best friend. On the outside I clung to God with all my strength. But on a deeper, subconscious level I was enraged with God that he would allow such a tragedy, that he would "take" my friend from me knowing how she was family to me when I had none of my own. I became convinced in my heart that God was just like my father—uncaring, cruel, a betrayer of trust.

It wasn't until I reached my thirties, married and with children of my own, that the eruption let loose. There were headaches and numerous viruses, outbursts of anger and times of depression. Then I began to experience panic attacks. I was terrified of what was happening to me. With the help of a highly skilled Christian therapist I began an emotional journey that has often seemed unendurable and endless. The feelings that had been pushed down inside of me for so many years gushed out all at once and threatened to overwhelm me.

A large part of my healing process has been to try to come to terms with God—no small task. I have challenged him, cried with him, raged at him, and

I try to see the dry period as a time of *waiting*. After all, I gladly wait for loved ones when their planes are delayed, wait on hold for computer help lines, wait in line for a concert I want to attend. Waiting need not kill time; it uses time, in anticipation of something to come.

I once heard a theologian remark that in the Gospels people approached Jesus with a question 183 times whereas he replied with a direct answer only three times. Instead, he responded with a different question, a story, or some other indirection. Evidently Jesus wants us to work out answers on our own, using the principles that he taught and lived. Prayer, I find, often operates

clung to him. In my quieter moments, I have searched for him, implored him, worshiped him, and meditated on his Word. I have asked the hard questions, laid it all out, and waited for his answers. My journal is thick with entreaties and longings and grief. I have cried more than I ever thought humanly possible and felt such intense pain that at times I felt my body simply could not endure it.

I have a quiet joy now, a kind of mysterious settledness to be able to say that God has met me. There are times when he answers me in a surprisingly direct way through his Word. There are other times when his answers are not a response to what I asked, but satisfy me anyway. It is as though God knows that there are questions underneath my questions and those are the ones he answers. Often he simply waits, lovingly waits, for me to get it all out and get to a place where I can hear him and comprehend what he wants to say.

God has, for the time being at least, settled many of my questions by answering my crucial one: Do you love me, God? That was at the heart of my turmoil and confusion and that was the one he has answered with a resounding "YES!!" Over and over and over again God has revealed his love for me in countless, varied, and creative ways. In those moments the tears of pain become tears of joy and grateful relief to finally, finally be loved — fully, freely, eternally.

My other questions will have to wait. And I can say that, while I still feel wounded and sore and even raw in some places, I have come to know that God will give me enough of an answer to enable me to live and even to live abundantly. I am looking forward to moving out of this period of grief and into more of that abundant life!

the same way. In the difficult and sometimes frustrating act of pursuing God, changes occur in me that equip me to serve God. Maybe what I sense as abandonment is actually a form of empowerment.

A final survival strategy is to lean on the faith of others. When the cloud descends, it heartens me to realize that not everyone is having the same experience. Indeed, the Bible gives a strong emphasis to the practice of praying along with others. Many of the psalms have notes indicating group worship rather than private meditation. "*Our* Father," Jesus taught us to pray, notably using the plural pronoun. "For where two or three come together in my name, there am I with them," he affirmed. After Jesus' departure, his followers continued the practice of praying together. At times when I have no words and my faith falters, I find solace in listening to the prayers of others and realizing that not everyone is sharing my sense of desolation.

In churches affected by the small group movement, the most meaningful prayer often takes place in homes, in circumstances that closely resemble those of the early church. I have been in groups where someone takes the vulnerable step of confessing a deep, recurrent failure in life and asking for help in dealing with it. The group quiets down, puts aside all distractions, and pours love and energy into lifting up a friend to the One who cares most.

Group prayer offers a place for those in the desert as well as those on the mountaintops, for some who simply say "Please pray for me" as well as those who gladly do it. A Jewish teacher of prayer said, "When I prepare myself to say my prayers, I unite myself with all who are closer to God than I am, so that, through them, I may reach God. And I also unite myself with all who may be farther away from God than I am, so that, through me, they may reach God."

I have a relative whom I'll call Diane who learned to pray with others while going through the protracted pain of a divorce. For months she prayed that God would repair the marriage. At one point she called together ten of the most respected members of her church and prayed with them in the chapel. Their faith uplifted hers, and she truly believed healing was on the way. Instead, more and more evidence of her husband's deception and adultery came out. He showed no interest in reconciliation.

Diane recalls: "That was such a devastatingly bleak period. Some days I couldn't stop crying. Our children felt torn. Not knowing the details, they sensed mainly the pain, and would switch loyalties back and forth between Michael and me.

"In desperation one day I called my mother and asked if she would pray with me. She lives in another city, and the first time we prayed together it was over the telephone. As she poured out her heart to God on my behalf, I realized that a mother knows her child's hurt better than anyone. She had been praying for me all these years anyway—and yet never before had I asked her to pray with me.

"The marriage unraveled, we got divorced, and I am still trying to put life back together. But I came away with this wonderful gift of praying with my mother. Her love buoyed me during that awful time. We've kept it up ever since. In fact, I've taken on a prayer partner in my neighborhood too, another woman I pray with every day. And as I've grown stronger, I've become a prayer coordinator for my church, encouraging others to link up during their own dark times.

"I've asked myself what kept me from praying with others during a time of need. Fear is the answer, I suppose. Fear and a sense of inadequacy. I still feel inadequate—and that's why I pray."

Free Partners

No one can reduce to a formula the secret to close communion with God. The English bishop Hugh Latimer wrote to a fellow martyr, "I am sometimes so fearful, that I would creep into a mouse-hole; sometimes God doth visit me again with his comfort. So he cometh and goeth." We may experience a spiritual high one day and spend the next month wandering in the desert. "The wind blows wherever it pleases," Jesus told Nicodemus. So he cometh and goeth.

On the hill behind my mountain home, each spring a pair of red foxes raises a litter of kits. The parents have grown quite accustomed to me roaming the hill and think it not at all strange that I stop in front of the den and whistle a greeting. Sometimes the young ones poke their faces out the crevice in the rock, sniffing the air and staring at me with alert, shiny eyes. Sometimes I hear them scrabbling around inside. Sometimes I hear nothing and assume them asleep. Once, when a visitor from New Zealand stopped by, I took him to the den, warning him that he may see and hear nothing at all. "They are wild animals, you know," I said. "We're not in charge. It's up to them whether they make an appearance or not."

A bold young fox did poke his nose out of the den that day, thrilling my visitor, and a few weeks later I received a letter from him, now back home in New Zealand. As he reflected on it, oddly enough, my comment about foxes helped him understand God. He had just gone through a long season of depression. Sometimes God seemed as close as his wife or children. Sometimes he had no sense of God's presence, no faith to lean on. "He is wild, you know," he wrote. "We're not in charge."

"Come near to God and he will come near to you," wrote James, in words that sound formulaic. James does not put a time parameter on the second clause, however. He reminds me that keeping company with God involves two parties, and I have an important role to play in the relationship. As James suggests, I can purify my heart and humble my spirit. I am learning to take responsibility for my part and then leave the rest to God.

In the process of becoming an adult, I have learned to conduct human relationships in a way that at first blush may seem inauthentic. When I get poor service in a restaurant, I don't throw a temper tantrum and break the dishes like a two-year-old. Talking on the telephone, I try to sound polite even when the caller has just interrupted me. I show up at work whether I feel like it or not. I look for ways to be attentive to my wife even when I'm more aware of my own needs. In other words, all relationships involve an act of will, and I likewise persevere through difficult times in prayer despite my feelings at the moment.

Sometimes I come to God out of sheer determination of will, which may seem inauthentic. When I do so, however, I need not put on a mask. God already knows the state of my soul. I am not telling God anything new, but I am bearing witness to my love for God by praying even when I don't feel like it. I express my underlying faith simply by showing up.

When I am tempted to complain about God's lack of presence, I remind myself that God has much more reason to complain about my lack of presence. I reserve a few minutes a day for God, but how many times do I drown out or ignore the quiet voice that speaks to my conscience and my life? "Here I am! I stand at the door and knock," have become familiar words from Revelation, often stretched into an evangelistic message. But Jesus addressed those words to a church full of believers. How many times have I failed to hear the soft knock on the door and thus missed God's invitation?

Every relationship involves two free partners. With my computer I have a mechanical bond: I turn it on and expect it to respond in predictable, programmed ways. No relationships with human beings work that way, whether between friends, husband and wife, work colleagues, or parents and children. Each involves missed cues, conflicting schedules, varying moods, and a dose of autonomy. Each goes through times of closeness as well as seasons that might be called arid. Indeed, I gauge the strength of a given marriage more by how the partners handle the rough patches than by their reports of romantic highs.

A relationship conducted through prayer, too, goes through rhythms. The prayer I prayed today represents one prayer of my whole lifetime. Many of the psalms of lament, those which most eloquently express the sense of God's absence, include the word "Remember!" The writers remind themselves (and God) in the process of writing that what they feel right now they have not always felt, and will not always feel. The very words they use—*hide, forsake, withdraw*—assume that God is free, God's presence variable. The cry "How long?" voices hope that a change will come.

> I waited patiently for the Lord;
>> he turned to me and heard my cry.
> He lifted me out of the slimy pit,
>> out of the mud and mire;
> he set my feet on a rock
>> and gave me a firm place to stand.
> He put a new song in my mouth,
>> a hymn of praise to our God.

A Leap of Trust

I may go through a period when it feels like God is absent, but if God were truly absent everything in the universe would cease to exist. I have learned to recognize that I am going through a particular season, and try not to judge reality based on how I am feeling right now.

As I read the Bible, I see a pattern operating between God and some of God's favorites. Abraham goes through tests of faith, Job suffers unjustly, Jacob wrestles through the night, and Jesus himself feels abandoned. I certainly exercise freedom in my relationship with God by disobeying, indulging myself, and neglecting prayer. Shouldn't I expect a similar measure of freedom, albeit expressed in different ways, from God? In Martin Luther's words,

> When we try to dictate to God the time, place, and manner for him to act, we are testing him. At the same time, we're trying to see if he

is really there. Doing that is putting limits on God and trying to make him do what we want. It's nothing less than trying to deprive God of his divinity. But we must realize that God is free — not subject to any limitations. He must dictate to us the place, manner, and time.

I used to wonder how I could muster up more faith. I yearned for the kind of faith that Jesus remarked on with approval, the faith that readily believes in miracles. Alas, I never found it. I found instead a realistic faith that developed as a by-product of spending time with God. I came to trust God, even trusting that God's will is the best way for me, though rarely the easiest. As the British convert Jonathan Aitken expresses it, "Trusting in God does not, except in illusory religion, mean that he will ensure that none of the things you are afraid of will ever happen to you. On the contrary, it means that whatever you fear is quite likely to happen, but that with God's help it will in the end turn out to be nothing to be afraid of."

Just as a scientist proceeds according to proven laws, I exercise faith based on what I have learned about God, primarily through the life of Jesus. Growth, however, calls for a leap beyond the known: a search for the cure to cancer, the first step on the moon's surface, a prayer for an end to a thirty-year feud in my family, or an end to poverty in my city. Though I cannot even imagine how the prayer will be answered, I take that step because I have learned to trust God. I believe in God's desire for healing and justice, whether or not I will ever see that desire realized in the particular way I want.

Prayer invites us to rest in the fact that God is in control, and the world's problems are ultimately God's, not ours. If I spend enough time with God, I will inevitably begin to look at the world with a point of view that more resembles God's own. What is faith, after all, but believing in advance what will only make sense in reverse?*

On my last visit with Karl, the paraplegic chaplain, he wanted to clarify that he still prayed and still believed strongly in prayer. "I am *sustained* by

---

* Austin Farrer gives this description of trust: "A Christian who knew his own heart might pray in some such fashion as this. My God, I wish to give you the gift you so much desire; I wish to commit myself to you once and for all, so there shall be no taking back. I cannot commit *myself* into your hands, O God, I cannot do it; but yet I can commit myself into *your* hands; for though I cannot keep myself there, your fingers can hold me there, your strong, gentle fingers always giving way and never letting go; your wise subtle fingers, wrestling so gently against my puny rebellions, that I tire myself trying to climb out of your hands, and come to rest at last in those wounded palms."

the prayers of others," he said. "I read the cards and expressions of support, some from strangers, and I lean on them for strength when my own strength gives out. After surgery on my spinal cord the anesthesiologist stopped by to tell me, 'I called my church in Louisiana and they've been praying for you.' Another time an African-American surgeon herself prayed the most beautiful, lilting prayer for me just before she worked to repair damage to my mouth from the accident.

"I don't doubt prayer. I just puzzle over why so much of the time I lack a sense of God's presence. I know about the ministry of presence. When deployed for Kosovo and the Persian Gulf, I would walk the flight line, praying with the pilots under the wings of the F16s before they took off. Some of them gave me letters for their loved ones, in case they never returned. God meets us at such hinge moments. Why is he not meeting me now?"

Motioning for me to follow, he wheeled down a hallway and into a bedroom. There he told me of a time when, after a pressure ulcer developed, he had lain in bed for several weeks. Having survived blood clots and a raging infection, now once again he was bed-bound. He interrupted the story to point out two Russian icons on the walls. "Icons aren't really part of my tradition," he said. "But somehow these two became windows to another world for me as I lay in bed feeling abandoned by God, wondering if he really cared and wondering if prayer meant anything or really changed anything.

"One icon shows the baptism of Jesus. As I stared at it, I was reminded that God fully entered into our world, our skin. Whatever I'm experiencing here, God experienced too. He even knew the experience of paralysis—nailed to a cross.

"The other icon shows Cristo Pontocrator, Christ the Almighty. Every few hours I would rotate over to my other side and this second icon would come into view. I would stare at it and ask, 'Where are you, Cristo Pantocrator, now that I need you?' The tension between the two images of Christ screamed at me as I stared first at one and then the other. Somewhere suspended between those two images, I live. I have a hope in the future based on Christ the Almighty, but every day I have to fight the battles of the flesh, in my case a damaged flesh.

"Ten years from now, I may look back on this period as a parenthesis in my spiritual life. Maybe I won't struggle with prayer then as I do now. And I know that God can use me even now when it feels like a void. At the nursing home the elderly connect with me because of my disability. When I roll up to their bedsides, I'm already at their level, I don't have to bend down. 'Karl will understand,' they say as they experience loss of function.

"A few months ago I spoke to fellow chaplains about my physical and spiritual journey after the accident. Then we conducted an anointing service for healing. 'This is for healing, not cure,' I told them. 'My condition is irreversible; I don't expect it to change. But I still need healing.' At this service, however, I was the one doing the anointing. A line of chaplains came forward and I dipped my fingers in oil and pressed it on their foreheads. The first few bent down to the level of my wheelchair. Then one man knelt. Soon they were all kneeling. And perhaps that is what I need to focus on right now. For the rest of my life, through no choice of my own, I'm at the level of one who kneels."

PART 4

PRAYER DILEMMAS

There comes an hour when begging stops,
When the long interceding lips
Perceive their prayer is vain.

EMILY DICKINSON

CHAPTER 16

UNANSWERED PRAYER: WHOSE FAULT?

When the gods wish to punish us,
they answer our prayers.
OSCAR WILDE

I am sitting in a comfortable chair looking through a plate glass window at a tricolored mountain lake. A white crescent of ice still clings to one shore even as a few floes break free and float daringly toward the center; the melted middle catches and reflects a sea-blue Colorado sky; in the coves, rivulets of spring snowmelt carve channels through cracked brown mud. I see not a single human-made object, hear no sound save a croaking chorus of young frogs. Migrating birds peck for food in the mud flats. A stand of Douglas firs thickens at the stream banks. A good time, a good place, I decide, to review the recent prayers I have voiced.

The week before Christmas a friend wrote a farewell note, stepped in the shower, pushed the barrel of a pistol inside her mouth, and pulled the trigger. For years I had prayed for her fight against alcoholism; this one skirmish proved fatal. Now I pray for her husband who fights the same addiction, with her support no longer and thus all the more tempted to surrender.

One relative in my extended family died of AIDS after an excruciating, decade-long struggle. Another died of diabetes before reaching the age of forty. An uncle lost his leg to the same disease and at this moment lies in a hospital bed recovering from a fall (he was found unconscious after five days). A cousin valiantly strives to overcome drug addiction. A dear friend's daughter cannot expunge the memories of sexual abuse that took place overseas where her parents served as missionaries.

Faces from other countries come to mind as well. A World Vision worker who heads an AIDS program in South Africa while battling the

215

disease himself, a result of a contaminated blood transfusion. Two friends in Lebanon, who with every bomb and terrorist act in the region flash back to the bloody civil war there. Aid workers in Guatemala who saw ten years' worth of development work wiped out in a deadly mudslide that barely made the news elsewhere.

"Each day has enough trouble of its own," said Jesus, an axiom of understatement that hangs over me like an avalanche chute as I gaze at a pristine scene and ponder the suffering and evil that afflict those close to me. I have prayed for each of these neighbors, friends, and relatives, and by any reasonable standard of judgment I must conclude that the prayers have gone unanswered.

My own emphasis in prayer has moved from petition to companionship, and I no longer agonize over the issue of unanswered prayer as I once did. Yet I know that for many people unanswered prayer forms a barrier that blocks any desire to keep company with God. What kind of companion who has the power to save a life or heal a disease would sit on the sidelines despite urgent pleas for help? In a sense every war, every epidemic or drought, every premature death or birth defect stands as an accusation against the teasing promise of prayer.

Gerard Manley Hopkins, a priest as well as a poet, sums up the tempting deduction about prayer:

> ... cries like dead letters sent
> To dearest him that lives alas! away.

A Threat to Faith

Unanswered prayer poses an especially serious threat to the faith of trusting children. Last night I read a hundred-page manuscript, written more to exorcise the past rather than for publication, by a young woman who as a child was raped almost nightly by her older brother. When their mother at last found them together, she slapped her daughter and called her a whore. "I cried out every night for God's help, to make it stop" the author recalls. "God never answered."

In *Of Human Bondage*, Somerset Maugham recounts an incident from childhood, slightly fictionalized in the novel, an incident from which his faith never recovered. The main character, Philip, has just discovered the verse in Mark which says, "Whatever you ask in my name, believing, you will receive it." He thinks immediately of his clubfoot:

216

He would be able to play football. His heart leaped as he saw himself running faster than any of the other boys. At the end of Easter term there were the sports, and he would be able to go in for the races; he rather fancied himself over the hurdles. It would be splendid to be like everyone else, not to be stared at curiously by new boys who did not know about his deformity, nor at the baths in summer to need incredible precautions, while he was undressing, before he could hide his foot in the water.

He prayed with all the power in his soul. No doubts assailed him. He was confident in the Word of God. And the night before he was to go back to school he went up to bed tremulous with excitement. There was snow on the ground, and Aunt Louisa had allowed herself the unaccustomed luxury of a fire in her bedroom, but in Philip's little room it was so cold that his fingers were numb, and he had great difficulty undoing his collar. His teeth chattered. The idea came to him that he must do something more unusual to attract the attention of God, and he turned back the rug which was in front of his bed so that he could kneel on the bare boards, and then it struck him that his nightshirt was a softness that might displease his Maker, so he took it off and said his prayers naked. When he got into bed he was so cold that for some time he could not sleep, but when he did, it was so soundly that Mary Ann had to shake him when she brought his hot water next morning. She talked to him while she drew the curtains, but he did not answer; he had remembered at once that this was the morning of the miracle. His heart was filled with joy and gratitude. His first instinct was to put down his hand and feel the foot which was whole now, but to do this seemed to doubt the goodness of God. He knew that his foot was well. But at last he made up his mind, and with the toes of his right foot he just touched his left. Then he passed his hand over it. He limped downstairs just as Mary Ann was going into the dining room for prayers, and then he sat down to breakfast.

"You're very quiet this morning, Philip," said Aunt Louisa presently.

Somerset Maugham's own ailment, stuttering, on which he based this scene, stayed with him all his life, a constant reminder of prayer unanswered. Maugham's friend and fellow novelist George Orwell likewise tells of offering up anguished, tearful prayers in boarding school that he not wet the bed. Often they went unanswered, and each time he had to undergo a caning. Both writers lost any shred of religious faith.

Augustine writes in *The Confessions* of his childhood prayers that the teachers at school not beat him. Invariably, he was beaten. Reading his account, I recalled my own prayers that I not get attacked by bullies at school. Nerdy and undersized, I made a perfect target, and no guardian angels appeared in answer to my prayers. I learned to run home from school as self-protection. Was anyone listening to those prayers?

One skeptical Englishman attempted to analyze prayer scientifically. Francis Galton (Charles Darwin's cousin) noted that *The Book of Common Prayer* included a petition for the long life of the British sovereign. He then compared the life spans of royalty to other groups in society and found them to be the shortest lived of all! A prayer repeated millions of times a day by Anglican believers had no provable effect. Expanding the survey, he found no significant difference in the life spans of the clergy compared to other professions. Missionaries, too, seemed as vulnerable as anyone else to shipwreck, tropical disease, and violence despite the many prayers on their behalf.

Magic or Faith

DAVID

I work as a grief counselor for a hospice program. While working with death and dying, I identified the challenge to my faith that had thrown me for a loop: the inconsistent intervention of God and his people.

In earlier years I found myself surrounded by people who viewed God as a genie in a bottle who granted their every wish (though I observed it was inconsistent deliverance, as in Hebrews 11, rescuing some from peril while allowing others to be sawn in two). The "successes" were often trumpeted from the housetops, while the failures were quickly buried in the backyard for no one to see. I saw in hospice that the rain fell on the just and unjust and that some Christians were delivered for God's purposes and others lost their lives and went to heaven giving glory to God.

I rebelled against an interpretation of life that had God rushing around the world answering prayers to clear away parking places for Christians tardy for appointments. I heard many of these people praying that God would magically intervene and help poor or sick people — never sensing they might be the answer to those prayers. It seemed more a belief in magic than in God.

Yesterday my son and his wife were involved in a freeway accident, spin-

218

I have a file drawer full of letters in response to a book I wrote titled *Disappointment with God*, and every so often I read through those letters. They would silence the mouth of any prosperity-gospel evangelist and break the heart of any sensitive soul. Some tell of relatively trivial unanswered prayers: for example, a baby that refuses to sleep and cries louder every time the harried mother prays for relief. Some tell of unanswered prayers with more serious consequences. Scars from abuse not by bullies but by family members. A child with cystic fibrosis. A mother with severe Alzheimer's who has suddenly turned violent. Breast cancer, a brain tumor, pancreatic cancer. The correspondents give a virtual diary of prayer, begun with high hopes, buoyed by support of friends and church, dashed into disappointment.

They are writing me, as they explain, because their faith dangles on the thread of unanswered prayer. Some blame themselves, following the cruel logic of fellow Christians who tell them that proper faith would achieve the desired result. Some, looking for bright spots, point to positive side-effects

---

ning out of control at 70 mph to avoid lumber falling off a truck in front of them. Somehow they escaped without injury, with only their car banged up. Witnesses testified to a miracle, and the state highway patrol marveled that they survived the accident without major injury or death. My other two adult sons came upon the scene moments later and witnessed what had happened.

Last night we gathered as a family and talked about the accident. One of my twenty-something sons (our skeptical Thomas) said his brother and wife were just plain lucky in a fallen world of random events and disorder. Another son wasn't so sure that something special hadn't happened but wasn't going to stake his reputation on it. The son who drove the car said God had delivered him. My daughter-in-law said, "We were just returning from planting flowers on Grandma's grave and she was a woman of prayer, and those she prayed for God to bless and protect them while she was living were answered today." My wife also believed they were "delivered."

After years of experience with catastrophes, I could only say with integrity: "God was there, he was with them, he was helping them. God would be with them if they ventured into the 'valley of the shadow of death,' and is also with them in life, granting them strength and grace each day." I wish I could have said more ... I understand the man's prayer in the Gospels, "Lord, I believe, but help my unbelief."

of prayers—relatives brought to faith, a church united—while the main request goes ignored. Others simply give up, concluding that prayer doesn't work.

The Inconsistency Problem

I hope by now I have made it clear that I believe in prayer and its power to change both people and events. Nevertheless, when I hear a person describe a remarkable escape from an airplane crash, I cannot help thinking about the people who died in the same crash, many of them praying just as fervently. And although I rejoice over reports of miraculous healings, I also remember with a pang the file drawer in my office bulging with stories of those who have not been healed. I do not doubt that God answers prayer. Rather, I struggle with the inconsistency of those apparent answers.

In fairness, Francis Galton's study of prayer's futility should be balanced by the reports that his contemporaries wrote in direct rebuttal. Two such books compiled 630 pages of accounts of answered prayers. Their titles tell the story: *Prayer and Its Remarkable Answers* and *The Wonders of Prayer: A Record of Well Authenticated and Wonderful Answers to Prayer*. George Müller alone claimed fifty thousand answers to prayer in his storied life as head of a faith-based orphanage.

I have similar books on my shelves, including recent accounts by Jim Cymbala of God's work at the Brooklyn Tabernacle Church in New York. In a survey of 5,600 people conducted by *U.S. News* and *Beliefnet.com*, 41 percent of respondents reported frequent answers to their prayers. I have personally interviewed individuals, such as a Costa Rican prostitute (see page 224), whose stories could confound the hardest skeptic. I have heard, and investigated as a journalist, numerous anecdotal accounts of answers to prayer. I believe them and take them at face value. More, I am aware of "unprayed answers" as well—occasions when God's providence or a guardian angel works on my behalf even when I don't get around to asking.

Yet these many accounts do not solve the problem of unanswered prayer. To the husband who lost his wife in a plane crash, the testimony of a survivor does little to encourage faith; to the family who lost a child to meningitis, it brings no solace to hear of another child's recovery. Many books on prayer include a statement like this: "God always answers prayer, but sometimes No is the answer." I read that statement and then think of specific friends and relatives who received the negative answer. Why? Were their prayers somehow deficient?

I have written of the effect of prayer on the collapse of Communism and the peaceful changeover in South Africa, and I believe that prayer played a crucial role in both events. But how many Russian priests and believers died in the Gulag Archipelago praying for deliverance before it came, and how many South Africans faced torture and execution by police hit squads before their prayers got answered?

Often when I turn the television to a religious channel, someone is reading letters about a viewer whose back miraculously straightened or who took her first steps after watching the program. How must that sound to a mother who spends every afternoon pounding the back of her sixteen-year-old son with cystic fibrosis to loosen the phlegm clogging his lungs? I know of no reported healing of cystic fibrosis.

The Dutch author Corrie ten Boom tells of a miraculous little bottle of vitamins in her Nazi concentration camp that kept yielding life-preserving drops for her sister as well as for two dozen cellmates long after it should have been depleted. Her sister Betsie likened it to the biblical story of the widow of Zarephath's supply of oil that did not run out. Later in Corrie's book we learn that Betsie died at the Ravensbrück camp. Did God answer a prayer about vitamins and not about Betsie?

I heard a survivor story of a couple from India who happened to be in separate towers of the World Trade Center on September 11, 2001. Miraculously, both made it down the stairways and out before the two towers collapsed, an escape which so impressed them that they converted to Christianity and the husband became a full-time evangelist. As I listened to his incredible story, though, I could not help thinking of the three thousand who died, many of whom were praying even as the tons of molten steel imploded on them.

Somehow we must offer our prayers with a humility that conveys gratitude without triumphalism, and compassion without manipulation, always respecting the mystery surrounding prayer.*

---

*Lutheran theologian Martin Marty said, "I find the most offensive kind of prayer when 250 Marines get killed ... and four survive, and their families go on television and say, 'We really prayed, so they were spared.' That's an unbiblical game. It's magic; it's superstition. I like the matter-of-factness of Jesus when asked about the man born blind, and Jesus says, "'Did he sin or did his parents?" you ask. He was just born blind.' Things just happen. It rains on the just and the unjust alike."

What We Do Wrong

Some prayers go unanswered because they are simply frivolous. "Lord, please give us a sunny day for the soccer match" trivializes prayer, especially when local farmers may at the same time be praying for rain. A last-ditch plea, "Help me get an A on this next test," will likely not succeed if the pray-er has not studied, just as a chain-smoker has no right to pray, "Protect me from lung cancer."

I have made several trips to Asia, where people are fascinated by my curly hair, worn in a finger-in-the-light-socket style. (Twice, in fact, giggly Japanese teenage girls have approached me after a speaking engagement and asked, very shyly, "Mr. Yancey, may we touch your hair?") For my part, I find sleek, black, shiny, and *straight* Asian hair very attractive. After enduring the nickname "Curly" all through grammar school, I would gladly have traded my mane for an Asian one. I believe I could pray every day for straight, black Asian hair, solicit all my friends to pray for it, even send in requests to television evangelists, and it would have no more effect than if I prayed for God to change my family of origin or the country of my birth. The laws of genetics largely determine our appearance, and prayers to reverse those laws, no matter how heartfelt, are ill-considered.

Athletes figure prominently in another set of frivolous prayers. Players in many sports will thump their chests, raise a finger to the sky and eyes toward heaven, as if thanking the Big One upstairs for the touchdown, goal, or home run. Boxer Floyd Patterson said, after knocking out Archie Moore to win the world heavyweight championship, "I just hit him and the Lord did the rest."

Rock star Janis Joplin used to growl, "Oh Lord, won't you buy me a Mercedes Benz." I once heard the Christian author Charlie Shedd say, only partly tongue-in-cheek, "I pray to the great God above every day that my books will sell a million copies and be a blessing to many people—and I'm still working to get that order right." Prison chaplains sometimes hear criminals confess that the only time they pray is when they feel in danger of getting caught (which would, in fact, make God an accessory to the crime).

The New Testament highlights several foolish requests made directly to Jesus. Peter, overwhelmed by the sudden appearance of Moses and Elijah on the Mount of Transfiguration, impetuously asked that shelters be built for the two time travelers and Jesus. The disciples James and John, along with their ambitious mother, once asked Jesus to reserve prominent positions for them in the kingdom. "You don't know what you are asking," Jesus replied, no doubt shaking his head over how badly they had missed his message. The same two vengefully asked for fire to fall from heaven to destroy a resistant Samaritan village.

Another disciple, Peter, earned a strong rebuke when he objected to Jesus' plan to suffer in Jerusalem. Peter's advice, naive though understandable, must have hit a nerve, for Jesus jumped on him: "Get behind me, Satan. You do not have in mind the things of God, but the things of men." That principle gets to the heart of the problem with inappropriate prayers: they are self-serving and not in accord with God's nature. They put the focus on *our* things, not the things of God. The apostle James would later reiterate this principle: "When you ask, you do not receive, because you ask with wrong motives, that you may spend what you get on your pleasures."

The Bible also makes clear that a prayer may go unanswered because of a flaw in the person praying, not the prayer itself. Adam and Eve experienced a blockage in their contact with God because of their disobedience, a blockage so severe that God had to come searching for them. Psalm 51 records David's plaintive plea for reconnection with God after his sins. And a rebellious King Saul inquired of the Lord and heard no answer, which led him to consult a witch.

Sometimes sin disrupts communication with God. In the midst of a jubilant psalm of praise, one author admits, "If I had cherished sin in my heart, the Lord would not have listened." No one expressed this truth more plainly than the prophet Isaiah, who reported these words from God:

> When you spread out your hands in prayer,
>   I will hide my eyes from you;
> even if you offer many prayers,
>   I will not listen.
> Your hands are full of blood;
>   wash and make yourselves clean.
> Take your evil deeds
>   out of my sight!
> Stop doing wrong,
>   learn to do right!
> Seek justice,
>   encourage the oppressed.
> Defend the cause of the fatherless,
>   plead the case of the widow.

Thus God flatly declares that, in addition to our private spiritual state, our social concern (or lack of it) — for the poor, for orphans and widows — also has a direct bearing on how our prayers are received. Other prophets, such as Malachi, get even more specific. Those who pay exploitative wages, who break marriage vows through adultery and divorce, who treat illegal immigrants badly, who refuse to share food with the hungry or provide shelter to the homeless, risk closing God's ears to their prayers. As a twenty-first century American, those warnings cut me to the quick.

The book of Proverbs states the principle bluntly: "If a man shuts his ears to the cry of the poor, he too will cry out and not be answered." In his letter, the apostle Peter urges that husbands be considerate to their wives and treat them with respect "so that nothing will hinder your prayers." It may seem strange that issues political and domestic would have a direct effect on

---

A Prostitute's Prayer

HILDA

My family in Costa Rica had no money, and so when I was four years old my mother sold me into sexual slavery. Men pay a lot of money to have their way with children. So while other kids my age went to school, I worked in a brothel, turning over all the earnings to my mother. All my life I felt ugly and dirty, ashamed. I learned to drink alcohol and use cocaine very early, as a way to dull the pain.

When I was a teenager I had two children of my own. My mother took them from me, saying a filthy person like me could not raise children. From then on I worked harder to earn money to support my children. It was the only way I could show my love for them.

Eventually the pimps started demanding more and more from us prostitutes. I sometimes worked a double shift, seeing a hundred men in a day. The men lined up outside the door and I had only ten minutes with each one.

One day a customer got furious when I wouldn't do what he asked. He pulled a knife on me, then hit me with a baseball bat, splitting my head open. They took me to the hospital and I lay in that bed plotting to kill myself. Maybe if I just pulled out all the tubes they had attached to me ...

prayer life, but not if prayer is viewed as keeping company with God. Every aspect of life, including how we treat those around us, affects an intimate relationship.

I cannot say to my neighbor, "I love you and enjoy spending time with you, but I hate your stupid dog and keep those bratty kids out of my yard, will you?" How I treat what belongs to my neighbor affects how he receives my love. The same applies to God: how I treat God's creation, God's children, will determine in part how God receives my prayers and my worship. Prayer involves more than bowing my head a few times a day; it pervades all of life, and vice versa.

The apostle John summed up the relation between prayer and behavior: "[We] receive from him anything we ask, because we obey his commands and do what pleases him." Martin Lloyd-Jones answered the question of why

---

Finally I got down on my knees beside the bed and pled with God. I wanted somehow to escape prostitution, to become a real mother to my children. And God answered that prayer with a miracle. He gave me a vision. I actually saw the words, "Look for Rahab Foundation." I was barely literate and didn't know the word Rahab. It's not a Spanish word. One of the nurses helped me find their phone number, though, and I called.

The phone rang and rang, and I prayed, "Lord, if you really exist, make somebody answer that phone." At last a woman named Mariliana answered. Turns out, she was the director of Rahab, which was closed for the day, but she had stopped by to pick up some papers.

"I need help," I told Mariliana. "I'm dying. I can't take it anymore." She told me that God loved me and would not leave me alone. She would help me get away from prostitution and start a new life. A few days later she brought me to her home, bruised and bandaged, fresh from the hospital. She welcomed me with a huge hug and said, "You're safe here, Hilda." She told me Rahab was named for a prostitute in the Bible, one who became a heroine.

I couldn't believe the hope on Mariliana's face. It felt like a dream. She gave me a clean bed, flowers in the room, and a promise that no men would harass me. She introduced me to other women who had left prostitution. She taught me how to be a real mother, and now I am studying a trade to live for the glory of God.

people like George Müller and Martin Luther received such spectacular answers to their prayers by saying, "We desire to receive all the blessings which saints have received; but we forget that they were saints. We ask, why does God not answer my prayer as He answered that man's prayer? We should ask, why is it that I have not lived the type of life which that man has lived?"*

Contradictory Prayers

Another set of prayer requests simply cannot be granted. If a dozen people pray to get the same job, eleven must ultimately come to terms with unanswered prayer. And if two "Christian" nations wage war against each other, some citizens' prayers will not be answered to their satisfaction.

Nothing draws a nation to prayer like war. During the Middle Ages, prayers in Europe used to end, "Lord, save us from the Vikings. Amen." We like to see ourselves as united in pursuing a just and righteous cause.† The problem is, our opponents usually see themselves the same way. The British poet John Betjeman captured this one-sided view of war in an ironic poem written during World War II, the so-called "good war":

> Gracious Lord, oh bomb the Germans.
> Spare their women for Thy Sake,
> And if that is not too easy
> We will pardon Thy Mistake.
> But, gracious Lord, whate'er shall be,
> Don't let anyone bomb me.

The most devastating war in American history, the Civil War, claimed pray-ers on both sides. The devout Southern general Robert E. Lee made a

---

* The pastor David Mains recommends the following checklist to make sure prayers are on target:
  1. *What do I really want?* Am I being specific, or am I just rambling about nothing in particular?
  2. *Can God grant this request?* Or is it against God's nature to do so?
  3. *Have I done my part?* Or am I praying to lose weight when I haven't dieted?
  4. *How is my relationship with God?* Are we on speaking terms?
  5. *Who will get the credit if my request is granted?* Do I have God's interests in mind?
  6. *Do I really want my prayer answered?* What would happen if I actually did get that girlfriend back?

† When the United States launched a military response to the September 11 terrorist attacks, the Pentagon labeled the action "Operation Infinite Justice" — that is, until Muslims objected to the overreaching name. Interestingly, I heard no Christians objecting.

startling contrast to his Northern opponent, the profane and sometimes-drunken Ulysses S. Grant. One of Lee's favorite generals, Stonewall Jackson, refused to fight on Sunday unless attacked, and held worship services for his troops. Confederate President Jefferson Davis called for Southerners to observe days of prayer, confident that "it hath pleased Almighty God, the Sovereign Disposer of events, to protect and defend the Confederate States hitherto in their conflict with their enemies, and to be unto them a shield."

Davis's counterpart in the North, President Abraham Lincoln, pointed out the incongruity of pious men fighting to preserve slavery. "It may seem strange that any men should dare to ask a just God's assistance in wringing their bread from the sweat of other men's faces," he said in his second inaugural address. But in typical irenic spirit he added, quoting Jesus, "let us judge not, that we be not judged." Lincoln's address shows an amazingly nuanced and humble view of the cause he led. "Both read the same Bible, and pray to the same God; and each invokes His aid against the other.... The prayers of both could not be answered; that of neither has been answered fully. The Almighty has his own purposes."

Lincoln's attitude stands in stark contrast to the triumphalism that normally accompanies war. Lincoln accepted the terrible cost of the Civil War as a just judgment on the evil of slavery the nation had perpetrated:

> Fondly do we hope, fervently do we pray, that this mighty scourge of war may speedily pass away. Yet, if God wills that it continue unto all the wealth piled by the bondman's two hundred and fifty years of unrequited toil shall be sunk, and until every drop of blood drawn with the lash shall be paid by another drawn with the sword ... so still must it be said that "the judgments of the Lord are true and righteous altogether."

Moreover, Lincoln called for a spirit of reconciliation, not vengeance, as the war drew to a close: "With malice toward none; with charity for all; with firmness in the right as God gives us to see the right, let us strive on to finish the work we are in; to bind up the nation's wounds; to care for him who shall have borne the battle, and for his widow and orphan — to do all which may achieve and cherish a just and lasting peace among ourselves and with all nations."

At the time, both Northern and Southern clergy were claiming God on their side. Lincoln gently cautioned them to inquire instead whether they were on God's side. Finite humans can never know the will of an infinite

227

God with absolute certainty. Following in the footsteps of Old Testament prophets, Lincoln viewed the nation's trauma as a time to reflect on and confess sins, rather than to rouse his side to a haughty self-righteousness. As he said, "I have been driven many times to my knees by the overwhelming conviction that I had nowhere else to go."

The Blessing of Unanswered Prayers

Apart from prayers impossible to answer—those that involve a logical contradiction such as opposing sides praying for victory, or farmers and athletes praying for conflicting weather patterns—what would happen if God answered *every* prayer?

By answering every possible prayer, God would in effect abdicate, turning the world over to us to run. History shows how we have handled the limited power granted us: we have fought wars, committed genocide, fouled the air and water, destroyed forests, established unjust political systems, concentrated pockets of superfluous wealth and grinding poverty. What if God gave us automatic access to supernatural power? What further havoc might we wreak?

I remember as a child reading the comic book stories of Superman, Batman, Spiderman, and the Invisible Man and yearning for their special powers. Oh, if I could only change costumes like Superman and get revenge on the bullies! Or think of the classroom tricks I could play if I had the power to make myself invisible. I would have used prayer as a genie in a bottle, a self-serving way of getting attention and of imposing my will on others.

Would adults act any differently? A large portion of the world's resources goes toward developing high-tech weapons that allow nations to dominate each other. What would happen if some of those nations, but not others, had access to *supernatural* power? Or what if God restricted such powers to the most devout pray-ers? In that case the armies of Robert E. Lee and not Ulysses S. Grant would have won the American Civil War. Christians would comprise a favored class who never got sick, never lost their jobs, never experienced a traffic accident. And how would that affect the Christian community, not to mention those outside it? The biblical history of Israel, a favored people who had access to God's supernatural power, gives a clue. Golden eras, such as the reign of Solomon, fostered pride and decadence while times of national humiliation brought about spiritual growth.

The movie *Bruce Almighty* presents a Hollywood version of what might happen if God entrusted supernatural power to an ordinary human being. Bruce Nolan (played by Jim Carrey), a television reporter from Buffalo, New York, rages against God after a series of mishaps. "He could fix my life in five minutes if he wanted to," Bruce complains. Summoned to an abandoned building, home of Omni Presents, Inc., Bruce encounters God himself (Morgan Freeman), who has decided to let Bruce try being God for a week to see if he can improve matters.

Bruce uses his divine power capriciously, a magic genie he can command to clear a path in traffic for his new sports car or get his dog to use the toilet correctly. He works revenge on fellow employees and on the ruffians who once beat him up. To impress his girlfriend (Jennifer Anniston), he lassoes the moon and pulls it near in order to enhance the romantic mood—simultaneously causing a tidal wave in Japan. He hears thousands of prayers in his head at once, these just from Buffalo residents, and tries to deal with the blizzard of requests. He answers yes to everyone who prays to win the lottery, thus creating 400,000 winners and diluting the grand prize to almost nothing.

In short, Bruce Almighty learns an appreciation for the complexity of prayer as well as a new humility and sense of inadequacy. Someone asked Mahatma Gandhi, "If you were given the power to remake the world, what would you do first?" He replied: "I would pray for power to renounce that power."

Jesus actually did renounce that power while on earth, refusing the tempter's three offers: to dazzle the crowds with a miracle, to rule the world, to protect himself from harm. He exercised supernatural power, yes, but on a local and not global stage, prompted by compassion and not spectacle, and never for self-promotion or self-protection. Jesus' life, in fact, shows the delicate balance required when supernatural power impinges on this world. Immature persons like the fictional Bruce Nolan and mature persons like Mahatma Gandhi soon realize they lack the wisdom to balance free will, divine intervention, and self-sacrifice—the very wisdom Jesus demonstrated during his time on earth.

Most of us learn, over time, that some prayers prove better off unanswered. As a child, Amy Carmichael used to pray for God to change her eyes from brown to blue. Later, as a missionary in India, she was grateful for brown eyes, which made her less foreign and intimidating to Indian children. I received a letter from a woman who once prayed for God to take away her

229

intellect. "It was a hindrance to my faith," she said, "as it enabled me from about age seven to see the hypocrisies in Christians and the church, to ask the unanswerable questions." She continued, "Fortunately, I now know God answers prayers in His own time and manner," for it was her intellect that eventually drew her back to faith.

Country singer Garth Brooks had a hit song in which he recalls his impassioned prayers for God to melt the heart of a high school sweetheart—later apparent to him as a terrible choice:

> Just because he doesn't answer doesn't mean he don't care.
> Some of God's greatest gifts are unanswered prayers.

No Fixed Formula

Even after spelling out some of what we do wrong in our prayers, however —*especially* after spelling that out—I must repeat that prayer does not work according to a fixed formula: get your life in order, say the right words, and the desired result will come. If that were true, Job would have avoided much suffering, Paul would have shed his thorn in the flesh, and Jesus would never have gone to Golgotha. Between the two questions "Does God answer prayer?" and "Will God grant my specific prayer for this sick child or this particular injustice?" lies a great pool of mystery.

Charles Edward White, a college professor in the state of Michigan, spent several terms as a visiting professor at the University of Jos in Nigeria. While there he visited a missionary graveyard in a quiet garden beside a chapel on Nigeria's Central Plateau. Most of the graves, he noticed, were small: two- and three-foot mounds to accommodate child-sized coffins. Thirty-three of the fifty-six graves, in fact, held the bodies of small children. The tombstones went back as far as 1928, and old-timers in the mission could tell him the stories of only the most recent deaths.

Two of the infants lived just one day. Others lived a few years, falling victim to the tropical diseases common in that part of the world. Melvin Louis Goossen was twelve when he and his brother fell off a suspension bridge over a rain-swollen creek. Their missionary father, Arthur Goossen, dived in the creek to save one son. But when he dived after Melvin, both father and son drowned.

Professor White listened to these and other accounts of missionaries who had come to Nigeria in full awareness of the dangers, and of their children who had no such choice and succumbed to those dangers. He imagined the sorrow of households that no longer heard the happy cries of a three-year-old, that lost a first-grader just as she was learning to read.

The graveyard at Miango tells us something about God and about his grace. It testifies that God is not a jolly grandfather who satisfies our every desire. Certainly those parents wanted their children to live. They pled with God, but he denied their request.

The graves also show us that God is not a calculating merchant who withholds his goods until we produce enough good works or faith to buy his help. If anyone had earned credit with God, it would have been these missionaries. They left all to spread the gospel in a hostile environment. But God does not hand out merit pay.

Not only do we learn about God's nature from the Miango graveyard, but we also discover truths about his grace. God's grace may be free, but it is not cheap. Neither purchasing our salvation nor letting us know of the gift was inexpensive.

Beginning with Abel, many of the witnesses to divine grace sealed their words with their blood. Jesus asked the Jews which of the prophets was not persecuted? When he first sent out his disciples, he promised them betrayal and death. Then, at the end of his ministry, he promised his followers that as they carried his word, they would face trouble and hatred.

"The only way we can understand the graveyard at Miango," White concluded, "is to remember that God also buried his Son on the mission field."

For a missionary couple who stand beside a mound of earth in a garden in Nigeria, no logical explanation of unanswered prayer will suffice. They must place their faith in a God who has yet to fulfill the promise that good will overcome evil, that God's good purposes will, in the end, prevail. To cling to that belief may represent the ultimate rationalization — or the ultimate act of faith.

CHAPTER 17

UNANSWERED PRAYER:
LIVING WITH THE MYSTERY

O that thou shouldst give dust a tongue
To crie to thee
And then not heare it crying!
GEORGE HERBERT

Some, but not all, unanswered prayers trace back to a fault in the one who prays. Some, but not all, trace back to God's mystifying respect for human freedom and refusal to coerce. Some, but not all, trace back to dark powers contending against God's rule. Some, but not all, trace back to a planet marred with disease, violence, and the potential for tragic accident. How, then, can we make sense of any single experience of unanswered prayer?

I take odd comfort in the fact that the Bible itself includes numerous prayers that went unanswered. Although we can only speculate why God does not answer a given prayer, these biblical examples lay down useful clues.

- After leading the Israelites through the wilderness for forty years, Moses pled with God to allow him to accompany them across the Jordan River before he died. God refused this request as punishment for Moses' past outbursts, which so rankled Moses that four times in his speeches to the Israelites in Deuteronomy he lashed out, blaming them for God's refusal. On other occasions Moses had talked God into "changing his mind." Not this time.
- King David spent a week, prostrate and spurning all food, praying that his infant son not die. As a consequence of his grievous sin, that prayer went unanswered: David and Bathsheba lost the child. Nevertheless, a later union led to the birth of Solomon, who would rule over Israel's Golden Age.

- Four characters in the Old Testament—Moses, Job, Jonah, and Elijah—actually prayed to die. Fortunately for them, God ignored their requests.
- Several times the armies of Israel prayed for victory over their enemies, only to suffer humiliating defeats. Each event prompted soul-searching. Did the army act precipitously, against God's orders? Had some soldier committed a war crime that displeased God?
- The prophet Habbakuk prayed for deliverance from the Babylonians; Jeremiah prayed that Jerusalem not be destroyed. Both prophets' prayers went unanswered, and each struggled to explain the reason to a defeated nation. "You have covered yourself with a cloud so that no prayer can get through," lamented the prophet in a book aptly titled Lamentations.

I have mentioned some of the twelve disciples' inappropriate prayers, such as calling for fire from heaven against a town. In one instance the disciples proved unable to perform a miracle of healing and seemed puzzled by the failure (see Matthew 17 and Mark 9). Jesus used the opportunity to rebuke their lack of faith. Although the disciples' prayers had gone unanswered, clearly it was God's will that the boy be healed, for Jesus then accomplished what they could not.

The apostle Paul had his share of unanswered prayers: you need only read his luminous prayers for churches and then read the sad record of those churches to realize how far short they fell of the ideal for which he prayed. In his most famous unanswered prayer, Paul pleaded with the Lord three times for the removal of the "thorn in my flesh." In a model response to a negative answer, he put behind him the disappointment of not getting what he wanted and instead accepted what he got:

> Therefore I will boast all the more gladly about my weaknesses, so that Christ's power may rest on me. That is why, for Christ's sake, I delight in weaknesses, in insults, in hardships, in persecutions, in difficulties. For when I am weak, then I am strong.

Not even Jesus was exempt from unanswered prayer. In Gethesemane Jesus prayed with both the faith of protest and the faith of acquiescence. He turned for help first to God, pleading "let this cup pass"; then to his friends, who were sound asleep; then to the religious rulers, who accused him; then to the state, which sentenced him; then to the people, who rejected him. Finally he uttered that awful cry of dereliction, "My God, why have you forsaken me?" For C. S. Lewis, that sequence of helplessness illustrates "the human situation writ large.... Every rope breaks when you seize it. Every door is slammed shut as you reach it."

From these unanswered prayers I gain a glimmer of insight into the riddle of prayer. What if David's son had lived and reigned as king instead of Solomon? What if the prophets' prayers had been answered and Israel had established itself as a world power, its citizens holding their religion tight to their chests, unshared with the world? What if Paul had been healed, making him a more agile missionary perhaps but one of insufferable pride as he feared? Finally, what if Jesus had received the answer he prayed for in a moment of dread? His rescue would have meant the planet's ruin.

C. S. Lewis observes:

> The essence of request, as distinct from compulsion, is that it may or may not be granted. And if an infinitely wise Being listens to the requests of finite and foolish creatures, of course He will sometimes grant and sometimes refuse them. Invariable "success" in prayer would not prove the Christian doctrine at all. It would prove something much more like magic.
>
> It is not unreasonable for a headmaster to say, "Such and such things you may do according to the fixed rules of this school. But such and such other things are too dangerous to be left to general rules. If you want to do them you must come and make a request and talk over the whole matter with me in my study. And then — we'll see."

Sweeping Promises

As Lewis acknowledged, the real problem lies not in the fact of refusal but in the Bible's lavish promises. In a nutshell, the main difficulty with unanswered prayers is that Jesus seemed to promise there need not be any.

Jesus could have said something like this: "I am bestowing the gift of prayer. You must realize, of course, that humans cannot have perfect wisdom, so there are limits as to whether your prayers will be answered. Prayer operates like a suggestion box. Spell out your requests clearly to God, and I guarantee that all requests will be carefully considered." That kind of statement about prayer I can easily live with. Instead, here is what Jesus said:

> I tell you the truth, if you have faith and do not doubt ... you can say to this mountain, "Go, throw yourself into the sea," and it will be done. If you believe, you will receive whatever you ask for in prayer.

Again, I tell you that if two of you on earth agree about anything you ask for, it will be done for you by my Father in heaven.

Therefore I tell you, whatever you ask for in prayer, believe that you have received it, and it will be yours.

You may ask me for anything in my name and I will do it.

These represent just a sampling of the New Testament's sweeping claims made in plain language. Some preachers seize on these passages as a kind of club, flogging the church for not taking them literally and faulting believers for having too little faith. But how to account for the unanswered prayers of Jesus and Paul? And how can we reconcile the lavish promises with the actual experience of so many sincere Christians who struggle with unanswered prayer?

One possible explanation centers in the specific group of people whom Jesus was addressing: the disciples. Could it be that Jesus gave the Twelve, handpicked to carry on the work after his death, certain rights and privileges in prayer that would not be normative for every follower? The Gospel writers do not explicitly say "These commands apply to the disciples only," but they do specify in each case that Jesus was speaking to his intimate disciples, not a large crowd.

Jesus invested in the disciples a unique discernment into God's will. "Everything that I learned from my Father I have made known to you," he told them at the Last Supper. After spending three years schooled directly by Jesus, they would presumably have a good idea of which prayers would further God's purpose on earth and which would be capricious or self-serving. (Yet the letters credited to Peter and John show that prayer did not operate like magic for the disciples either. Those two, like Paul, expressed frustration over developments in the church contrary to their prayers. And historians tell of the martyrdom of ten of the disciples. Surely the prayer "let this cup pass" must have run through their minds at some point.)

Another explanation focuses on the "fine print" that modifies the lavish promises. Virtually all of them contain a qualifier, such as "whatever you ask *in my name*," or "*If* you remain in me and my words remain in you." The assurance of answered prayers, still sweeping in its scope, comes with conditions. Am I abiding in Christ? Am I making requests according to his will? Am I obeying his commands? Each of these underscores the relationship, the companionship with God. The more we know God, the more we know God's will, the more likely our prayers will align with that will.

After pondering this problem for years and discussing it with "about every Christian I know, learned or simple, lay or clerical, within my own Communion or without," C. S. Lewis finally concluded that the kind of dauntless faith called for by Jesus "occurs only when the one who prays does so as God's fellow-worker, demanding what is needed for the joint work. It is the prophet's, the apostle's, the missionary's, the healer's prayer that is made with this confidence.... Something of the divine foreknowledge enters his mind." In other words, one who works in close partnership with God grows in the ability to discern what God wants to accomplish on earth, and prays accordingly.

Prayer for a Prodigal

JANIS

I've been a single mom for twelve years, shouldering the bulk of the responsibility of raising my four daughters. My youngest resented her father's absence from our lives more than her sisters, and rebelled against me because he wasn't around. I became worn out trying to keep peace at home and keep her from disaster.

Finally, I realized I was carrying the load of being both mom and dad, and God wasn't asking me to. One day I bowed my head in despair and said, "Lord, I can't go on with her anymore. I love my daughter dearly, but you love her more. I'm letting go and asking you to do what it takes to bring her heart to you." I cried because I knew it might take a difficult time to bring her to Jesus, and I would have to keep my hands off her so he could do his best work. My job was to continually pray for my daughter and for her friends, whom I disliked.

Did it take a difficult time to bring her back? Yes. She's pregnant and broken. Her friends recommended an abortion, but she decided to keep the baby. Six months into her pregnancy she came to me and said, "I know God's calling me, and he's going to use this baby to help me straighten out my life."

After my shock wore off, I heard that wonderful, still small voice whisper, *Remember, I love her, and my plans are not your plans. I want to bring healing to the broken parts of her life you don't even know about.* Peace flooded my soul. I'm so thrilled to know God's at work in her life, and I can trust him to continue the process.

236

A Time to Wait

In no way do I mean to dilute the majestic promises about prayer given by Jesus, James, John, and others in the New Testament. God knows—truly, God knows—I need more of the bold and simple faith those passages call for. On the other hand, considering them in isolation leads to a "name it and claim it" mentality that ignores much other revelation. The same Jesus who spoke of faith as a mustard seed also gave us the story about a widow wearing down a judge with her persistence. And all through the Bible spiritual giants wrestle with God in their prayers.

As we have seen, Jesus himself set limits to the requests he made. "Take this cup," he asked, and then added the modifier about the Father's will. He prayed that Peter's faith would hold firm, but not that Peter avoid all testing. He declined to pray for angels' help in rescuing him from execution.

So, too, do we all set limits to our prayers. Some things we can ask for unconditionally, such as forgiveness, and compassion for the poor, and progress in growing the fruit of the Spirit. Other requests are conditional, such as Paul's plea for relief from the "thorn." Some we refrain from asking out of respect for the natural laws that govern the planet. I pray that God will help my uncle cope with diabetes, but not that God restore his amputated leg. Nor do I pray that God would shift the orbit of planet Earth to counteract global warming. Instead, I ask what my own role should be in helping my uncle and in addressing environmental concerns.

I also learn, as I ponder the mystery of unanswered prayer, simply to wait.

The Lord is good unto them that wait for him.

But they that wait upon the Lord shall renew their strength; they shall mount up with wings as eagles; they shall run, and not be weary; and they shall walk, and not faint.

And let us not be weary in well doing: for in due season we shall reap, if we faint not.

Daniel waited three weeks for an answer to his prayer. Seeking guidance in the midst of war, Jeremiah waited ten days before receiving an answer. After climbing Mount Sinai to receive the Ten Commandments, Moses waited six days before hearing God's voice. Jesus, too, waited. When he performed an impressive miracle, his followers wanted to spread the word immediately. Jesus hushed them: "My time has not yet come." He understood something about God that we impatient types overlook: God acts *slowly*.

Think of the centuries that passed between the disruption caused by Adam and the reconciliation brought by Jesus: centuries that included Abraham's waiting for a child, the Israelites' waiting for liberation, the prophets' waiting for Messiah. Biblical history tells a meandering, zigzag tale of doglegs and detours. God's plan unfolds like a leisurely opera, not a Top 40 tune. For those of us caught in any one phrase of the opera, especially a mournful phrase, the music may seem unbearably sad. Onward it moves, at deliberate speed and with great effort.

The very tedium, the act of waiting itself, works to nourish in us qualities of patience, persistence, trust, gentleness, compassion—or it may do so, if we place ourselves in the stream of God's movement on earth. It may take more faith to trust God when we do not get what we ask for than when we do. Is that not the point of Hebrews 11? That chapter includes the poignant comment that the heroes of faith were "commended for their faith, yet none of them received what had been promised." It then intertwines their frustrated destiny with ours: "God had planned something better for us so that only together with us would they be made perfect." Faith calls us to trust in a future-oriented God.

Scoffers will call such a pledge into question, as the Bible freely admits. "They will say, ' ... Ever since our fathers died, everything goes on as it has since the beginning of creation.' ... But do not forget this one thing, dear friends: With the Lord a day is like a thousand years, and a thousand years are like a day. The Lord is not slow in keeping his promise, as some understand slowness. He is patient with you, not wanting anyone to perish, but everyone to come to repentance." With all the time in the world, God waits, tolerating the insults of human history out of mercy, not impotence.

Even Psalms, the Bible's prayer book so profuse with groans and laments, circles back repeatedly to the theme of God's faithfulness. No matter how circumstances appear at any given moment, we can trust the fact that God still rules the universe. The divine reputation rests on a solemn pact that one day all shall be well.

The Surprise Factor

I have a friend in Japan who provides resources to the underground church in China and often worships among them. One day I asked her, "How do Chinese Christians pray? Do their prayers differ from what you hear in the U.S. or Japan?" She replied that the prayers closely follow the pattern of the

Lord's Prayer. The church has spread most widely among the lower classes, and when they ask for daily bread and deliverance from evil, they mean it literally.

She continued, "I've heard Chinese Christians pray for the leaders of their government, but never for a change in the government — even in areas that persecute the unregistered churches. They pray very practically, thanking God for today's grace, asking for tomorrow's protection. They tell us visitors, 'Don't pray for me to get out of prison, please pray for courage and strength so that I can witness boldly in the prison and not lose faith.'"

When I visit places like Nepal and China, I come upon a paradox of answered and unanswered prayers. On the one hand, I hear remarkable stories of miracles. For example, the first Nepalese became a Christian in 1950. Now the church numbers more than half a million, and Nepalese church leaders estimate that 80 percent of the converts have resulted from physical healings: a Christian prays for a sick neighbor who then gets well. I have interviewed European and American doctors who work there as missionaries, and they admit that they have no scientific explanation for some amazing recoveries they have seen. David Aikman's book *Jesus in Beijing* reports a similar pattern of apparent miracles in China.

On the other hand, Christians in Nepal and China tell horrific stories of oppression, imprisonment, and torture. My Japanese friend introduced me to a Chinese pastor revered as one of four patriarchs in the unregistered church, a giant of faith who spent twenty-three years in prison because he refused to halt his church activities. Pastor Yuan told me with great excitement of a miracle: during his long sentence in a prison near Mongolia, he worked daily outdoors wearing nothing but a light jacket in the harshest winter weather and never caught a common cold or influenza. I marveled at his story, but inwardly I could not help wondering why God answered that prayer and not the thousands of prayers from church members pleading for his release.

I asked my Japanese friend how to reconcile this strange combination of miraculous answers to prayer in the midst of intense persecution. If God can heal sick people or prevent illness, then why not protect suffering Christians? (As soon as I phrased the question, I had to smile, for that replicates the pattern of the book of Acts.) She thought for a moment and said, "I know this is a 'textbook' answer, but everything is in our Lord's hands. And he shows his glory in each occasion."

In all my prayers, whether I get the answers I want or not, I can count on this one fact: God can make use of whatever happens. Nothing is irredeemable. "Teach me, O God, so to use all the circumstances of my life today that they may bring forth in me the fruits of holiness rather than the fruits of sin," prayed the British author John Baillie:

> Let me use disappointment as material for patience.
> Let me use success as material for thankfulness.
> Let me use trouble as material for perseverance.
> Let me use danger as material for courage.
> Let me use reproach as material for long suffering.
> Let me use praise as material for humility.
> Let me use pleasures as material for temperance.
> Let me use pain as material for endurance.

By selfish nature I tend to pray for successes, happy outcomes, and relief from difficulties. And I must say, with gratitude, I have experienced my share of the good things life offers. But in the Beatitudes Jesus calls "blessed" those who experience the very opposite: poverty, mourning, hunger, persecution. How would my faith survive, and my prayers change, if life took a dramatic turn for the worse — if I came down with a degenerative disease or lost my home or landed in prison because of my beliefs? Could I fill in the blanks of John Baillie's prayers with details of my own newly lapsed state? Would I humbly allow the Spirit to accomplish God's purposes in me even through such unwelcome agents?

I have a book titled *Prayers of the Martyrs*, which reproduces actual prayers of martyrs from AD 107 (Ignatius of Antioch) to 1980 (Archbishop Oscar Romero). I find it shocking how few prayed for deliverance as in the background lions roared, gladiators sharpened their swords, or, in Romero's case, assassins fastened ammunition clips onto their automatic weapons. The martyrs prayed for families left behind, for steadfastness of faith, for strength to endure death without shame. Some thanked God for the privilege of suffering, surprised they would be counted worthy. Some forgave their persecutors. Very few asked for a miracle.

God's Smile

Theologian Ronald Goetz calls himself an "occasionist": God acts in response to prayer, he believes, but with baffling unpredictability. (Of course, most of us pray with baffling unpredictability, too.) Review the alternatives, though. God could act alone, ignoring us and our prayers. Or God could leave matters entirely in our hands with no direct involvement in human history. The first option contradicts the whole motive behind creating personal beings made in God's image; the second option is too ominous to contemplate.

We have, instead, a relationship with God based on constant negotiation. We inform God what we think should be done in the world, and in the process God reminds us of our own role in doing it. Rarely do we get everything we want, and I imagine the same holds true for God.

The trail of God at work rarely follows a straight line, which means our prayers may well produce different answers than we expect. For whatever reason—God's sense of irony, antagonistic spiritual powers, the vicissitudes of a fallen planet—prayers get answered in ways we could neither predict nor imagine.

Each December actors in Christmas pageants recite the jubilant responses of two cousins, the elderly infertile Elizabeth and the young virgin Mary, as they learn news of their surprise pregnancies. How must Mary have looked back on her great prayer, the Magnificat, as she saw Jesus crucified by the very rulers she had hoped he would vanquish? And Elizabeth's husband Zechariah, who had prophesied "salvation from our enemies and from the hand of all who hate us"—what did he think as he watched his son John grow into an insect-eating dissident who got beheaded by one of those enemies? Both families prayed fervently, and neither got the answer they expected.

Sometimes, though, an unanswered prayer opens the door to something far better. For fifteen years Monica prayed for her son Augustine as he indulged his senses and investigated exotic philosophies. When Augustine finally converted, these were the very experiences that gave depth and richness to his writings, allowing him to set the course of Christian thought for centuries. Once, Monica prayed all night that God would stop her son from going to wicked Rome, but he tricked her and sailed away. It was on that trip, in fact, that Augustine became a Christian. Reflecting later, he said that God denied his mother once in order to grant her what she had prayed for always.

Edith Schaeffer, the daughter of missionaries, tells of Dr. Hoste, the successor to Hudson Taylor as director of China Inland Mission, praying daily on a walk that lasted four hours. He counted that task his chief responsibility as leader of the mission and mentioned each missionary and child by name. Within a few years, however, Chairman Mao would evict all seven thousand missionaries from China, including all those for whom Hoste prayed. They relocated to places like the Philippines, Hong Kong, and Singapore, dismayed at what might happen to the fledgling church in China now bereft of outside help. In their absence, under a dictatorial regime that forbade Christian evangelism, the greatest numerical revival in history broke out. What happened in China, and is happening now, exceeds beyond all dreams the prayer requests of the missionaries of 1950.

"If you want to see God smile, tell him your plans," goes an old saying.

Human Agents

In answering prayers, God normally relies on human agents. On a visit to Holland I heard the story of strict Dutch Calvinist farmers who, during the devastating floods of the 1950s, climbed onto the roofs of their barns but refused to be rescued. "God's will be done," they said.

War Prayers

JOHN

My family lived in Beirut, Lebanon, all through the civil war of the 1980s. A hundred and fifty thousand people died in that war, which went on for years, and I tell you that changes the way you pray. I led Bible studies in various parts of the city, and each night we would try to determine from the tracer bullets where the snipers were firing that night and schedule our meetings around them.

I am Lebanese, married to an American, and her family and our friends in the U.S. pled with us to leave until the violence calmed down. We both felt called to stay, though, sensing clearly that God wanted us there. I felt God should lead us *to* something else, not just *away* from something. What would happen if Christians always packed up and left when trouble broke out?

In wartime, prayers get very practical. *Keep my kids safe, Lord. Bring us some peacemakers. Please, may the bombing not start up again. Don't let this hatred get passed on to the next generation. Lord, don't let my kids find me dead someday.* Many nights my wife went to bed praying Psalm 91:3-5. The young people I worked with saw sights no one should see: bodies tied to the bumpers

Someone made a joke about one such farmer who sat on his roof with flood waters swirling around him. A neighbor in a rowboat offered him help, which he declined, insisting, "God will protect me." A helicopter buzzed overhead, its rescue party lowering a rope and ordering through a loudspeaker, "Grab the rope, and we'll pull you to safety." The farmer stubbornly shook his head no.

Soon the water engulfed the barn and swept the farmer away. In heaven he demanded an explanation from God. "I counted on you to protect me! Why didn't you answer my prayers?"

God replied, "I sent you a rowboat and then a helicopter. What more did you want?"

Those of us who struggle with unanswered prayer dare not overlook an important theological truth about how God acts in this world today. The church is the body of Christ, and as such it does God's work. As Ronald

---

of cars and pulled along the cobblestone streets, a severed head mounted like a hood ornament on a Mercedes. I prayed that somehow those images not scar these kids forever.

You pray these things, and then sometimes it seems the war drags on under its own power, oblivious to any prayers and any forces for peace. You live with a permanent knot in your stomach. You jump when a door bangs shut.

I could tell stories of God's protection, such as the time a militia installed missile batteries down the road from our apartment (which would, of course, attract return fire) and they all misfired harmlessly into an embankment. Yet I also know many friends who lost family members. My deaf neighbor didn't hear a command to stop and got shot, leaving his family fatherless. A South African missionary was shot point blank; a Muslim convert died when a bomb intended for Dutch missionaries exploded in his face. These people, too, prayed for protection.

Lebanon is peaceful now, and sometimes I look back on the war as a time of closeness with God. We were pressed to God every day. I learned to live each day by faith, whether I had the emotional feeling or not, whether life made sense or not.

Rolheiser expresses it, "A theist believes in a God in heaven whereas a Christian believes in a God in heaven who is also physically present on this earth inside of human beings.... God is still present, as physical and as real today as God was in the historical Jesus. God still has skin, human skin, and physically walks on this earth just as Jesus did."

To pray "God, please help my neighbor cope with her financial problems," or "God, do something about the homeless downtown" is the approach of a theist, not a Christian. God has chosen to express love and grace in the world through those of us who embody Christ.

As a journalist I see this principle at work in inspiring ways. While writing this book I have made trips to several different countries. I visited a church in South Africa, 35,000 members strong, which runs outreach programs including a prison ministry, a hospital, and a rehabilitation farm for addicts. In the same city I visited a woman who recruits volunteers to come in daily and act as surrogate mothers to children afflicted with AIDS. Two months later I traveled to Nepal where I met with health workers from fifteen nations who serve under a mission specializing in leprosy work. Historically, most of the major advances in leprosy treatment have come from Christian missionaries—mainly because they were the only ones willing to treat the dreaded disease.

A few months later, in Wisconsin, I attended a conference on ministry to women in prostitution that attracted representatives from thirty different nations. They work to counter illegal sex trafficking and also to liberate women from prostitution, which in poor nations constitutes a modern form of slavery. From there I went to a Salvation Army conference where I heard stories from the world's third-largest standing "army"—this one mobilized to help the poor and downtrodden—then to Roanoke, Virginia, where I visited a sprawling complex that began as a rescue mission and, through the help of sixty churches, grew into a shelter, education center, and clinic.

As I interviewed the leaders of these ministries, I learned that many began with a crisis of faith, indeed a crisis of prayer. *God, why don't you do something about the homeless families in Roanoke . . . or the AIDS orphans in Johannesburg? Don't they break your heart?* Inevitably, there followed a prayer echoing the one prayed by Bob Pierce, founder of the global charity World Vision: "Lord, may my heart be broken by what breaks your heart." Those who responded became the answers to their own prayers.

Children view God as a celestial version of Santa Claus who sits on a cloud considering requests and funneling answers like presents down a chimney. A better model might be the president of a large corporation who must occasionally step in to manage a crisis but prefers to delegate tasks to trusted managers and employees. Or better yet, the metaphor the New Testament relies on: a human body, in which all parts of the body are organically joined and cooperate to carry out the will of the head.

An Apostle's Prayer

The apostle Paul had one overriding desire: that fellow Jews would embrace the Messiah he had encountered on the road to Damascus. "I have great sorrow and unceasing anguish in my heart," he said. "For I could wish that I myself were cursed and cut off from Christ for the sake of my brothers, those of my own race, the people of Israel." No doubt Paul prayed to that end daily, yet seldom saw it answered. In city after city his fellow Jews rejected him and he turned to the Gentiles.

I see in Paul's response to that disappointment an ideal pattern of coping with an unanswered prayer. In the first place, he did not simply make a request and resign himself to God's decision. Paul the human agent put feet to his prayer, making a habit of going first to the synagogue when he entered a new town, often at great personal cost as his visits led to riots.

Furthermore, Paul persevered, even when it became increasingly clear that his prayer was not being answered. John Calvin said, "We must repeat the same supplications not twice or three times only, but as often as we have need, a hundred and a thousand times.... We must never be weary in waiting for God's help."

Apparently, however, Paul did grow weary. In his most elegant letter, he sets as his centerpiece (Romans 9–11) a passionate passage, a verbal wrestling match with God in which he struggles openly with this the great unanswered prayer of his life.

Paul acknowledges one important side benefit (the "surprise factor") of this most distressing development: the Jews' rejection of Jesus led to his acceptance by the Gentiles. It seems strange, he admits, that the Gentiles who did not pursue God's gift attained it whereas the Jews who did pursue it have not attained it—not yet, anyway.

Paul is trying to make sense of history, a very personal history. Sometimes his passion interrupts: "Brothers, my heart's desire and prayer to God for the Israelites is that they may be saved." He plows over the same ground, looking for something he may have missed. And he concludes that God hasn't rejected the Jews; to the contrary, they have the same opportunity as Gentiles. God has widened, not closed, the embrace of humanity.

The prose begins to soar as Paul steps back to consider the big picture. And then comes this burst of doxology in the midst of Paul's dissertation on an unanswered prayer:

> Oh, the depth of the riches of the wisdom and knowledge of God!
> How unsearchable his judgments,
>> and his paths beyond tracing out!
> "Who has known the mind of the Lord?
>> Or who has been his counselor?"
> "Who has ever given to God,
>> that God should repay him?"
> For from him and through him and to him are all things.
> To him be the glory forever! Amen.

In a flash Paul has gained a glimpse of the view from the top of the mountain, not timberline, the view from Andromeda, not Rome.* In that glimpse, somehow the doleful events of history and theologians' mind-numbing theodicies, the unsolved mysteries and unanswered prayers all fade to grey against the Technicolor panorama of God's plan for the ages. God is the potter, we are the clay. God is the Father, we are the children.

Perhaps more accurately, God is the playwright, we are the actors. That prayer exists at all is a gift of grace, a generous invitation to participate in the future of the cosmos.

In the end, unanswered prayer brings me face-to-face with the mystery that silenced Paul: the profound difference between my perspective and God's.

> "For my thoughts are not your thoughts,
>> neither are your ways my ways,"
>> declares the Lord.

> "As the heavens are higher than the earth,
>> so are my ways higher than your ways
>> and my thoughts than your thoughts."

---

* William Sloane Coffin says of this passage about God's unsearchable judgments, "Christianity is less a set of beliefs than a way of life, and a way of life that actually warns against absolute intellectual certainty."

A Senior Citizen's Prayer

As I was writing this chapter, my wife recommended that I interview some senior citizens about prayer. "Most of them pray, and they've been at it a long time," she said. "Surely they'll have some wisdom for you."

She was right. I accompanied her to the retirement center where she assists as a chaplain, and that morning I heard one miracle story after another. One of the seniors had felt a sudden urge to leave a card game and go home. As she walked in the door she saw that a candle had burned to the nub, igniting a bouquet of plastic roses—a fire she was able to smother with a pillow just in time. Another told of remarkable survival stories from World War II. Another told of her husband choking on a homemade cinnamon roll, just as two paramedics walked past who saved his life by performing the Heimlich maneuver.

I heard, too, of prayers for world peace and against injustice. Those prayers saw seniors through the scary times of a world war and then a cold war that threatened the very survival of the species. One African-American senior reminisced about praying while growing up as a second-class citizen in the South. Who could imagine then the changes she would live through?

Although I probed for accounts of unanswered prayers, most of the seniors preferred to talk about answered prayers. All of them could tell of family tragedies and health breakdowns, but somehow these events did not shake their faith in prayer.

After our meeting, however, I wandered through a portion of the facility that cares for seniors who need more assistance. They lay in beds or sat in wheelchairs. One man was so slouched over that his chin rested on the wheelchair tray. Some wore orthopedic boots, some hummed nervously, some drooled, some snored. One woman with a vacant stare waved a banana in her hand. Another repeated the same phrase over and over. I tried talking to these seniors, too, but the lights in their minds had gone out. Any secrets they had learned about prayer lay hidden beyond retrieval.

I drove away from the facility more convinced than ever that the only final solution to unanswered prayer is Paul's explanation to the Corinthians: "For now we see through a glass, darkly; but then face to face: now I know in part; but then shall I know even as also I am known." No human being, no matter how wise or how spiritual, can interpret the ways of God, explain why one miracle and not another, why an apparent intervention here and not there. Along with the apostle Paul, we can only wait, and trust.

CHAPTER 18

PRAYER AND PHYSICAL HEALING

Behind me he says, "Your sins are forgiven."
I think "That's good but not why I came."
I turn and say "Am I also cured?"
He comes close but looks down. He says "That too ..."

REYNOLDS PRICE

More than half the spontaneous prayers I hear in church pertain to the sick. In the broader picture of prayer, that gives the same imbalance as a pastor preaching from the book of Job every Sunday. At the same time, it also shows how instinctively we turn to prayer when illness strikes.

When asked to speak to my church on the topic, "What I Have Learned About Suffering," I pulled out the thick folders of letters I have received in response to my books on suffering. On Sunday I set the letters on a table onstage beside me. They made a large pile, perhaps a thousand letters in all, each one representing a story, usually a tragic story, most of them asking poignant questions about physical healing.

One of the letters comes from a couple who were leaders in their church. In 1991 their twenty-one-year-old son, a scholarship athlete and youth leader in the church, fell asleep at the wheel while driving a green Datsun pickup truck. The accident severed his aorta and caused paralysis from the waist down. Thirty thousand people in the close-knit community prayed for divine healing, elders anointed him with oil, and a national television minister prayed over him. Fifteen years later, the young man is still paralyzed. "Where was the answered prayer that I longed to share with my friends?" writes the mother. "Where was my Father in heaven who sees the sparrow that falls and loves my son even more than I?" The father minces no words. "What is the value of prayer?" he asks.

A woman in New Zealand tells of her eighteen-month-old son who has Down syndrome. Like a small percentage of others with that affliction, he suffers from an incurable condition called megakaryoblastic leukemia, which thickens the marrow so that his body cannot produce blood cells. His spleen enlarges, filling the pelvic area so that he cannot sit up. Already the toddler has had nine complete blood transfusions. She prays, yes, pleading to God for mercy while she holds her son tight against her body to control his convulsive sobs as the doctor probes for a vein.

Two different letters describe the onset of Huntington's chorea, a nerve-destroying disease that afflicts 50 percent of the carrier's offspring and leads to a slow, debilitating death. One woman first learned she carried the gene when her thirty-year-old daughter came down with the disease. Now her twenty-seven-year-old son has begun to show symptoms. He is very angry at God, she says. He knows exactly what will happen to him because for three years he has been watching his sister's health deteriorate. Another man writes that his brother was just diagnosed with Huntington's, which means he has a 50 percent chance of getting it too, and his three teenage children likewise have a 50 percent chance. So far, he has declined to be tested. Does prayer carry any weight against a defect scripted into the genes at conception?

Most of the letters tell of judgment and confusing messages received from the church. Some Christians, it seems, presume that suffering betrays a flaw in the afflicted person: either the sufferer is being punished for some sin or lacks healing because of inadequate faith. These suggestions, reminiscent of Job's comforters and coming at a time of such vulnerability, may hurt worse than the physical pain itself.

I would never want to dampen someone's faith, because bold faith surely impressed Jesus. Yet the stack of letters from my file cabinet convinces me that we can do equal harm by holding out false hope of physical healing. Believe me, there is nothing I would rather say to parents of a Down syndrome child or to families waiting on edge for Huntington's chorea to manifest itself than, "Just believe, and you will be healed." But I know of no miraculous healings of those conditions, and to offer false hope would be even more cruel.

I am left to struggle with the dilemma of prayer and physical healing. Many books and articles report physical healings and hold out extravagant hope. However, I mostly hear from earnest believers whose prayers go unanswered, and for this reason I present a perspective that may well seem unbalanced, focusing on those who do not readily find healing.

From Cultic to Mainstream

In my lifetime a sea change has taken place: physical healing has moved from the realm of cultism, the domain of Pentecostals and superstitious Catholics, to mainstream acceptance.

During my childhood, each summer "faith healers" would come to the suburbs of Atlanta and set up tents. Posters promised deliverance from disease, and sometimes I would stand at the edge of the tents listening to the strange sounds of tongue-speaking and slayings in the Spirit inside. They spooked me, and I regarded the healers as urban cousins to the snake handlers operating in the hills of northern Georgia just up the road. I also remember, as a tourist in my twenties, visiting shrines in France and Mexico where pilgrims had hung tiny metal replicas of body parts—eyes, ears, legs, lungs, kidneys, breasts, stomachs—as tokens of their prayers for healing. In earlier times Catholics had designated particular saints to address particular ailments: St. Apollo for toothache, St. Roch for plague, and so on.

As a young journalist I had encounters with faith healing both farcical and tragic. In the heyday of the PTL Club television program, I heard Tammy Faye Bakker tearfully describe the trauma of her little dog Chi Chi, who ate too many lima beans and fell over dead. "I thought my world had come to an end," said Tammy Faye. When her prayers that God raise Chi Chi from the dead went unanswered, Tammy Faye came to terms with it by realizing, "The fact was that Chi Chi was a naughty little dog.... God knew that if he took him then that would be the end of wetting all over the room."

Later, I interviewed parents who attended a Faith Assembly church in Indiana and accepted the church's teaching that faith alone can heal any disease and that to look elsewhere for help—for example, to medical doctors—demonstrates a lack of trust in God. Two such parents, Larry and Lucky Parker, watched their eleven-year-old son die of diabetic complications, which led to their arrest for involuntary manslaughter and child abuse. (They later renounced their theological error in a book, *We Let Our Son Die.*) Medical researchers determined that the infant mortality rate for Faith Assembly churches was three times normal—at least 126 children died after medical treatment was withheld—and the mortality rate associated with childbirth was a hundred times greater.

In the 1970s and 1980s, mainstream media pounced on such stories. National magazines did profiles of remorseful parents and dutifully reported the court cases. CBS television made a movie about the Parkers' tragic story. The news programs 60 Minutes and Frontline highlighted abuses by Benny Hinn and other prominent faith healers.

A remarkable shift has taken place in recent years, however. In the last decade each of the three largest U.S. news magazines has featured a cover story detailing the effects of prayer on health. Books by prominent physicians such as Larry Dossey, Herbert Benson, Harold Koenig, and Bernie Siegel have climbed the bestseller charts, touting scientific studies that prove the relation between prayer and physical healing. Seventy medical schools, with prestigious Duke and Harvard at the forefront, now offer courses examining the role of spirituality in health.

A 2003 survey reported five hundred clinical studies documenting correlations between religious practices, including prayer, and better health. Eight in ten Americans believe that miracles can happen today, and more than half of all doctors report observing miracles in their patients that defy medical explanation.

What happened to bring faith healing from the cultic to the mainstream? And does the new appreciation for spirituality in the healing process offer any hope to those — like the people who wrote me letters — who have seen no results from their prayers?

The Inbuilt Miracle

The change in attitude came about because for the first time researchers applied the research techniques of double-blind studies to measure the effect of prayer on health. Volunteers agreed to pray for one set of patients but not another, with neither patients nor medical staff knowing who was being prayed for. To the astonishment of medical researchers, one study after another indicated that even anonymous prayers organized for an experiment have an effect. In one famous study, volunteers prayed for half of 393 heart-attack patients at a San Francisco hospital. Among the group prayed for, significantly fewer died, most had a faster recovery requiring the use of fewer potent drugs, and none had to be put on life support.

Not everyone finds these studies convincing; some are methodologically flawed, and other studies have yielded contradictory results. One statistic seems incontrovertible, though. It "blew my socks away," says the epidemiologist who reviewed the various studies. "People who regularly attend church have a 25 percent reduction in mortality—that is, they live longer—than people who are not churchgoers."

Dr. Harold G. Koenig, a psychiatrist who directs Duke University's Center for the Study of Religion/Spirituality and Health, reports on many of these findings in the book *The Healing Power of Faith*. Selected chapter titles alone signal his conclusions:

Religious People Have Stronger Marriages and Families

Religious People Have Healthy Lifestyles

Religious People Cope Well with Stress

Religion Offers Protection from Depression and Helps Those Afflicted to Recover Quickly

---

A Partial Miracle

VINCE

If you met me on the street, scooting around in my wheelchair, you probably wouldn't think of me as a specimen of physical healing. But compared to who I was in June 2003, I've been healed.

I packed a lot into my life before the accident. I traveled to five of the seven continents, scuba dived the Great Barrier Reef, worked as an electrician at the South Pole, and took mission trips to Mexico and Indonesia. Nowadays I'm stumped by a doorway less than twenty-eight inches wide and a step more than four inches high. If I let myself look backwards instead of looking to the future, I get stuck in a mud-pit of depression.

I was returning from climbing one of Colorado's 14,000-foot mountains when my motorcycle slid out from under me. For the next eight days I lay in a deep coma, with traumatic injury to both my brain and spinal cord. I would not blink when a cotton swab was placed on my eyeball. I could not breathe on my own. The doctors suggested taking me off life support since, they said, I'd never regain brain function and would probably remain in a permanent vegetative state.

My family would have none of it. The night of the accident, they claimed Psalm 57 for me. On the eighth day God answered their prayers from the verse that says, "Awake my soul, awake harp and lyre, I will awaken the dawn." That dawn I started to open my eyes and the doctors told them to

Religious People Live Longer, Healthier Lives

Religion May Protect People from Serious Cardiovascular Disease

Religious People May Have Stronger Immune Systems

Religious People Use Fewer Expensive Hospital Services

As Koenig acknowledges, many of these results show the overall effect of religion on health rather than the specific impact of prayer. Lifestyle choices account for much of the benefit: regular churchgoers smoke less, drink less alcohol, engage in less promiscuous sex and drug use, and have a supportive community to rely on in coping with life problems.

Yet prayer can indeed help a person cope with stress and have a greater sense of well-being, more hope, and a readiness to forgive—all of which

---

forget the life-support issue. That verse came to mean a lot to me, too. The year I spent in Antarctica I experienced four months of complete winter darkness. Unless you've been there, you can't imagine what it's like to see that first golden glow of sun sneaking up the horizon.

Most of my "healing" took place slowly and painfully, step by step. I cried out to God to stop the phantom pain from severed nerves for which doctors have no remedy. It took months for sensation and movement to come back to my hands. I had to learn to read again. Even now two-thirds of my body doesn't work right. I even lack the sensation of hunger. Should I pray for complete healing or accept my condition?

Physical healing involves a lot of other people. I had to move back home, and I now rely on my brother, my family, and my friends for basic things. I've been through many hours of physical therapy. I now realize that it's okay to ask for help. You don't always have to smile and put on a happy face. The world tries to convince you that you don't need help, you can be independent, and weakness is not an option. That's not the way God wants us to be. When the accident happened, it was amazing how people came out of the woodwork to support us, to bring food, to pray with us at the hospital, or even just to share in our sufferings.

My brother tells me that the first few weeks I was at the hospital, they kept getting in trouble with the staff because so many people had gathered to pray, taking over the whole waiting room. I just don't know how people go through tragedies without that kind of support.

affect health in positive ways. And machines that monitor brain waves, breathing, heart rate, and blood chemistry record dramatic changes when a person prays. How we think and feel has a direct effect on bodily health because the mind regulates the body's natural healing systems. People who take quiet times during the day and force themselves to relax learn to control stress in a way that fosters health. A sense of gratitude calms the heart. (On the contrary, fear, loneliness, hostility, worry, grief, and helplessness are enemies of recovery.) We are still learning how the brain accomplishes these feats, in part by producing endorphins that control pain and alter body chemistry.

Skeptical scientists and physicians use the word *psychosomatic* to explain away reports of supernatural healings, implying the recovery was due more to autosuggestion than to any miracle. I wrote three books with the renowned surgeon Dr. Paul Brand, who said, "It doesn't diminish my respect for God's power in the slightest to realize that God primarily works through the mind to summon up resources of healing in a person's body. The word *psychosomatic* carries no derogatory connotations for me. It derives from two Greek words, *psyche* and *soma*, which mean simply *mind* (or *soul*) and *body*. The cure of such diseases demonstrates the incredible power of the mind to affect the rest of the body."

In fact, Dr. Brand coined a new word, *pneumapsychosomatic*, adding the Greek word for "spirit" to acknowledge the role of the spirit in health. A person experiences maximum health when all three, body-soul-spirit, are aligned in a way that expresses the will of the Designer. Brand comments, "Those who pray for the sick and suffering should first praise God for the remarkable agents of healing designed into the body, and then ask that God's special grace give the suffering person the ability to use those resources to their fullest advantage. I have seen remarkable instances of physical healing accomplished in this way. The prayers of fellow Christians can offer real, tangible help by setting into motion the intrinsic powers of healing in a person controlled by God. This approach does not contradict natural laws; rather, it fully employs the design features built into the human body."

A person who is at peace, surrounded by loving support, will quite literally heal better, drawing on the resources of body, mind, and spirit. Such healing is not inferior to a direct intervention by God that reverses physical laws. Rather, the Spirit uses the natural milieu—the mind, nerves, and hormonal systems that govern all cells—to accomplish the work.

Suspending Nature

I can predict the reaction of some Christians to crediting the "inbuilt miracle" in our physical bodies: "Yes, yes, I understand all that. But what about *miracles?* What about the times when a disease is incurable, when the doctors give no hope, when the science of medicine has nothing to offer. Does God intervene then? Does God overrule nature to answer prayers of faith?"

First I must say a few words in defense of the laws of nature. Scientists and theologians alike agree that the universe runs by faithful, consistent laws. The sun always appears first in the east, low pressure systems bring storms, species give birth to their own kind, the planets follow dependable orbits. Because of its very predictability, the natural world allows us to adapt to it. Build a house on an earthquake fault line or in a flood zone, and the odds of being a victim of nature rise exponentially—just as they rise if you smoke tobacco or drink alcohol to excess.

In many instances of human suffering, if we look carefully enough we can trace the problem to a basic cause and effect. Suffering may stem from something I do wrong, such as overeating, or something another does wrong, such as driving while drunk. Or perhaps I sit too close to a person coming down with influenza and a germ flies into my mouth. To avoid influenza entirely I must shun all people or wear a mask, as many Japanese commuters do.

It puzzles me that some Christians who accept the regularity of natural laws in other areas resist them when it comes to health. For example, I have heard extreme faith healers encourage people to pray and not seek medical treatment in the event of illness. But I have heard no one recommend planting a farm in the middle of the Sahara Desert. If a farmer plants rice in the Sahara and prays for rain, he simply has a wrong view of the way God has ordered the world.

Each of us learns to adapt our prayers to natural laws.* A child may pray that a dead cat be brought back to life, that the teacher cancel a scheduled test, that his team win the World Cup or the Super Bowl, that she suddenly will have green eyes rather than blue—but over time learns that God is not

---

*I have prayed about the direction of winds driving a forest fire, as smoke filled my Colorado house and rescue helicopters clattered overhead, but I have not prayed that God suspend gravity. George Buttrick expresses this difference in a general principle: "The greater the apparent constancy in nature, the less the power of petitionary prayer: we cannot change the tides by praying. The greater the apparent variability and flexibility, the more instant our prayers: we shall continue to pray about the weather and about physical health."

a magician who rearranges life to fit our whims. In terms of physical health, you could say that the power of prayer has limits: no prayer will reverse the aging process, banish death, or eliminate the need for nourishment. Or you could say that God has set certain rules in motion and within those rules there exists much potential for physical healing.

According to the Bible, on occasion God did intervene spectacularly. For example, God provided manna to the Israelites for a time and Jesus supplied loaves and fishes for a hungry crowd. But I know no one today who refuses all natural sources of food, waiting instead for a similar miracle. Jesus did not waste miracles; I doubt he would have provided food for the five thousand if food stalls had been readily available nearby.

Some twenty years ago I coauthored an article on physical healing with Dr. Paul Brand which was published in *Christianity Today* magazine. In it he remarked, "From my own experience as a physician I must truthfully admit that, among the thousands of patients I have treated, I have never observed an unequivocal instance of intervention in the physical realm. Many were prayed for, many found healing, but not in ways that counteracted the laws governing anatomy. No case I have treated personally would meet the rigorous criteria for a supernatural miracle."

Dr. Brand had, after all, devoted his life to the treatment of leprosy and had never met a single patient who claimed to be cured miraculously of leprosy. Fortunately, excellent drugs can halt the progress of the disease, and as a surgeon Brand worked to reverse some of its worst effects. Usually it required two or three years of successive surgeries and gradual rehabilitation to free one hand from a frozen, useless state into something more usable. Not once did a missing finger suddenly grow back. "If all that the television evangelists claim is true, then I am in the wrong business," he wrote. "Have I wasted my life doing slowly and painstakingly what could have been done in the twinkling of an eye?"

We received many letters in response to that article. Some commended Dr. Brand's honesty while others, outraged, accused him of deficient faith. A few physicians wrote in to report miracles of healing, such as the complete disappearance of all signs of bone cancer in one patient, and in another a spinal cord injury that should have led to quadriplegia but did not. Following up on these cases, Dr. Brand concluded that some indeed appeared to represent supernatural intervention. Before he died in 2003, he was working on a revision of his philosophy of physical healing that began with praise for the inbuilt miracle designed into the human body and also allowed for miraculous exceptions.

Most doctors acknowledge cases that appear to defy the normal course of nature. The book *Spontaneous Regression of Cancer* by the former president of the American College of Surgeons details 176 such cases. Even so, these remissions represent a very small percentage of the people with cancer who have been prayed for. The medical literature now estimates that perhaps two or three out of every thousand people with cancer will experience such "cures" apparently unrelated to treatment.

Many times I have asked Christian doctors if they have seen a supernatural miracle. Most think for a few minutes and then describe one or two cases that may qualify. Like Dr. Brand, they allow for the exceptions while stressing their infrequency. A famous faith healer confided to me that he had seen only two or three cases he would classify as true miracles. A medical board supervising the shrine at Lourdes in France has examined nearly seven thousand claims of healing in two centuries, and has authenticated only sixty-seven as miraculous cures, only one since 1987.

What Makes the Difference?

Reported miracles are far more common in developing countries. As I have mentioned, the church in Nepal grew dramatically as a direct result of physical healing. I interviewed several European doctors in Nepal, and each one told me accounts of healings that defy explanation: a baby born dead who began breathing, a woman's severed facial nerve that still functions normally, a withered hand that straightened, an inoperable tumor that disappeared. Similar things happen in China.

Confronted with a serious medical condition, Christians in the developed world pray for divine intervention just as passionately. What makes the difference? Could it be that we in the West, with a scientific world view, lack the faith necessary for miracles? Could the explanation lie with the spirit world, a deployment of resources in which supernatural forces concentrate in some places but not others? I do not know.

Nonetheless, I do believe that what many people think of when you say the words "divine healing"—supernatural interventions in the laws of nature governing our bodies—are extremely rare. They are *miracles*, not ordinaries. However we present divine healing, let us not stir up false hopes so that a suffering person stakes his or her faith on belief in miraculous healing at this level.

In Jesus' day miracles abounded. He changed the weather at least once and performed many miraculous healings. I notice, though, a selective quality to Jesus' miracles. In his first miracle he turned water into wine in order to salvage a wedding celebration. Why this occasion, this particular use of his powers? He brought a young girl back to life, but how many others died in Israel that day? He healed a paralyzed man by the pool of Bethesda, but John says nothing of what happened to the other disabled persons lying around the same pond.

As I read the Gospels, I keep wanting Jesus to be more systematic. I want him to solve world hunger, not just feed five thousand who happen to be listening to him one day. I want him to destroy the polio virus, not merely heal an occasional paralytic. Such thinking only leads to frustration. Clearly Jesus did not come to earth in order to reverse the laws of nature and establish better laws—not in his first coming, at least. Indeed, Jesus resisted that temptation as posed by Satan in the wilderness.

I have come to see the very selectiveness of biblical miracles as a sign of God's personhood. Jesus healed people he encountered in the course of a day. He may have set out to accomplish one task, and the people he met along the way presented new challenges. I understand this tendency, for the same thing happens to me nearly every day. Though I begin with goals to accomplish, interruptions along the way cause me to modify those goals. Jesus had access to power that allowed him to overrule natural laws on those occasions.

We keep expecting God to act in immovable, fixed patterns, but the Bible shows a tendency for God to act in a way that seems almost arbitrary. God chose Jacob not Esau, and David not his older brothers, for reasons that defied comprehension at the time. God miraculously rescued both Peter and Paul from prison, yet eventually both were re-imprisoned and executed. I question any system that attempts to explain each of God's acts in suspending the laws of nature. God showed preferences that, if made by anyone but God, would seem, well, quirky.

I have concluded that our strict division between natural events and supernatural miracles—or general and special providence, as the theologians term it—have much more significance to us than to God. Biblical scholars diagram levels of God's interventions on earth. The top level includes such obviously supernatural events as the burning bush and the ten plagues of

Egypt. A middle level includes dreams, messages, and even visitations to people like Abraham and Jacob, who didn't always recognize their celestial visitors. A bottom level would include "natural" events accomplished by human beings. Deborah led an army, Solomon designed a temple, Nehemiah supervised a construction project, Paul preached in synagogues—all these and many more carried out God's will in normal, everyday ways. I suspect, however, that as God reviews history, any such distinctions seem insignificant. If anything, God delights in delegating the mission to human agents.

Checklist for Healing

When I fall sick, or learn of physical suffering in a friend or loved one, I bring that request to God, whom the Bible describes as "the Father of compassion and the God of all comfort." Sickness, not health, is the abnormality that Jesus came to expose. While not solving all the problems on earth, Jesus' miracles gave a clear sign of how the world should be, and someday will be. His acts of healing restored to specific individuals what had been spoiled on the planet as a whole.*

At the same time, I have seen great damage that results when we presume upon God. The Bible gives examples of prayers answered and unanswered, of illnesses healed and unhealed. We dare not raise expectations so high as to virtually guarantee a crashing disappointment. In search of the proper balance, when I desire and pray for a miracle I ask myself a series of questions.

Am I expecting a miracle as an entitlement?

I think again of the letters in my file cabinet, many of them from people who prayed urgently for a miracle. One couple joyfully announces that God has answered their longsuffering prayers for a baby while another gives up and begins the arduous process of adopting a Chinese baby. My pastor once heard a woman stand in church and breathlessly tell of her two-year-old

---

* A third of the healings in the New Testament involved exorcism of evil spirits, and the Bible often presents illnesses as afflictions of Satan; even Paul's malady is termed "a messenger of Satan." In the words of James Kallas, "We see polio or crippling and we piously shake our heads and cluck all the trite absurdities of a non-thinking people by saying 'it is the will of God ... hard to understand ... providence writes a long sentence, we have to wait to get to heaven to read the answer.' ... Jesus looked at this and in crystal clear terms called it the work of the devil, and not the will of God."

son who fell in a swimming pool, was revived by artificial respiration, and recovered completely. "Isn't God wonderful!" she exclaimed. Sitting in the audience was another woman whose son also fell in a swimming pool, was pulled from the water, and never regained consciousness.

God neither protects Christians with a shield of health nor provides a quick, dependable solution to all suffering. Christians populate hospital wards, asylums, and hospices in approximate proportion to the world at large. I asked Dr. Vernon Grounds, a seminary chancellor and one of the godliest men I know, "Have you ever seen an undeniable miracle of physical healing?" Without a flicker of hesitation he responded, "No, but I'm still hoping!" He told me of a friend diagnosed with an untreatable kidney condition. Grounds prays daily for the man's miraculous healing, fervently believing in God's power to perform such a miracle even though in ninety years he has never observed one.

I prefer Vernon Grounds's approach of humble, expectant faith to one that promises too much. Consider an incident from the 1990s, a scene described to me by a church leader who had witnessed it firsthand. A faith healer from the U.S. scheduled a crusade in Cambodia, a country with a tiny minority of Christians. Posters went up promising healing and deliverance for any problem. Peasants sold their cows, even their houses, and traveled to Phnom Penh for the rally. As a result of landmines left over from the Vietnam war, one in two hundred Cambodians is an amputee, and many of these flocked to the crusade as well. When the amputees were not healed, a riot broke out in the stadium. The evangelist had to be rescued by an army helicopter, which whisked him to the safety of a hotel. When the angry crowd poured out of the stadium and surrounded the hotel, the faith healer departed the country and returned to the U.S.

"You cannot imagine the impact on the struggling church in Cambodia," said the church leader. "It has set us back at least fifty years. We may never recover credibility here."

Am I using the benefits of God's "common grace" — the healing built into our bodies and the medical knowledge we have gained?

One disease, smallpox, killed 500 million people in the nineteenth century — many times more lives than are threatened by AIDS today. In the next century it became the first disease ever to be eradicated fully, thanks to the dedicated work of researchers and medical professionals. Sad to say, some prominent Christians opposed the smallpox vaccine when first released because they thought it interfered with "God's will." In direct opposition, I see brave souls like Edward Jenner, developer of the vaccine, as *fulfilling* God's will by bringing healing and wholeness to people whom God loves.

Jesus held up the example of a Good Samaritan (note, neither Jewish nor in any sense a "Christian") who bandaged the wounds of a robbery victim, poured on him oil and wine, and took him to an inn. The Samaritan did not simply pray for the victim but ministered to him medically in the best way known to that day. In doing so he loved his neighbor as himself, fulfilling one of the two most essential commandments.

I see in the Good Samaritan a prototype of the doctors and scientists who dedicate their lives to bringing health. Only in the last century have we discovered treatments effective against the great scourges of history: polio, bubonic plague, diphtheria, influenza, malaria, yellow fever, and many others. In some diseases, Christian missionaries led the way in discovering the best treatments, for they alone were willing to risk infection by living among and ministering to patients.

The studies I've cited on faith and healing demonstrate that the best healing takes place when a person lives so that a properly aligned soul and spirit can direct the bodily healing prompted by good medicine. In the words of Dr. Paul Brand,

> My profession of surgery depends entirely on the body's own healing system. When I set a fracture, I merely align two ends of bone properly; the body must lay down the calcium needed for them to rejoin, or my work would prove futile. The Christian heals because he or she has the kind of body that was designed by God to be equipped to overcome injury and infection. The non-Christian body is likewise equipped, but may be more misused so that its healing functions may not be as well focused. Yet, like the sun which God makes to shine on the righteous and the unrighteous, so the osteoblast heals righteous bones as well as unrighteous bones.
>
> The real direction of prayer for the sick and the suffering should be, first to praise God for the wonderful mechanisms of healing and recovery that God has designed and placed in the person's body, and then to pray that God's special grace will take hold of his or her whole person and give the ability to use these resources to their fullest advantage; and also that the church will rally round and lay their healing hands on the one who needs support, faith, hope, and love.

Do I wrongly blame God for causing the suffering?

I have met many people who torment themselves over some tragedy. To mention one recent example, the rate of sudden infant death syndrome dropped 40 percent in the U.S. in fifteen years, mainly because doctors began cautioning parents to place their sleeping babies on their backs, not their stomachs, lest they suffocate. I think of all the parents in past years who cried out to God after losing a child, *Why did God take my child?* That is the wrong question, I believe. The babies' deaths came about simply because we did not know the danger of babies sleeping on their stomachs.

Hanging On

JACQUELINE

I learned about prayer during a period of depression that lasted six months. Nothing prepared me for the overwhelming pain. To someone who hasn't experienced true clinical depression, it must feel strange to talk about physical pain. In one sense nothing was wrong with my body. In another sense, everything was wrong. I might as well have been run over by a truck, I felt that bad.

I remember lying on the floor and pleading with God for the pain to go away. The prayers went about as high as the top fibers on the carpet. I could hardly relate to another human being—how could I relate to God? I spent most days curled up in bed in a fetal position.

I felt ashamed because I knew my pain was nothing compared to a woman in Sudan holding her starving baby or a person with a terminal illness. Yet I learned that all pain is pain. You can't measure it on a scale and rate how "worthy" it is.

Rare moments of relief would come, like grace notes. One night I went to the refrigerator to get an orange and suddenly, standing there in the eerie light that spilled out the refrigerator door, I felt peace. The pain had passed. The next day I was back in bed, fetal. Some Sundays I would sneak into the back of church, close my eyes and listen, then sneak out before anyone noticed me. That relief usually faded by Monday, and I began to distrust every respite, knowing it would soon pass.

Similarly, during the worst years of the Black Death, or bubonic plague, long-haired prophets roamed the streets of London—eerily empty as a third of the residents had died and a third had fled the city—and pronounced the plague as God's judgment on wickedness. For half a millennium, in fact, prophets pronounced such judgment on Europe. In the end, rat poison made the dreaded plague disappear.

A similar advance in knowledge exposed the danger of tobacco-related illnesses. The Dutch once considered smoking healthy, a sign of a spiritual Christian, and only the rebellious refused to smoke. Now we know that

---

I went on suicide websites to see if other people had experienced something similar. I now understand why people kill themselves: suicide is the only way to end the pain. "God, keep Jackie from suicide," my husband would pray. "Let her see that you still love her." To me, that prayer seemed the most remote of all. I would say the words, "God, help me see that you still love me," but it seemed as impossible as asking to win the lottery.

Though blind to it at the time, looking back now I can see how God answered our prayers. My sister hopped on the first plane and stayed with me for an entire week. She sat by my bed, sometimes singing hymns softly, sometimes praying wordlessly, sometimes just brushing my hair.

"Jackie, when you look in a mirror, what do you see?" she would say. "Worthlessness, a failure, a spiritual nothing," I would answer her. "Jackie, let me tell you what God sees. He *adores* you." I could not feel God's love directly, but in time I felt it through her.

I credit my therapist as another answer to prayer, not to mention the medicines he prescribed for me. God often works through people to accomplish his healing. Once a week I got a card from someone who quoted an encouraging Bible verse and added the line, "We're praying for you." I still don't know who sent those cards, but every verse was exactly what I needed that day.

I survived depression, but it changed me forever. It took away all cockiness, any sense that I can make it on my own. I think of myself as having a spiritual disability now—I have to rely on God all day long every day. I can't count on myself, because I failed myself. I used to see prayer as my way of trying to get God to do what I wanted. Now I see it as my way of being in on what God is doing, and just hanging on.

smoking harms the body. Pious Dutch Calvinists who accepted their lung cancer and emphysema as God's will could, in fact, have prevented it by dousing their pipes.

I know a missionary whose wife and seven-month-old daughter were killed by a single bullet when the air force in a South American country mistook their plane for that of a drug runner and opened fire. "God guided the bullet," the surviving husband and father said to the press. We have held long discussions about that quote, because I do not believe the "Father of compassion" guides bullets into the bodies of babies. Jesus himself refuted those who blamed human tragedies on God.

At the church I attended in Chicago, the pastor would sometimes offer a time for people to come to the front for prayer. "The worst thing that can happen to you is that you will have an experience of being profoundly loved. That's not so bad, is it? And you just might hear the Master's voice, 'Your faith has made you whole. Go in peace, freed from your suffering.'" Each time, he emphasized that we in the church should offer love and support to those who suffer, not guilt and self-doubt. Over the years many people reported healings, not just from physical conditions but from addictions and sexual wounds. And all of us went away with an important reminder that God is a source of comfort, not torment.

Am I prepared for the possibility that physical healing may not take place?

The apostle Paul had the power to heal a man crippled from birth and even raise another from the dead. Yet three times in the New Testament he refers to friends (Epaphroditus, Trophimus, and Timothy) who suffered from serious illness, not to mention his own ailment. One friend he left behind, ill; for another he counseled treatment. We have no record of their physical healings.

In its most detailed passages on suffering, the New Testament moves the emphasis to what we can learn from the difficulty and the good that can be produced. By such a standard we should honor, not demean, the disabled and chronically ill. Jesus never promised to erase all poverty, all suffering, all human need. Rather, he announced a kingdom that values the needy above the beautiful and powerful and self-sufficient. In my own experience, those who most readily recognize their dependence on God are the ones who have no other choice: the disabled, the suffering, and those who care for them.

Whatever we conclude about physical healing, we must not add to the burden of guilt and sorrow borne by those who do not find healing. Many Christians who roll about in wheelchairs, who awake each day to the scarred stumps of amputated limbs, who cope with debility and chronic illness, have prayed for healing. Some have attended healing services, felt a sudden rush of hope, and kneeled for an anointing of oil—yet still they live unhealed. For them, divine healing feels like the cruelest joke of all, a taunting accusation that in spiritual as well as physical health they do not measure up.

Some television and radio preachers promise that healing is always available for believers. If that were true, need any Christian wear eyeglasses, grow bald, or show other signs of aging? A combination of disease and lowered cellular efficiency is leading each of us—including every faith healer—toward death, and no amount of prayer and faith will reverse the process. Despite much prayer, the nerves controlling author Joni Eareckson Tada's legs have not spontaneously regenerated. And I have never yet read an account of miraculous healing of pancreatic cancer (which has a 100 percent mortality rate), or of cystic fibrosis, or ALS.

I have heard from Christian leaders in Africa that "health and wealth theology," once widespread on that continent, has undergone a sobering change since the onset of AIDS. There are no verified instances of AIDS being healed either, and in some African countries the infection rate approaches 40 percent. The church has had to change its message from "Simply believe you'll be healed" to a more difficult message of preaching against risky behavior, caring for the sick and dying, and looking after the millions of orphans resulting from the disease.

One of the most revealing scientific studies of illness focused not on suffering people themselves but on caregivers. Researchers who studied parents of young children with chronic illnesses—juvenile diabetes, juvenile rheumatoid arthritis, cystic fibrosis, epilepsy, and spina bifida—found that the parents' ability to derive comfort and strength from religion was the single most important factor in their coping ability. From the very beginning, the church has honored this calling: the first Christians distinguished themselves by remaining behind to nurse victims of the plague, rather than fleeing it.

I will never forget sitting in the bedroom of a tiny house in Columbia, South Carolina, watching Robertson McQuilkin feed homemade soup to his wife, spoonful by spoonful, laughing, talking to her, stroking her cheek, wiping off the spilled food. She could still raise one arm and wave it, though she made no sounds and showed no sign of recognizing her husband of forty years. McQuilkin had resigned as president of a Christian college to care for Muriel, a teacher and media personality in her own right before the onset of Alzheimer's disease. For twenty years he took on that responsibility, canceling most speaking engagements and interrupting his own projects to remain available to her. Why? "I took a vow before God," he told me. "In sickness and in health. Isn't this what love is about?"

A woman in Ontario gave me her family's journal of caring for her husband during his seven-year bout with ALS (Lou Gehrig's disease). His brother, mother, grandfather, aunt, and cousin had died of the same disease, so he knew well what lay ahead. He knew, too, that there are no reports of healing from the disease.

"The Lord is my shepherd, and so I lack nothing," the family wrote in a paper handed out at the funeral, and just across from it, "My God! My God!... Why have you forsaken me." Words from the two adjacent psalms, 22 and 23, summarized their seven years of caregiving.

The daughter's journal entries record the progression of the disease. "Dad can't tie up his own shoes anymore.... Dad can't sign his name anymore. Dad breaks his collar bone and stops going to work. Dad falls in the parking lot and has to wait on the ground until someone picks him up.... Dad can't have his corn flakes for breakfast anymore. Dad can't put his arms around us anymore.... Dad has trouble swallowing puréed peas.... Dad can't hold his head up anymore."

After seven years comes this entry: "Lying beside Dad as he sits in his chair working for breath. Praying for peace. Wiping his nose. Rubbing his shoulders. Watching Mom love Dad. Saying goodbye. Hearing Dad express his love for Mom and his love for their life together. Watching Dad gaze heavenward and take his last quiet breath.... The Lord is our shepherd."

In the midst of the man's suffering, and their own anguish, his family was able to provide the strength and comfort that he needed in order to die gracefully. "The God of all comfort," one of the most beautiful descriptions of God, appears in Paul's letter to the Corinthians. God offers us a minimum of protection and a maximum of support, as one minister wryly put it. Paul, however, moves the emphasis to us: God "comforts us in all our troubles, so that we can comfort those in any trouble with the comfort we ourselves have received from God. For just as the sufferings of Christ flow over into our lives, so also through Christ our comfort overflows."

CHAPTER 19

WHAT TO PRAY FOR

We do not want to be beginners [at prayer].
But let us be convinced of the fact
that we will never be anything
but beginners, all our life!

THOMAS MERTON

Unanswered prayers and unanswered questions about God and physical healing can leave us feeling confused and mute about the requests we present. What exactly should we pray for?

From interviews with suffering people and ordinary pray-ers, from the experience of caregivers, chaplains, and helpers, I have gathered the following guidelines on prayer. They offer a template of how to pray, not only for a person who suffers but for all of us who cry out to God at a time of need. These prayers we can count on, and pray with confidence.

Heart Desire

I have learned to tell God exactly what I want regardless of how impossible it may sound. I pray for peace in the Middle East, for justice in Africa, for religious freedom in China and other countries, for an end to homelessness and racism in the U.S., because I earnestly desire those things—and moreover, I believe God does too.

A friend of mine in Chicago tried to recruit some colleagues in urban ministry to join him in a season of prayer for an end to poverty in that city. Almost everyone he asked balked. "Why pray for something so idealistic and impossible?" they objected. My friend had a different view. What is the point of prayer if not to express our heart's desire, especially when it matches what we know to be God's will on earth? Who knows what will happen when we pray what we know God desires? Remember the many prayers of Christians behind the Iron Curtain and in an apartheid South Africa, prayers that also seemed impossible and idealistic.

God invites us to ask plainly for what we need. We will not be scolded any more than a child who climbs into her parent's lap and presents a Christmas wish list. Dr. Vernon Grounds says that when he hears of someone in need of healing, he prays like this: "God, I know you have your own purposes and undoubtedly have a plan for this person, but I'll tell you straight out what I would like to see happen."

If diagnosed with a serious illness, I would ask directly for physical healing. We are commanded to pray for healing, Jesus decisively demonstrated God's desire for human health and wholeness, and dozens of studies have borne out the effectiveness of prayer in the healing process. Faith works. It aligns body, mind, and spirit, and galvanizes the healing processes built into our bodies.

Sometimes Jesus asked a person, "Do you want to be healed?" That was no idle question: as doctors testify, some patients can hardly imagine an identity apart from their unwell condition. In prayers for healing, as in all prayers of request, we should honestly present the problem and tell God our heart's desire.

Lament

"Lord, the one you love is sick," Mary and Martha informed Jesus about their brother Lazarus in a form of prayer. Preachers like to accent the personality differences between the scurrying, type A Martha and her contemplative sister Mary. What strikes me in the story is their twin response to Jesus when he shows up, apparently too late to help Lazarus. "Lord, if you had been here, my brother would not have died," Martha says after rushing out to meet Jesus. A while later, at a slower pace Mary arrives and says: "Lord, if you had been here, my brother would not have died." Suffering and grief cut across personality differences and reduce us all to lamenters. Sometimes we have nothing to offer in our prayers but complaint.

Jesus' response follows, not a rebuke but a spasm of compassion ("he was deeply moved in spirit and troubled") punctuated by the shortest verse in the Bible: "Jesus wept."

A man who serves as the grief pastor of a large church in Colorado reminds me of the value of tears. John spends much of his time visiting the sick and dying, and most weeks he conducts at least one funeral. In addition, he has two children of his own with life-threatening genetic disorders. "Evangelicals tend to want to get to the happy ending," John says. "Sometimes there is no happy ending, and we're simply suspended in grief. When I'm with suffering people, I feel like a deep-sea diver accompanying them into the depths. Come up too fast, and you'll dangerously decompress. We need to stay with the grief for a while, feel it, let it out. Maybe we can see things through tears that we can't see dry-eyed."

Not only does God tolerate complaint in our prayers, the Scriptures fill in the words for us. Eugene Peterson calculates that two-thirds of the psalms qualify as laments. The Bible does not rush to a happy ending.

A dead-end marriage that seems to offer no way out. A surly teenager who saps the family finances and shows resentment, not appreciation. A spouse who has no interest in sex. Global terrorism. A national election that goes the wrong way. A bitter and divided church. A parent with dementia. Each of these circumstances rightly calls for prayers of lament.

Robertson McQuilkin, as patient a man as I know, confessed the temptation to scream at, even slap, his Alzheimer's-afflicted wife when irritation reached a certain level. Prayer offers a better alternative, just as the psalms' fierce prayers against enemies offer a better alternative than personal revenge. We need feel no guilt over such prayers of frustration, for God welcomes them.

Confession

Sin can disrupt the relationship between ourselves and God in a way that jars the alignment of body, soul, and spirit. Confession restores the channel of communication with God while at the same time flushing away anxiety, guilt, fear, and other obstacles to health.

I have mentioned the inner conversation that we all conduct at a level inaudible to those around us. When I struggle with guilt, I find that inner conversation revolving around myself: attempts to rationalize or explain away my behavior, resentment against others who caused it, feelings of self-pity and remorse. Only confession can clear away that self-absorption and open my spirit to God's soft voice.

Ed Dobson, the well-known pastor of Calvary Church in Grand Rapids, Michigan, grappled with confession after contracting the terminal disease ALS. "When I was diagnosed, I thought, *If I'm going to die, I want to die with a clear conscience and whole relationships.* I knew there were people I had offended, people I needed to ask for forgiveness. So I made a list and began calling."

Dobson had his roots in the fundamentalist movement and in right-wing Moral Majority politics but later moved in a different direction, especially in his outreach to the local homosexual community. When he learned of his illness he called colleagues from the past—Jerry Falwell, Bob Jones, James Dobson (no relation)—and asked for forgiveness if he had offended them. After that, he prayed with a clear conscience and sensed a new freedom in his prayers.

Clearing obstructions in a relationship with God allows us to take a giant step toward wholeness and health. And we can have confidence that a prayer of confession God will always answer, with guaranteed forgiveness. Writes the apostle John, "But if anybody does sin, we have one who speaks to the Father in our defense—Jesus Christ, the Righteous One."

Jaime Cardinal Sin, the Catholic archbishop of Manila who played a key role in the People Power revolution there, liked to tell the story of a woman who attended his weekly audience to inform him she had a message from

---

By the Fire

VERNON

I would estimate that 80 percent of the prayer requests I hear in church center in physical healing. I can understand that—suffering tends to chase away everything else—but I wish I heard more prayers about poverty and persecution and injustice, a different kind of pain.

My wife watches some of the television ministries faithfully, and I don't know what to think about the miracles stories I hear on TV. Some question them, but could they be manufacturing the specificity of those stories? I'm ninety years old now, and it would do an aged soul good to witness an undeniable, certified healing. I haven't really seen one, though I've prayed for many.

For some reason, God's failure to answer all my prayers doesn't shake my faith. We've been together too long, God and I. And surely I've seen God work. I prayed for a brother-in-law for forty years when he showed no spiritual interest whatsoever. Then suddenly, *not* to my surprise, he began attending and eventually joined an evangelical church.

For me, the controlling principle in prayer comes out of Jesus' model

God. He brushed her off several times, but she kept coming back. Finally he said, "We Catholics have strict rules governing visions and messages from God. I need to test your authenticity. I want you to go back and ask God about a particular sin I recently confessed in private. If you ask God and he tells you the answer, I'll know your vision is genuine."

The next week she returned and he quizzed her, a bit nervously, "Well, did you ask God about my sin?"

"I did."

"And did God answer?"

"Yes."

"What did he say?"

"God said that he couldn't remember."

Peace

Roy Lawrence, a vicar and adviser on prayer to a British bishop, says that we make a mistake to think that effective prayer must involve great effort.

---

in Gethsemane: Remove this cup ... nevertheless, thy will be done. I have unquestioning confidence in God's ability to accomplish whatever God wants—the resurrection proves that—but I also believe that other spiritual forces are trying to frustrate the forces of good. I accept mystery and paradox. When you've been around as long as I have, you must.

We shouldn't expect a relationship with God to remain on a constant plane all the time. Not long ago I celebrated my sixty-fifth wedding anniversary. Believe me, when you've been married that long, you don't stay on a plane of ecstasy all the time. Romance starts as a blazing bonfire—you know, "You light up my life." After a few decades it settles into something more like a heap of glowing coals. Sure, some of the heat dissipates, but coals are good, too: you can roast marshmallows, or warm your feet. A different level of companionship opens up.

For as long as I can remember I've spent at least a half-hour daily in prayer. There have been experiences when, as the old hymn puts it, "heaven came down and glory filled my soul." Those are rare. Most of the time I persist because I value the relationship with God, just as I value my marriage relationship. I gratefully warm my feet by the fire.

"We think of it as hard work, as striving.... That is the way I myself used to think. In fact, often after praying for somebody's healing, I would find the imprints of my own nails on my palms because I had been clenching my fists so tightly as I agonized in prayer."

Lawrence became convinced that prayer has more to do with resting than with striving. "Come to me, all you who are weary and burdened, and I will give you rest," Jesus said—or, as another translation has it, "and I will refresh you." For guidance on prayer, Lawrence now looks to the passage in John 15 in which Jesus holds up the image of a vine and branches. The branch bears fruit not by striving or agonizing, simply by "abiding" or resting.

I wrote earlier about changing the direction of prayer. Rather than begin with my own requests and demands, I can begin with God, first getting to know who God is and then positioning myself in the stream of God's own love and power. When praying for a person who is sick or troubled, I try to begin not by presenting a list of requests, as urgent as they may be, but rather by meditating on how God must already feel about the person I am praying for.

I know how God feels because of Jesus: I see the tears of compassion he wept for Mary and Martha; I see the physical healing Jesus provided every time he was asked; I see the transformations he worked in prostitutes and tax collectors and social outcasts. I gain peace when I realize that I do not have to talk God into caring. God cares more than I can imagine, and has ultimate control over all that happens.

"Peace I leave with you; my peace I give you," Jesus told his disciples. Any doctor will agree that the absence of peace, in the form of stress, fear, tension, or worry, endangers physical health as much as a disease microbe. The persecuted church also needs peace. Parents of newborns need peace. College students need peace. Caregivers and relief workers in the world's hot spots need peace. As a farewell gift, the Prince of Peace presented to us the one thing we most need on a turbulent planet.

How exactly should you pray in a given circumstance? Will your prayers lead to divine healing, or should you rather come to terms with a chronic, even terminal condition? Will you get released from prison or should you look for ways to redeem the time? Should you pursue intensive premarital counseling or simply break off the engagement? Again, Paul's soothing promise about the Spirit relieves that pressure, making possible peace in the midst of confusion:

In the same way, the Spirit helps us in our weakness. We do not know what we ought to pray for, but the Spirit himself intercedes for us with groans that words cannot express. And he who searches our hearts knows the mind of the Spirit, because the Spirit intercedes for the saints in accordance with God's will.

God's Presence

In the same Last Supper conversation in which Jesus bequeathed his peace, he also promised a far greater gift: the presence of God, who would live not in some faraway heaven but inside us, in our very souls. He promised us the Holy Spirit, and the title he chose, the Counselor (or Comforter), itself indicates one of the Spirit's main roles. The *sense* of God's presence may come and go. Yet the believer can have confidence that God is already present, living inside, and need not be summoned from afar.

I have seen evidence of God's presence in the most unexpected places. During our trip to Nepal, a physical therapist gave my wife and me a tour of the Green Pastures Hospital, which specializes in leprosy rehabilitation. As we walked along an outdoor corridor, I noticed in a courtyard one of the ugliest human beings I have ever seen. Her hands were bandaged in gauze, she had deformed stumps where most people have feet, and her face showed the worst ravages of that cruel disease. Her nose had shrunken away so that, looking at her, I could see into her sinus cavity. Her eyes, mottled and covered with callus, let in no light; she was totally blind. Scars covered patches of skin on her arms.

We toured a unit of the hospital and returned along the same corridor. In the meantime this creature had crawled across the courtyard to the very edge of the walkway, pulling herself along the ground by planting her elbows and dragging her body like a wounded animal. I'm ashamed to say my first thought was, *She's a beggar and she wants money.* My wife, who has worked among the down-and-out, had a much more holy reaction. Without hesitation she bent down to the woman and put her arm around her. The old woman rested her head against Janet's shoulder and began singing a song in Nepali, a tune that we all instantly recognized: "Jesus loves me, this I know, for the Bible tells me so."

"Dahnmaya is one of our most devoted church members," the physical therapist later told us. "Most of our patients are Hindus, but we have a little Christian chapel here, and Dahnmaya comes every time the door opens.

273

She's a prayer warrior. She loves to greet and welcome every visitor who comes to Green Pastures, and no doubt she heard us talking as we walked along the corridor."

A few months later we heard that Dahnmaya had died. Close to my desk I keep a photo that I snapped just as she was singing to Janet. Whenever I feel polluted by the beauty-obsessed celebrity culture I live in—a culture in which people pay exorbitant sums to shorten their noses or plump up their breasts to achieve some impossible ideal of beauty while nine thousand people die each day from AIDS for lack of treatment and hospitals like Green Pastures scrape by on charity crumbs—I pull out that photo. I see two beautiful women: my wife, smiling sweetly, wearing a brightly colored Nepali outfit she had bought the day before, holding in her arms an old crone who would flunk any beauty test ever devised except the one that matters most. Out of that deformed, hollow shell of a body, the light of God's presence shines out. The Holy Spirit found a home.

Compassion

During hard times my vision narrows so that I think only of myself and my problems. Then, more than ever, I need to widen that vision, to expand the circle of God's love. I need to review Paul's words about God who comforts us "so that we can comfort those in any trouble with the comfort we ourselves have received from God." I need to remember that the weakness and discomfort I feel temporarily, some people must cope with every day.

I used to spend a lot of energy asking God questions. Why must poverty persist in a rich country like the U.S.A.? Why does one continent, Africa, absorb like a sponge so many of the world's disasters? When will "peace on earth" ever arrive? Ultimately, I came to see these questions as God's interrogations of us. Jesus made clear God's will for the planet—what part am I playing to help fulfill that will?

When I pray for the healing of AIDS in Africa, I pray for the campaigns by World Vision and World Concern and Tear Fund to raise awareness, for the rock star Bono and his prophetic challenge to the church, for the boards of the pharmaceutical companies as they make sacrificial decisions to donate drugs, for government leaders as they debate funding, for doctors and relief workers and educators on the ground in Africa who minister directly to patients and scout out homes for orphans. In this small way, through my prayers, I contribute.

When I pray for my friends with debilitating diseases such as Alzheimer's and ALS, I try to remember to pray also for the caregivers who bear many of the same stresses, and sometimes bear abuse as well. I pray for their strength and courage and their long-term endurance. Most caregivers tell of a burst of support from relatives, friends, and church members at the onset of the condition. Over time, such support tends to fade away: because of a weak theology of suffering, many churches tend to view unhealed people as an embarrassment, a token of failure.

I also pray for practical resources: provision for the physical needs of life, for meals and volunteer helpers and medical insurance and financial help. Of course, as I pray those prayers I also have to listen for God's message to me. Should I actively join the stream of God's love and comfort? Should I become one of those helpers? (Of the accounts of individuals being healed in the Gospels, all but seven were brought to Jesus by someone else.) To pray is a dangerous act.

For some people, illness itself may prevent much direct activity. But at least we can pray. After three devastating strokes the author Corrie ten Boom, formerly a globe-trotting "tramp for the Lord," found herself confined to bed in a single room overlooking a garden. She had her helpers mount photos of friends and missionaries on every wall. Even when her limbs no longer functioned, her eyes moved from one photo to another and others in the room knew what that meant: Corrie was praying.

Gratitude

Life is a gift. I heard a stirring speech from a young man, David Rothenberg, who has undergone more than sixty major surgeries and faces the prospect of scores more. As a six-year-old he suffered third-degree burns over 90 percent of his body when his father gave him a sleeping pill, poured kerosene over him, and set him afire. What gives you the courage to keep going? he was asked. David replied, "I am alive! I am alive! I am alive! I didn't miss out on living and that is good enough for me."

Medical research is discovering that gratitude is the one emotional trait most likely to benefit physical health and recovery. Grateful people tend to be happier and more satisfied with their lives, and may actually live longer. "A grateful heart might be a healthy heart," one researcher concluded after studying the effect of gratitude on relieving stress and hypertension.

I have a vivid memory of two back-to-back nights in Chicago. One evening I met with a good friend who informed me she was leaving her husband, also a close friend. "He doesn't meet my needs," she said. "I know he tries to be a good husband and good father, but I've found someone better. I'm leaving him." After listening to her, I talked about the difficulties all marriages face and reminded her of her husband's good qualities and all that she would be losing. She agreed with everything I said but had already made up her mind. I left that meal with a heavy heart, knowing my wife and I had lost one of our best couple friendships.

The very next night I attended a celebration organized by a young widow whose husband had died of brain cancer. On the night that would have been Chuck's thirty-second birthday, she was holding a party in his memory. I

Available

BUD

Peter Marshall, former chaplain of the U.S. Senate, once remarked that God has equipped us to go deep-sea diving and instead we wade in bathtubs. What makes the difference, I firmly believe, is how seriously we take prayer. I see prayer as the process of becoming available for what God wants to do on earth through us.

Somebody asked me if I've ever experienced a bona fide miracle. Oh, yes. Several times. We live in one of the poorest neighborhoods in Chicago. And miracles abound, or we would not be here. I organize work teams to rehab buildings so that homeless and underprivileged people can own their own homes. One day I was working with a sandblaster, with air piped in through my helmet, and the compressor started leaking carbon monoxide, a poisonous gas you can't taste or smell. I soon passed out. A friend of mine was driving on a highway at the other end of the state and he unmistakably heard God tell him, "Ken, you need to check on Bud." It seemed so strange and so inconvenient — he was five hours away! — that he passed up the two best routes to Chicago and only after God kept pressing him did he turn back toward Chicago. He found me unconscious, dragged me to a hospital, and literally saved my life.

Why didn't God speak to someone closer by? Well, maybe God did, to scores of people, but maybe they weren't listening. My friend Ken made him-

knew the agony they had been through during his surgery and prolonged treatment. Lynn now faced the double burden of paying off medical bills and supporting two children as a single mother. Still reeling from the news of my friend's impending divorce, I went to Lynn's house with a sense of foreboding.

I heard not a word of complaint or regret that night. Lynn passed around photos and had each of us call up memories of her husband. We laughed, and cried, and Lynn pulled out a guitar and sang some of his favorite songs. She talked about the good times they had shared together, his corny jokes, the cartoons he drew, the intimacy of walking together through the progression of his illness. "I will always miss him," she said, "but I'll always be grateful for the exciting few years we shared together. Chuck was a gift to me."

---

self available (albeit a little reluctantly). God wants to do miracles every day through us, if only we make ourselves available.

We live amid spiritual warfare and only God's love will overcome the power of evil, poverty, and injustice. There have been five murders in my neighborhood this year. People ruin their lives on drugs and alcohol. Some turn their lives around, then slide back into addiction. Every year, though, people are resurrected. We hold an annual Easter service on the beach as the sun rises over Lake Michigan. This year a woman testified, "Last year I was dead, now I'm alive." That's the real miracle of prayer, the miracle of new life.

Our homeless shelter for women and children, in fact, is named New Life. Before eating together, we gather in a circle, hold hands, and sing a prayer: "Our God is good to us. And so we thank our God, for giving us the things we need, the sun and the rain and the food we eat." A visitor once asked if that kind of song was appropriate for homeless people. Let me tell you, it is abundantly clear that the people in that room have more sense of thanksgiving and praise than many people in the average suburban pew. They pray unashamedly, just to survive, and thank God for every little blessing that comes their way.

The poor know grassroots things about the gospel that the rest of the church needs. I learn to pray by listening to them, and then by asking God to make me constantly available for whatever we can do to serve one another and Christ's reign.

On consecutive nights I saw a stark difference in two approaches to life. One resents loss and wants more. One celebrates life as a gift, something to remember with gratitude. I ask God for that spirit regardless of my circumstances.

Faith

The Bible puts forward two different kinds of faith. The one kind—bold, childlike faith—impressed Jesus, and several times such faith from the most unlikely sources "astonished" him. Another kind, I term *fidelity*, a hang-on-by-the-fingernails faith against all odds, no matter the cost. Abraham, Joseph, Job, and others of God's favorites in the Old Testament demonstrated this faith, and the tribute in Hebrews 11 honors them.

Scientific studies have amply proved the value of positive, hopeful faith on overall health. A belief in healing, in transcendent power, has a salutary effect on the body's actual cells. Millions can testify to that effect.

For others, however, there comes a time when it seems clear that no amount of faith will gain the desired healing. "I have lived with Crohn's disease for twenty-three years," writes Stephen Schmidt. "I know the disappointment, the rage, the ongoing reality that I will not get better. Period."

> So I come to the question of prayer with a very personal bias. I can pray my heart out and shout my defiance into eternity, but I will not be healed of Crohn's disease, at least not now, until some new medical insight or drug is found. I have stopped asking God for a miracle. That has not happened for me in twenty-three years, and for whatever length of time I still have to be and live, it is not helpful, reasonable, or faithful to ask of God that which is not possible. That would be magic. I am too old for magic, too experienced for sentimentality, and too angry and frustrated to waste time on a specific kind of prayer which in my life would be a prayerful placebo, practicing the piety of prayerful impossibility.

Schmidt goes on to say that he has accepted suffering as part of being human. He had to be healed of the need to be healed. Now he prays for strength to endure, for meaning in his suffering, for faith to believe in a good and loving God even when he has to go in once again for a painful surgical procedure. Each day he must live out fidelity faith.

As I have admitted, I need more of the childlike faith that impressed Jesus. By temperament I accept too readily what life throws me and start to make adjustments. Instead, I should ask God for the vision to see what can be changed.

For all its benefits, though, childlike faith has one major flaw: it stakes everything on the future, on a desired change. For some, that change never comes. If you wait until you are well or employed or married or whatever new state you are asking for, you may never get there. I have learned that I have no time in which to live out Christ's life other than *now*. This very moment is all I can count on.

In one of his letters Paul described himself as afflicted but not crushed, perplexed but not driven to despair, persecuted but not forsaken, struck down but not destroyed. He learned a different level of faith, one that does not remove difficulty but nevertheless withstands, a fidelity in which weakness transforms into strength and prayers for healing melt into prayers of acceptance.

Grace

By definition no one deserves grace and yet it descends, dropping "as the gentle rain from heaven," to borrow Shakespeare's comment about mercy. In response, human spirits ascend beyond heights they could ever achieve on their own.

Grace allowed Nelson Mandela to emerge from twenty-seven years of prison with a spirit of magnanimity and reconciliation, rather than the resentment and revenge to which he was entitled.

Grace allowed George Chen, arrested for his "barefoot evangelist" activities in China, to find a most unlikely prayer closet while serving an eighteen-year sentence at hard labor. Guards forced him to work in the prison cesspool, where he spent his days knee-deep in human waste, turning it with a shovel to make compost. "They thought I'd be miserable, but actually I was happy," said Chen. "It smelled so bad that no one could come near me, so I could pray and sing aloud all day."

Grace allows the mother of a severely disabled child to live without the self-pity such a state might normally produce. A woman in Michigan told me of her son, born with spina bifida and hydrocephalus, who requires constant care. The financial burden alone caused her to abandon most of her dreams. Yet, she told me, "Though my son has never spoken a word, no master of theology could teach more about unconditional love."

By mentioning this woman I do not mean to compound the guilt of a mother who might wake up every day resenting the demands of her child and blaming God for the curse of disability. Grace descends as the gentle rain from heaven. It does not divide, does not rank. It floats like a cloud high in the sky, and the thirsty pray for it as desert nomads pray for rain.

One man daily grows embittered by his paralysis; another prays for the grace to cope. One abused child harbors hatred and resentment; another rejoices that "I am alive!" One estranged family lets the walls remain in place; another begins the laborious task of dismantling them. Prayer for grace offers the chance for a deep healing, or at least a way to cope with what cannot be fixed.

Lee Van Ham, a Presbyterian pastor, kept a prayer journal during a battle with testicular cancer. At first he wrote many pages, both listening and talking to God during the initial shock of illness. After surgery, the communication simply stopped. He leaned on the prayers of others but found no ability to pray himself. He began to lose heart, overwhelmed with grief at the prospect of life that would likely be cut short before his children grew up and before grandchildren arrived.

"How do I live these days of low energy in which I'm more aware of having to let go of things than doing them?" he prayed, asking the same question over and over. One day an answer came: "With love. With great love."

> I began to practice doing the simple things with love. I loaded and unloaded the dishwasher with thoughts of love. It was very different from thoughts such as "If I didn't have to do dishes, I could do more important things." Or, "It seems I'm doing more than my share of this mundane stuff." I practiced waiting in love while the computer started up instead of fidgeting and scolding the machine's sloth. On days when I could drive, yellow lights at the intersections became reminders to brake, to stop and to refocus my life in love, not accelerate and hurry....
>
> I realized how dark the theater had been for several weeks. Now it was apparent that in that darkness and in the vast emptiness behind the stage of my soul, God had been forming divine and eternal thoughts to present to me: "With love, Lee. Live these days with great love." It chanted inside of me many times throughout the day ... and still does.

Grace had descended on a parsonage in Illinois. It followed Lee to California, where he serves a new parish, with love. Through illness, he learned an attitude that can last a lifetime.

Preparations

Flannery O'Connor, a brilliant writer struck down before the age of forty after a battle with lupus, lamented, "I have never been anywhere but sick. In a sense sickness is a place, more instructive than a long trip to Europe, and it's always a place where there's no company, where nobody can follow." She added these words, amazing in light of the suffering she endured: "Sickness before death is a very appropriate thing and I think those who don't have it miss one of God's mercies."

Not everyone will reach the exalted plateau of acceptance shown in those words. We go through stages and manifest the works of God in distinct and unique ways. Sometimes we never attain the faith for which we strive. And that is why we pray. As a prayer in the Roman Missal states it, "May what comes to us in our time be for our healing in the everlasting years. Amen."

The apostle Paul described a personal dilemma. As he sat in a Roman prison, reflecting on all the hardships he had endured, death loomed as a welcome relief. At least he would be with Christ, which is far better. At least his "eternal glory" would outweigh all the troubles. At least he would get a new body, healed of stripes and bruises. He had one prayer, that "Christ will be exalted in my body, whether by life or by death." Paul had found a way to fulfill Jesus' command, "do not worry about your life." He had come to terms with mortality and had no obsession with physical health. He realized that the time we spend on earth, with all its joys and griefs, triumphs and failures, is mere preparation. Paul was ready to die.

I have mentioned that my wife worked for a time as a hospice chaplain. A hospice has a 100 percent mortality rate; just to be admitted, a patient must have a doctor's diagnosis of advanced terminal disease. On average, most patients in this hospice lived less than two weeks. Working in a hospice affects one's view of life and health, Janet found, and especially it affects a way of praying. Imminent death offers a chance for old wounds to be healed, grudges forgiven, legacies passed on. Sometimes that happens, sometimes it doesn't.

Janet found that the obstacles to a good death were the very same obstacles to physical health: anxiety, tension, worry, guilt, fear. She sought to help patients express these emotions and come to terms with them. And for patients of faith, she saw the actual, practical help of belief in an afterlife, especially its promise of reunion with the loved ones who preceded and those who will follow.

For everyone death involves a process of letting go. Attachments, relatives, friendships, possessions, identity—everything that defines life for us, we let go in death. For a person in hospice, the deadline most of us try to ignore forces itself into view.

For the Christian, death also involves an anticipation of new beginning. We let go bodies that have served us, not perfectly but well enough, in exchange for new bodies. We let go a known life, touched with grace and pleasure but also evil and pain, in exchange for the promise of a life perfected. We let go the muddle of doctrine and wavering faith in exchange for sure knowledge at last. And during the rest of life we prepare for that exchange.

PART 5

THE PRACTICE
OF PRAYER

The greatest tragedy in life
is not unanswered prayer,
but unoffered prayer.

F. B. Meyer

CHAPTER 20

PRAYER AND ME

Prayer, in short, is the field hospital
in which the diseased spirituality
that we have contracted from the Powers
can most directly
be diagnosed and treated.

WALTER WINK

On safari in South Africa I soon learned to respect the instincts of our African scout, Lawrence. He sat in a jump seat that folded down by the front grille of the Land Rover, from which perch he looked for scat, tree rubbings, hoof prints, and other clues that a large animal had recently passed by. Whenever he spotted something he raised his hand for the driver to stop. Then he would sniff the air and point in a certain direction. "Rhino — that way. Very close." Or, "Two giraffes passed by here maybe one hour ago." Lawrence never missed.

Once, however, the white driver seemed irritated when Lawrence raised his hand without showing any sign of having detected an animal. "Back up," Lawrence ordered, and the driver reluctantly obeyed. Lawrence then pointed to a modest bush abloom with yellow flowers. "That is the weeping wattle bush," he said in a reverential tone. "It is very important to my people."

He went on to tell of the days when white South Africans imported black workers from neighboring countries to work in the gold mines. It was hot, dangerous work. The miners descended in cages down shafts as deep as two miles below the surface where, in near darkness at temperatures found only in the fiercest deserts, they would swing picks at rocks too hot to touch with their bare hands. They lived in dormitories surrounded by barbed wire. Most of them came from illiterate families and so never got mail from home. They had no calendars or watches. The miners' days passed in a monotony of grueling labor underground, dinner in a mess hall, and a card game or other diversion before turning in to rest for another day just like the previous one.

"They saw their families only two weeks a year," Lawrence said. "At Christmastime. And the weeping wattle blooms in early December. When the men saw these yellow blossoms, oh, how their hearts lifted. They knew that soon they would see their wives and children."

Lawrence's story had particular poignancy because we knew that his contract with the game preserve permitted him to visit his own family only twice a year. The weeping wattle bush was for him, too, a marker of hope. In less than a month he would be reunited with his wife and see an infant son for the first time.

Tuning In

By nature I resist techniques, especially those relating to spiritual disciplines. I would prefer to keep my relationship with God impromptu. The problem is, every time I proceed down such an idealistic path God gets pushed to the side. I need markers, like the weeping wattle bush, to remind me of another world out there, a hidden reality on which my life should center. And, like the African guide Lawrence, I need to take note of ordinary clues that might easily go overlooked. If prayer is my response to God's presence, first I must tune in to that presence.

Henri Nouwen suggests that we "create space in which God can act." God, who made space in the most literal sense, the universe, needs us to protect a God-space, to prevent our lives from filling up with other things. For control freaks like me, that means sheltering space in which something unexpected and unplanned may happen. Although I cannot control the sense of God's presence — on an emotional level, it will come and go — I can actively wait for it and attend to it.

While he was working among the poor in Bolivia, Nouwen took an evening off during Advent season to see a movie. "The movie was so filled with images of greed and lust, manipulation and exploitation, fearful and painful sensations, that it filled all the empty spaces that could have been blessed by the spirit of Advent." *How often do I let that happen?* I asked myself when I read that passage. I enter a motel room and switch on the television. I have CNN going when I eat lunch and the radio playing when I drive the car. I'm always reading a newspaper, magazine, computer manual, Internet blog, *something.* I fill up spaces.

"He who has ears to hear, let him hear," Jesus said. Any parent knows about ears that hear not. "But I didn't hear you," a child protests, after clear

286

instructions not to wander beyond the driveway. A revealing comparison, it occurs to me, for we often fail to "hear" God's clear commands.*

Listening is an art, and I must learn to listen to God just as I have had to learn to listen as a journalist. When I interview people, I ask a question and they give an answer. Early on, especially when the interview subjects were nervous and halting, I would jump in and finish their sentences. I learned, though, that if I don't interrupt or move quickly to a follow-up question, if I sit in silence for a while, they may speak again, filling in details. Counselors know this too.

God often speaks quietly. Memories, phrases from the Bible, images of friends in need drift into my mind unsummoned. Hope stirs to life where previously I felt despair. A spirit of forgiveness rather than revenge settles in after a wrong. I feel a call to engagement and not passivity. These things tend to happen, though, only when I'm tuned in to God.

A seminary professor wrote a book titled *Wasting Time with God* that deals with the notion of simply being with God. It speaks volumes about modern life that the publisher chose that clever title, for during much of history whole armies of monks and nuns did nothing but "waste time" with God. It was their vocation. I have learned, and I'm sure the book's author would agree, that time with God is not wasted, even when it seems so. Do I waste time by visiting a nursing home? By sitting in an ICU ward with a dying friend? By staying up all night with a sick child? Being present with someone I love is never a waste of time, especially if God is the one with whom I am present.

Martha complained about Mary wasting time at Jesus' feet while work piled up. Judas groused about the same Mary wasting expensive perfume by pouring it on Jesus. Indeed, any time spent in prayer seems wasted to someone who has other priorities than a relationship with God. For one who loves God, however, there is no more productive, or necessary, act.

Prayer as Therapy

All too often I crowd out prayer because in other activities I see tangible results. With prayer much of the benefit takes place behind the scenes, beneath the level of conscious awareness, in ways difficult to measure.

---

*Pamela Grey once commented, "For one soul that exclaims 'Speak, Lord, for thy servant heareth,' there are ten that say 'Hear, Lord! For thy servant speaketh.'"

The very process of "wasting time" with God changes me on the inside. A child does not decide, "I think I will imitate Dad," and then go about practicing posture, mannerisms, and voice inflections that bear an uncanny resemblance to his dad. He absorbs family traits unconsciously, by sustained contact.

Dr. Alexis Carrel, a French physician awarded the Nobel Prize in Medicine, published a book in 1936 extolling the therapeutic value of prayer. Pray regularly, he advised, and you will find your life improved. The bodily posture itself—relaxing, joining hands, bending knees—has health benefits. Prayer helps us resolve emotional conflicts, purge guilt, and overcome negativism. And by verbalizing what goes on inside, the pray-er practices a kind of self-induced therapy.

Carrel assured his readers that these benefits accrue whether or not prayer is addressed to God or indeed any god, and regardless of its content. Dr. Carrel's theories, since adopted by many New Age advocates, may well be correct, but they miss the main point of Christian prayer. Whom we pray to matters more than how or what we pray. As E. Stanley Jones observed, "If prayer were only autosuggestion, I would still pray. It's a better hypothesis with better results. But I would find it difficult to pray for long, for we cannot

---

One Rare Moment

BEN

I have had at least one supernatural experience while praying, and I look back on it as a holy moment. I was visiting a friend, a hemophiliac, who had contracted AIDS from contaminated blood. Everyone knew he was dying, and I went to his hospital room with my associate pastor to serve him Communion.

My friend was gaunt, his skin pale and bruised, and thrush had broken out in his mouth. He swallowed the Communion elements with some difficulty. I expected him to be anxious over death, but he wasn't. He told us a very moving story. Earlier in the week an angel had visited him in the hospital room. "Don't be afraid," said the angel. "You'll be seeing your daughter soon" (a daughter who had died in infancy).

As I sat by his bed, I could hear the television in the next room. The setting, with its industrial furniture and humming machinery, was anything

give ourselves to an unreality. I do not want to live in a paradise if it turns out to be a fool's paradise."

Any therapeutic value to Christian prayer comes as an outgrowth, not a goal. As Jesus promised, the fruit will grow if we remain attached to the vine. Our job is to remain attached, to "abide."

I recall a time early in our marriage when Janet and I were at loggerheads about, well, almost everything. We were still sorting out power issues, and neither of us was giving much ground. Every decision, major or minor, escalated into a tug-of-war. Stymied, we agreed to try something that had never before worked for us: we would pray together. Each day we sat on a couch and spilled out our inner selves to God. We prayed about those decisions, about the people we would contact that day, about our friends and family members. Our own power issues took on an entirely new light as we subjected ourselves to a Higher Power. We were now side by side before God, not facing each other in opposition. Twenty-five years later we keep up the practice.

Has that practice been therapeutic? Yes, certainly. Even more important, though, it gives us as a couple a daily reminder of a reality we might otherwise ignore. We made our vows before God, after all, and it seems only

---

but mystical. After he finished his story, I felt a need to prolong the moment. "We need to be silent," I said. And in that setting, for the first and only time, I spoke in tongues. I had been around charismatics and even prayed for the gift of tongues but had never received it. Now it happened to me, as a spontaneous response to the *gravitas* of that moment, the glory we had glimpsed as he told us of God's mercy to him on his deathbed.

I now serve as a chaplain to university students. And I must say that around them I hesitate to mention that experience, though for me it was profound. We get such moments rarely. I hear students speak of God so casually: "God told me to start a Bible study.... God told me to date this girl." To someone who doesn't know the lingo, it sounds like the Christian life is one big mystical experience after another.

I wouldn't trade my experience with my friend in the hospital for anything—but that was one moment out of a lifetime of showing up, of waiting on God. I had been in ministry for years before I experienced anything like that. I tell the students that 90 percent of praying is showing up.

appropriate to welcome God as an interested party into the ordinary, and sometimes stormy, workings of our marriage.

"Nobody has to prove to me that prayer makes a difference," wrote Henri Nouwen during his stay in South America. "Without prayer I become irritable, tired, heavy of heart, and I lose the Spirit who directs my attention to the needs of others instead of my own. Without prayer, my attention moves to my own preoccupation. I become cranky and spiteful and often I experience resentment and a desire for revenge." Nouwen admitted that his hour a day in a chapel was full of distractions, restlessness, sleepiness, confusion, and boredom. But he noticed in retrospect that the days and weeks were different, positively different, when he prayed: "Without this one-hour-a-day for God, my life loses its coherency and I start experiencing my days as a series of random incidents and accidents."

A few years ago I wrote a book on the Old Testament, *The Bible Jesus Read*, in which I discussed the cursing psalms that called for revenge on enemies. I described a practice of taking a weekly "anger walk" on the hill behind my home, during which I would present to God the resentment I felt toward people who had wronged me. Forcing myself to open up deep feelings to God had a therapeutic effect. "Usually I come away feeling as if I have just released a huge burden," I wrote in that book. "The unfairness no longer sticks like a thorn inside me, as it once did; I have expressed it aloud to someone—to God. Sometimes I find that in the process of expression, I grow in compassion. God's Spirit speaks to me of my own selfishness, my judgmental spirit, my own flaws that others have treated with grace and forgiveness, my pitifully limited viewpoint."

I came across that passage just today and had the startling feeling that someone else had written it. You see, it has been several years since I have taken an anger walk. I still stroll on that hill, usually on Sunday afternoons. I check the fox den, look for signs of beetle damage on the Ponderosa pines, follow animal tracks in the snow. And I still pray, though now it would be more accurate to call them "praise walks." In time, the anger melted away. Healing took place, even without my conscious awareness.

Fear

Ultimately prayer proves its power by producing changes in us the pray-ers. "Prayer is taking time to let God recreate us, play with us, touch us as an artist who is making a sculpture, a painting, or a piece of music with our lives," writes Don Postema. Looking back, I can see several specific ways in which the power of prayer has helped re-create me. Fear is one example.

I take a refresher course in fear every summer as I try to climb some of the more difficult mountains in Colorado. Since I get queasy when I clean the gutters on my house, edging my way across a narrow ledge with a thousand-foot drop on either side requires some major self-therapy. On a mountain fear can be your enemy, by paralyzing you and tempting you to make rash decisions, or your friend, by teaching you responsible limits. Last summer after a five-hour climb I turned back a mere sixty feet from the summit of Wetterhorn Peak. Each step of the final ascent was coated with hard-packed snow, and a single misstep would have sent me hurtling to certain death. Made wise by fear, I postponed the ascent to a warmer day.

Sometimes the fear is only *apparent*: a granite face that looks perilous turns out to have good ledges and handholds. Sometimes the fear is fully appropriate, and then trust is the only sure antidote. Whenever possible I climb with partners because it helps to vocalize fear and get counsel from others. Which route seems safest? Is this move foolhardy? Can we make the summit before that thunderstorm rolls in? I practice with an ice axe during the winter so that I can trust my self-arrest instincts in case of a slide down a snowfield. I trust ropes when they prove necessary.

On two of the hardest peaks my wife and I hired a professional guide, which did wonders for fear. As it happened, the guide who led us had summited Mount Everest three times and Mount Denali thirteen times. I transferred all my insecurities to crusty old Bob, who knew these two Colorado peaks as well as I know my backyard. Thanks to him, I experienced less fear crossing the notorious Knife Edge on Capitol Peak than climbing a less difficult peak on my own.

Prayer introduces a very different set of fears than what I confront on a mountain, and yet there are some parallels. For years I labored under a huge *apparent* fear: the image of a stern, judgmental God as a sort of cosmic Enforcer. Who would want to pray to that God? With such a fearsome partner, how could I pursue an intimate relationship? My defenses lowered over time as I experienced grace, as I met trustworthy guides, and then supremely as I got to know Jesus.

For a recovering fundamentalist, it takes courage to trust that the gospel truly is good news from a God who is love. I sought out guides who believed this most fundamental and yet seldom-realized fact of faith. For ten years I followed around Dr. Paul Brand, who brought healing and grace to some of the lowest people on the planet, low-caste Hindus afflicted with leprosy. Sometimes we prayed together and always I marveled at his simple faith. He showed a spirit of thanksgiving even as he worked for near-poverty wages in trying conditions. He faced into old age with anticipation, not fear. Even at the end, he saw death as a true homecoming, not an interruption but a culmination.

Henri Nouwen proved another trustworthy guide, one who demonstrated that a true image of God calms, rather than provokes, fear. Despite his own inner fears, Nouwen put his trust in the character of God. He learned about fear that "you do not run away from it but feel it through and stand up in it and look it right in the face.... So I am praying while not knowing how to pray. I am resting while feeling restless, at peace while tempted, safe while still anxious, surrounded by a cloud of light while still in darkness, in love while still doubting." Ultimately he placed his trust in a God "who holds me, who loved me long before I came into life [and] will love me long after I have died."

If I am ever sent to prison and tortured, thought Nouwen, I hope and pray they let me keep a copy of Psalms. Those prayers calmed his fears. "They are more than ideas, images, comparisons: They become a real presence. After a day with much work or with many tensions, you feel that you can let go in safety and realize how good it is to dwell in the shelter of the Most High." You transfer your fears to God. "I will fear no evil, for you are with me," wrote the psalmist.

I marvel that many of the exalted prayers of the apostle Paul appear in the prison epistles, composed in a dungeon. Prayer served as a way for Paul to rise above the fears of the present circumstances into a radical trust in God's tender care. In the same way, ministers and civil rights protestors in the 1960s used their prison time to pray aloud and sing hymns. A skeptic could see those prayers as reality-denial of the worst kind. A believer sees them as faith in a reality that transcends circumstances and disarms fear.

A friend who bicycled across China in 1984 told me of staying with a couple, both university professors, who were just beginning to talk openly about their faith. During the years of the Cultural Revolution they had landed on a blacklist because of their education status. Worse, Red Guards harangued children to turn in their parents if they showed any sign of religious faith. Not wanting to put their own children in an impossible position, the man and his wife decided for a time to remove all religious symbols from their house and to stop praying in public or talking about their faith. They did agree to continue one practice, though. At night, as they lay in bed, they held hands and repeated silently the Lord's Prayer. By squeezing hands at the end of each line, they worked through the phrases together. Then they continued to hold hands for a time of silent prayer, especially for their children. That nightly silent ritual allayed their fears and bonded their faith during the darkest days of the revolution.

Finally, when it appeared that the political climate had truly changed, the couple decided to talk with their children. They feared that through their self-imposed silence they had forfeited all opportunity to raise their children in a Christian home. Within a year all five children, who had grown up under militant atheism, accepted the faith of their parents. "Our prayers were answered," the parents told my friend. "We had nothing to fear after all."

Anxiety

John of the Cross warns of the *Spiritus vertiginis* that tempts us as we pray, a whirling spirit like vertigo that leaves the head spinning and the stomach churning. That spirit besets me when deadlines approach and family members go through crises and mechanical devices stop working. I want to fidget and fix things, and prayer seems entirely too slow and unproductive a response. Watching the news can bring on the same spirit, as it stirs up new objects for worry: terrorist threats, the dwindling oil supply, bird flu, global warming, a downturn in the economy.

Then I read with amazement Paul's words to the Philippians: "Do not be anxious about anything, but in everything, by prayer and petition, with thanksgiving, present your requests to God." A quick review of Paul's biography—prison, harrowing escapes, public debates, beatings, illness, shipwreck—makes that advice almost incomprehensible, especially when I note this was one of the letters Paul composed from a prison "in chains." He continues, "And the peace of God, which transcends all understanding, will guard your hearts and your minds in Christ Jesus."

In a letter written to people undergoing persecution, the apostle Peter gave similar advice: "Cast all your anxiety on him because he cares for you." I had been letting anxiety keep me from prayer. Instead I need to see prayer as a place to *deposit* my anxiety, by naming my concerns as specifically as possible and asking for God's help in relieving me of the burdens. Can I trust

God's promise to replace anxiety with a spirit of peace that will "guard" my heart and mind?

Paul's description of a peace that transcends all understanding echoes Jesus, who said, "My peace I give you. I do not give to you as the world gives." Defeating the *Spiritus vertiginis* means exposing as a lie the peace dangled before me by the world. When I turn on the television, every few minutes I hear lavish assurances of peace: if only I buy a certain pill (after checking with my doctor for side effects which flash on the screen too fast to read), drink a new low-carb beer, climb in the driver's seat of a safety-rated automobile, or sign up for life insurance to guarantee my family's financial security. Jesus must have had a very different peace in mind because he had none of those indulgences and died at a young age after a turbulent career.

Hailed as a miracle worker and Savior of Israel, Jesus was pressed by crowds of people begging him to solve their family problems, heal their illnesses, bless their children, rescue their nation, exorcize their demons. Sometimes after a full day surrounded by anxieties Jesus would get up early in the morning, long before sunrise, and pray; sometimes he would escape the madding crowd and row across a lake in search of peace and quiet. For him, prayer served as a refuge. He left his own anxiety over suffering and death behind in a garden before reporting to the trial and crucifixion he knew awaited him. Jesus knew the secret of anxiety-transfer.

Letters from the Desert by Carlo Caretto tells of a busy Italian executive who in 1954 joined the Little Brothers of Jesus in the desert of Algeria to help establish a place of peaceful prayer in a hostile Muslim land. Before then, Caretto had worked as an activist, a doer. He felt the anxiety of a person doing a busy and important work for God.

> For many years I had thought I was "somebody" in the Church. I had even imagined this sacred living structure of the Church as a temple sustained by many columns, large and small, each one with the shoulder of a Christian under it. My own shoulder too I thought of as supporting a column, however small.... There was never enough time to get everything done. One raced continually from one project to another, from one meeting to another, from one city to another. Prayer was hurried, conversations frenzied, and one's heart in a turmoil.

As he knelt on the desert sand one day, Caretto reports,

> I drew back suddenly, as though to free myself from this weight. What had happened? Everything remained in its place, motionless. Not

a movement, not a sound. After twenty-five years I had realized that nothing was burdening my shoulders and that the column was my own creation—sham, unreal, the product of my imagination and my vanity.... The weight of the world was all on Christ Crucified.

I am learning that prayer need not be "productive" in the normal sense of the term. I spend most of my waking hours trying to make it through the designated tasks for that day. Prayer offers a time to set aside that list of concerns—or rather to present them to God—to relax, to let the mind roam freely, to drink deeply, to insert a pause in the day, to trust. A strange thing happens, though. I find that when I reserve that time, I become more productive. I make clearer decisions and fewer impulsive mistakes. I waste less time worrying. I seem less bothered when things go wrong. The vertigo slips away.

A week ago as I headed to the mountains to write this chapter I drove into a blizzard. As the highway climbed steeply toward the Eisenhower Tunnel west of Denver, cars were spinning tires and skidding left and right across the icy pavement. Some lost control and slid to the shoulder or into retaining ditches beside the road. I engaged four-wheel-drive and slowed my speed, but even so the driving snow, which made dazzling patterns like fireworks in my headlights, obscured the highway lane markers. I could hardly see where to steer. I felt acid churning in my stomach and sweat pooling on my hands.

My mind raced through the possibilities. I could turn around and abandon the trip. I could plow ahead despite the anxiety, hoping for the best. Suddenly a thought came to me: I could pray. For the next forty-five minutes I prayed aloud for every relative and friend and missionary and prisoner and suffering person I could think of. That very act somehow disengaged me from the anxiety. Although my foot kept touching the brake and my hands turned the steering wheel as needed, the rest of my concentration poured into my prayers. I was floating above life, just as my car was floating above the pavement, cushioned by a layer of snow.

I would not recommend such an exercise in any winter driving manual, but I did arrive safely at my destination remarkably free of tension and fear. "Cast all your anxiety on him because he cares for you," wrote the apostle Peter, quickly followed by the admonition, "Be self-controlled and alert." Somehow both took place that night on Interstate 70.

Impatience

When I moved to Colorado I soon learned about noxious weeds. Unwelcome species such as dandelion, oxeye daisy, Russian thistle, and toadflax are spreading like botanical viruses in my part of the state, threatening the survival of native species. Wanting to be a good citizen, I bought a hardy weed-puller and began a routine I have kept up through each spring and summer. I take an afternoon walk on the hill behind my home in search of the noxious invaders. As it happens, that walk presents an ideal opportunity for prayer. For a few minutes in the middle of the day I am alone in the beauty of nature, away from the distractions of my home office.

One day when my wife accompanied me I had an epiphany about my weed walks and also my prayers. Her keen eyes helped in the process of spotting weeds, yes, but more importantly she changed the entire nature of the walk by pointing out more than twenty species of wildflowers. I had been so intent on finding the weeds that my eyes had skipped right past the wildflowers adorning the hills—the very flowers my weed-pulling endeavored to protect!

It occurred to me that I do something similar in my prayer practice. I tend to bring a tangled mess of problems to God, not unlike the snarl of weeds I carry home in my collection bag, while overlooking opportunities for praise and thanksgiving. My prayers are essentially selfish, an effort to employ God to help me accomplish my ends. I look on God as a problem-solver (a weed-puller) while overlooking the striking evidence of God's work all around me. And when nothing much seems to happen, I grow impatient.

There is a cure for impatience in prayer, I have found: Keep praying. You will likely grow so frustrated that you will either give up the practice or change your approach to prayer. Jean Nicolas Grou, a mystic from the eighteenth century, prescribed that healthy prayer should be humble, reverent, loving, confident, and persevering—in other words, the exact opposite of impatient.

I like to see the results of my labors. I work on an article and several months later it appears in print. I climb a mountain and reach the summit. Prayer operates by different rules, God's rules. We do it in secret, so that no one notices the effort, and the results—God's results, not ours—come in surprising ways, often long after we expected them. Prayer means opening myself to God and not limiting God through my own preconceptions. In sum, prayer means letting God be God.

Many prayers in the Bible come out of the act of waiting. Abraham and Sarah waiting for just one child. Jacob waiting seven years for a wife and then seven more years after being tricked by her father. The Israelites waiting four centuries for deliverance, and Moses waiting four decades for the call to lead them, then four more decades for a Promised Land he would not enter. David waiting in caves for his promised coronation. Prophets waiting for the fulfillment of their own strange predictions. Mary and Joseph, Elizabeth and Zechariah, Anna, Simeon waiting like most Jews for a Messiah. The disciples waiting impatiently for Jesus to act like the power-Messiah they longed for.

God, who is timeless, requires of us a mature faith that may, as it did for many of these, involve delays that seem like trials. Patience is one sign of that maturity, a quality that can develop only through the passage of time.

Children want things *now*: "Are we there yet?... But I want dessert now!... Now can we open our presents?... Is my time-out over?" In contrast, lovers learn to wait: "So Jacob served seven years to get Rachel, but they seemed like only a few days to him because of his love for her." Medical students wait through ten years and more of training before setting up a practice. Parents wait for years in hopes that the prodigal will return. Waiting is not the goal, but may be a necessary stage in attaining the goal. We wait for what is worth waiting for, and in the process learn patience.

"My soul waits for the Lord more than watchmen wait for the morning," wrote one of the psalmists. The picture comes to mind of a watchman counting the minutes for his shift to be over. I pray for the patience to endure times of trial, to keep anticipating, keep hoping, keep believing. I pray for the patience to be patient. As another psalmist wrote,

> My eyes fail, looking for your promise;
>   I say, "When will you comfort me?"
> Though I am like a wineskin in the smoke,
>   I do not forget your decrees.
> How long must your servant wait?

Stopping Time

Anthony Bloom struggled to learn patience, with good reason. He lived a tumultuous life in a tumultuous century. After spending early years in Russia and Persia (now Iran), he fled as a refugee with his parents to France, where he served in World War II and trained as a surgeon.

Having no religious background, Bloom professed atheism until he experienced a dramatic conversion while reading the gospel of Mark. Later he resigned his medical practice, entered the priesthood, and eventually rose to become the Russian Orthodox Metropolitan for Western Europe. In his book *Beginning to Pray* he tells of the crucial step of conquering his impatience and creating space for God by "stopping time."

As a physician, Bloom was always focusing on the future. While examining one patient he would peer behind her into the next room to count the heads of those waiting to see him. By the end of his surgery hours, he had not the slightest recollection of the people he had seen. Furthermore, he found himself asking the same questions twice or three times, not remembering what he had just done. He decided he had to change his approach, by treating the patient before him as the only person who existed. Whenever he felt the urge, "I must be quick," he forced himself to sit back and engage in small talk for a few minutes in order to keep himself from hurrying. Surprisingly, he found that he actually had *more* time during the day because he no longer had to repeat questions and procedures.

Primary Wonder

DENISE LEVERTOV, FROM *SANDS OF THE WELL*

Days pass when I forget the mystery.
Problems insoluble and problems offering
their own ignored solutions
jostle for my attention, they crowd its antechamber
along with a host of diversions, my courtiers, wearing
their colored clothes; cap and bells.

And then
once more the quiet mystery is present to me, the
throng's clamor recedes; the mystery
that there is anything, anything at all, let alone
cosmos, joy, memory, everything,
rather than void: and that, O Lord,
Creator, Hallowed One, You still,
hour by hour sustain it.

We must deliberately stop time that is trying to move too fast, Bloom decided. Say, "No," and you will discover that time passes perfectly well and without the inner tension. "Can you imagine that only one minute goes by every minute? That is exactly what happens. It is strange, but it is true, though from the way we behave one might think that five minutes could rush by in thirty seconds."

The practice of stopping time gradually transformed Bloom's life with God. He concentrated on living in the present, recognizing that the past is irremediably gone and the future is irrelevant because who knows whether it will happen or not. *Now*, a fleeting instant, represents the intersection of eternity with time.

At certain times in the day Bloom would pause and say, "I am seated, I am doing nothing, I will do nothing for five minutes ... I am here in the presence of God, in my own presence and in the presence of all the furniture that is around me, just still, moving nowhere." He practiced this for short periods, two to five minutes, when tempted to fidget. Then he extended the few minutes to a longer time, learning to be calm and serene in those intervals, before resuming his busy schedule.

To his amazement Bloom found that the rest of the world could, in fact, wait five minutes while he was not busy with it. He learned that even the most pressing tasks, which normally would fill up his mind, could be postponed for three, five, or ten minutes—and in fact he did those tasks more calmly and quickly after the interludes. Eventually he linked these stop-time moments to a protracted time of prayer in the morning and evening.

He began each day in quiet and stillness, acknowledging that the day itself was a gift of God, something that had never existed before, a chance for a new start. It stretched before him like a vast expanse of unspoiled snow in his native Russia. "This is the day the Lord has made; let us rejoice and be glad in it." He prayed to enter that day as God's own messenger, carrying God's presence to everyone he met. Then at night he would review all that had happened, committing both the progress and the failures to a gracious God. The day is now spent; it rests in God's hands.

Intervals of stillness and prayer became for Bloom a series of markers, strung together like pearls in a necklace, reminding him of the true nature of reality. Life is not a meaningless sequence of actions but an arena in which to live out the will of another world, the kingdom of heaven. Prayer is a state as much as an act, a fact that easily gets forgotten when we confine it to one or two isolated instances a day.

I point to Anthony Bloom (who died in 2003) because I would be dishonest to pretend to achieving the discipline he recommends. When I sense that my activity means something and has worth, and so move faster and faster trying to accomplish more and more, at that moment I give in to pride and a feeling that all depends on me. What a foolish thought. My heart could stop beating within the hour, my brain could fail from an aneurysm. This present moment itself is a gift from God—I would live more realistically, and at the same time accomplish far more, if I allowed that fundamental truth to pervade my day.

How can I stop time? How can I learn to listen during silence? How can I trust my actions less and God's stillness more? How can I transfer my fear and anxiety to God? How can I frame my day by aligning it with the reality that begins and ends with God? What markers in a day call me back to the truth that busyness conspires against? If I can answer those questions, I may find the other questions that obsess me receding in urgency.

CHAPTER 21

PRAYER AND OTHERS

The purest form of love is given with no expectation of return.
Measured by this standard, earnest prayer for others
is a magnificent act of love.
DAVID HUBBARD

Knowing of my interest in prayer, a friend forwarded to me an email and asked for my opinion. I had received chain-letter emails about golf balls and money-making schemes, but never one pertaining to prayer.

An American soldier in Iraq had learned that his wife back home had been diagnosed with stage four cervical cancer. Doctors gave a bleak prognosis. Feeling helpless, separated by half the world from his distraught wife, the soldier sent an email message to his church. Members of the church then forwarded his prayer request to all their contacts:

> Pray and forward. It only takes a second to hit "forward." Please do it and don't delete this, your prayer can and perhaps will save her life. Please pray and ask everyone you know to pray for the HEALING of Cindy, removal of all cancer in her body so she may enjoy all that life has to offer, and to continue to be the wonderful mother to our 5-year-old son.

The email raised questions for my friend. Does prayer operate like a pyramid scheme — the more people who pray, the more likely the answer? Does a sick woman who happens to have praying friends stand a better chance for recovery than an equally deserving person who does not? Exactly how does prayer benefit someone other than the pray-er? And how can something I pray have an impact on another person without infringing on his or her free will?

Some of these questions, such as whether quantity matters, no one can answer with certainty.* I learned of an earlier email campaign in which the sender promised that if one million Christians prayed, then Saddam Hussein would resign voluntarily, forestalling the impending war in Iraq—a prayer that obviously went unanswered. Surely prayer does not operate according to a mathematical formula in which God calculates the total amount of prayer-pressure being applied.

Yet in places like South Africa and Eastern Europe, mass prayers did seem to make a difference. The Bible itself includes some examples, such as God responding to Israelite slaves in Egypt because "I have heard them crying out." The prophets pleaded with entire nations to repent and in some cases (notably Jonah's Nineveh) they did. Paul solicited group prayers from places like Corinth, Ephesus, and Rome. Apparently the shared concern of many people has an effect.

As God Sees

Intercession—praying for others—introduces some of the most puzzling issues of prayer. The more I mull over intercession, the more it calls for a shift in how I look at the world.

Thanks to the scientific method, most people in "developed" countries have an outlook of mild deism. We assume things like weather and disease operate according to fixed natural laws. Every so often, though, problems impinge on us so directly that we stretch beyond that mildly deistic stance and ask God to intervene. When a drought drags on too long, we pray for rain. When a young mother gets a diagnosis of cervical cancer, we solicit prayers for her healing. We beseech God as if trying to talk God into something God otherwise might not want to do.

My understanding of prayer calls me to recast that perspective on the world. I take as my starting point what I learn about God in the person of Jesus. The Gospels make clear that Jesus wants all people everywhere to experience the love of God, because he devoted his life to conveying

---

*Not for lack of trying, however. Historian Paul Johnson reports that "at the University of Louvain, where Erasmus spent some time, teachers and students were in 1493 debating the topics: do four five-minute prayers on consecutive days stand a better chance of being answered than one twenty-minute prayer? Is a prayer of ten minutes, said on behalf of ten people, as efficacious as ten one-minute prayers? The debate lasted eight weeks, longer than it had taken Columbus to sail to America the previous year, 1492."

that message. They also make clear that Jesus desires physical health for us, because not once — *not once* — did he turn down a request for physical healing.

I begin, then, with the central core of reality: God is love, and desires the best for us. True, not all people welcome or even care about God's love, and not all people enjoy physical health. That means something must be interfering with God's ideal for this planet, but it does not change the prime fact of God's love.

God is looking for a beachhead of presence in the world — a *body*, we might say, and indeed that is the very image Paul seizes upon in his letters. We the "body of Christ" have formed a partnership to dispense God's love and grace to others. As we experience that grace, inevitably we want to share it with others. Love does not come naturally to me, I must say. I need prayer in order to place myself within the force field of God's love, allowing God to fill me with compassion that I cannot muster on my own.

This way of viewing the world changes how I pray for others. Crudely put, I once envisioned intercession as bringing requests to God that God may not have thought of, then talking God into granting them. Now I see intercession as an increase in *my* awareness. When I pray for another person, I am praying for God to open my eyes so that I can see that person as God does, and then enter into the stream of love that God already directs toward that person.

Something happens when I pray for others in this way. Bringing them into God's presence changes my attitude toward them and ultimately affects our relationship. I pray for the neighbor who is always trying to sneak out of paying his share of neighborhood assessments and begin to see him not as a conniver but as a friendless man who lives with constant financial worries. I pray for my drug-addicted relative and see past the irresponsible behavior to a wounded, desperate soul.

In short, prayer allows me to see others as God sees them (and me): as uniquely flawed and uniquely gifted bearers of God's image. I begin seeing them through Jesus' eyes, as beloved children whom the Father longs to embrace. I know that God wants their marriages to grow stronger and their children to stay out of trouble; God wants them healthy, and strong to resist temptation, capable of reaching out to others in need. I bring those prayers to God because I know God wills the very same thing. What I desire in the people I pray for, God desires all the more.

Praying for those whom I love gives me a glimpse of how God must feel. I cannot impose my own wishes; God, who probably could, chooses not to out of respect for human freedom. In many cases I can see behavior that needs to change, for *their* sakes. I see relatives and friends making choices that hurt others in addition to themselves. Yet, as every parent knows, we have limited influence over any other free person unless we resort to some coercion that will likely backfire. In the Prophets, and in Jesus' parable of the prodigal son, God expresses the exact same dilemma.

Once I catch a glimpse of another person through the eyes of God, I feel a prod to respond as part of Christ's body—God's incarnate presence—on earth. And, of course, what changes me *does* change the other person. I begin to treat my neighbor and relative in a different way, tinged by God's grace. I write my troubled friends notes of encouragement and ask how I can help. I pray for those in other countries who work with prostitutes, prisoners, and orphans and find myself digging deeper to send financial help. Nothing spurs compassion in me like prayer.*

I look back with special fondness on an early morning prayer time held weekly when I worked for *Campus Life* magazine. We convened at 7:00 a.m., an hour before work began, and the gathering was strictly voluntary. Over time, though, the handful of us who met learned each other's secrets. We got to know each other's stories, including the colorful family members and the private pains and struggles. Then, after praying about each of the specifics of those lives, we would join together in the combined task of putting out a magazine.

You treat a typist differently during the day, I found, after listening to her describe her self-image problems—"Will I always be just a secretary?"—and praying with her that morning. You are less likely to judge a computer programmer for his irritating mistake when you hear how deeply that mistake affected him. In short, you begin to see fellow workers not as cogs in a machine but as human beings graced and loved by God. That hour in the morning brought us together in a new kind of order, not one based on ranking and salary, but as men and women with hopes and longings, fears and struggles, dreams and devastations. It brought us together in the orbit of God's searing love.

---

* *The Book of Common Prayer* includes a lovely prayer for "the poor and the oppressed, for the unemployed and the destitute, for prisoners and captives, and for all who remember and care for them."

A Widening Circle

"Christ stands between us, and we can only get into touch with our neighbours through him," wrote Dietrich Bonhoeffer. When I bring others before God, I bear in mind that God is present both to me and to the people for whom I am praying. Starting from the center point of God's love, my prayers move outward in widening circles, like ripples in a pond, from those closest to me to those in the distance.

I know my family and my good friends best. I try to be as specific as possible, praying for my niece's problem pregnancy, my cousin's battle with alcohol, my neighbor's prodigal daughter—again, not telling God anything new but involving a third party in the relationship, a Person who cares more about each of them than I do. I ask that God will use my love and concern, my prayer, to help bring about the good that we both desire.

Sometimes intercession produces change in the person prayed for and sometimes in the pray-er. Virginia Stem Owens tells of her practice of laying out requests before God in evening prayers and then listening for God's response. She waited in the darkness one night, hearing nothing before finally drifting off to sleep. In the early morning hours, just before dawn, she started awake and found herself weeping. A memory had come to her subconscious of a spinster aunt who had moved in with her family when Virginia was a young adolescent. Virginia had been promised a room of her own, but with her aunt's arrival her brother got the private room and Virginia got the consolation prize: a semi-invalid aunt as a roommate.

Over the weeks and months that followed, Virginia barely concealed her bitterness, showing it in a thousand subtle and caustic ways. That night in bed, years later, she realized she had harbored the grudge her whole life:

> But now, in this early morning light, I was feeling for the first time the scalding shame this elderly woman must have felt. Moving from house to house, never having one of her own. Totally dependent on the good graces of nieces and nephews for the very necessities of life. Never in all my years at home, or indeed until now, had I given a single thought to how she felt in the situation. But now I was getting a full dose of it—the pride that had to be swallowed daily in a galling gulp. It was more bitter than I could bear.

The next evening Owens repeated the exercise, offering her petitions to God and then listening awhile before falling asleep. Something similar happened the following morning: another incident resurrected from her past, again with shattering results. Prayer became a time of confrontation and then healing as she brought her relationships into the presence of a Mediator.

For years I have kept a list of people I pray for on a set of note cards. One day I pray for family members by name. On alternating days I pray for friends, neighbors, fellow writers, and those ministering in the inner city or other countries, and then I use one day as a spiritual checklist for myself. Like Virginia Stem Owens, I find that my attitude changes in the very act of praying. Instead of writing off my cousin as an irresponsible bum, I begin to see him through the compassionate eyes of Jesus. I think of ways in which I can offer personal help for the very problems I am praying about.

On the Edge

MIKE

I learned about the importance of intercessory prayer when, as a college sophomore, I got the crazy idea of leaving school for five months to live on the street. A friend caught the vision too, and after some serious negotiating with our parents we left the fine California campus of Westmont College and its multigrain cafeteria and set out for cities like Denver, Washington, D.C., Portland, and Phoenix. We ate whatever we could rummage out of garbage cans or whatever we could buy from the coins people tossed into our guitar cases as we stood on street corners and sang praise songs.

It's a different world out there. We didn't shave or shower, and from our scraggly appearance no one could guess we were really college students, not a regular part of street culture.

Every two weeks I tried to find a library or some place with a free computer we could use, and file a report to a group who had agreed to pray for us. The first email went to forty or fifty people. At the end of five months, ten times that many were on our list. I can think of half a dozen times when I heard from someone who said they'd felt a sudden urge to pray for us. For example, one friend said she woke up at three o'clock in the morning and felt she needed to pray for me. I worked out the time zone difference, and that was the very night someone tore through my backpack and stole my jeans.

Some twenty years ago I wrote a well-known author that I would pray for her one day a week because I imagined the kind of pressures she would face. "No one had ever once said he was praying for me," she told me later. "Consequently I felt obligated to be worthy of your prayers, to remain a Christian writer, to do it as well as I could." I know that feeling, because I too have been on the receiving end of prayers. A reader who had read one of my books as her three-year-old daughter underwent surgery for a brain tumor sent me an extraordinary gift: a Prayer Journal in which she had filled in the blank pages—365 of them—with handwritten prayers for me. Sometimes on an odd day, say March 3 or August 19, when I am feeling discouraged or lethargic, I'll turn to a prayer she wrote on my behalf several years ago and find it eerily relevant to that day's struggles. I tried writing the woman recently

---

I looked on those email contacts as a kind of life-support line back to a world of people who cared, who shared something of our vision. The streets can be rough. And I met so many needy people who have no one, not a single person in the world, who prays for them. I'd estimate a quarter of the homeless I met have an active faith. But for the most part they're out there alone, unsupported.

We were playing guitars and singing "As the Deer Panteth for the Water" when a street guy named David started weeping. "That's what I want, man," he said. "I want that water. I'm an alcoholic, but I want to be healed." As I spent more time with David, I realized that connecting with God is his only hope for healing. He simply doesn't have the inner strength. Really, he needs a group around him supporting him in prayer, like I had.

I wrote about some of my adventures in a book (*Under the Overpass*), but of course I had the ability to leave the streets and return to a more secure, comfortable life. I hope I never forget what I learned there. Some of the people I met put my faith to shame. Like Rings, a former drug addict who got converted and now spends his entire Social Security check on food that he distributes to people still stuck on the street. I hope I never forget hearing some of them pray—just like they live, on the edge, without clichés, with no pretense at all. They are what they are, before the rest of the world and before God too.

and got a postal notice that she had moved, with no forwarding address. Her prayers live on: I, too, seek to be worthy of them.

When I study the prayers of the apostle Paul, I see clearly the widening circle of God's love. Paul prays constantly, night and day, for his fellow worker Timothy and often mentions other individuals by name. He prays for a slave owner, Philemon, even as he presses for the slave's release. He prays for close friends, yes, but also offers passionate prayers for churches he has visited and even some, like Rome and Colosse, he has not. He prays for an entire race, his fellow Jews who cannot accept Jesus as Messiah.

I think about parallels in my own life twenty centuries later. I hear a report on AIDS in Africa. Better yet, I visit Africa on a writing assignment and see in person the abandoned babies with stick-figure limbs and orangish hair lying motionless in bed, and hear in accented English the stories of women infected by their adulterous husbands and now ostracized from the community. That night I pray for the faces I have seen, and they become not just faces but fellow human beings who have fallen victim to evil on this planet. As I pray, their pain becomes mine, and I bring their plight before God. I search my soul for ways in which I, one person who lives an ocean away, can convey God's own love and concern for them. Who might best embody that love, and how can I help?

Or, closer to home, I hear that a friend of mine in another city is consulting a divorce lawyer. I know the circumstances well enough to know that no physical abuse or adultery is involved, just two people who have grown weary of the hard work of marriage. I bring the two, husband and wife, before God. All too easily I jump in with my own strong ideas of what should happen and pray for that result, but this time I confess I do not know all the facts. I hold out my hands, cupped in an open position, and present the couple to God. I try to imagine what healing would encompass: many tears, perhaps counseling, exposed secrets, the slow wash of forgiveness. I ask for that, and ask what role I can play as their friend. Aware that the marriage may have fractured beyond repair, I pray for them and for my response in that event as well.

At its best, my prayer does not seek to manipulate God into doing my will—quite the opposite. Prayer enters the pool of God's own love and widens outward.

Pushing the Boundaries

Frank Laubach, the founder of the modern literacy movement and a missionary to the Philippines, describes how he sought to pray for everyone he met, keeping an undercurrent of prayer going throughout his busy day. "One need not tell God everything about the people for whom one prays," he said. "Holding them one by one steadily before the mind and willing that God may have His will with them is the best, for God knows better than we what our friends need, yet our prayer releases His power, we know not how."

Laubach applied the same principle to people who lived beyond the circle of acquaintance, to world leaders he would never meet. After all, the New Testament commands prayer for such people. According to Laubach, we would accomplish more for the world by praying faithfully than by walking into the White House or Whitehall or the Kremlin with suggestions. Our personal advice would most likely be misguided, but prayer for leaders summons an invisible spiritual force that can have real effects—not by persuading God to try harder, but by persuading the leaders to try harder.*

"Love your enemies," Jesus said, widening the circle of prayer beyond anyone's comfort zone: "Pray for those who persecute you." During most of my life, Russians and Chinese were enemies, representing what seemed an implacably violent threat to the West. Now we cooperate with both nations and trade and cultural exchanges flourish. Our former enemies have human faces.

On a trip to Russia in 1991 I participated with a group of Christians who actually prayed with officers in the KGB. "We invited you because we need to learn the meaning of the word *repentance*," said the presiding colonel. After we left, he proceeded to distribute two million copies of the New Testament to Russian army troops. With shame I realized that during the Cold War not once had I prayed for Russian leaders. Perceiving them as mere

---

*In one famous instance in U.S. history, the leaders themselves turned to prayer after reaching an impasse. In four contentious weeks the Constitutional Convention had failed to write a single word. Benjamin Franklin, a man not known for his piety, rose to address George Washington: "The longer I live, the more convincing proofs I see of this truth, that God governs in the affairs of men." He went on to state his fear that the various factions would argue their own interests and reach no agreement: "Without his [God's] concurring aid, we shall succeed in this political building no better than the builders of Babel." Franklin then made a motion, "That henceforth prayers, imploring the assistance of Heaven and its blessing on our deliberations, be held in this assembly every morning." That practice continues in the U.S. Congress to this day.

enemies, I never took the step of bringing them before God and asking for God's point of view.

What about Islamist radicals who now oppose the West with violence? What effect might it have if every Christian church adopted the name of one Al-Qaeda member and prayed faithfully for that person?

More, should we be searching our souls prayerfully for the very symptoms in our society that arouse such opposition in the first place? The evening of September 11, 2001, my church filled with several hundred members who spontaneously assembled with no prior announcement of a service. Stunned, we pondered such questions as, *Why do they hate us?* At such a moment we instinctively turned to prayer, for our nation, for the future, for the families affected by the tragedy, for our leaders. A few days later the leaders themselves held a public prayer service in Washington's National Cathedral. For

---

The Long View

ARAM

"You must be hungry after shoveling so hard! Let me get you a piece of apple pie. Do you like apple pie? You stay right there and let me get you some pie."

She was an eighty-year-old widow, and I knew it would take at least ten minutes for her to make it into the kitchen, never mind dishing out the pie. I sat at the table, wondering how long she would make me sit before I got my pay and was out of there.

The offering was quintessential New England: light golden brown crust, piping hot apples, and cold milk in a tall glass. I devoured it.

She had barely sat down at the head of the table to enjoy her slice when she noticed my bare plate. "Let me get you another piece!" There was no declining the offer: she was into the kitchen before I could open my mouth. Funny how quickly she could move at times. The pie was good, the milk cold, and I made quick work of her second offering.

But she kept talking and talking. It was the unspoken dread of our neighborhood—getting caught with Mrs. Back. We all have a Mrs. Back in our lives. Even at that young age, I began to reflect, *How could someone be so oblivious to the cues before her—how could she not notice that I wanted out of there?*

310

a brief time Americans turned inward. Prayer in awareness of enemies, not to mention prayer *for* enemies, offers an opportunity for self-reflection; in a strange way, our enemies help to define us as much as our friends do.

In a letter to his brother, C. S. Lewis mentioned that he prayed every night for the people he was most tempted to hate, with Hitler, Stalin, and Mussolini heading the list. In another letter he wrote that as he prayed for them, he meditated on how his own cruelty might have blossomed into something like theirs. He remembered that Christ died for them as much as for him, and that he himself was not "so different from these ghastly creatures."

Almost everyone has an enemies list. For some in the United States it may include fundamentalists and right-wing Republicans; for others, secular humanists and the ACLU. Elsewhere, Christians face outright persecution

---

About ten years later, on a Monday afternoon, something inside me said, *You need to tell Mrs. Back.* For on that previous Friday night, at a bachelor party in Harvard Square, I gave myself to Jesus. I still hadn't told anybody. But somehow I knew: I was supposed to tell Mrs. Back.

It was a lovely spring afternoon in May, and Mrs. Back was hanging out her laundry to dry. I walked up to the fence. "Mrs. Back, do you know what it means to be "born again"?

She dropped everything and looked at me in sheer surprise and delight. "Why, yes I do." She had been a pastor's wife, after all.

"Well, the other night, I was born again."

She looked at me and said with a firm voice, "You stay right there!" I stood on the driveway, at the fence, watching her hobble up to the back door, up the steps with her cane.

Ten minutes later she came out from the back door, walked over to me, and handed me the biggest, most delicious piece of chocolate cake I had ever eaten in my life. She smiled and said, "Eat it!" And I devoured that piece of chocolate cake as she stood there and gazed at me. Celebrating with me. Rejoicing for me.

Finally, she spoke. "For the last fifteen years, since you moved in, I have prayed every day for you and for Paul (my friend who lived on the other side of her house) — I prayed every day that you would come to know Jesus."

311

from governments and religions. True followers of Jesus, however, hold in common his stunning command to love our enemies and pray for those who mistreat us. In so doing, we join together to extend the widening circle of God's love to those who may experience it in no other way.

In a passage from *The Cost of Discipleship*, the German pastor Dietrich Bonhoeffer contemplates that most difficult command. Jesus' enemies were no distant threat from overseas; they followed him around (probably listening to him as he spoke those very words), plotting against him and reporting on him to another set of enemies, the Roman occupiers. Bonhoeffer found himself in a parallel situation as Hitler's spies stalked him, scrutinized his sermons for signs of disloyalty, censored his writings, and looked for excuses to arrest him.

"We are approaching an age of widespread persecution," Bonhoeffer warned prophetically. "The Christians will be hounded from place to place, subjected to physical assault, maltreatment and death of every kind." By praying for such enemies, he continued, we do vicariously for them what they cannot do for themselves. Who needs our love more than those who are consumed with hatred? Through prayer we stand beside our enemies and plead to God on their behalf. (In the Gospels, the demon-possessed never asked Jesus for a cure; they were incapable. Instead, other people brought them to Jesus.)

Members of the religious orders the Little Brothers and the Little Sisters of Jesus take a vow to live among the very poor, especially in slums, places of armed conflict, and in Islamist areas where Christians are not welcome. They seek ordinary jobs such as cleaning houses or factory work, and spend their spare time in communal prayer. They do not preach or even get involved in much social work. They simply live alongside their neighbors, quietly showing them love, and they pray, believing that by doing so they will "drop by drop" allow the gospel to penetrate the world around them.

We are called to widen the orbit of God's love beyond friend and family and acquaintance, beyond even the boundaries of propriety and justice, to enemies themselves. We do this because God's love already extends that far: "Father, forgive them, for they do not know what they are doing," Jesus prayed for those who were in the act of killing him. A few months later one of Jesus' followers faced similar straits and responded as Jesus had, praying for those who were executing him, "Lord, do not hold this sin against them." Among those who heard Stephen's haunting words was a young man named Saul, an enemy of Jesus who would become the greatest missionary of all time.

"God loves his enemies," concludes Bonhoeffer; "that is the glory of his love." We defeat our enemies by loving them, and prayer activates that love. If I nurse a grudge and have not the strength to forgive, I present to God that wound, along with the one who inflicted it, and ask for strength I cannot supply on my own. (Could this be why Jesus *prayed*, "Father forgive them . . ." from the cross rather than pronouncing, "I forgive you"?) In effect, I transfer the wearisome burden to One far better equipped to carry it. Over time, the wound shows tender signs of healing. God works in me what I could not work in myself.

When a Christian magazine asked its readers to reflect on their most difficult prayers, it received the following response from a woman in Arkansas:

> Several years ago, when my daughter married, she revealed to me that my brother-in-law had repeatedly molested her when she was four. My first response was to pray for her healing from this man's evil. But the more I read about sexual abuse, the more I learned many abusers have been victims of abuse as well. I felt compelled to pray for my brother-in-law. Where I got the strength to pray this prayer, only God knows. It's not natural for a mother to pray for those who hurt her children. But I realized he'd never change without God healing what probably were very old wounds in his life. I struggle daily to forgive him, and worry that by doing so, I'll minimize the pain and suffering he's caused—but who else is going to pray for this man?

CHAPTER 22

PRAYER AND GOD

We pray best when we are
no longer aware of praying.
CASSIAN

I met with one of the few people I know personally who takes prayer as seri-ously as did Martin Luther, George Müller, and other giants of prayer. Marcia has a designated prayer closet in which she follows the interior castle model set forth by Teresa of Avila. Yet when I asked her about prayer, to my surprise she talked about all the other hours in her day:

"Conversation can be a prayer. Think of the Samaritan woman at the well, talking with Jesus about water and mountains and Jerusalem—wasn't that a prayer? I like to think of my conversations with people as prayer. I speak to Jesus within a person. I ask, Lord, let this lunch or tea or whatever be a prayer. When I read the Bible, that's a prayer. I don't read Psalm 73, I *pray* Psalm 73. I willingly refer my actions to God, and in so doing they become a prayer.

"'How's your prayer life?' people sometimes ask. For a Christian, how does that question differ from 'How's your life?' Our problem is that we separate, we compartmentalize.

"I'm a painter. I pray as I paint, and my painting becomes a kind of prayer. If someone asks me for help in prayer, I tell them to find what they most *enjoy* and do that, only do it for the glory of God. For you it may be writing or climbing a mountain. For me, it's painting. Start with what really energizes you and touches your heart: flowers, music, hiking, birds, gardening, what-ever. Ask God to remind you, as you do it, that you're doing it for him.

"Sometimes I pause in the midst of my painting and give God five min-utes, or more. Sometimes I don't—the whole afternoon of painting becomes a prayer. And often as I'm doing what I enjoy, specific requests come to mind. My friends studying in England. A missionary in China. I never make a list of what to pray for. I pray instantly, as soon as something comes to mind, and I trust God to bring it to mind.

"Spending time with God is what's important. We spend the time anyway. Why not recognize that we spend it with God, and then act like it?"

Listening to Marcia, I realized how easily I compartmentalize my life. I had the notion of prayer as a spiritual act oddly unrelated to the rest of my life. Out of a sense of duty I would put in the time, sometimes gladly and sometimes not, then get on with the real business of the day. I have since come to see prayer as something like a warm-up exercise, not an end in itself but a means to an end: to increase awareness of God at all other times.

Without Ceasing

I am learning the difference between saying prayers, which is an activity, and praying, which is a soul attitude, a "lifting up of the mind to God." Praying in that sense can transform every task, from shoveling snow to defragmenting a computer's hard disk.

Be joyful always; pray continually; give thanks in all circumstances.

Let us continually offer to God a sacrifice of praise.

… always giving thanks to God the Father for everything, in the name of our Lord Jesus Christ.

Pray in the Spirit on all occasions with all kinds of prayers and requests.

I used to read such passages in a fog of guilt, imagining saints who prayed through the night, building up calluses on their knees.* I read them differently now, not as a perpetual guilt-trip but as a call to a Godward orientation. Prayer means keeping company with God who is already present. My very concern about the people and issues I pray for actually manifests God's presence within me. I need not jump up and down like a child, shouting, "Look at me!" God is close by, if only I tune in.

---

* A group called the Messalians decided the only way they could "pray without ceasing" was to recruit surrogate pray-ers on their behalf while they slept. Meanwhile, a group of nuns in Wisconsin have been praying in shifts nonstop since 1878.

"Prayer consists of Attention," wrote Simone Weil. "It is the orientation of all the attention of which the soul is capable toward God." How do we pray "without ceasing" in Paul's phrase? Our minds have the potential to attend to more than one thing at once, and I have found it possible to give God attention even while doing something else: to pray *simultaneously* as other activities are going on. I simply try to direct Godward the inner dialogue that is taking place all the time. To pray without ceasing taps into the mind's multitasking ability.

When I speak before a group, part of my mind is concentrating on the words and expressions of my speech, while another part — hopefully in a manner undetected by the audience — is sorting out how much time I have left, whether my ticklish throat will require a distracting sip of water from the cup on the podium, how engaged the folks on the front row appear to be. A young mother can conduct a lucid conversation with her four-year-old in the supermarket while mentally ticking off a grocery list and calculating price-per-item. A teenager can carry on instant-messaging conversations with four friends on the Internet while simultaneously listening to the latest MP3 download and doing homework.

If I let it drift, my inner dialogue will usually revolve around me. I think about things like what kind of impression I'm making on the people around me, whether a salesperson is telling the truth about the product I'm interested in, if I'm dressed appropriately for the social occasion. Mental prayer moves the focus of this inner conversation from me to God. If I remember — no small feat — I can refer experiences to God at the moment they are happening. Indeed, I find it easier to praise God while I am snowshoeing through snow-laden trees or snorkeling a reef rather than later, reflecting back on the experience. And an undercurrent of prayer while standing in a checkout line can transform how I treat the clumsy trainee who made me wait.

The Quaker theologian Thomas Kelly called this practice "mental habits of inward orientation." The prayerful person takes ordinary things that happen and moves them "into the Light." Everything gets realigned. The panhandler becomes a child of God. The opening for revenge becomes an opening for grace, the temptation to greed a temptation to generosity. At first it seems a split life to perceive things on two levels at once. With practice, it seems the only whole life.

Sue Monk Kidd, a contemporary novelist, describes a way this might work. She first encountered the ancient Jesus Prayer by reading *The Way of the Pilgrim*, the account of an anonymous Russian peasant in the nineteenth century who sought to pray one simple prayer from the Gospels all day long.

"Lord Jesus Christ, have mercy on me," I said a little shyly. Then I said it again. I said it for nearly five minutes, just letting the words happen to me. Below the window I watched the traffic, the squirrels jumping under a tree, students hurrying to class, and I said the prayer blending it with my breathing as the pilgrim had done. "Lord Jesus Christ," on the in-breath ... "have mercy on me," on the out-breath. I said it slowly, silently finding a rhythm that seemed to slow everything down and focus naturally in Christ.

Kidd found, with practice, that the prayer took on a life of its own. She could continue to pray at one level even while carrying on a conversation or doing chores. She would apply the prayer to a stranger on the road or when talking to a friend: "Lord Jesus Christ, have mercy on *him*."

It comes when there are no other words, when you don't know how to pray or what to say.

I have come to think of this prayer as living within me, beating like a heart. It is not in my thoughts all the time. That would be an utter distraction to have it constantly in my heart even when I am unaware of it. It returns during the days, sometimes rising up spontaneously. Other times I call it up when I dress or sit at a stop sign, or wait at the hairdresser. Any place at all we can breathe it in and out, always with gentleness.

Inappropriate Prayers

The New Testament emphasizes God's intimate involvement with every detail of our lives. "Even the very hairs of your head are all numbered," Jesus assured his listeners. Frankly, I find it hard to comprehend such sweeping claims of God's personal interest, let alone apply them to prayer. As one friend said to me, "I cannot imagine *anyone*, much less God, caring that much about my life. God has far more to worry about than my petty concerns."

Some people, like my friend, muzzle their prayers because of a poor self-image, while others do so out of a sense of piety. The mystic Meister Eckhart refused to "pray the rich and loving God for such trifles" as to help him recover from an illness. Catherine of Genoa took pride in never asking anything for herself in thirty-five years of constant prayer. Sometimes I feel tempted to follow their example, to squelch all prayers that might seem selfish or inappropriate. Then I turn again to prayers in the Bible.

The Bible records with approval all sorts of "selfish" prayers: an infertile woman who wants a baby, a widow who needs more cooking oil, a soldier who begs for victory in battle. People pray for rain during a drought, for vengeance on their enemies. The Lord's Prayer itself includes a plea for daily bread. Paul prays about safe travels, prosperous work, relief from a physical ailment, and boldness in preaching. James urges prayers for wisdom and physical healing.

After reviewing the prayers contained in the Bible, I have stopped worrying about inappropriate prayers. If God counts on prayer as a primary way to relate to me, I may block potential intimacy by devising a test for appropriateness and filtering out prayers that may not meet the criteria. According to Jesus, nothing is too trivial. Everything about me — my thoughts, my motives, my choices, my moods — attracts God's interest.

I recognize a similar pattern in relating to my friends. With professional contacts I keep the conversation on a business track and don't bore them with stories about my aches and pains and bouts with insomnia. Only with my best friends will I assume an interest in the trivia, let alone the deep secrets, of my life.

In a charming passage from *The Seven Storey Mountain*, Thomas Merton tells of walking the streets of New York "in the incomparable agony of a new author waiting to hear the fate of his first book — an agony which is second to nothing except the torments of adolescent love." I remember well that agony, and feel a twinge every time I send off a book or article manuscript. Having submitted his novel to a publisher, Merton debated whether he should pray about such a selfish matter. Yes, he decided:

> After all God does not care if our prayers are [self-]interested. He wants them to be. Ask and you shall receive. It is a kind of pride to insist that none of our prayers should ever be petitions for our own needs: for this is another subtle way of trying to put ourselves on the same plane as God — acting as if we had no needs, as if we were not creatures, not dependent on Him and dependent, by His will, on material things too.

Having resolved the issue, Merton knelt in a little Mexican church in Lower Manhattan and prayed with intense desire for the acceptance and successful publication of the novel. (Merton goes on to tell the results of that prayer: the publisher rejected the manuscript! Years later he saw that deci-sion as God's superior answer to his request. The rejection, a wise publishing decision which saved him much embarrassment, drove Merton back to his vocation as a monk and thus opened the gate to all his future writings.)

My own concern about inappropriate or irrelevant prayers melts away as I view prayer less as a technique than as a relationship, a way of keeping

---

Bodily Thanksgiving

PHILIP

My mentor and coauthor Dr. Paul Brand began the day by offering a "Litany of Thanksgiving" for life and the wonders of the human body. He would call to mind various parts of the body — the heart, the brain, cells, the immune system — and praise God for the intricacies that made life possible. "As a doc-tor, I hear about the few parts of the body that don't work as designed," he told me. "I need a constant reminder of the miracle that so many trillions of cells in my body function flawlessly every day."

Brand also employed prayer as a first-line defense against chronic pain. If he had trouble sleeping, he would get out of bed, slip on a robe, and walk around the paths of the leprosarium in his bare feet. He deliberately chose to walk on paths made of sharply-edged shell gravel, which caused mild pain. The sensations of gravel, then wet grass, on bare feet, combined with the night sounds of a Louisiana swampland, competed with and partially drowned out the pain signals from his ailing back or gall bladder.

Dr. Brand recalled one particular night: "I'm not sure when the singing began. I think I spoke at first, expressing aloud to God my wonder and appre-ciation for the good earth around me and the stars blazing overhead. Then I found myself singing a few bars of a favorite hymn. Birds started and flew away in disorder. My dog Nell cocked her ears and looked quizzical. I glanced around, self-conscious, suddenly aware how it would look if a night watch-man caught the senior staff surgeon outdoors at 2:00 a.m., barefoot, wearing pajamas and singing a hymn."

Brand assured me that the experience worked wonders on pain, which did not disappear but became much more tolerable than what he had felt in a dark, quiet bedroom.

company with God. Every lover longs to know the needs, the desires, and yes, even the trivia of the beloved. For people we care about, simply spending time together is the most relevant act of all. Why else do we cuddle children, play catch in the yard, or rack up extra charges on a mobile phone with a boyfriend or girlfriend?

Again, Jesus likened prayer to a child approaching the Father. A child who crawls into her father's lap with a fantasy Christmas list may not get everything she desires. But the very fact that she crawled into his lap, making known her deepest desires, helps cement the bond of love the father cherishes above all else. We do far better to act like a trusting child, presenting foolish requests and letting the Father make judgments, than to fret in advance over appropriate petitions.

Fittingly, some of the most articulate prayers come from the mouths of children. *God, help that man we saw at the red light find a place to sleep tonight.... Please don't let my cat suffer any more.... Help Grandmommy to stop feeling sad all the time.... Teach me how to get along with my mean brother.*

My neighbor Elizabeth, age four, was staying with her grandmother while her parents went to New York City on business. Kneeling by her bed that night, she prayed, "Help Mommy and Daddy to come home safely. And if they don't want to come home—" Her grandmother interrupted, "Honey, of course they want to come home." Elizabeth set her straight with a sharp reply, "I'm talking to God!" With the wisdom of a child, she knew that in prayer it is perfectly appropriate to voice fear, anger (think of the imprecatory psalms), insecurity, doubt, or anything else we need to get out.

Praise

Books on prayer, including this one, tend to probe the effect of prayer on us the pray-ers to the neglect of the other party in the relationship. God is the one who has invited, even commanded prayer. What does God desire from it? Why should it matter to God whether we paltry humans pray?

The word *praise* leaps to mind and reflexively I flinch. For me, praise once represented a most troubling part of prayer. It seemed odd, if not offensive, to imagine God as someone like the queen in the fairy tale *Snow White*: "Mirror, mirror on the wall, who is the fairest one of all?"

First, I tried to understand by recalling how much praise means to me. I ski better and hit golf balls straighter when accompanied by friends who look for things to compliment rather than those who point out my every mistake.

That line of thinking did not go far, however, because unlike me God does not battle insecurity. When God said to the Israelites, "If I were hungry I would not tell you, for the world is mine, and all that is in it," that was a plain statement of fact, not a brag. God hardly needs our affirmation.

Why praise, then?

"The heavens declare the glory of God," begins one famous psalm. "Day after day they pour forth speech; night after night they display knowledge." And another: "Let the sea resound, and all that is in it; let the fields be jubilant, and everything in them. Then all the trees of the forest will sing for joy." Fine poetry but metaphorical, of course. Trees do not sing, the heavens do not speak, and the only knowledge they display is their creator's, not their own. The grand works of nature reveal something of God's own self passively; they cry out for an observer to exclaim over them. Although rivers may clap their hands and mountains shout, only men and women can supply the words.

No message comes through more forcefully in the Bible than that the human species matters profoundly to God. God created the world with humanity in mind, set us at its center, continued to love us despite our failings, and even sent the Son on a rescue mission.* And our response to all these gifts has an actual and deep effect on God. What pleasure has God in giving if we the recipients don't acknowledge it? Jesus implied as much in his reaction when only one of ten men healed of leprosy returned to thank him.

Children receive constant reminders to thank someone for a gift: "What do you say to the nice lady?" Like children, we must form the habit in order to overcome a tendency toward spiritual amnesia.

To develop this habit, devout Jews practice reciting at least one hundred blessings every day, and in Orthodox neighborhoods you can actually hear the low murmurs of praise in the background. The Talmud spells out blessings for hearing thunder or seeing lightning, for the variety of tastes, for sunrise and sunset, for fragrances, for trees and lakes and mountains. One of my favorites expresses gratitude to God "who makes the creatures so very different." Perhaps if I memorized these blessings and recited them each day,

---

*Orthodox theologian David Hart points to humanity's unique position as a "boundary or frontier" between the physical and spiritual realms, "the priesthood of creation that unites earth to heaven." The apostle Paul hints at our cosmic significance in Romans 8: "The creation waits in eager expectation for the sons of God to be revealed."

I might stay more mindful of God's presence in the ordinary. (I wonder, though: How often do I take seriously the blessing I say before a meal?)

Of the recorded prayers of Jesus, about half burst out spontaneously in response to what had just happened: the return of the seventy disciples, the provision of food, the resurrection of Lazarus. Paul, too, broke into prayers of thanksgiving in the midst of his letters, sometimes even interrupting a correction or warning. "Thanks be to God!" he interjects, his thoughts rising like a bird set free from a cage as one of God's good gifts comes suddenly to mind.

Who, indeed, deserves our praise but the God who originated every good and perfect gift. We need not invent a compliment to make God feel good, rather we need only give credit where credit is due. When I yell for encores at a concert or line up to watch a champion marathoner race past, I do so voluntarily, exuberantly, forgetting myself for a moment in my enthusiasm over someone whose skills far exceed mine. In the face of true greatness, competitive instincts fall away.

For fifteen years I had season tickets to the Chicago Symphony Orchestra, one of the world's great ensembles. I paid extra one year to attend a private rehearsal of the orchestra and chorus preparing for a performance of the magnificent *German Requiem* by Johannes Brahms. Wired for sound, the conductor Margaret Hillis entertained us guests even while spurring on the musicians. "You altos, if he had wanted an E-flat he would have asked for one — give me an E!" Her background with church choirs showed. "Legato, legato! This isn't Brahms's version of 'Onward, Christian Soldiers,' you know," she muttered at one point. Later, "Be good Presbyterians and believe in predestination: anticipate the next line!"

For the perfectionist Hillis, even compliments had a hortatory ring. "That's good enough for every other chorus in the world," she said after one exalted passage. She waited two beats, and added "... but not for the Chicago Symphony." Finally, as if reaching for the ultimate prod, she implored the assembly of superb musicians, "If you don't believe in God, at least believe in Brahms!"

A few nights later I sat in the balcony and listened to a performance in which the musicians onstage seemed to attain Madame Hillis's ideal. The piece begins solemnly, almost mournfully, colored by Brahms's own grief over the double loss of his mother and his friend Robert Schumann. It considers the plight of humanity — "All flesh is as grass" — in light of our only hope, the forgiveness and resurrection promised by God in Christ.

As the words and music filled the dome above, a surround-sound that no technology can duplicate, I turned the performance into an act of praise, as I knew it was for several of my friends singing in the chorus, and perhaps for those in the orchestra who at least believed in Brahms, and surely for the composer himself. To those of us swept up in the music, nothing else mattered—the work we had left undone at home, worries over health and family and finance.

Whether artfully enacted in Orchestra Hall, Chicago, or feebly croaked by senior citizens in a storefront church a few blocks west, praise allows a free surrender to a supreme good. I have seen Bono of the band U2 hush 20,000 screaming fans to silence, then lead them in a psalm and a reverent refrain of "Hallelujah." Some who thundered in applause were praising only Bono; he and others deflected that praise to God, for whom he intended it.

We do it, this act of praise, feebly or majestically, privately or corporately. We kneel, only to find that we rise taller because praise does not diminish but fulfills, by establishing our true place in the universe, and also God's. In George Herbert's words, we are "secretaries of praise."

The First Rule

When the resurrected Jesus appeared to Peter, who had betrayed him three times, he asked three questions which were really the same question: "Do you love me?" Somehow our love means something incalculable to the God of the universe.

Once, when asked to identify the most important rule in life, Jesus immediately replied, "Love the Lord your God with all your heart and with all your soul and with all your mind." In those words he summed up what God most wants from us. Our most treasured gift to God, that which God can never force, is love. Every parent knows it as the one response most valued in their children and the one they are least able to compel.

How strange, I have thought, to *command* love. I do not normally will myself to love another person. Love springs up naturally as in the case of family, sweeps me off my feet as in romance, or grows as a relationship develops. Yet Jesus marks love for God as the single most important goal in life. How can I possibly learn to love God with all my heart, soul, and mind?

In the midst of one of the most exhaustive books on prayer ever written, Teresa of Avila made this summary statement: "The important thing is not

323

to think much but to love much." Only in prayer can we learn to love God with heart, mind, and soul.

Love God with all your heart, Jesus said. Listen to your life: to its passion, its dreams and disappointments, its tedium as well as its drama. It came to you as a gift and each day, too, unravels as a gift. God wants an invitation to share in its every detail.

Neal Plantinga remarks on a subtle change Jesus introduced in the first commandment. Deuteronomy charges us to love God with all our heart, soul, and strength; Jesus changed that last word to *mind*. Take that as a charter for Christian intellectual life, says Plantinga, a member of a family that includes a philosopher, several musicians, a theologian, a webmaster, and a seminary president. Love God with all your mind. Plantinga explains,

> In other words, you shall love God with everything you have and everything you are. Everything. Every longing, every endowment, each of your intellectual gifts, any athletic talent or computer skill, all capacity for delight, every good thing that has your fingerprints on it — take all this, says Jesus, and refer it to God. Take your longing, and long for God; take your creaturely riches, and endow God; take your eye for beauty and appreciate God. With your heart and soul and mind, with all your needs and splendors, make a full turn toward God.

To love God with all the soul may be the most difficult part of the command. What is a human soul? We can neither see it nor measure its activity on graph paper as we can the mind and heart. Skeptics even doubt its existence. But for the believer at prayer, nothing matters more than the soul. We also pray to prepare ourselves for the life that continues after heart and mind fall still.

It changes perspective in prayer, to love God with all the soul. The difficulties over which we obsess fall into a different place. The apostle Paul dismissed his grueling ordeals as "light and momentary troubles" because he had in mind an "eternal glory that far outweighs them all." The French mathematician Blaise Pascal hesitated to pray for relief, much less healing, when he fell sick:

> I know not which is most profitable to me, health or sickness, wealth or poverty, nor anything else in the world. That discernment is beyond the power of men or angels, and is hidden among the secrets of your Providence, which I adore, but do not seek to fathom.

To adore but not seek to fathom—perhaps in those words lies a clue to loving God with all my soul. So often I line up my prayers like the closing arguments of an attorney, in an attempt to fathom. Why are some people blessed and some cursed? Why does God permit so much evil and violence? How can I trust what I do not see? What is the meaning of life?

By bringing us into the presence of God, and giving us a glimpse of the view from above, prayer radically changes how we experience life. Faith during affliction matters more than healing from affliction. Submitting to God's will is preferable to a rescue from crucifixion. Humility counts more than deliverance from a thorn in the flesh.

In the advanced school of prayer, where one loves God with the entire soul, doubts and struggles do not disappear, but their effect on us diminishes. "If you, then, though you are evil, know how to give good gifts to your children, how much more will your Father in heaven give good gifts to those who ask him!" Jesus said, in a statement that provokes a thousand rebuttals. Yet if I love with all my soul, the rebuttals do not convince. My questions about prayer recede in urgency as I learn to trust the ultimate goodness of God, who can transmute whatever happens into a "good gift."

Resuming the Conversation

I recently read the memoir of Helmut Thielicke, a great German preacher of the last century who lived a life that might rival Job's. He lost his university positions for opposing Hitler, endured humiliating interrogations by the SS, and faced the constant threat of imprisonment. As the war growled to a close, he walked to his Stuttgart church one day only to find it bombed to rubble and returned home to find his house destroyed. His heart nearly broke when he came across his famished children licking the pictures of food in recipe books. And each week he stood in a pulpit and tried to bring a message of hope to a demoralized congregation, standing now amid the crushed stones of their former sanctuary.

"The one fixed pole in all the bewildering confusion is the faithfulness and dependability of God," Thielicke declared to his congregation, remarkable words considering their context. He assured them that God's faithfulness can never falter, and that through the labyrinth of history and the disorder of personal lives there runs the constant thread of God's purpose.

One day, perhaps, when we look back from God's throne on the last day we shall say with amazement and surprise, "If I had ever dreamed

325

when I stood at the graves of my loved ones and everything seemed to be ended; if I had ever dreamed when I saw the specter of atomic war creeping upon us; if I had ever dreamed when I faced the meaningless fate of an endless imprisonment or a malignant disease; if I had ever dreamed that God was only carrying out his design and plan through all these woes, that in the midst of my cares and troubles and despair *his* harvest was ripening, and that everything was pressing on toward his last kingly day—if I had known this I would have been more calm and confident; yes, then I would have been more cheerful and far more tranquil and composed."

Thielicke gently turned his parishioners to the example of Jesus who saw like no one else the anguish and injustice, the terror, of this planet. Shouldn't such awareness have filled his every waking hour and robbed him of sleep at night? Shouldn't it have shaken his very soul?

No, Jesus left the global concerns in the care of his Father and spent his time instead among nobodies: tax collectors, fishermen, widows, prostitutes, outcasts. Speaking to the Father—praying—notes Thielicke, was more important to Jesus than speaking to crowds; he would pass through their midst in search of time with the Father. "And that's why he has time for persons; for all time is in the hands of his Father. And that too is why peace and not unrest goes out from him. For God's faithfulness already spans the world like a rainbow: he does not need to build it; he needs only to walk beneath it."

Those of us who follow Jesus also believe that God's faithfulness spans the world like a rainbow, with Jesus himself offering one of the best proofs of that faithfulness. Times will come, as they did for Thielicke in Stuttgart (and Jesus at Gethsemane and Gologtha), that test such belief to the limit. When I face my own version of those times, I cry a prayer of desperation, a thrust in the dark in hopes of regaining trust in the big picture, a renewed glimpse of God's point of view. And when things are going well, ironically, I have to work even harder to keep the conversation going, to believe that God cares about the details of my life.

I pray in astonished belief that God desires an ongoing relationship. I pray in trust that the act of prayer is God's designated way of closing the vast gulf between infinity and me. I pray in order to put myself in the stream of God's healing work on earth. I pray as I breathe—because I can't help it. Prayer is hardly a perfect form of communication, for I, an imperfect, material being who lives on an imperfect, material planet am reaching out for a perfect, spiritual Being. Some prayers go unanswered, a sense of God's presence ebbs and flows, and often I sense more mystery than resolution. Nevertheless I keep at it, believing with Paul that "now I know in part; then I shall know fully, even as I am fully known."

O Gracious and Holy Father

BENEDICT OF NURSIA

O gracious and holy Father,
give us wisdom to perceive Thee,
intelligence to understand Thee,
diligence to seek Thee,
patience to wait for Thee,
eyes to behold Thee,
a heart to meditate upon Thee,
and a life to proclaim Thee;
through the power of the Spirit
of Jesus Christ our Lord.

The book of Revelation describes a time of full restoration when "they will be his people, and God himself will be with them and be their God. He will wipe every tear from their eyes. There will be no more death or mourning or crying or pain, for the old order of things has passed away." Revelation mentions there will be no need for sun or moon in that new order, for the presence of God will provide its light. Of all the magical descriptions of heaven, this one brings me up short. I have grown so accustomed to fleeting sensations of God, to the feints and thrusts of prayer, that I cannot imagine a state of God's unrestrained presence.

Prayer itself will necessarily change — not end, exactly, but realize its rightful place as conversation. Prayer now is a kind of awkward rehearsal, like talking on a mobile phone to someone in Africa, the connection garbled and staticky, the English broken and accented. God "has never acquiesced in the break which was brought about in Adam," wrote Jacques Ellul. Indeed God has not. The entire Bible chronicles God's effort to renew what was lost on that day in the garden when Adam hid and no longer conversed with God as a friend. One day we will all have that chance.

Sometimes I think about my first face-to-face conversation with God. I have so many unresolved questions, so many laments and regrets. Where should I begin? Various openings play out in my mind, until I remember with a start whom in fact I will be talking to, the One who spun out galaxies and created all that exists. Objections fade away, doubts dissolve, and I imagine myself falling back on words akin to Job's: "Oh, now I get it." And then the conversation resumes.

EPILOGUE

The last weekend of February 2007, I spoke at a historic church in Los Alamos, New Mexico. In the 1940s the U.S. government built a large laboratory on forested mesas as part of the Manhattan Project, and as a town sprang up to support the laboratory, believers from various denominations joined together to form the United Church. Los Alamos has the highest concentration of Ph.D.'s in the world, and my hosts lined up a meeting with scientists from the lab, including some who had witnessed the original hydrogen bomb explosion.

When I spoke to the community on the subject of prayer that evening, I related some of the mountain-climbing adventures I allude to in this book. For instance, on the day my wife and I summited Mt. Wilson, we were still well above the safety of timberline when dark clouds moved in and the skies opened up to pelt us with sleet and hail. Lightning struck closer and closer. "What do we do?" I asked our experienced companion.

"There's really not much you can do," he replied. "The granite rock conducts electricity. I'd recommend separating by at least a hundred yards or so —that way if one of us gets hit, another can go for help. And squat down with your feet together to make yourself as small a target as possible."

My wife and I looked at each other. Finally I shrugged and said, "Honey, we've had a good life. Let's go together." We ditched our buzzing hiking poles and squatted down, as our friend suggested, but side by side, holding hands. For the next hour we got pummeled by rain, hail, sleet, snow, and a mixture of all at once, all the while counting the seconds between each lightning bolt that crashed around us and the blast of thunder that followed.

"I learned an important life lesson," I told the folks who had gathered in the United Church. "I am not in control. What transpired on the mountain that day had nothing to do with me. I was in the hands of far larger forces. I must tell you, as a freelance writer I'm something of a control freak. I have to be. Since I have no boss telling me what to do, I have to organize my own life and most of the time I go around feeling like I'm in control. As I learned atop Mt. Wilson, that's an illusion."

I went on to say that this mountain-climbing lesson actually applies all the time. "Even when I think I'm in control, I'm not. I could die of a heart attack right in front of you before finishing this sentence." Some in the audience laughed nervously. "Or I could have an auto accident driving back to Denver tomorrow—probably far more likely than getting hit by lightning on Mt. Wilson." More laughter.

How eerily prophetic those words would prove to be. Sunday morning, driving back from Los Alamos to Denver, I turned down a small, remote road just over the Colorado border, more for variety in scenery than anything else. Like many roads in Colorado, it curved back and forth around streams, hills, and mountain passes. Snow had fallen a few days before, and several times I was surprised by patches of ice on the road. Suddenly, as I headed downhill into one curve, my Ford Explorer began to fishtail. I fought it, steering left, then right, then left again until the right rear tire slipped off the pavement and grabbed soft dirt. Then the Explorer rolled sideways, over and over, five times in all.

The noise was deafening, a crescendo of glass, plastic, and metal breaking all at once. The radio console shot out of the dashboard. Every window shattered, spilling skis, boots, ice skates, my laptop computer, and luggage across the Colorado countryside. As I rolled, two things came to mind. *Philip, you've always managed to pull out of these close scrapes before, but not this time.* And, *Whatever you do, keep your hands on the steering wheel so your arms don't flop around and get broken.*

Finally the rolling stopped, with the vehicle in an upright position. The engine was still running, and I recalled scenes from movies in which wrecked cars burst into flames. I turned off the ignition, unbuckled my seat belt, and ducked under the collapsed roof to stumble to the ground. My nose was bleeding, I had cuts on my face, legs, and arms, and I felt a searing pain in my upper back, just below the neck. My belongings were strewn over a hundred feet, and I wandered the desert landscape searching for my laptop and cell phone.

Within five minutes a car pulled over and a portly middle-aged man got out. "Are you okay? We saw the dust cloud from the rollover," he said. "Man, oh man. Shouldn't you be sitting down? Shouldn't you put on a coat?" I stared at him, dazed, and finally did what he said, putting on a coat and sitting back in the driver's seat, holding a tissue to my nose and dabbing the facial cuts. The pain in my back kept me from finding a comfortable position.

I started thinking of appointments and trips I would need to cancel and other details I would have to deal with—insurance, computer repair, shopping for a new vehicle, police reports. These were chased out by a shock of gratitude that I was alive, my fingers and toes still moving, my brain still functioning. "You wouldn't be here now without that seat belt," said the driver who had stopped to help. I looked around at my smashed Explorer and had to agree.

A few minutes later a second car pulled over. A well-dressed couple got out, ran to the scene, and started giving orders rather than asking questions. I soon learned why: they were both certified Emergency Medical Technicians, and the husband headed up the ambulance corps for the county. They led me to their car, called for an ambulance, and sat beside me holding my head in a fixed position. "How did you happen to come down this remote road early on a Sunday morning?" I asked after they had stabilized my neck.

"We're Mormons," the woman replied. "We've just started a mission church in the tiny town of San Luis, and we're driving over to help them get on their feet."

Thus began one of the longest, most memorable days of my life. When the ambulance came, attendants strapped me into a rigid body board, taping my head still and immobilizing it with a neck brace. We drove almost an hour to reach the town of Alamosa, where I was transferred with much jostling and bumping onto a gurney and into a hospital emergency room.

The Alamosa hospital, which has no radiologist on duty on weekends, had outsourced diagnosis to an outfit in Australia. As a result, digitized CAT-scan images had to be sent via satellite to Australia (where it was Monday, a normal work day) for interpretation. The images were so dense that high-speed transmittal took an hour, and the Australian radiologists needed another hour to properly analyze the images. For those two hours I lay in a most uncomfortable position on the body board, awaiting results. I could have nothing for pain, and no water or nourishment, until results came back. Hospital personnel, who knew I had been walking around after the accident, did not seem overly concerned and mostly left me alone. I stared at the perforated tile ceiling and listened to the sounds around me: a crying baby, a squeaky wheelchair, metal bars on a bed being raised and lowered, the changing pitch of a siren as an ambulance approached.

When the results came back from Australia, everything changed. The doctor came in with prefatory words that no patient wants to hear: "There's no easy way to say this, Mr. Yancey ..." I had a broken neck, specifically the C–3 vertebra in a "comminuted" or pulverized fashion. The good news was that the break did not occur in the spinal cord channel itself. If it had, I would likely have ended up paralyzed like Christopher Reeve. The spinal column has three channels, one for the spinal cord and two for arterial blood supply, which is where my fractures occurred. The bad news was that due to the splintered nature of the break, a bone fragment may well have nicked or penetrated a major artery.

"We have a jet standing by if needed to airlift you to Denver," the doctor explained. "We'll do another CAT scan, this time with an iodine dye solution to reveal any possible leakage from the artery. I must emphasize, this is a life-threatening situation. You may want to contact your loved ones."

My wife, Janet, whom I had phoned from the ambulance, had scrambled to throw some clothes in an overnight bag and begin the four-hour drive to Alamosa to join me. A Good Samaritan neighbor insisted on going with her, a magnificent gift as it freed her to make phone calls and compose herself during that tense drive. They had driven exactly halfway when the doctor called her with the initial diagnosis, explaining that if the dye scan revealed arterial leakage they could not hold the plane for her; I would be airlifted to Denver immediately.

Cell phones in mountainous Colorado are an imperfect technology: about every third word drops and the call cuts off every thirty seconds or so. My own cell phone was running low on battery power and tended to drop calls whenever hospital machines kicked on. Janet was trying to decide whether to turn around and drive back to Denver in the event I needed surgery or continue on to Alamosa with the possibility of watching my jet contrails in the sky above her. When I reached her by phone, staticky and barely audible because of hospital machinery, I insisted she come to Alamosa: "You've got to pick up my laptop computer! It's got all my weekend work on it." She took that as a sign of stubborn male rationality and made the uneasy decision to keep driving.

Technicians rolled me in for the iodine-dye scan, and then left me alone again to wait for the transmission to Australia and the next set of results. In all, I lay strapped onto that body board for seven hours, plenty of time to think through my life. I've written articles on people whose lives have been instantly changed by an accident that left them paraplegic or quadriplegic. Evidently I had narrowly missed that fate (and I mean narrowly—my break was about one-half inch from the spinal cord). But if my artery was leaking, an artery that feeds the brain, or if it formed a blood clot, well, I soon faced a fate worse than paralysis.

I stayed calm throughout, my pulse hovering around 70, as the monitor flashed in LED lights. As I lay there, contemplating what I had just been teaching in Los Alamos about prayer, and facing for the first time the imminent possibility of death, I felt surprisingly peaceful. I reflected on what a wonderful life I have had, with a life-giving marriage partner of thirty-seven years, all but three of Colorado's fifty-four 14,000-foot mountains under my belt, adventures in more than fifty countries, and work that allows me both meaning and near-total freedom, connections through my writing with people I've never met. (The morphine drip a nurse had just attached to my arm may well have contributed to this sense of calmness!)

I looked back on my life and felt little regret. And as I thought of what may await me, I felt deep trust. Although no one raised in the kind of church environment I grew up in totally leaves behind the acrid smell of fire and brimstone, I had an overwhelming sense of trust in God. I have come to know a God of compassion and mercy and love. Although I have no clue what heaven or an afterlife will be like, I felt sustained by that trust.

Those were the hours of strange suspension: Janet speeding down the highway with our neighbor, feeling helpless and unsure, imagining how her life would change with a dead or paralyzed husband; and me strapped on a table, utterly helpless, with the images that would determine my future bouncing off a satellite en route to Australia.

As it happened, thank God—oh, yes, thank God—the results turned out far better than either of us could hope. The scans revealed no arterial leakage. The hospital released me within an hour of Janet's arrival, fitted with a stiff neck brace that would keep my head from moving for the next twelve weeks. If all goes well (and I am still recovering as I write this), the fractures and misaligned vertebrae may heal back appropriately on their own; if not, I may need surgery for spinal fusion sometime down the road.

Looking back now, I see many coincidences—God-incidences?—that contributed to a good outcome. The EMT-trained Mormons traveling that route early on a Sunday morning. The most experienced X-ray technician, normally off-duty on weekends, filling in for a sick colleague. The emergency room doctor, featured that day in the local paper as a star graduate of an elite medical school returning to his small Colorado town to be of service. And most of all, the injury itself, serious but not nearly as catastrophic as the alternatives.

I remember sitting in the Ford Explorer as it finally stopped rolling, its engine still running, and thinking, "This begins chapter two of my life." Indeed it did, though with considerably brighter prospects than it seemed at the time. I hope to ski long mogul runs again, to climb more fourteeners and gaze at the wildflowers along the way, to cherish friends and love my wife and family and thank God for every minute of this precious gift of life.

I now look back on that long day, spent strapped to a body board in an ambulance and then emergency room, as a unique gift. All of us will face death, some through a long degenerative illness like cancer and others through an abrupt accident. I had something in between, a window of time in which I lay suspended between life and nonlife, with the very real possibility of death within a few minutes or hours and yet an opportunity to emerge with overwhelming good news and another chance at life. Samuel Johnson said that when a person knows he is about to be hanged, it concentrates the mind wonderfully. Any near-death experience does that.

I hope that I never forget that window of time or what I saw through it. For a few weeks after the accident I walked around in a "daze of grace," looking at the sky, trees, grass, my wife, my friends, with newly washed eyes. Even as my battered body brought new aches and pains to my attention, life held surprises around every corner, fresh promptings to gratitude and joy. Each day I awoke with a profound sense of gratitude for the simplest things: birds flitting from tree to tree, the sound of a creek flowing around rocks and ice near our home, the ability to move a finger, to dress myself.

Then the sleepless nights in a neck brace began to take their toll; woodpeckers hammered holes in the west wall of our house; in an electronic conspiracy the television, microwave, and refrigerator all stopped working. Life also grinds you down.

I am trying to keep before me the crystalline vision I had while lying strapped down for seven hours. I have learned how thin is the thread that separates life from nonlife, and how comforting is the knowledge that I am not alone on this journey. I have learned these things in a way that I doubt I will ever forget. What we spend so much time and energy on (finances, image, achievement) matters so little in the face of imminent death. What matters reduces down to a few basic questions. *Who do I love? Who will I miss? How have I spent my life? Am I ready for what's next?* The challenge is, How do I keep those questions in the forefront as I come to my desk each day and face piles of paper and blinking electronic messages?

Word of the accident got out, and over the next few months I was overwhelmed by support from friends, family, and people I have never met. In the act of writing I spill something of my soul onto the printed page, and through the cards and letters that came in I realized a remarkable link can forge even with strangers. The month of the accident, I was leading an online discussion on this book hosted by a Quaker publisher. One of the participants wrote me that Quakers have a phrase they were exercising on my behalf: "holding you in the light." I felt held, truly.

One more thing: on that scary day in February and during the days that followed, I learned to put into practice what I have written about in the pages of this book. I have used the phrase "keeping company with God," which was indeed my working title of the book as I wrote it. Recently, a spate of authors have been trumpeting a kind of triumphalist atheism. I can understand why someone would choose atheism, but I cannot understand why such a stance might seem like good news, something worth trumpeting. Lying helpless, strapped to a body board, I would have felt utterly and inconsolably alone, except for my faith that I lay in the hands of a God who loves me and promises a future beyond death. And over the next few months I felt the sure sense of, as the Quakers had expressed it, being held in the light.

My wife, while working as a hospice chaplain, observed a striking difference in the way that believers and unbelievers face death. Both feel fear, and pain, and grief. But Christians have an almost palpable contribution in the mysterious linkage that comes through prayer. It's the difference between a hospice visitor saying, "I will pray for you—honest, every day," and someone saying, "Good luck. Best wishes."

I have referred to "coincidences" the day of the accident: my vehicle happening to end its tumble upright (with a broken neck, undoing my seat belt while upside down could have proved fatal), the Mormons happening to take that remote road early Sunday morning, the hospital personnel, my neighbor volunteering to drive Janet to the hospital. Of course, a skeptic could look at the same set of events and say, "Wait a minute. What about the accident itself? If God orchestrated these things you call mini-miracles, why couldn't God have kept you on the road in the first place?"

It's a good question, I admit, exactly the kind of question that prompted this book in the first place. The subject of prayer will always remain full of mystery. Someone asked me if I wished I had written this book *after* the accident rather than before. I said no. I might have been tempted to over-emphasize the "happy ending" aspect of prayer, whereas so many people live with the kind of ongoing struggle that fills this book. I must say, though, that the process of wrestling with the puzzle of prayer for several years served as excellent preparation for what I went through in February 2007, just a few months after its publication. Does prayer make a difference? Even more now than when I wrote this book, I believe it does.

Philip Yancey
August 2007

I value your thoughts about what you've just read.
Please share them with me. You'll find contact information
in the back of this book.

PRAYER RESOURCES

There are thousands of resources on prayer, ranging from Richard Wagner's *Christian Prayer for Dummies* to Friedrich Heiler's scholarly *Prayer* and the recent bestseller *Prayer: A History* by Philip and Carol Zaleski. I can only mention a sampling, most of which can be located by an Internet search.

Prayer: Finding the Heart's True Home, by Richard Foster, examines twenty-one different kinds of prayer. Foster's organization, Renovaré, publishes *Spiritual Classics* and *Devotional Classics*, which contain time-tested writings on the spiritual disciplines.

Peter Kreeft's *Prayer for Beginners* answers basic questions, as does Marjorie J. Thompson's *Soul Feast*. Donald Bloesch's *The Struggle of Prayer* and P. T. Forsyth's *The Soul of Prayer* investigate obstacles the serious pray-er may encounter. Simon Tugwell and Thomas H. Green have written several encouraging books for those who struggle with frustration and dryness in prayer. *The Art of Prayer* by Tim Jones takes a more personal and pastoral approach. *Prayer and Temperament*, mentioned in chapter 14, gives guidance to different personalities, following the Myers-Briggs Type Indicator test (MBTI). Others I recommend: *Contemplative Prayer*, by Thomas Merton; *Dimensions of Prayer*, by Douglas Steere; *The Problem with Prayer Is*, by David Hubbard; *The Still Hour*, by Austin Phelps; *Prayer, The Divine Dialog*, by Carroll Simcox; *The God Who Speaks*, by Ben Campbell Johnson; *With Christ in the School of Prayer*, by Andrew Murray.

Hans Urs von Balthasar and Karl Rahner have contributed insightful (though dense) books from a Catholic perspective. Orthodox theologian

337

Anthony Bloom penned several rewarding books on prayer. E. M. Bounds wrote eight (rather repetitive) books on prayer in the nineteenth century, now published in one volume. George A. Buttrick's *Prayer* is no longer in print but will prove worth the hunt if you can find a used edition. Esther de Waal sheds light on a rich tradition in *The Celtic Way of Prayer*.

Www.24–7prayer.com, a website based in the U.K., offers a global perspective on prayer. Indeed, any Internet search engine can lead you to a host of websites specializing in prayer.

The Upper Room, based in Nashville, Tennessee, publishes numerous resources on spiritual disciplines, most notably the journal *Weavings* and excellent workbooks on prayer by Maxie Dunnam. *Armchair Mystic* by the Jesuit priest Mark E. Thibodeaux gives a short and immensely practical guide to meditative prayer. Alice Fryling's *The Art of Spiritual Listening* approaches the same subject from an evangelical perspective.

For those more philosophically inclined, *Providence and Prayer* by Terrance Tiessen explores every angle of the Calvinist/Arminian/Open Theology debates on prayer. And C. S. Lewis's *Letters to Malcolm: Chiefly on Prayer* brilliantly tackles both practical and theoretical issues. I also recommend *Creative Prayer* by Brigid E. Herman, *Doors into Prayer* by Emilie Griffin, *Gratefulness, the Heart of Prayer* by Brother David Stendl-Rast, and *When God Doesn't Answer Your Prayer*, by Jerry Sittser.

In *Bless This House* Gregory and Suzanne M. Wolfe assemble a delightful collection of prayers for families to use in teaching children the art of prayer. Betty Shannon Cloyd's *Children and Prayer: A Shared Pilgrimage* also addresses this need.

Collections

Some collections focus on individuals: *The Prayers of Kierkegaard*, edited by Perry D. LeFevre; *Lancelot Andrewes and His Private Devotions*, translated by Alexander Whyte; *The English Poems of George Herbert*, edited by C. A. Patrides; *Prayers from* The Imitation of Christ *by Thomas à Kempis*, edited by Ronald Klug; and John Donne's *Devotions*. The website *www.wordamongus.org* has information on the "Praying with" series that features prayers by such notables as C. S. Lewis, Ignatius of Loyola, and Dorothy Day.

Catholics produce *Christian Prayer: Liturgy of the Hours* while Anglicans and Episcopalians rely on *The Book of Common Prayer*, both excellent resources designed for liturgical use. *A Guide to Prayer for All Who Seek God* follows a similar format, drawing on both contemporary and classic writings; and many denominations publish their own prayer guides. See also the *Book of Common Worship* by Westminster John Knox Press; *A Treasury of Prayers* by Stephen Fortosis; and *The Oxford Book of Prayer* edited by George Appleton.

Phyllis Tickle has streamlined the Divine Hours liturgy in a popular trilogy of books. Kathleen Norris's *Cloister Walk* and Robert Benson's *Living Prayer* give the story behind two people who encounter the liturgy; Benson later did his own collection in *Venite: A Book of Daily Prayer*.

The Lion Prayer Collection compiled by Mary Batchelor groups more than 1300 prayers according to topic. Ken Gire's *Between Heaven and Earth* includes many sample prayers as well as brief reflections on the subject. John Baillie's *A Diary of Private Prayer* offers contemporary prayers, one for morning and evening, with blank pages for the reader's own notes. Benedict Groeschel's *Praying to Our Lord Jesus Christ* brings together written prayers and meditations from the second to the twentieth century, most by Catholic luminaries.

Bible Meditation

Thelma Hall's *Too Deep for Words: Rediscovering Lectio Divina* includes five hundred Scripture texts that can be prayed in a contemplative way. Eugene Peterson's *Eat This Book* includes several chapters on the *lectio divina* style of meditating on Bible passages, while Richard Peace's *Contemplative Bible Reading* tailors the method to small group study.

Eugene Peterson has also written several books on the Psalms, including one that gives a year of daily prayers and reflections. *Christ in the Psalms*, by the Orthodox priest Patrick Henry Reardon, goes through the psalms one by one.

THANKS

When I first started contemplating a book on prayer, I knew I would need a lot of help. I began by reading through letters I've received over the years and interviewing friends and acquaintances about their experiences with prayer. They asked such articulate questions and gave such good insights that I decided to use many of their stories as inserts dropped into chapters throughout the book. I thank all of those who allowed me to probe what is usually a most private act, and then to present the results in a public form. Others, whose stories are not included in inserts, helped guide the path I took in this book.

I also spent many hours in libraries in the daunting shadow of shelves full of books about prayer. I would probably still be there reading had not my assistant, Melissa Nicholson, done yeoman's work of scanning scores of those books and marking portions that deserved special attention. Somehow she also kept track of the scraps of paper and bits of data that are woven together in a research-heavy book like this one.

The draft you are reading, despite its length, is far less cumbersome than earlier drafts (and hopefully more coherent) in large part due to patient readers like David Graham, Susan McQuilkin Grey, and John Topliff. David Moloney, Bob Hudson, Tim Stafford, and Katherine Helmers weighed in with their expert professional opinions (and scissors). And John Sloan, bless his heart, read every word in every incarnation, offering superb advice in his inimitable Barnabas style. It's rare indeed to find an editor who cares about a project as much as the author. I am grateful for all who contributed so selflessly, and especially to my wife, Janet, who manages to tolerate with grace the neuroses that seem endemic to those who make a living by the introverted task of writing.

SOURCES

Frontmatter

Book Epigraph: William James, quoted in "The Power of Prayer," by Jeffery L. Sheler, *US News & World Report* (Dec. 20, 2004), 54.

Part 1: Keeping Company with God

Epigraph: Patricia Hampl, *Virgin Time* (New York: Ballantine, 1992), 35.

1: Our Deepest Longing

Epigraph: Albert Einstein, cited in *Leadership Journal* (Winter 1983), 43.

pg. 13: *"red corner"*: David Remnick, *Lenin's Tomb* (New York: Random House, 1993), 81.

pg. 13: *Pravda:* Quoted in Paul Johnson, *Modern Times* (New York: Harper & Row, 1983), 454.

pg. 13: *Merton:* Thomas Merton, quoted in Mark E. Thibodeaux, S.J., *Armchair Mystic* (Cincinnati: St. Anthony Messenger, 2001), ix.

pg. 13: *Gallup:* George H. Gallup, Jr., *Religion in America 1996* (Princeton, NJ: The Princeton Religion Research Center, 1996), 4, 12, 19.

pg. 14: *Edwards:* Jonathan Edwards, quoted in Austin Phelps, *The Still Hour* (Carlisle, Penn.: Banner of Truth Trust, 1979), 11.

pg. 14: *Küng:* Hans Küng, cited in Ben Patterson, *Deepening Your Conversation With God*, Chapter 2, n.p., *www.ctlibrary.com/lebooks/pastossoul.soulconverstation*.

pg. 15: *Buttrick:* George Buttrick, *Prayer* (New York: Abingdon, 1942), 26.

pg. 16: *Lloyd-Jones:* Martyn Lloyd-Jones, *Why Does God Allow War* (Wheaton, Ill.: Crossway, 2003), 15.

pg. 16: *May:* Gerald May, *Addiction & Grace* (San Francisco: HarperSanFrancisco, 1988), 1.

2: View from Above

Epigraph: George Marshall, source unknown.

pg. 19: *"One of the psalms . . . thunder"*: Psalm 29:3.

pg. 20: *"Let me know"*: Psalm 39:4.

pg. 21: *"When I consider"*: Psalm 8:3–4.

pg. 21: *"O Lord"*: Psalm 8:1.

pg. 22: *"Where were you"*: Job 38:4.

pg. 22: *"Who is this"*: Job 38:2.

pg. 22: *"[God] is not far"*: Acts 17:27.

pg. 23: *Wilder:* Thornton Wilder, "Our Town," from *Three Plays* (New York: Harper & Brothers, 1957), Act 1, 45.

pg. 23: *"Let justice roll"*: Amos 5:24.

pg. 23: *"poor, bare"*: Shakespeare, *King Lear*, 3.4, line 106.

pg. 24: *Schmemann:* Alexander Schmemann, cited in Alan Jones, *Soul Making* (San Francisco: Harper & Row, 1985), 53.

pg. 24: *"Be still"*: Psalm 46:10.

pg. 24: (footnote) *Merton:* Thomas Merton, quoted in Ronald Rolheiser, *The Shattered Lantern* (New York: Crossroad, 2001), 40.

pg. 25: *Hampl:* Hampl, *Virgin*, op. cit. 217.

pg. 25: *"know that"*: Psalm 46:10.

pg. 25: (footnote) *"Almighty God"*: cited in Jonathan Aitken, *Prayers for People Under Pressure* (London: Continuum, 2005), 176.

pg. 25: *"You would have"*: John 19:11.

pg. 26: *Tugwell:* Simon Tugwell, *Prayer: Living With God* (Springfield, Ill.: Templegate Publishers, 1975), 35.

pg. 27: *Milton:* John Milton, *Paradise Lost*, Book VIII, line 103.

3: Just As We Are

Epigraph: C. S. Lewis, *Letters to Malcolm: Chiefly on Prayer* (London: Geoffrey Bles, 1964), 109.

pg. 31: *"a broken and contrite"*: Psalm 51:17.

pg. 31: *"a desire to lay"*: Cyril Connolly, quoted in Paul Johnson, *Intellectuals* (New York: Harper & Row, 1988), 315.

pg. 32: (footnote) *Buechner:* Frederick Buechner, *Whistling in the Dark* (San Francisco: Harper & Row, 1988), 96.

pg. 32: *"Search me"*: Psalm 139:23–24.

pg. 32: *Wangerin:* Walter Wangerin Jr., *Whole Prayer* (Grand Rapids, Mich.: Zondervan, 1998), 95–6.

pg. 33: *Hallesby:* Ole Hallesby, *Prayer* (Minneapolis: Augsburg, 1975), 16–17.

pg. 33: *"Apart from me"*: John 15:5.

pg. 34: *Nouwen:* Henri Nouwen, *With Open Hands* (New York: Ballantine/ Epiphany Edition, 1985), 54.

pg. 35: *Adams:* Henry Adams (pseudonym Frances Snow Compton), *Esther: A Novel* (New York: Henry Holt, 1884), 299.

pg. 36: *"The Lord Upholds"*: Psalm 105:4.

pg. 36: *"God opposes"*: 1 Peter 5:5–6.

pg. 36: *"God, have mercy"*: Luke 18:13.

pg. 36: *"For everyone"*: Luke 18:14.

pg. 37: *Hawk:* Daniel Hawk, source unknown.

pg. 38: *"German poet"*: Rainer Maria Rilke, *Rilke's Book of Hours* (New York: Riverhead, 1996), 143.

pg. 40: *Hillesum:* Etty Hillesum, *An Interrupted Life* (New York: Washington Square Press, 1981), 264.

pg. 40: *"Then in his joy"*: Matthew 13:44.

pg. 41: *"The Lord does not look"*: 1 Samuel 16:7.

pg. 42: *Lewis:* C. S. Lewis, *Malcolm*, op. cit., 35.

pg. 43: *Heschel:* Abraham Joshua Heschel, *I Asked for Wonder* (New York: Crossroads, 2000), 18.

pg. 43: *"Can a mother"*: Isaiah 49:15–16.

pg. 43: *Milton:* John Milton, *Paradise Lost*, Book XI, line 148ff.

pg. 43: *Ford*: David Ford, *The Shape of Living* (Grand Rapids, Mich.: Baker Books, 1997), 55.

pg. 44: *"that you, being"*: Ephesians 3:17.

4: The God Who Is

Epigraph: Nancy Mairs, *Ordinary Time* (Boston: Beacon, 1993), 54.

pg. 45: *"Tech-savvy Buddhists"*: Cited in Philip Zaleski & Carol Zaleski, *Prayer: A History* (New York: Houghton Mifflin, 2005), 4.

pg. 46: *Aitken*: Jonathan Aitken, *Pride and Perjury* (London: Continuum, 2004), 12.

pg. 47: (footnote) *MacDonald*: George MacDonald; quoted in Rolland Hein, *The Heart of George MacDonald* (Wheaton, Ill.: Harold Shaw, 1994), 373.

pg. 47: *"Another friend"*: Esther Elizabeth, from the *Journey Into Freedom* newsletter.

pg. 48: *Augustine*: Saint Augustine, *Sermons*, #117.5, quoted in Gary Wills, *Saint Augustine* (New York: Viking, 1999), xii.

pg. 48: (footnote) *Price*: Reynolds Price, *Letter to a Man in the Fire* (New York: Scribner, 1999), 84.

pg. 48: (footnote) *"For God so loved"*: John 3:16.

pg. 49: *Jeremias*: Joachim Jeremias, *The Prayers of Jesus* (Naperville, Ill.: Alec R. Allenson, Inc., 1967), 78.

pg. 49: *"Because you are sons"*: Galatians 4:6.

pg. 49: *"We do not know"*: Romans 8:26.

pg. 49: *Dante*: Dante Alighieri, *Paradiso*, Canto 33.

pg. 49: *"a thousand years"*: Psalm 90:4.

pg. 50: *"the glory I had"*: John 17:5.

pg. 50: *"we live and move"*: Acts 17:27.

pg. 51: *Hillesum*: Etty Hillesum, *Interrupted*, op. cit., 255, 238, 189.

pg. 53: *Heschel*: Abraham Joshua Heschel, quoted in Terry W. Glaspey, *Pathway to the Heart of God* (Eugene, Ore.: Harvest House, 1998), 53.

pg. 53: (footnote) *Farrer*: Austin Farrer, *The Essential Sermons* (London: SPCK, 1991), 157.

pg. 54: *Eckhart*: Meister Eckhart, David O'Neal, ed., *Meister Eckhart, from Whom God Hid Nothing* (Boston: Shambhala, 1996), 15.

pg. 55: *"account of a spiritual seeker"*: Cited in Thibodeaux, *Armchair*, op. cit., 173–4.

pg. 55: *"Hallowed"*: Matthew 6:9.

pg. 55: *Rilke*: Rainer Maria Rilke, *Rilke's Book*, op. cit., 81.

pg. 55: *"the eyes of the Lord"*: 1 Peter 3:12.

5: Coming Together

Epigraph: Blais Pascal, *Pensées* (New York: Dutton, 1958), 123.

pg. 56: *Stafford*: Tim Stafford, *Knowing the Face of God* (Grand Rapids, Mich.: Zondervan, 1986), 130–31.

pg. 57: *"the glory"*: John 17:5.

pg. 57: *"O unbelieving generation"*: Mark 9:19.

pg. 57: *"your will be done"*: Matthew 6:10.

pg. 58: *"You are my Son"*: Mark 1:11.

pg. 58: *"The Son can"*: John 5:19.

pg. 58: *"Your Father knows"*: Matthew 6:8.

pg. 58: *Stafford*: Tim Stafford, *Knowing*, op. cit., 134.

pg. 59: *"You are my friends"*: John 15:14–15.

pg. 61: *"your Father knows"*: Matthew 6:8.

pg. 62: *"My God"*: Matthew 27:46.

pg. 62: *Lewis*: C. S. Lewis, *Malcolm*, op. cit., 32.

pg. 62: *"keeping company with God"*: Clement of Alexandria, quoted in Simon Tugwell, *Prayer*, op. cit., vii.

pg. 63: *Ecclestone:* Alan Ecclestone, *On Praying,* quoted in John V. Taylor, *The Go-Between God* (London: SCM Press, 1972), 235.

pg. 63: *"Teach us":* Luke 11:1.

pg. 64: *"slow of speech":* Exodus 4:10.

pg. 64: *"panting . . . thirsting . . . longing":* Psalm 119:131, Psalm 42:2, Psalm 63:1.

pg. 65: *Teresa:* Mother Teresa, *Everything Starts From Prayer* (Ashland, Ore.: White Cloud Press, 1998), 35.

pg. 66: *"What profit":* Job 21:15 KJV.

pg. 66: *Brueggemann:* Walter Brueggemann, *The Message of the Psalms* (Minneapolis: Augsburg, 1984), 80, 52.

pg. 68: *"with loud cries":* Hebrews 5:7.

pg. 68: *"Do those who are dead":* Psalm 88:10.

pg. 68: *Reb Dovid Din:* An oral tradition cited in *Hasidic Tales,* 149.

Part 2: Unraveling the Mysteries

Epigraph: George Herbert, "Longing," *The English Poems of George Herbert,* (Totowa, N.J.: Rowman and Littlefield, 1974), 158.

6: Why Pray?

Epigraph: R.S. Thomas, "Folk Tale," in *Experimenting with an Amen* (London: Macmillan, 1986), 53.

pg. 73: *Tolstoy:* Leo Tolstoy, *War and Peace* (Baltimore: Penguin, 1957), Vol. 1, 588.

pg. 74: *"one philosophy professor":* Quoted in Nancey Murphy, "Of Miracles," *Bulletin of the Center for Theology and the Natural Sciences,* vol. 10, no. 2, Spring 1990, 16.

pg. 78: *"Now my heart":* John 12:27.

pg. 78: *"Abba":* Mark 14:36.

pg. 78: *"Eloi":* Mark 15:34.

pg. 78: *"he offered up prayers":* Hebrews 5:7.

pg. 78: *"Take this cup":* Mark 14:36.

pg. 79: *"the people":* John 11:42.

pg. 79: *"Father, forgive":* Luke 23:34.

pg. 79: *"I have food":* John 4:32.

pg. 79: *"Counselor":* John 14:16.

pg. 80: *"skeptical Greeks":* Joachim Jeremias, *The Prayers of Jesus,* op. cit. 66.

pg. 80: *"Anyone":* John 14:9.

pg. 80: *" Your will":* Matthew 6:10.

pg. 80: *"O unbelieving":* Mark 9:19.

pg. 80: *"Do not put":* Matthew 4:7.

pg. 80: *"My God, my God":* Matthew 27:46.

pg. 81: (footnote) *Rousseau:* Jean-Jacques Rousseau, quoted in Harry Emerson Fosdick, *The Meaning of Prayer* (New York: Association Press, 1917), 62.

pg. 81: *"Ask":* John 16:24.

pg. 81: *"that all of them":* John 17:21.

pg. 81: *"Jesus went out":* Luke 6:12.

pg. 81: *"Judas Iscariot":* Luke 6:16.

pg. 81: *"Satan":* Matthew 16:23.

pg. 82: *"How long":* Matthew 17:17.

pg. 82: *Anderson:* Ray S. Anderson, *The Gospel According to Judas* (Colorado Springs: Helmers & Howard, 1991), 51–53.

pg. 83: *"follow in his steps":* 1 Peter 2:21.

pg. 84: *"Simon, Simon":* Luke 22:31.

pg. 84: *"Then Satan":* Luke 22:3.

pg. 84: *"Friend, do":* Matthew 26:50.

pg. 85: *"Quench not":* 1 Thessalonians 5:19 KJV.

pg. 85: *"Grieve not":* Ephesians 4:30 KJV.

pg. 85: *Donne:* John Donne, "Divine Meditation 14" from *The Complete English Poems* (New York: Penguin, 1987), 314.

pg. 85: *"Do you think":* Matthew 26:53.

pg. 86: *"Abba, Father . . . what you will"*:
Mark 14:36.

pg. 86: *"You would have"*: John 19:11.

pg. 86: *Robinson:* Haddon Robinson,
in *Focal Point* magazine, quoted by
Paul Robbins in "The Back Page,"
Leadership, vol. 8 (1987), n.p.

pg. 87: *"O Jerusalem"*: Matthew 23:37.

pg. 88: *"for the joy"*: Hebrews 12:2.

pg. 88: *"Therefore he is able"*: Hebrews
7:24–25.

pg. 88: *"And then the lawless"*: 2 Thessalonians 2:8.

7: Wrestling Match

Epigraph: Walter Wink, "Prayer and the
Powers," *Sojourners*, vol. 19, no. 8
(October, 1990), 13.

pg. 89: *Mandela:* Nelson Mandela, *Long
Walk to Freedom* (New York: Little,
Brown, 1995), 265.

pg. 90: *Sojourner Truth:* Sojourner Truth,
quoted in Hugh T. Kerr and John M.
Mulder, Eds., *Conversions* (Grand
Rapids, Mich.: Eerdmans, 1983), 117.

pg. 90: *"Will a son"*: Genesis 17:17.

pg. 91: *"After I am worn out"*: Genesis
18:12.

pg. 91: *"Shall I hide"*: Genesis 18:17.

pg. 91: *"Far be it"*: Genesis 18:25.

pg. 91: *"For the sake of ten"*: Genesis 18:32.

pg. 91: *"The Lord is slow"*: Numbers 14:18.

pg. 92: *"remembered"*: Exodus 2:24.

pg. 92: *"The cry"*: Exodus 3:9.

pg. 94: *"stiff-necked"*: See Exodus 32:9, 33:3,
33:5, 34:9 and many more.

pg. 94: *"Let me alone"*: Deuteronomy 9:14.

pg. 94: *Luther:* Martin Luther, quoted in
Walter Wink, *Engaging the Powers*
(Minneapolis, Minn.: Fortress, 1992),
301.

pg. 94: *"Go up to the land"*: Exodus 33:3.

pg. 94: *"Did I conceive"*: Numbers 11:12.

pg. 95: *Trench:* Archbishop Trench, quoted
in Donald Bloesch, *The Struggle of
Prayer* (San Francisco: Harper & Row,
1980), 73.

pg. 95: *"What would we gain"*: Job 21:15.

pg. 95: *"I am worn out"*: Psalm 69:3.

pg. 95: *"Woe to me"*: Isaiah 6:5.

pg. 95: *"I do not know"*: Jeremiah 1:6.

pg. 96: *"Ah, Sovereign Lord"*: Jeremiah 4:10.

pg. 96: *Heschel:* Abraham Joshua Heschel,
A Passion for Truth (New York: Farrar,
Straus & Giroux, 1973), 265, 269.

pg. 96: *"I have heard"*: Acts 9:13.

pg. 97: *"Go!"*: Acts 9:15.

pg. 98: *"Let me go"*: Genesis 32:26.

pg. 98: *"I will not"*: Genesis 32:26.

pg. 99: *Waskow:* Arthur I. Waskow,
Godwrestling (New York: Schocken
Books, 1978), 1–2.

pg. 99: *"To see your face"*: Genesis 33:10.

pg. 100: *Bounds:* E.M. Bounds, *The
Complete Works of E.M. Bounds*
(Grand Rapids, Mich.: Baker Book
House, 1990), 322.

pg. 100: *Lawrence:* Roy Lawrence, *How to
Pray When Life Hurts* (Downers Grove,
Ill.: InterVarsity, 1990), 28.

8: Partnership

Epigraph: Abraham Joshua Heschel, *The
Prophets* (New York: HarperCollins,
Perennial Classics Edition, 2001), 253.

pg. 101: *"God's fellow workers"*: 1 Corinthians 3:9.

pg. 101: (footnote) *Julian:* Julian of
Norwich, *Revelations of Divine Love*
(London: Methuen & Co., 1901), 90.

pg. 102: *"the word of the Lord"*: 1 Samuel
3:1.

pg. 102: *"A time is coming"*: John 4:23.

pg. 102: *"Unless I go away"*: John 16:7.

pg. 103: *"Work out your salvation"*:
Philippians 2:12.

pg. 103: *"I worked harder"*: 1 Corinthians 15:10.

pg. 103: *"I no longer live"*: Galatians 2:20.

pg. 103: *"For we are God's"*: Ephesians 2:10.

pg. 104: *Lewis:* C. S. Lewis, *The Screwtape Letters* (New York: Time, 1961), 97.

pg. 104: *Lewis:* C. S. Lewis, *Miracles* (New York: Macmillan, 1947), 187.

pg. 104: *Lewis, "Only faith":* C. S. Lewis, *Malcolm*, op. cit., 70.

pg. 105: *Franciscan Benediction:* from many sources.

pg. 106: *Temple:* Archbishop William Temple. Quoted in Alister Hardy, *The Biology of God* (New York: Taplinger, 1975), 130.

pg. 106: *"God-incidents":* Phrase borrowed from Donald DeMarco in *The Heart of Virtue* (San Francisco: Ignatius Press, 1996), 147.

pg. 106: *Rabbi:* Rabbi Shlomo Carlebach, quoted in *Christianity Today* (June 10, 2002), 47.

pg. 108: (footnote) *Tiessen:* Terrance Tiessen, *Providence & Prayer* (Downers Grove, Ill.: InterVarsity, 2000), 339 – 40.

pg. 108: (footnote) *Kierkegaard:* Søren Kierkegaard, cited in Charles E. Moore, *Provocations: Spiritual Writings of Kierkegaard* (Farmington, Penn.: Plough, 1999), 345.

pg. 108: *Hampl:* Hampl, *Virgin*, op. cit., 217.

pg. 108: *"Your will be done":* Matthew 6:10.

pg. 109: *"If we are thrown":* Daniel 3:17. (emphasis mine)

pg. 109: *"Not my will":* Luke 22:42.

pg. 109: *Peterson:* Eugene Peterson, *Working the Angles* (Grand Rapids, Mich.: Eerdmans, 1987), 30 – 31.

pg. 110: *"I will build":* Matthew 16:18.

pg. 110: *"the head cannot say":* 1 Corinthians 12:21.

pg. 110: *"because they were harassed":* Matthew 9:36.

pg. 111: *"Ask the Lord":* Matthew 9:38.

pg. 112: *Carey:* William Carey, story cited in Brad Long & Doug McMurry, *Prayer that Shapes the Future* (Grand Rapids, Mich.: Zondervan, 1999), 60.

pg. 112: *"Your kingdom come":* Matthew 6:10.

pg. 112: *"In Christ":* Cited in Brennan Manning, *Lion and Lamb* (Old Tappan, N.J.: Chosen Books, 1986), 86.

pg. 112: *"Because you are sons":* Galatians 4:6. (emphasis mine)

pg. 112: *"And he who searches":* Romans 8:27.

pg. 113: *"Continue to work":* Philippians 2:12.

pg. 113: (footnote) *O'Casey:* Sean O'Casey, "Juno and the Haycock," from *The Sean O'Casey Reader* (New York: St. Martin's, 1968), Act II, 29.

pg. 113: *Peterson:* Eugene Peterson, *The Contemplative Pastor* (Grand Rapids, Mich.: Eerdmans, 1989), 103 – 4.

9: What Difference Does It Make?

Epigraph: William Shakespeare, *Richard III*, Act 4.4, line 75.

pg. 115: *Lenin:* Vladimir Lenin. Quoted in Stephanie Courtois, et. al., *The Black Book of Communism* (Cambridge, Mass.: Harvard University Press, 1999), 124.

pg. 115: *Stalin:* Joseph Stalin. Quoted in Winston Churchill, *The Gathering Storm*, Vol. 1, (Boston: Houghton Mifflin, 1948), 135.

pg. 116: *Mouw:* Richard Mouw, told in a private conversation.

pg. 117: *Thielicke:* Helmut Thielicke, *Our Heavenly Father: Sermons on the Lord's Prayer* (New York: Harper & Brothers, 1960), 109.

pg. 117: *"For our struggle"*: Ephesians 6:12.

pg. 117: *"But the prince"*: Daniel 10:13.

pg. 118: *"the god of this age"*: 2 Corinthians 4:4. Gregory Boyd, *God At War*, and David Bentley Hart, *The Doors of the Sea*, develop this concept.

pg. 118: *"the ruler"*: Ephesians 2:2.

pg. 118: *Barth:* Karl Barth, quoted in Kenneth Leech, *True Prayer* (San Francisco: Harper & Row, 1980), 68.

pg. 120: *"We want God!":* Cited in Robert Barron, *The Strangest Way* (Maryknoll, N.Y.: Orbis, 2004), 156.

pg. 121: *"He will strike"*: Isaiah 11:4.

pg. 121: *Ray McCauley Story:* From a personal interview.

pg. 123: *Tutu:* Bishop Desmond Tutu, quoted in Antjie Krog, *Country of My Skull* (New York: Three Rivers Press, 2000), 202.

pg. 124: *Bono:* Cited in *Bono in Converstation with Michka Assayas* (New York, Riverhead Boods, 2005), 272.

pg. 124: *Bonhoeffer:* Dietrich Bonhoeffer, quoted in Geffrey B. Kelley & F. Burton Nelson, *The Cost of Moral Leadership: The Spirituality of Dietrich Bonhoeffer* (Grand Rapids, Mich.: Eerdmans, 2003), 228.

pg. 125: *founder of the Center:* Richard Rohr, *Everything Belongs: The Gift of Contemplative Prayer* (New York: Crossroad Books, 1999), 92.

pg. 125: *Dickens:* Charles Dickens, *Martin Chuzzlewit* (New York: Knopf, 1907), 145.

pg. 125: *"Suppose a brother"*: James 2:15.

pg. 125: *Sir Thomas More:* Cited on *www.saintthomasmoresociety.org*, and numerous other places.

pg. 127: *"Awake, awake! Clothe"*: Isaiah 51:9.

pg. 127: *"Awake, awake, O Zion"*: Isaiah 52:1.

pg. 128: *Barth:* Karl Barth, *Church Dogmatics II, The Doctrine of God,* part 1, translated by T.H.L. Parker, W.B. Johnston, Harold Knight and J.L.M Haire, ed. G.W. Bromley and T.F. Torrance (Edinburgh: T & T Clark, 1957), 265.

pg. 128: *Catholic Worker:* From "God's Work, Not Ours" by Sandi Huckaby, *The Other Side* Jan./Feb. 1998, 45.

pg. 130: *"and there came peals"*: Revelation 8:5.

pg. 130: *Wink:* Walter Wink, *Engaging the Powers,* op. cit., 299.

10: Does Prayer Change God?

Epigraph: Andrew Murray, *With Christ in the School of Prayer* (Greenville, S.C.: Ambassador Publications, 1998), 215.

pg. 131: *Origen:* "On Prayer," in *Origen: An Exhortation to Martyrdom, Prayer and Selected Works,* trans. Rowan Greer, *Classics of Western Spirituality* (New York: Paulist, 1979), 92.

pg. 131: *Kant:* Immanuel Kant, quoted in Friedrich Heiler, *Prayer* (New York: Oxford University Press, 1932), 89.

pg. 132: *Edwards:* Jonathan Edwards, "The Most High: A prayer-hearing God," in *Works of Jonathan Edwards,* Edward Hackman, Ed., (Edinburgh: The Banner of Truth Trust, 1974), 2:115–16, cited in John Sanders, *The God Who Risks.*

pg. 132: *Calvin:* John Calvin, *Institutes of the Christian Religion* (Grand Rapids, Mich.: Eerdmans, 1964), 148.

pg. 132: *Hardy:* Thomas Hardy, quoted in Timothy George, "What God Knows," *First Things* (June/July 2003), 8.

pg. 132: *Vonnegut:* Kurt Vonnegut, *Slaughterhouse-Five* (New York: Delacorte, 1969) 52.

pg. 132: *Lord's Prayer:* Matthew 6:9–13.

pg. 133: *"And when you pray"*: Matthew 6:7–8. (emphasis mine) pg. 133: *Ellul:* Jacques Ellul, *Prayer and Modern Man* (New York: Seabury, 1973), 177.

pg. 133: *"delights in those":* Psalm 147:11.

pg. 133: *"For a long time":* Isaiah 42:14.

pg. 133: *"Ask and it will":* Matthew 7:7.

pg. 133: *"And the prayer":* James 5:15.

pg. 133: *"The eyes":* 1 Peter 3:12.

pg. 133: *"You do not have":* James 4:2.

pg. 134: *"Forty more days":* Jonah 3:4.

pg. 134: *"when God saw":* Jonah 3:10.

pg. 134: *"relented," "changed his mind":* Exodus 32:14, Psalm 106:45, Amos 7:3, Amos 7:6.

pg. 134: *Finney:* Charles Finney, *Prevailing Prayer* (Grand Rapids, Mich.: Kregel, 1965), 41.

pg. 134: *Pinnock:* Clark Pinnock, *The Openness of God* (Downers Grove, Ill.: InterVarsity, 1994), 48.

pg. 134: *Murray:* Andrew Murray, *With Christ,* op. cit., 127.

pg. 136: *"We do not know":* Romans 8:26.

pg. 136: *"For through him":* Ephesians 2:18.

pg. 136: *Lewis:* C. S. Lewis, *God in the Dock* (Grand Rapids, Mich.: Eerdmans, 1970), 104–5.

pg. 136: *Pascal:* Blaise Pascal, *Pensées* #513, op. cit., 140.

pg. 137: *Lewis:* C. S. Lewis, *Dock,* op. cit., 105–6.

pg. 138: *Lewis:* C. S. Lewis, *Miracles,* op. cit., 185–6.

pg. 138: (footnote) *de Molina:* Luis de Molina, cited in Tiessen, *Providence,* op. cit., 153–8.

pg. 139: *"Your will be done":* Matthew 6:10.

pg. 141: *"I am coming":* John 17:13.

pg. 141: *"My prayer":* John 17:15.

pg. 142: *"And now, Father":* John 17:5.

pg. 142: *"before the creation":* John 17:24.

pg. 142: *"Was given us":* 2 Timothy 1:9.

pg. 142: *"chosen before":* 1 Peter 1:20.

pg. 142: *"before the beginning":* Titus 1:2.

pg. 142: *"Because I have said":* John 16:6.

pg. 142: *"But I tell you":* John 16:7. (emphasis mine)

pg. 143: *Barth:* "He is not deaf": Karl Barth, *Prayer* (Philadelphia: Westminster, 1952), 21.

pg. 143: *Barth:* "The fact that": Karl Barth, quoted in Steven Mosley, *If Only God Would Answer* (Colorado Springs: Navpress, 1992), 150.

pg. 143: *"your Father knows":* Matthew 6:8.

pg. 143: *"Do not be anxious":* Philippians 4:6.

pg. 144: (footnote) *Lewis:* "For he seems": C. S. Lewis, *The World's Last Night* (New York: Harcourt Brace Jovanovich, 1960), 9.

pg. 144: (footnote) *Lewis:* "Creation seems to be": C. S. Lewis, *Malcolm,* op. cit., 95–6.

11: Ask, Seek, Knock

Epigraph: *Milton:* John Milton, *Paradise Lost,* book XI, lines 307–10.

pg. 14: (footnote) *Bailey:* Kenneth Bailey, *Poet & Peasant* and *Through Peasant Eyes* (Grand Rapids, Mich.: Eerdmans, 1983), *Poet & Peasant,* 122.

pg. 146: *"who watches over you":* Psalm 121:3.

pg. 146: *"to show them":* Luke 18:1.

pg. 147: *Bailey:* Kenneth Bailey, *Through Peasant Eyes* quoting H.B. Tristram, *Eastern Customs in Bible Lands* (London: Hodder and Stoughton, 1894), 228ff.

pg. 147: *"Even though I don't fear":* Luke 18:4–5.

pg. 148: *"Where is this 'coming'":* 2 Peter 3:4.

pg. 149: *Thielicke:* Helmut Thielicke, *Christ and the Meaning of Life* (Grand Rapids, Mich.: Baker Book House, 1975), 85.

pg. 150: "the gates of hell": Matthew 16:18 KJV.

pg. 150: Sittser: Jerry Sittser, When God Doesn't Answer Your Prayer (Grand Rapids, Mich.: Zondervan, 2003), 115.

pg. 151: "Lord, if you had": John 11:21.

pg. 151: "Send her away": Matthew 15:23.

pg. 151: Kierkegaard: Søren Kierkegaard. Quoted in Zaleski, Prayer, op. cit., 99.

pg. 152: Cicero: Cicero, quoted in A.L. Lilley, Prayer and Christian Theology (London: Billing & Sons Ltd., 1924), 4.

pg. 152: MacDonald: George MacDonald, Creation in Christ (Wheaton, Ill.: Harold Shaw, 1976), 315.

pg. 153: Nouwen: "Why should I": Henri Nouwen, Primacy of the Heart (Madison, Wis.: St. Benedict Center, 1988), 9.

pg. 153: Nouwen: "We must pray": Henri Nouwen, The Road to Daybreak (New York: Doubleday, 1988), 117.

pg. 153: Nouwen: "sitting in the presence": Henri Nouwen, Primacy, op. cit., 9.

pg. 153: Weil: Simone Weil, The Notebooks of Simone Weil, vol. 2 (New York: Putnam, 1956), 574.

pg. 154: Augustine: St. Augustine, quoted in Friedrich Heiler, Prayer, op. cit., 200.

pg. 154: "If you then": Luke 11:13. (emphasis mine)

pg. 154: "If you then": Matthew 7:11. (emphasis mine)

pg. 154: "For we are": Ephesians 2:10.

Part 3: The Language of Prayer

Epigraph: Frederick Buechner, Godric (New York: Atheneum, 1981), 142.

12: Yearning for Fluency

Epigraph: Nouwen: Henri Nouwen, Reaching Out (New York: Doubleday, 1975) 126.

pg. 158: Buechner: Frederick Buechner, Now & Then (San Francisco: Harper & Row, 1983), 32.

pg. 161: "Teach us to pray": Luke 11:1.

pg. 161: Teresa: Mother Teresa, Everything Starts, op. cit., 39, 40.

pg. 161: Weatherhead: Leslie Weatherhead, A Private House of Prayer (Nashville: Abingdon, 1958), 28.

pg. 162: Nouwen: Henri Nouwen, The Genesee Diary (Garden City, N.Y.: Image Books/Doubleday, 1981), 140.

pg. 163: Postema: Don Postema, Space for God (Grand Rapids, Mich.: Bible Way/ CRC Publications, 1983), 17.

pg. 163: Morford: Judy Morford, quoted in Terry Muck, Liberating the Leader's Prayer Life (Carol Stream, Ill.: Christianity Today/Word Books, 1985), 67.

pg. 164: Yankelovich: Daniel Yankelovich. Cited in Joseph M. Champlin, Behind Closed Doors: A Handbook on How to Pray (New York: Paulist Press, 1984), 63–4.

pg. 165: "full armor": Ephesians 6:11.

pg. 166: Virgil: Cited in Simon Tugwell, Prayer, op. cit., 5.

pg. 166: "Blessed are the pure": Matthew 5:8.

pg. 166: "renewing": see Romans 12:2.

pg. 168: Nouwen: Henri Nouwen, quoted in Terry Muck, Liberating op. cit., 138.

pg. 169: Patterson: Ben Patterson, Waiting (Downers Grove, Ill.: InterVarsity, 1989), 109.

13: Prayer Grammar

pg. 170: *"Deaf children babble"*: Cited in Morton Hunt, *The Universe Within* (New York: Touchstone, 1982), 222–3.

pg. 171: *The Lord's Prayer*: Matthew 6:9–13.

pg. 172: *Calvin*: John Calvin, from the Author's Preface to John Calvin's *Commentary on Psalms, Volume 1*, (*www.ccel.org*).

pg. 173: *Bonhoeffer*: Dietrich Bonhoeffer, cited in Geffrey B. Kelley, "The Prayerbook of the Bible: Dietrich Bonhoeffer's Introduction to the Psalms," in *Weavings*, vol. vi, no. 5 (Sept./Oct., 1991), 36.

pg. 174: *"my sin"*: Psalm 51:3.

pg. 174: *"against you"*: Psalm 51:4.

pg. 175: *"The sacrifices of God"*: Psalm 51:17.

pg. 176: *Peterson*: Eugene Peterson, *Answering God* (San Francisco: HarperSanFrancisco, 1991), 7.

pg. 177: *"he who began"*: Philippians 1:6.

pg. 177: *"against the powers"*: Ephesians 6:12.

pg. 178: *Rienstra*: Debra Rienstra, *So Much More* (San Francisco: Jossey-Bass, 2005), 144.

pg. 179: *Patterson*: Ben Patterson, *Deepening*, chapter 4, op. cit., n.p.

pg. 179: *Milton*: John Milton, quoted in Buttrick, *Prayer*, op. cit., 230.

pg. 179: *Lewis*: C. S. Lewis, *Malcolm*, op. cit., 22.

pg. 180: *Rinker*: Rosalind Rinker, *Communicating Love Through Prayer* (Grand Rapids, Mich.: Zondervan, 1966), 90–95.

pg. 181: *De Sales*: Francis de Sales, "Introduction to a Devout Life," quoted in William Adams Brown, *A Life of Prayer in a World of Science* (New York: Scribner's, 1927), 153–155.

pg. 182: *Tickle*: Phyllis Tickle, *Prayer is a Place* (New York: Doubleday, 2005), 256.

pg. 183: *Lamott*: Anne Lamott, *Traveling Mercies* (New York: Pantheon, 1999), 82.

pg. 183: *"Create in me"*: Psalm 51:10.

pg. 183: *"Restore to me"*: Psalm 51:12.

pg. 183: *"The wind blows"*: John 3:8.

14: Tongue-Tied

Epigraph: George MacDonald, *Creation*, op. cit., 328.

pg. 184: *Luther*: Martin Luther, from Luther's exposition of John 16:23, cited in *What Luther Says*, Ewald M. Plass, ed. (St. Louis: Concordia, 1959), 2:1083.

pg. 185: *The Cloud of Unknowing*, anonymous, cited in Thomas H. Green, S.J., *When the Well Runs Dry* (Notre Dame, In.: Ave Maria Press, 1998), 136.

pg. 186: *Kempis*: Thomas à Kempis, *The Imitation of Christ* (Nashville: Thomas Nelson, 1979), 159.

pg. 186: *Donne*: John Donne, *Sermons on the Psalms and Gospels*, Evelyn M. Simpson, Ed. (Los Angeles: University of California Press, 1963), 226.

pg. 186: *"lifting up of the mind"*: St. John Damascene, cited in F.P. Harton, *The Elements of the Spiritual Life* (New York: Macmillan, 1943), 222.

pg. 187: *McCabe*: Herbert McCabe, *God, Christ and Us* (London: Continuum International Publishing Group, 2005). Quoted in L. Roger Owens "Don't Talk Nonsense," *Christian Century* (January 25, 2005), 21.

pg. 190: *Luther*: Martin Luther, *By Faith Alone* (Grand Rapids, Mich.: World Publishing, 1998), March 9.

pg. 190: *Merton*: Thomas Merton, *New Seeds of Contemplation* (New York: New Directions, 1961), 31.

pg. 190: *Bondi:* Roberta Bondi, *To Pray and to Love* (Minneapolis.: Fortress, 1991), 49.

pg. 191: *"Let us then":* Hebrews 4:16. (emphasis mine)

pg. 191: (footnote) *Moltmann:* Jürgen Moltmann, *The Source of Life* (Minneapolis: Fortress, 1997), 126–30.

pg. 192: *"In one project":* Chester P. Michael and Marie C. Norrisey, *Prayer and Temperament:* (Charlottesville, Va.: The Open Door, Inc., 1991).

pg. 192: *Underhill:* Evelyn Underhill, *Concerning the Inner Life,* quoted in Kathy Callahan-Howell "Mary Heart, Martha Brain," *Leadership* (Fall 2001), 57.

pg. 192: *"O Lord,":* Psalm 139:1.

pg. 193: *"the Spirit himself":* Romans 8:26.

pg. 193: *"in my name":* John 14:13.

pg. 196: *Ambrose:* Quoted in Eugene Peterson, *Angles,* op. cit., 58.

pg. 196: *Marty:* Martin Marty, *Cry of Absence* (Grand Rapids, Mich.: Eerdmans, 1997), 41.

pg. 197: *Muck:* Terry Muck, *Liberating,* op. cit., 175.

pg. 197: (footnote) *Muck:* Ibid., 105.

pg. 197: *Lewis:* C. S. Lewis, *Malcolm,* op. cit., 149.

15: The Sound of Silence

Epigraph: Georges Bernanos, *The Diary of a Country Priest* (Garden City, N.Y.: Image, 1954), 80–81.

pg. 199: *"How long":* Psalm 13:1.

pg. 200: *"But if I go":* Job 23:8.

pg. 200: *"O my God,":* Psalm 22:2.

pg. 200: *". . . my foes":* Psalm 42:10.

pg. 200: *"I spread out":* Psalm 143:6.

pg. 200: *"My God, my God":* Matthew 27:46.

pg. 200: *"Imagine the disciple Peter":* Suggested by Patrick Henry, *The Ironic Christian's Companion* (New York: Riverhead Books, 1999), 130.

pg. 201: *Green:* Thomas Green, *When,* op. cit., 84–5.

pg. 201: *Cowper:* William Cowper, quoted in Fosdick, *Meaning,* op. cit., 81.

pg. 201: *Herbert:* George Herbert, *Poems,* op. cit., 168–9.

pg. 202: *Bonhoeffer:* Dietrich Bonhoeffer, *Life Together* (San Francisco: HarperSanFrancisco, 1954), 84.

pg. 203: *"thorn in my flesh":* 2 Corinthians 12:7.

pg. 203: *"Every branch":* John 15:2.

pg. 204: *Blackaby:* Henry Blackaby, *Experiencing God* (Nashville: Broadman & Holman Publishers, 1994), 115.

pg. 205: *"183 times":* From a personal conversation with Richard Rohr.

pg. 206: *"For where two or three":* Matthew 18:20.

pg. 206: *"A Jewish teacher of prayer":* Cited in David Steindl-Rast, *Gratefulness, the Heart of Prayer* (New York: Paulist Press, 1984), 52.

pg. 207: *Latimer:* Hugh Latimer, quoted in Fosdick, *Meaning,* op. cit., 82.

pg. 207: *"The wind":* John 3:8.

pg. 208: *"Come near":* James 4:8.

pg. 208: *"Here I am!":* Revelation 3:20.

pg. 209: *"I waited patiently":* Psalm 40:1.

pg. 210: *Luther:* Martin Luther, *By Faith,* op. cit., August 17.

pg. 210: *Aitken:* Jonathan Aitken, *Pride,* op. cit., 277.

pg. 210: (footnote) *Farrer:* Austin Farrer, *Sermons,* op. cit., 183–4.

Part Four: Prayer Dilemmas

Epigraph: Emily Dickinson, *The Complete Poems of Emily Dickinson*, ed. Thomas H. Johnson (Boston: Little, Brown, 1961), 709.

16: Unanswered Prayer: Whose Fault?

Epigraph: Oscar Wilde, "An Ideal Husband," from *The Best of Oscar Wilde: Selected Plays and Writings* (New York: New American Library, 2004), 212.

pg. 216: *Hopkins:* Gerard Manley Hopkins, "I Wake and Feel the Fell of Dark," from *The Poems of Gerard Manley Hopkins* (New York: Oxford University Press, 1970), 101.

pg. 217: *Maugham:* Somerset Maugham, *Of Human Bondage* (New York: Bantam Books, 1991), 48–9.

pg. 218: *Galton:* Cited in Rick Ostrander, *The Life of Prayer in a World of Science* (New York: Oxford University Press, 2000), 23, 33, 42.

pg. 220: *"survey of 5,600":* Sheler, "Power," op cit., 56.

pg. 221: (footnote) *Marty:* Martin Marty, quoted in Jim Castelli, "Prayer," in *USA Weekend* (December 23–25, 1994), 5.

pg. 222: *Patterson:* Floyd Patterson, quoted in "The Sanctification of Sport: Can the Mind of Christ Coexist with with the Killer Instinct?" by Shirl J. Hoffman, *Christianity Today* (4 April 1986), 18.

pg. 223: *"You don't know":* Matthew 20:22.

pg. 223: *"Get behind":* Matthew 16:23.

pg. 223: *"When you ask":* James 4:3.

pg. 223: *"If I had":* Psalm 66:18.

pg. 223: *"When you spread":* Isaiah 1:15–17. See also Isaiah 58:3–9, 59:2, and Malachi 2–3.

pg. 224: *"If a man shuts":* Proverbs 21:13.

pg. 224: *"so that nothing":* 1 Peter 3:7.

pg. 225: *"receive from him":* 1 John 3:22.

pg. 226: *Lloyd-Jones:* Martin Lloyd-Jones, *Why,* op. cit., 21.

pg. 226: (footnote) *Mains:* David Mains, from personal conversation.

pg. 226: *Betjeman:* John Betjeman, from "In Westminster Abbey, 1940," quoted in John Bartlett, *Bartlett's Familiar Quotations* (Boston: Little, Brown, 1980), 866:17.

pg. 227: *Davis:* Jefferson Davis, quoted in Alfred Kazin, *God and the American Writer* (New York: Vintage, 1998), 135.

pg. 227: *Lincoln:* Abraham Lincoln, "Second Inaugural Address," delivered March 4, 1865. Reprinted online: *www.bartleby.com/124/pres32.html.*

pg. 228: *"I have been driven":* Abraham Lincoln, quoted in Woodrow Kroll, *When God Doesn't Answer* (Grand Rapids, Mich.: Baker Book House, 1997), 179.

pg. 229: *Gandhi:* Mahatma Gandhi, quoted in E. Stanley Jones, *Victory Through Surrender* (Nashville: Abingdon, 1971), 68–9.

pg. 230: *Brooks:* Garth Brooks, "Unanswered Prayers," written by Patrick Alger, Larry B. Bastian, and Troyal Garth Brooks. 1991 Major Bob Music/Mid-Summer Music, Inc./ Universal Music Publishing Group/ Universal Polygram International Publishing, Inc.

pg. 231: *White:* Charles Edward White, "Small Sacrifices," in *Christianity Today* (June 22, 1992), 32–3.

17: Unanswered Prayer: Living With the Mystery

Epigraph: George Herbert, "Deniall," *Poems*, op. cit., 96.

pg. 233: *"You have covered"*: Lamentations 3:44.

pg. 233: *"thorn"*: 2 Corinthians 12:7.

pg. 233: *"Therefore I will boast"*: 2 Corinthians 12:9–10.

pg. 233: *"let this cup pass"*: Matthew 26:39 KJV.

pg. 233: *"My God"*: Matthew 27:46.

pg. 233: *"the human situation"*: C. S. Lewis, *Malcolm*, op. cit., 64.

pg. 234: *"The essence of request"*: C. S. Lewis, *World's*, op. cit., 4–5.

pg. 234: *"I tell you the truth"*: Matthew 21:21.

pg. 235: *"Again, I tell you"*: Matthew 18:19.

pg. 235: *"Therefore I tell you"*: Mark 11:24.

pg. 235: *"You may ask"*: John 14:14.

pg. 235: *"Everything that I learned"*: John 15:15.

pg. 235: *"whatever you ask"*: John 14:13. (emphasis mine)

pg. 235: *"If you remain"*: John 15:7. (emphasis mine)

pg. 236: *Lewis*: Lewis details this quest in the essay "Petitionary Prayer: A Problem Without an Answer," in Lewis, *Christian Reflections* (Grand Rapids, Mich.: Eerdmans, 1967), 142–151.

pg. 237: *"The Lord is good"*: Lamentations 3:25 KJV.

pg. 237: *"But they that wait"*: Isaiah 40:31 KJV.

pg. 237: *"And let us not be weary"*: Galatians 6:9 KJV.

pg. 237: *"My time"*: John 2:4.

pg. 238: *"commended for their faith"*: Hebrews 11:39.

pg. 238: *"God had planned"*: Hebrews 11:40.

pg. 238: *"They will say"*: 2 Peter 3:4, 8.

pg. 239: *Aikman*: David Aikman, *Jesus in Beijing* (Washington, D.C.: Regnery, 2003).

pg. 240: *Baillie*: John Baillie, quoted in George Appleton, *Journey for a Soul* (Glasgow: William Collins, 1974), 222.

pg. 240: *Beatitudes*: Matthew 5:3–11.

pg. 240: *Prayers of the Martyrs*: Duane W.H. Arnold, ed., (Grand Rapids, Mich.: Zondervan, 1991).

pg. 240: *Goetz*: Ronald Goetz, "Lord, Teach Us to Pray," in *The Christian Century* (November 5, 1986), 975.

pg. 241: *"salvation from our enemies"*: Luke 1:71.

pg. 244: *Rolheiser*: Ronald Rolheiser, *The Holy Longing* (New York: Doubleday, 1999), 81.

pg. 245: *"I have great sorrow"*: All quotes from Paul are from Romans 9 to 11.

pg. 245: *Calvin*: John Calvin, *Sermons on the Epistle to the Ephesians* (Edinburgh, Scotland: Banner of Truth Trust, 1975), 683.

pg. 246: (footnote) *Coffin*: William Sloane Coffin, *Credo* (Louisville: Westminster/John Knox, 2004), 40.

pg. 246: *"For my thoughts"*: Isaiah 55:8–9.

pg. 247: *"For now we see"*: 1 Corinthians 13:12 KJV.

18: Prayer and Physical Healing

Epigraph: Reynolds Price, *The Laws of Ice* (New York: Atheneum, 1987), 67.

pg. 250: *Bakker*: Tammy Faye Bakker, quoted in "Theologian of the Year: Tammy Faye Bakker," *The Wittenberg Door*, vol. 58 (December, 1980–January 1981), 3.

pg. 251: *"more than half"*: A full survey of physicians is given online at *www.jtsa.edu/research/finkelstein/surveys/physicians.shtml*

pg. 251: *An epidemiologist:* Cited in "Faith & Healing," *Newsweek* (November 10, 2003), 48.

pg. 251: *Koenig:* Dr. Harold G. Koenig, *The Healing Power of Faith* (New York: Simon & Schuster, 1999), 9.

pg. 255: (footnote) *Buttrick:* George Buttrick, *Prayer*, op. cit., 114–15.

pg. 256: *Brand:* Dr. Paul Brand, reprinted as a booklet co-authored with Philip Yancey, *Healing* (Portland, Ore.: Multnomah, 1984).

pg. 259: *"the Father of compassion":* 2 Corinthians 1:3.

pg. 259: (footnote) *"Messenger of Satan":* 2 Corinthians 12:7.

pg. 259: *Kallas:* James Kallas, *The Significance of the Synoptic Miracles* (Greenwich, Conn.: Seabury, 1961), 63.

pg. 261: *Brand:* Dr. Paul Brand, from an unpublished article.

pg. 265: *"One of the most revealing scientific studies":* Cited in Dale A. Matthews, M.D., *The Faith Factor* (New York: Viking, 1998), 149–50.

pg. 266: *"The God of all comfort":* 2 Corinthians 1:3.

19: What to Pray For

Epigraph: Thomas Merton, *Contemplative Prayer* (New York: Doubleday, 1996), 37.

pg. 268: *"Do you want":* John 5:6.

pg. 268: *"Lord, the one":* John 11:3.

pg. 268: *"Lord, if you had":* John 11:21.

pg. 268: *"Lord, if you had":* John 11:32.

pg. 268: *"he was deeply":* John 11:33.

pg. 268: *"Jesus wept":* John 11:35.

pg. 269: *Peterson:* Eugene Peterson, *Christ Plays in Ten Thousand Places* (Grand Rapids, Mich.: Eerdmans, 2005), 138.

pg. 269: *Dobson:* Ed Dobson, "Leave Room for God," in *Leadership* (Fall 2001), 31.

pg. 270: *"But if anybody":* 1 John 2:1.

pg. 270: *Jaime Cardinal Sin:* From a private conversation with Leighton Ford and others.

pg. 272: *Lawrence:* Roy Lawrence, *How*, op. cit., 69–70.

pg. 272: *"Come to me":* Matthew 11:28.

pg. 272: *"Peace I leave":* John 14:27.

pg. 273: *"In the same way":* Romans 8:26.

pg. 274: *"so that we can":* 2 Corinthians 1:4.

pg. 275: *A grateful heart:* From Robert A. Emmons, "Gratitude and Mind-Body Health," *Spirituality & Medicine Connection*, vol. 5, issue 1, Spring, 2001, 1.

pg. 278: *Schmidt:* Stephen A. Schmidt, "Theologies of Prayer: A Christian perspective," *Stauros Notebook*, vol. 20, no. 2 (September 2001), 3.

pg. 279: *"afflicted but not crushed":* 2 Corinthians 4:8.

pg. 279: *"as the gentle rain":* William Shakespeare, *The Merchant of Venice*, Act 4.1, line 183.

pg. 279: *Chen:* George Chen, cited in "China's Dynamic Church," *Christianity Today* (July 13, 1998), cover story, accessed online.

pg. 280: *Van Ham:* Lee Van Ham, "Some Benefits of Losing Heart," *Faith at Work* (Spring 1998), 6–7.

pg. 281: *O'Connor:* Flannery O'Connor, *The Habit of Being* (New York: Vintage, 1979), 163.

pg. 281: *Roman Missal:* Aitken, *Prayers*, op. cit., 68.

pg. 281: *"eternal glory":* 2 Corinthians 4:17.

pg. 281: *"Christ will be":* Philippians 1:20.

pg. 281: *"do not worry":* Matthew 6:25.

Part Five: The Practice of Prayer

Epigraph: F. B. Meyer. Quoted in Jerry Sittser, *When God*, op. cit., 11.

20: Prayer and Me

Epigraph: Walter Wink, *Engaging*, op. cit., 298.

pg. 286: *"create space"*: Henri Nouwen, "Moving from Solitude to Community to Ministry," in *Leadership* (Spring 1995), 81.

pg. 286: *"The movie was so filled"*: *Nouwen: Henri Nouwen, Gracias!* (Maryknoll, N.Y.: Orbis, 1993), 57.

pg. 286: *"He who has ears"*: Mark 4:9.

pg. 287: (footnote) *Grey*: Pamela Grey, quoted in Carroll E. Simcox, *Prayer: The Divine Dialog* (Downers Grove, Ill.: InterVarsity, 1985), 32.

pg. 287: *A seminary professor*: Klaus Issler, *Wasting Time With God* (Downers Grove, Ill.: InterVarsity, 2001).

pg. 288: *Carrel*: Dr. Alexis Carrel, *Prayer and Modern Man* (New York: Morehouse-Gotham, 1948), cited in Ellul, *Prayer & Modern Man*, op. cit., 42–3.

pg. 288: *Jones*: E. Stanley Jones, *The Way* (New York: Abingdon-Cokesbury, 1946), 206.

pg. 290: *Nouwen*: Henri Nouwen, *Gracias!*, op. cit., 44, 69.

pg. 290: *Postema*: Don Postema, *Space*, op. cit., 110.

pg. 292: *"you do not run"*: Henri Nouwen, quoted in Christopher de Vinck, *Nouwen Then* (Grand Rapids, Mich.: Zondervan, 1999), 134–5.

pg. 292: *"They are more"*: Henri Nouwen, *Genesee*, op. cit., 100.

pg. 292: *"I will fear"*: Psalm 23:4.

pg. 293: *"Do not be anxious"*: Philippians 4:6.

pg. 293: *"Cast all"*: 1 Peter 5:7.

pg. 294: *"My peace"*: John 14:27.

pg. 294: *Caretto*: Carlo Caretto, *Letters from the Desert*. Quoted in Eddie Askew, A Silence and a Shouting (Guilford, Surrey, England: Eagle Publishing, 2001), 25–6.

pg. 295: *"Cast all"*: 1 Peter 5:7.

pg. 297: *"So Jacob served"*: Genesis 29:20.

pg. 297: *"My soul waits"*: Psalm 130:6.

pg. 297: *"My eyes fail"*: Psalm 119:82.

pg. 297: *Bloom*: Anthony Bloom, *Beginning to Pray* (Mahwah, N.J.: Paulist Press, 1970), 88–9.

pg. 298: *"Primary Wonder"*: Denise Levertov, *Sands of the Well* (New York: New Directions, 1996), 129.

21: Prayer and Others

Epigraph: David Hubbard, *The Problem With Prayer Is . . .* (Wheaton, Ill.: Tyndale House, 1972), 14.

pg. 302: (footnote) *Johnson*: Paul Johnson, *A History of Christianity* (New York: Atheneum, MacMillan, 1976), 270.

pg. 302: *"I have heard"*: Exodus 3:7.

pg. 304: (footnote) *The Book of Common Prayer*: (New York: Oxford University Press), 384.

pg. 305: *Bonhoeffer*: Dietrich Bonhoeffer, *The Cost of Discipleship* (New York: MacMillan Co., 1959), 88.

pg. 305: *Owens*: Virginia Stem Owens, "Prayer—Into the Lion's Jaws," in *Christianity Today* (November 19, 1976), 17–21.

pg. 309: *Laubach*: Frank Laubach, *Man of Prayer* (Syracuse, N.Y.: Laubach Literacy International, 1990), 45.

pg. 309: (footnote) *Franklin*: Benjamin Franklin, quoted in E. Stanley Jones, *The Way*, op. cit., 207.

pg. 309: *"Love your enemies"*: Matthew 5:44.

pg. 311: *Lewis:* C. S. Lewis, quoted in Michael Ward, "Knights & Martyrs," *Christian History,* vol. 88, 30–31.

pg. 312: *Bonhoeffer:* Dietrich Bonhoeffer, *Cost,* op. cit., 135.

pg. 312: *"Father, forgive":* Luke 23:34.

pg. 312: *"Lord, do not hold":* Acts 7:60.

pg. 312: *Bonhoeffer:* Dietrich Bonhoeffer, *The Cost of Discipleship,* op. cit., 135.

pg. 312: *Christian magazine:* Phyllis, "Forgiving the Unforgivable," *Today's Christian Woman* (Nov.–Dec. 2005), 63–64.

22: Prayer and God

Epigraph: Cassian, quoted in Robert Bonazzi, *Man in the Mirror* (Maryknoll, N.Y.: Orbis, 1997), 160.

pg. 315: *"lifting up of the mind":* Cited in F.P. Harton, *Elements,* op. cit., 222.

pg. 315: *"Be joyful":* 1 Thessalonians 5:16.

pg. 315: *"Let us continually":* Hebrews 13:15.

pg. 315: *". . . always giving thanks":* Ephesians 5:20.

pg. 315: *"Pray in the Spirit":* Ephesians 6:18.

pg. 315: (footnote) *Messalians:* Cited in Frederica Mathewes-Green, *The Illumined Heart* (Brewster, Mass.: Paraclete, 2001), 71.

pg. 316: *Weil:* Simone Weil, *Waiting on God* (New York: Putnam's, 1951), 68.

pg. 316: *"without ceasing":* 1 Thessalonians 5:17 KJV.

pg. 317: *Kidd:* Sue Monk Kidd, *God's Joyful Surprise* (New York: Guideposts Associates, Inc., 1987), 222–224.

pg. 317: *"Even the very hairs":* Matthew 10:30.

pg. 317: *Eckhart:* Meister Eckhart, quoted in Friedrich Heiler, *Prayer,* op. cit., 192.

pg. 318: *Merton:* Thomas Merton, *The Seven Storey Mountain* (New York: Harcourt Brace and Co., 1948), 246–7.

pg. 321: *"If I were hungry":* Psalm 50:12.

pg. 321: *"The heavens declare":* Psalm 19:1.

pg. 321: *"Let the sea":* Psalm 96:11.

pg. 321: (footnote) *Hart:* David Bentley Hart, *The Doors of the Sea* (Grand Rapids, Mich.: Eerdmans, 2005), 63.

pg. 323: *Herbert:* George Herbert, "Providence," *Poems,* op. cit., 129.

pg. 323: *"Do you love me":* John 21:15.

pg. 323: *"Love the Lord":* Matthew 22:37.

pg. 323: *"Avila":* Teresa of Avila, *The Interior Castle* (New York: Image/Doubleday 1989), 76.

pg. 324: *Plantinga:* Cornelius Plantinga, Jr., "Pray the Lord My Mind to Keep," in *Christianity Today* (August 10, 1998), 50.

pg. 324: *"light and momentary":* 2 Corinthians 4:17.

pg. 324: *Pascal:* Blaise Pascal, quoted in William James, *The Varieties of Religious Experience,* (New York: The Modern Library, 1936), 281.

pg. 325: *"If you, then":* Matthew 7:11.

pg. 325: *Thielicke:* Helmut Thielicke, *The Waiting Father* (San Francisco: Harper & Row, 1959), 87–89.

pg. 327: *"now I know":* 1 Corinthians 13:12.

pg. 328: *"they will be":* Revelation 21:3.

pg. 328: *Ellul:* Jacques Ellul, *Prayer and Modern Man,* op. cit., 125.

CREDITS

What's So Amazing About Grace?

Philip Yancey, Author of
The Jesus I Never Knew

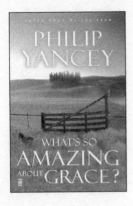

In 1987, an IRA bomb buried Gordon Wilson and his twenty-year-old daughter beneath five feet of rubble. Gordon alone survived. And forgave. He said of the bombers, "I have lost my daughter, but I bear no grudge.... I shall pray, tonight and every night, that God will forgive them."

His words caught the media's ear—and out of one man's grief, the world got a glimpse of grace.

Grace is the church's great distinctive. It's the one thing the world cannot duplicate, and the one thing it craves above all else—for only grace can bring hope and transformation to a jaded world.

In *What's So Amazing About Grace?* award-winning author Philip Yancey explores grace at street level. If grace is God's love for the undeserving, he asks, then what does it look like in action? And if Christians are its sole dispensers, then how are we doing at lavishing grace on a world that knows far more of cruelty and unforgiveness than it does of mercy?

Yancey sets grace in the midst of life's stark images, tests its mettle against horrific "ungrace."

In his most personal and provocative book ever, Yancey offers compelling, true portraits of grace's life-changing power. He searches for its presence in his own life and in the church. He asks, How can Christians contend graciously with moral issues that threaten all they hold dear?

And he challenges us to become living answers to a world that desperately wants to know, what's so amazing about grace?

Available in stores and online!

The Jesus I Never Knew

Philip Yancey, Author of
What's So Amazing About Grace?

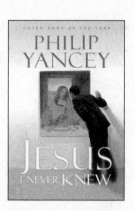

"There is no writer in the evangelical world that
I admire and appreciate more."
— Billy Graham

Philip Yancey helps reveal what two thousand
years of history covered up

What happens when a respected Christian journalist decides to
put his preconceptions aside and take a long look at the Jesus described in the Gospels? How does the Jesus of the New Testament
compare to the "new, rediscovered" Jesus — or even the Jesus we
think we know so well?

Philip Yancey offers a new and different perspective on the life
of Christ and his work — his teachings, his miracles, his death and
resurrection — and ultimately, who he was and why he came. From the
manger in Bethlehem to the cross in Jerusalem, Yancey presents a
complex character who generates questions as well as answers; a disturbing and exhilarating Jesus who wants to radically transform your
life and stretch your faith.

The Jesus I Never Knew uncovers a Jesus who is brilliant, creative,
challenging, fearless, compassionate, unpredictable, and ultimately
satisfying. "No one who meets Jesus ever stays the same," says
Yancey. "Jesus has rocked my own preconceptions and has made me
ask hard questions about why those of us who bear his name don't do
a better job of following him."

Available in stores and online!

Where Is God
When It Hurts?

Philip Yancey

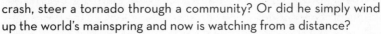

If there is a loving God, then why is it that ...?
You've heard that question, perhaps asked
it yourself. No matter how you complete it, at
its root lies the issue of pain.

Does God order our suffering? Does he decree an abusive childhood, orchestrate a jet
crash, steer a tornado through a community? Or did he simply wind
up the world's mainspring and now is watching from a distance?

In this Gold Medallion Award-winning book, Philip Yancey reveals
a God who is neither capricious nor unconcerned. Using examples
from the Bible and from his own experiences, Yancey looks at pain —
physical, emotional, and spiritual — and helps us understand why we
suffer. *Where Is God When It Hurts?* will speak to those for whom life
sometimes just doesn't make sense. And it will help equip anyone who
wants to reach out to someone in pain but just doesn't know what
to say.

Disappointment with God

Three Questions
No One Asks Aloud

Philip Yancey

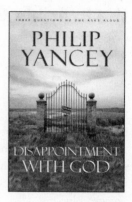

Philip Yancey has a gift for articulating the knotty issues of faith. In *Disappointment with God*, he poses three questions that Christians wonder but seldom ask aloud:

- Is God unfair?
- Is he silent?
- Is he hidden?

This insightful and deeply personal book points to the odd disparity between our concept of God and the realities of life. Why, if God is so hungry for relationship with us, does he seem so distant? Why, if he cares for us, do bad things happen? What can we expect from him after all? Yancey answers these questions with clarity, richness, and biblical assurance. He takes us beyond the things that make for disillusionment to a deeper faith, a certitude of God's love, and a thirst to reach not just for what God gives, but for who he is.

Available in stores and online!

Reaching for the Invisible God

What Can We Expect to find?

Philip Yancey

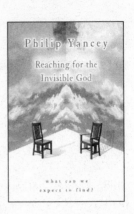

Life with God doesn't always work like we thought. High expectations slam against
the reality of personal weaknesses and un-
welcome surprises. And the God who we've
been told longs for our company may seem remote, emotionally
unavailable.

Is God playing games? What can we count on this God for?
How can we know? *How can we know God?*
This relationship with a God we can't see, hear, or touch — how
does it really work?

Reaching for the Invisible God offers deep, satisfying insights that
affirm and dignify the questions we're sometimes afraid to ask. Award-
winning author Philip Yancey explores six foundational areas: our thirst
for God, faith during times when God seems unavailable, the nature
of God himself, our personal relationship with God, stages along the
way, and the end goal of spiritual transformation. Honest and deeply
personal, here is straight talk on Christian living for the man or woman
who wants more than pat answers to life's imponderables. Ultimately,
Yancey shifts the focus from our questions to the One who offers
himself in answer. The God who invites us to reach for him — and find.

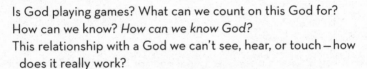

"I love Philip Yancey's work. He is a brilliant, graceful writer."
> — Anne Lamott, author, *Traveling Mercies*

*"This passionate book, unflinching in its honesty, will build your faith
by helping you wrestle authentically with your doubts. Join Philip
Yancey in this quest and you'll come closer still to our invisible but
very real God."*
> — Lee Strobel, author, *The Case for Faith*

The Bible Jesus Read

Philip Yancey

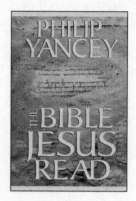

With his candid, signature style, Yancey interacts with the Old Testament from the perspective of his own deeply personal journey. From Moses, the amazing prince of Egypt, to the psalmists' turbulent emotions and the prophets' oddball rantings, Yancey paints a picture of Israel's God—and ours—that fills in the blanks of a solely New Testament vision of the Almighty.

Probing some carefully selected Old Testament books—Job, Deuteronomy, Psalms, Ecclesiastes, and the Prophets—Yancey reveals how the Old Testament deals in astonishing depths and detail with the issues that trouble us most. The Old Testament, in fact, tackles what the New Testament often only skirts. But that shouldn't surprise us. It is, after all, the Bible Jesus read.

Join Philip Yancey as he explores these sometimes shocking, often cryptic, divine writings. You will come to know God more intimately, anticipate Jesus more fervently, and find a wonderful, wise companion for your faith journey.

Rumors of Another World

What on Earth Are We Missing?

Philip Yancey

What on earth are we missing? Philip Yancey believes we are missing the supernatural hidden in everyday life.

In *Rumors of Another World*, Yancey investigates the natural world and discovers the supernatural hiding in plain view. He grapples with why God made the world and what our role truly is and seeks to answer the question, "How do I live in the natural world while expressing the values of the supernatural?"

Philip writes, "I have come to understand faith as the highest form of integrated encounter. Faith puts together, assembles, re-orders, accepting the entire world as God's handiwork. We live among clues, like rescuers sifting through pieces of stained glass shattered by a bomb, and only with a blueprint or some memory of original design can we begin to connect the shards, to assemble them into a pattern that makes sense of our world.

"Nature and supernature are not two separate worlds, but different expressions of the same reality. To encounter the world as a whole, we need a more supernatural awareness of the natural world."

Yancey invites readers to join him on a journey of discovery. He challenges us to tune into "rumors of another world" and connect the seen with the unseen. He promises that the grace-filled result will be a life of beauty, purpose, freedom, and faith.

Grace Notes

Daily Readings
with a Fellow Pilgrim

Philip Yancey

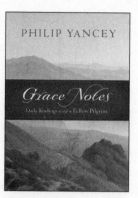

*"There is no writer in the evangelical world that
I admire and appreciate more."*
— Billy Graham

Philip Yancey's words — captured in his many bestselling books — have influenced the lives of millions of readers by strengthening their faith, building their hope, sparking their creativity, and challenging their comfort zones. If you're one of those readers, you know personally how his insights have affected your mind and heart. And if you're new to Yancey, you're in for a life-altering experience.

These meditations — all drawn from the beloved and bestselling writings of the author — will take you through an entire year of Yancey's insight and imagination, covering a broad range of topics:

- How to rediscover God through the wonders of nature, music, and romantic love
- Why grace means you can't do anything to make God love you more or less
- What happens when you cut through preconceptions to encounter the "real" Jesus
- How to renew your understanding and practice of prayer
- Where you can see God in unexpected people and places
- How to cope when life crashes in around you

Every day, experience the best from a beloved author who, with freshness, clarity, and energy, has so brilliantly articulated God's wonderful but mysterious relationship with you.

Available in stores and online!

ZONDERVAN®
.com

Share Your Thoughts

With the Author: Your comments will be forwarded to the author when you send them to *zauthor@zondervan.com*.

With Zondervan: Submit your review of this book by writing to *zreview@zondervan.com*.

Free Online Resources at
www.zondervan.com

Zondervan AuthorTracker: Be notified whenever your favorite authors publish new books, go on tour, or post an update about what's happening in their lives at www.zondervan.com/authortracker.

Daily Bible Verses and Devotions: Enrich your life with daily Bible verses or devotions that help you start every morning focused on God. Visit www.zondervan.com/newsletters.

Free Email Publications: Sign up for newsletters on Christian living, academic resources, church ministry, fiction, children's resources, and more. Visit www.zondervan.com/newsletters.

Zondervan Bible Search: Find and compare Bible passages in a variety of translations at www.zondervanbiblesearch.com.

Other Benefits: Register yourself to receive online benefits like coupons and special offers, or to participate in research.

ZONDERVAN®

ZONDERVAN.com/
AUTHORTRACKER
follow your favorite authors